# THE KID OF
# CONEY ISLAND

# THE KID OF
# Coney Island

## FRED THOMPSON
### AND THE
## RISE
### OF
## AMERICAN AMUSEMENTS

Woody Register

OXFORD
UNIVERSITY PRESS

2001

## OXFORD
UNIVERSITY PRESS

Oxford  New York

Athens Auckland Bangkok Bogotá Buenos Aires
Cape Town  Chennai  Dar es Salaam  Delhi  Florence  Hong Kong  Istanbul
Karachi  Kolkata  Kuala Lumpur  Madrid  Melbourne  Mexico City  Mumbai
Nairobi  Paris  São Paulo  Shanghai  Singapore  Taipei  Tokyo  Toronto  Warsaw

*and associated companies in*

Berlin  Ibadan

Published by Oxford University Press, Inc.
198 Madison Avenue, New York, New York 10016

Oxford is a registered trademark of Oxford University Press, Inc.

Library of Congress Cataloging-in-Publication Data is available.

ISBN: 0-19-514493-7

Parts of chapter 4 originally appeared in *Inventing Times Square: Commerce and Culture at the
Crossroads of the World*, edited by William R. Taylor, ©1991 Russell Sage Foundation, New York,
New York; parts of chapter 6 originally appeared in *Men and Masculinities* 2 (October 1999), Sage
Publications, Thousand Oaks, Calif.; lines from "Peter Pan, or the Boy Who Would Not Grow
Up," from *The Plays of J. M. Barrie*, are reprinted with permisssion of Scribner, a Division of
Simon & Schuster, New York, New York.

Book design and composition by Susan Day

1 3 5 7 9 8 6 4 2

Printed in the United States of America
on acid-free paper

B
Thompson
FRED
R

*For my parents*

# CONTENTS

## ACKNOWLEDGMENTS

THIS book began longer ago than I like to admit, but the extended incubation has been well worth the wait because of the aid I have received along the way. My first debts are to the historians who taught and inspired me in college and graduate school: the late Anita Goodstein, Bill Leach, and, most recently, Jack Thomas, my faithful supporter and great intellectual friend. I also am grateful to Roger Horowitz, John Sullivan, Carl Estabrook, Mary Gluck, Jim Patterson, the late Bill McLoughlin, John Kasson, the late Bob Wiebe, Bill Taylor, Gary Cross, and Gail Bederman, all of whom have lent important support, advice, or criticism to the project. Martha Hodes and Gayle McKeen read the manuscript at a crucial stage, and their encouragement and insights were indispensable. Luckily for me, the review process brought my work under the scrutiny of Karen Halttunen and David Nasaw, and I cannot thank them enough for the important additions they made to the final product. Peter Ginna, my editor at Oxford, has been this manuscript's (and writer's) best friend, as intelligent, sensible, and respectful a reader as I could have wished for. In countless ways this book benefited from the skill and dedication of the people at Oxford University Press, including John Sullivan (again), Rudy Faust, and especially Aimee Chevrette, who efficiently shepherded it to a swift completion. I was particularly fortunate to have my manuscript entrusted to Jane Lincoln Taylor, whose sharp and sensible copyediting resulted in a better book than the one she had received. Mariana Johnson, Jenny Johnson, Barbara Tholfsen, Larry Reid, and my extended family at the Sewanee Children's Center also have lent a hand at various stages of this project. Donna Ewald Huggins generously shared her knowledge about and artifacts from the Panama-Pacific Exposition. Nor have I forgotten all that Penny Register did to help me with an earlier version of this work, and I thank her for that.

Many archivists and librarians have contributed, but I wish especially to thank the staff of the Billy Rose Theatre Collection at the New York Public Library, who have been my partners in this enterprise. Bob Rubic lent excellent work with photographs. At Sewanee, Sue Armentrout and Andrew Moser have made interlibrary loan work for me. I am grateful, too, to the helpful people at the University of California's Bancroft Library, the San Francisco Public Library, the Museum of the City of New York, the Shubert Archive, the New-York Historical Society, the Brooklyn Museum of Art, the Brooklyn Public Library, and Brown University's Rockefeller Library. I also benefited from the generous and extraordinary assistance of Jean Coffey and the late Ron Mahoney at California State University, Fresno.

My colleagues in history and American studies at Sewanee have been an essential web of support, especially Sue Ridyard, Johan Åhr, Elizabeth Grammer, Scott Wilson, Charles Perry, and my fellow Americanists, Houston Roberson and John Willis. The encouragement of Bill Clarkson and Wyatt Prunty was welcomed and appreciated. The dean of the college has provided generous financial assistance for travel and research, and I am grateful to Bob Keele and Tom Kazee for backing me in this way.

Three thoughtful and unselfish friends have made this book possible: Bruce Dorsey, John Grammer, and Peter Laipson. I cannot imagine it without them, nor would I want to. Julie Berebitsky missed out on most of this book's history, but the ways in which she has encouraged, prodded, teased, and, most of all, loved me during its most critical stages of development are apparent, to me, on every page I have written. Sophie Register, who has patiently endured my scholarly oddities, lovingly reminded me to work hard as she dozed off to sleep each night, and joyfully awakened me each day at sun-up, has been my constant inspiration for seven years. Above all, I am grateful to my first and best teachers, my beloved parents, Barbara and Bill Register, who know better than anyone else what has gone into this book and what writing it has meant to me. It is my gift to them.

# THE KID OF
# CONEY ISLAND

*I see the av'rage business man a-working hard all day,*
*He does not need more dough, he likes to hustle though.*
*He's got the habit, hates to see a nickel get away,*
*He's trying now to snare, some other fellow's share.*

*At fifty he's a wreck, dyspepsia, gout and heart disease.*
*He can't have any fun, but, say, he has a son;*
*And Willie gets his papa's cash and blows it in with ease,*
*While daughter spends her share to buy a titled piece of cheese.*

*They are a joke, ha, ha, ha, ha! a lovely joke, ha, ha, ha, ha!*
*They are better than a pantomime to me.*
*How I laugh in royal glee,*
*Ha, ha, ha, he, he, he, he!*
*Oh what fools, oh my what fools these mortals be.*

*—"What Fools We Mortals Be"*

ONE

# Uncle Sam's a Boy at Play

KING Morpheus of Slumberland issued the foregoing lyrical indictment of the paragons of American civilization—the "av'rage" businessmen—near the beginning of the 1908 Broadway spectacle *Little Nemo*.[1] Connoisseurs of drama recognized that the king had borrowed Puck's amused observation on lovers and lunatics in *A Midsummer Night's Dream*. But the "fools" targeted by the monarch of Slumberland were of a different order, and the audience in the New Amsterdam Theatre did not have to catch the Shakespearean reference to see what was so funny. American men were forever hustling after the main chance; they were tooth-and-claw competitors, dauntless enemies of pleasure and frivolity, and to what end? Riches they could not bear to spend, an unstrung body to go with a surly disposition, and a generation of children who blew their fathers' hard-earned wealth with scarcely a thought of tomorrow.

*They are a joke, ha, ha, ha, ha! a lovely joke, ha, ha, ha, ha!*

This barbed indictment of contemporary men appeared during act 1 of the most expensive production to date in Broadway history. The show was based on Winsor McCay's popular comic strip *Little Nemo in Slumberland*. The feature had run since October 1905 in the Sunday color "funny paper" section of the *New York Herald* and had been syndicated

3

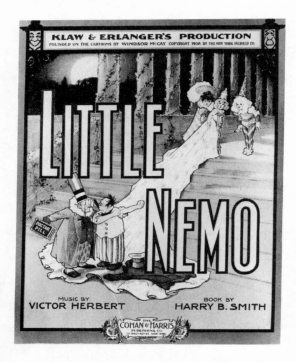

Fig. 1.1. Winsor McCay's graphic style and antic sensibility are evident in this cover illustration of a song sheet from the 1908 spectacle *Little Nemo. (Theatre Collection, Museum of the City of New York.)*

in newspapers across the nation soon afterward. McCay's Nemo was an ordinary middle-class Brooklyn boy, who was launched each week on a dream-quest to be the playmate of the Princess of Slumberland. Throughout the twentieth century, the cartoonist's many admirers have found the story line less inspired than McCay's innovative exploitation of the visual forms of mass entertainment culture (fig. 1.1). He used vibrant colors as a visual language, and burst, enlarged, or stretched the boundaries of the conventional square frame of the comic strip to render a narrative of intense anticipation, delayed consummation, and aching disappointment. In each episode the little adventurer attained a brilliantly hued world of unlimited and unexpected delights, only to lose the tantalizing vision as it evolved into a terrifying nightmare or disintegrated on the verge of fulfillment when a parent peremptorily awakened the dreaming child to get ready for Sunday school.[2]

The theatrical businessmen who sought to translate this endlessly mutating and irresistible Slumberland to the stage pledged that *Nemo* would "not be a 'baby play' to interest the nursery occupant only." They

Fig. 1.2. Fred Thompson, the "boy-wonder of Broadway producers," poses here as he usually appeared and preferred to be seen: informally attired, fidgeting coins in one hand, a cigar in the other. (*Billy Rose Theatre Collection, The New York Public Library for the Performing Arts, Astor, Lenox and Tilden Foundations.*)

targeted an adult audience and promised "the most elaborate and artistic spectacle of its kind ever presented in this country." The "idea of dream illusion has got to obtain throughout," explained producer Marc Klaw, "and the scenes must be presented so effectively that the auditor will believe in the reality of dreams."[3] Audacious and realistic fantasy was a standard that money could buy, and *Little Nemo* had the backing of the most powerful figures in American theater: Marc Klaw and his partner, Abraham Lincoln (A. L.) Erlanger. To the embarrassment of their ledger sheets, they delivered on their pledge. *Little Nemo* rang up astronomical preproduction costs, which ensured a river of red ink even as the show consistently filled theaters in New York and other American cities.[4]

Klaw and Erlanger may have provided the big money, but the real architect of *Little Nemo*, and the one responsible for its landmark status as an almost surreally disastrous investment, was Fred Thompson, the "boy-wonder of Broadway producers"[5] (fig. 1.2). Thompson owned a quarter of the show, but his more important contribution was in masterminding the "dream illusion," designing and producing the superabundance of stage tricks that was its undoing as a business proposition.[6]

In Thompson's hands, *Little Nemo* was one of the era's most extravagant representations of the promise of modern life in a culture of consumption, and of the new "man" who would prosper there. The stage pictures composed a lavish alternative to the cheerless dead end caricatured by King Morpheus. From start to finish, its sheer material excess—ten boxcars of scenery and 655 different costumes for waves of chorus girls—mocked the prescriptive authority of the Victorian bourgeoisie's moral order of prudential saving, moderation, work, and self-denial. The theatrical *Little Nemo* itself was out of control, excessive, improvident. It was, in McCay's own excited words, "Frederic Thompson's wildest fancies." The profusion of costumes, color, and light systematically demonstrated the enticements of twentieth-century industrial society and dramatized, with irrefutable and dazzling logic, that Americans were fools to resist them, to remain loyal to the values and priorities of a threadbare past (fig. 1.3). In the "distant heaven" of Slumberland, compulsive toil and pointless sacrifice yielded to effortless abundance and pleasure. "Do you believe in dreams, dear?" asked one of the concluding numbers,

*for if you do I'll tell*
*About a land a distant strand where happiness must dwell—*
*There's no such thing as work there and O it would be grand*
*If we could go and always live in dreamy Slumberland.*

The stage "ablaze with whirling pinwheels and exploding firecrackers," *Little Nemo* declared a new Independence Day in America, when, as one of its most sensational choruses announced, "Uncle Sam is once again a boy at play." What did a man have to do to exchange his earthbound existence for a paradise of dancing teddy bears, Fourth of July fireworks, flag-draped chorus girls, Coney Island amusement parks, and fanciful playgrounds? Simple: become a child again and relearn what he had forgotten—how to play.[7]

This piece of advice and the hyperkinetic manner in which it was staged owed less to McCay's light-handed and dreamily paced fantasy than to the boy wonder of Broadway and the amusement empire that he tried to amass during the first decade of the twentieth century. During

Fig. 1.3. Although outfitted with the paraphernalia of bourgeois childhood, *Little Nemo*, as these fetching nursery-rhyme figures suggest, was designed with grown-up boys' tastes in mind. (*Billy Rose Theatre Collection, The New York Public Library for the Performing Arts, Astor, Lenox and Tilden Foundations.*)

this period, Thompson was the marvel of the new American economy of urban mass amusements. In 1902–3, when only twenty-eight years old, he had designed and, with his partner Elmer "Skip" Dundy, built Luna Park, a twenty-two-acre amusement park on Coney Island on the edge of New York City. Luna was unlike any place Americans had ever seen: a cityscape of narrow avenues lined with brilliantly white palaces, playfully ornamented with spewing fountains, onion domes, glittering towers, and minarets that served no purpose other than to humor anyone who paid ten cents to cross its threshold (fig. 1.4). Luna founded a new and lasting paradigm for outdoor amusements—an architecturally unified and exotic garden of enchantment, which mocked the drab circumstances of everyday life and specialized in the experience of imaginative escape and thrilling fantasies. When it opened for the first time, at precisely eight o'clock on 16 May 1903, the main electrical switches in

Fig. 1.4. This panoramic view of Luna Park shows Fred Thompson's "Oriental dream" as it appeared in 1903, its first summer of business. (*Theatre Collection, Museum of the City of New York.*)

the park were thrown and the outlines of its buildings burst out of the early evening darkness, limned with thousands of small incandescent lights. As the *Brooklyn Daily Eagle* reported the next day, "it seemed that a huge mantle of light had been let down from the sky to disclose the domain of an unknown world." Never, the newspaper added, "here or elsewhere has there been such an opening to a pleasure park."[8] Mobbed during its first summer, Luna Park ignited entrepreneurial energies in cities throughout the United States, where speculators threw up larger and smaller versions of the park's "Oriental" or "fairy-tale" buildings and amusements. For years Coney Island had been notorious for its illicit economies of drinking, prizefighting, gambling, and prostitution. "In Texas and Colorado towns," noted one well-known writer, "the lowest dive is apt to be called 'the Coney Island.'" Luna's amazing popularity revised the island's identification with vice by establishing a new reputation for hearty, joyful, innocent childhood so widely recognized that in 1913 a department store in Oakland, California, named its indoor children's playground after the Brooklyn resort. By 1915 Luna Parks were operating in Berlin, Buenos Aires, Rome, and Melbourne, Australia. None of these parks was affiliated with Thompson, but all of them bore the imprint of his original amusement.[9]

Less than two years after Luna's debut, Thompson unleashed a similar enthusiasm for outsized theatrical spectacle by opening the largest theater in the world, the New York Hippodrome on Sixth Avenue near Times Square. The critical and popular acclaim for the fifty-two-hundred-seat theater and its inaugural production, *A Yankee Circus on Mars*, seemed to certify that the showman had discovered an untapped mass market for affordable theatrical luxury and fantasy. In the afterglow of *A Yankee Circus*, investors and impresarios promised Hippodromes for other American cities, and London as well. The promises went unfulfilled, but Thompson had identified a model of luxurious middle-class entertainment, which the movie studios would replicate with the picture palaces of the 1920s and 1930s. By 1909, he had achieved further unexpected and prodigious success as a Broadway producer and stage director with a string of hit plays, making such important contributions to American popular culture as *Brewster's Millions, A Fool There Was*, and *Little Nemo*. The next year, veteran Broadway observer Robert Grau praised Thompson as "thoroughly illustrative of the modern type of theatrical business man," with a record that others in the field could ill afford to ignore.[10]

Thompson's astonishing success in the art of catering to the millions was not all that distinguished him. Part of what made him a modern businessman can be seen in *Little Nemo*'s pyrotechnic pictures of a merry nation at play and its spirited upbraiding of men who "can't have any fun." During the first decade and a half of the twentieth century, perhaps no American man relished the opportunity or calculated the dividends of living according to Little Nemo's recipe of eternal childhood more than this self-described grown-up "boy at play." Today we regard amusement parks, and the uplifting renditions of folk and fairy tales produced by the major entertainment conglomerates, as fun for the whole family. Middle-class American parents have come to feel morally obligated to share the pilgrimage to Orlando's Magic Kingdom with their children. Although Fred Thompson deserves some credit for outlining the ethos of fun that underlies the post–World War II theme park recognizable today, the fantasy getaways he invented differed in fundamental ways, the most important of which was this: he conceived all of his ventures for middle-class adults, not for the poor, or children, or families. In its inaugural season, Luna offered a nursery service "For Tired Mothers" and guaranteed, "Babies No Longer a Bar to Pleasure ... You Get a Check—We Do the Rest." The promise underscored the origins of his amusements as temporary shelters from the encumbrances of respectable middle-class adulthood.[11] Photographs from the period show children in the crowds, but the little ones were not the hardship cases he targeted. Thompson's amusements, as a newspaper writer observed near the end of the showman's life, were "for grown-ups and Peter Pans who never will grow up."[12]

## The Toymaker of New York

In all his ventures, as his wife recalled after his death in 1919, Thompson insisted that he was not a "business man" but "a showman with a mission" to restore play and delight to the dyspeptic lives of Americans. The showman cast himself as a Santa Claus for adults and promoted his ventures—from "The Biggest Playground on Earth" (Luna Park) to "New York's Gigantic Toy" (the Hippodrome)—as playthings for "grown-up children" like himself, who longed to return to the carefree times of their childhoods. "I shall be happy," he had declared in 1909, "if I can be known as the toymaker of New York." It would be reasonable to discount such claims as the hackneyed sentimentalism of a cynical showman if Thompson were not among the most visible and imaginative figures giving shape and assigning meanings to the booming marketplaces of entertainment and leisure in cities across the United States at the time. The showman may well have wanted to camouflage the essential commercialism of his amusements as gift giving, but there are other issues that also deserve attention—namely, how he put this disguise to work and why this particular marketing strategy worked so well in selling him, his goods, and his conception of how life ought to be.[13]

Thompson's vision of the good life and the dazzling but short-lived empire of play that he built between 1900 and 1915 were at the center of important historical transformations in the United States. New York City, where he burst brilliantly onto the scene in 1903, was in the lead of a national revolution in urban commercial amusements that catered to the rapidly expanding population of middle-class patrons. During these years the city flourished with new, popularly priced theaters and vaudeville houses, rival opera companies at war with each other, dance halls and fantastic restaurants, amusement parks and ballparks, nickelodeons and picture palaces. New York itself had become the manufacturing center of theatrical entertainments, its leading entrepreneurs—the Klaw and Erlanger "Theatre Syndicate," the Keith and Albee vaudeville chain—controlling theatrical houses throughout the United States and producing as many as five hundred touring shows annually by 1900. Beyond Broadway, and largely as a result of Thompson's initiatives, Coney Island was overrun with visitors during this decade, with as many as twenty million packing the streets, parks, and beaches in the summer of 1909 alone. The appetite for such fare was not limited to New York or to the Northeast.[14] The theatrical and amusement boom occurred in small and large cities throughout the United States, with hundreds of theaters and amusement parks built between 1890 and 1910. In 1908 Fred Thompson's publicity man, Glenmore Davis, called the new amusement economy "the billion-dollar smile," and cheerily reported that "it is spread to-day from Seattle to New York, from Bangor to the Gulf."[15]

The emphasis on the cash value of smiles was no idle metaphor. Beyond the growing national markets for commercial leisure, Thompsonian amusements such as *Little Nemo* heralded a new era of expressive, pleasure-oriented urban culture. From "family" vaudeville to outdoor amusements such as Luna Park, a new expectation gradually supplanted genteel Victorian assumptions that respectable recreation would elevate the spirit, instruct the mind, and purify the body. Like many others in the business at the turn of the century, Fred Thompson cared less about instructing the conscience of his customers than about selling pleasure and manufacturing the kind of fun that people would pay for. Whether at Luna Park or at the Hippodrome, Thompson surrounded his patrons with visions as different from the everyday world of denied or delayed gratification as he could allow himself to imagine. His amusements did not remind people of their insuperable shortcomings, but shouted "yes" to their wishes. In the "playgrounds" he created on Coney Island and in Manhattan, amusement was composed of nonstop action, unceasing variety and novelty, pleasures without end, unlimited abundance. To see what he meant, he encouraged people to "picture many white steeples, and numerous minarets, and innumerable highly-decorated buildings of every conceivable architecture, from the prototype of a Turkish mosque to the styles obtaining among the more imaginative of the Japanese, with a strain of the architectural fashions which are creditably supposed to obtain in fairyland." Then, "imagine swirling things, and tortuous things, and very quickly moving things," and "countless crowds of women in white and quite as many men in many colors, strolling, waiting, peering, laughing; being borne off in curious contrivances that rush and dash; being carried again by other curious contrivances that jump and dance."[16] Imagine life, in other words, as a perpetual and hyperactive carnival of plenty.

Thompson's determination to encourage visions of surplus and luxury placed him at the center of the development of early-twentieth-century consumer capitalism. Between 1890 and 1930, Americans laid the institutional foundation of this economy—department stores, advertising agencies, grand hotels and lavish saloons, restaurants, dance halls, and the great "world's fairs"—which showcased the marvelous array of consumer goods and technologies produced by the new industrial order. The architects of the urban marketplace enlisted these institutions and the social roles and practices associated with them not just to sell goods in new or more-effective ways, but to make consumer goods the very marrow of American life. The great merchants and theatrical businessmen of the era well understood that they had to overthrow the authority of deeply rooted ethical and religious traditions and proscriptions that encouraged work and self-denial and fostered a suspicion of material luxury and secular pleasures. Instead of making him exceptional, Thompson's love of fairy tales allied him with an array of middle-class men—and some women—who were mining the imagined terrain of child life for ways to entice customers and to conceive of marketable goods and services. These entrepreneurs of childhood and play were associated with diverse and important institutions: not just amusement parks, but universities, department stores, theaters, museums, and toy manufactories. Besides showmen, their ranks included ethnologists, psychologists, artists, actors, department store buyers and window dressers, writers of modern fairy tales, cartoonists, architects, press agents, composers, puppeteers, and makers and sellers of toys. They deployed a new strategic vocabulary—words such as play, thrills, pleasure, personal satisfaction, toys, games, neverending childhood, and fun—to frame the promise of the economic world of goods.

Recalling the description of Thompson's audiences as "grown-ups and Peter Pans" underscores another historical development that was indispensable to these enterprises: the emergence of a new and enduring ideal, fostered by and for that culture, of the boy who never grows up. Thompson's simultaneous concern for play, profits, and the unhappiness of "av'rage" businessmen made him one of the era's most important exponents of the commercial culture of *Peter Pan*, to borrow the title of J. M. Barrie's play. Peter Pan is the boy who never grows up and

Fig. 1.5. *Peter Pan*, a spectator remarked, takes men back to "the time when the universe was but our playground." Here the American actor Maude Adams appears as the eternal boy in the 1905 New York premiere. (*Theatre Collection, Museum of the City of New York.*)

shuns the restraints of adulthood for a life of high adventure with the other Lost Boys in Never Land. Although British in origin, Barrie's story has been among the most popular in the United States from its first performances on Broadway in 1905–6 through its many revivals on film, stage, and television (fig. 1.5). There are many reasons for the story's resonance in modern American culture. But one asserted by *Theatre* magazine at the time of the play's American debut deserves attention: that the story contains both an essential hostility to the dehumanizing commercialism and materialism of the twentieth century and a resource for restoring vivacity, sweetness, and warmth to modern life through the recovery of one's childhood. When critics in 1906 asserted that people who do not fall under the play's spell are the ones who need it—and him—the most, they made the claim that has resounded for the rest of the century: *Peter Pan* "has the effect of rejuvenating all who witness it."[17]

At first glance, Fred Thompson, who was one of the era's most celebrated capitalists and a man unembarrassed by his enthusiasm for
spending money, seems anything but compatible with Never Land's
antimaterialist symbol of guileless make-believe and perpetual innocence. And yet the figure of Peter Pan made perfect sense to a man
such as Thompson, especially when Barrie's eternal boy "passionately"
crowed his peculiar declaration of independence: "I don't want to go to
school and learn solemn things. No one is going to catch me, lady, and
make me a man. I want always to be a little boy and to have fun."[18]
Thompson, like many of his contemporaries, embraced Peter's rebellion against duty and responsibility to justify the hedonistic imperative
of twentieth-century consumer culture, to enliven the fantastic settings
in which he staged his wares, and to show how to restore zest to the
lives of average men. The showman saw himself as a new kind of man
in business, one who kept lively and young at heart because he avoided
seriousness and never lost sight of what mattered most—being cheerful and having a good time. Contemporaries, who were astounded by
his achievements, attributed his personal vitality and genius as an en-
tertainer, the popularity of his amusements, and the speed with which
he had raced to the center of the urban consumer marketplace to one
fact above all others: he had never grown up; he was a boy at heart who
lived every day in "dreamy Slumberland." *His work was play.* Thompson
encouraged his "Peter Pan" celebrity and urged contemporaries to join
him in full-scale rebellion against the enfeebling prudence, restraint,
and solemnity of growing up.

Speaking of the commercial culture of Peter Pan draws particular attention to twentieth-century businessmen who enlisted the figure of the
eternal child—or, more accurately, the eternal boy—to explain themselves and to dramatize and legitimate consumer culture's enticing invitation to be like Peter, who plays and does whatever he wants, with scant
regard for anyone else. It also reveals how the ideal of the eternal child
became embedded in the way Americans, especially middle-class men,
have come to think about work, consumption, and the world of goods.
While some men of that generation were mounting serious challenges
to the unprecedented power of industrial corporations, the central narrative of Peter Pan culture promoted consumer goods and services as
the "gateway to the good life." This vision promised middle-class men
that there were profits as well as pleasures awaiting them in the market-

place of goods—if, that is, they overcame their foolish aversion to pleasure and spending money and embraced the good life of play by seeing
the world through the marveling, desiring eyes of children.[19] Echoes of
older Romanticist celebrations of the aesthetic potential of the playing
child can be heard in this counsel. Yet, as elaborated by Thompson and
other entrepreneurs of childhood, the image of Uncle Sam indulging
his boyish play impulse was a product less of the nineteenth than for the
twentieth century. The idea that a man, in order to achieve and enjoy the
full benefits of American life, should never stop playing or being a boy,
would become one of the most important cultural fictions used by
"av'rage" businessmen to justify and give an institutional, aesthetic, and
moral foundation to consumer capitalism.

### Too Much Work, Too Little Play

As Thompson put it, "the trouble with this present age" is "too much
work and too little play. We need to be educated up again to the child
spirit." In its most obvious sense, his pedagogy brought new commodities of material pleasure and delight to the consumer marketplace. But
his mission also involved rethinking or even reinventing middle-class
expectations of what a man naturally should be and do. In the nineteenth century, the main elements of identity and citizenship for white
men in America were grounded in work and workplace loyalties and in
religious and civic obligations. For many American men, an economy
shifting rapidly toward the manufacturing and marketing of consumer
goods and services offered thrilling and unprecedented opportunities
for profit, not to mention pleasure. Yet, accustomed to regarding
wealth, power, and manliness in terms of business ownership, land,
workplace accomplishment, and civic and religious duty, many also
were reluctant to give their full loyalties to an economic order built
principally on spending money for goods, salesmanship, and unrestrained desire. Such men were beset by corresponding concerns that a
world of "consuming identities" was culturally subversive, inherently
insubstantial, personally compromising, even unmanly.[20] Fred Thompson was like many middle-class American men in this respect; he, too,
was unable to dismiss those nagging reservations from his mind. But
rather than stopping him, his qualms about play and consumption
made him all the more insistent that a man could prosper and should

have fun in a consumer economy. Recognizing the centrality of play to his cultural perspective is especially important in examining how he and other entrepreneurs of childhood helped create new ways of thinking about gender—what I call consuming or Peter Pan manhood—which demarcated and lent respectability to new social roles for men in a culture of consumption.

What made Peter Pan manhood more than merely another way of expressing the eternal youth of the American nation was the way in which Thompson and other men put this gendered concept to work. Scholars have often noted that the rise of a consumer culture undermined Victorian gender and sexual norms. As helpful as this argument is, it tends to separate consumer culture and gender into discrete categories of cause and effect. This approach underestimates the complex ways in which the new market culture and the new ideas about manhood interacted, produced, undermined, and reinforced each other. Many of these men often felt like Barrie's orphans, the Lost Boys of Never Land, adrift in a world of unbounded desires and liquidity of identity. At the same time, an economy shifting rapidly toward the manufacturing and marketing of consumer goods offered thrilling opportunities for gain. For Thompson, such contending emotions and concerns did not pose a crippling "crisis of masculinity." Nor was he merely seeking to escape from the "frustrations, the routine, and the sheer dullness of an urban-industrial culture." Rather, he and other Peter Pans seized the situation as opportunities to explore and exploit what historian Jackson Lears calls the fundamental "pattern of tensions in commercial culture: between control and release, stability and sorcery." They did not flee the artificiality and theatricality of consumer culture, but operated within its pattern of tensions. Their struggles to secure their identity as men indicate that the form of masculinity they invented and performed was as tension-ridden as Peter Pan himself: frozen by the playwright in a condition of arrested development, yet conventionally represented on stage by a grown woman. At the same time, embracing Never Land did not amount to infantilization. By cultivating the "boy inside," men were devising new ways of exercising power, using the concepts of play and childhood to build markets, defuse the worst associations of consumerism with women and effeminacy, and reconcile their expectations of social, political, and cultural priority with the tendencies of the new economic world.[21]

Focusing on Thompson and the ways in which he reflected and contributed to the commercial promise of Never Land also modifies how we imagine the importance of popular amusements to the evolution of consumer culture in the twentieth-century United States. Some scholars have argued that the amusements built by Thompson and others like him were escapist diversions, "brief bouts of relief from industrial routine, reinforcing rather than undermining the hierarchies of the developing managerial order." In this view, Coney's amusement parks, which sold the illusion of liberation, were prototypes for the managed freedom and shopping-mall merchandising techniques of mid- and late-twentieth-century consumer capitalism. Although generally accurate, such accounts tend to emphasize how commercial amusements such as Luna Park were reflections of greater historical changes. We also need to consider how such enterprises may have shaped, even as they were shaped by, the larger contours of the twentieth-century market economy. The two major recent works on the history of consumption in the United States after the turn of the century, William Leach's *Land of Desire* and Jackson Lears's *Fables of Abundance*, address subjects that were at the heart of the new outlook promoted by the culture of Peter Pan—artificiality, theatricality, carnival, magic, light, color, and play. Yet neither work treats commercial amusements as anything more than symptoms of larger transformations.[22]

From another perspective, David Nasaw's excellent survey of "going out," which examines many of the enterprises that were part of Thompson's universe of play and that became important to the lives of urban Americans between 1900 and 1945, paradoxically marginalizes them. Nasaw encourages the tendency to view amusements as part of a separate "leisure" culture or economy that Americans "went out" to; in other words, commercial amusements were aspects of but in most ways ancillary to America's larger transformation into a consumer society. But the careers of Thompson and his fellow play entrepreneurs reveal more than the rapidly expanding opportunities for leisure in American cities and the rise of a new expressiveness in public behavior. They also elucidate central aspects of the utopian promise of consumer abundance in the early twentieth century and beyond. Thompson's amusements and shows were among the most popular urban middle-class entertainments of the era; they created and interpreted many of the important images, forms, and narratives of the commercial playground of consumption. They also contributed to the relocation of play and the dream worlds associated with childhood from the margins to the vital core of American middle-class life, constructing a new culture and with it a new cultural outlook.[23]

Any number of commonsense problems arise when one studies people such as Thompson—a "producer" of mass culture—to deduce how actual Americans actually felt about what they were purchasing or why. Yet the supply side of the consumption equation still has much to tell us about the demand side, especially in the case of Thompson, who was never solely or even predominantly a producer of amusements. Tagging him as such reduces him to a socioeconomic abstraction and distorts the broad context of his historical experience. The historian Lawrence Levine has suggested that, in making sense of the past, we should avoid relying on "ideal types" of all-powerful producers and "passive, hopeless consumers" who are affected by history without ever affecting the world around them. According to Levine, "What people can do and do do is to refashion the objects created for them to fit their own values, needs, and expectations." Levine's principal concern is with consumers, or audiences, but the same approach can be applied to the suppliers. Thompson should be regarded as one of these people, as someone who acted on his own values, anxieties, and wishes when he designed amusements and identified his audiences. Unable to distance himself from either his commodities or his audiences, he sold thrills that promised to excite and please himself. When he called his audiences fickle and insatiable, he was describing himself. He was always his first and best customer. The persistent problem was that his ideal customer was a spendthrift who thought little of tomorrow. To be sure, Thompson did not stand for all Americans or even all American men, but his desires and fears do have much to tell us about people, especially men, like him. His self-presentation as Peter Pan was a calculated marketing strategy that, for a time, brought him acclaim and wealth. But it also was an involuntary reflection of what he actually believed himself to be. The uncertain boundary between these two aspects of his identity generated a potent and creative confusion, which enabled Thompson to identify and to exploit his own and other men's alienation from and longing for what another contemporary Peter Pan called the "joy of living and the world of delight."[24]

## An Hour in the Scheme of Days

By just about any standard of the twentieth century, Fred Thompson was an extraordinary man, someone who stood above the crowds to whom he catered and who made a lasting mark on American and even European culture. Yet his life and career do not lend themselves easily to biography. Recently the prolific biographer Peter Ackroyd, writing in the *New York Times Book Review*, contended that a biographer must "intuit the personal stirrings of the individual consciousness" and bring the subject to life "upon the page."[25] As a practical matter, such a study of the Coney Island showman would be impossible to accomplish. Thompson, as the consuming public knew him and as the historical record has left him, was as fleeting, insubstantial, and superficial as the plaster façades of his amusements. He grew up not in a place, but in many places. He did not write letters; he sent telegrams. What he wanted known, he or his publicity men fed to the newspapers. What he did not want known was kept hushed until the clamor of his creditors or the reports of his breakdowns became too public to keep private. There is a consistency to the few brief writings published under his name, which suggests that he actually wrote them, but his authorship remains uncertain. The biographical details available in newspaper and magazine accounts of his exploits usually hold up under scrutiny, but there are few details to begin with. There are no diaries or collections of personal letters, either to or from Thompson. His second wife attempted to write his life, but that manuscript seems to have disappeared with her death. In all my research, I have seen his actual signature fewer than a dozen times. Like the child he claimed to be, he seems to have skipped in and out of history. His only lasting monument is a ponderous headstone, which his former associates placed on his grave three years after his death. Everything else, like Luna Park, has virtually disappeared.

Even if no amount of imagination can render Thompson's story in the form of an intimate biography, his story is nonetheless a rich resource for thinking about twentieth-century America and Americans, especially if we keep a certain critical distance that enables us to examine his life as itself a commodity devised for public consumption and for encouraging the additional consumption of his amusements. In this light, the very evanescence of his accomplishments and existence—brilliantly in demand today, forgotten tomorrow—was one of the most lasting aspects of consumer capitalism and culture in twentieth-century

19

America. Thompson arrived in New York in 1898 in the midst of the city's emergence as the financial, commercial, retail, advertising, and entertainment center of the United States. Virtually overnight he became one of the era's most boisterous and visible traffickers in a renovated urban marketplace of color, light, festivity, and play. Just as important, Thompson himself came to represent that culture. The "toymaker of New York" arose simultaneously with, and with the same care and precision that went into the design of, Luna's entertainments. Thompson claimed to shatter the developmental myth of self-denial, thrift, and industry, and offered his child-self as a model for the new century. His youthful achievements cast his enterprises as reflections of his wondrous personality and childlike passions, and pictured him as a paragon of the modern imagination, impervious to history, limitations, and age. The public manufacture of self in which he was engaged was indistinguishable from his manufacture of amusements. As Thompson observed in 1910, stating a twentieth-century marketing truth that could have served as his epitaph, "The life of your average summer [amusement] device is ephemeral—an hour in the scheme of days."[26]

What I offer here, then, is not an intimate biography of one human being, but an intensive examination of a figure who left little record of his personal self other than as an instrument for publicizing and selling his enterprises. The chapters are arranged in the chronological order of his major ventures, with those concerning his New York years overlapping to a degree in time: the world's fair projects through 1901, the debut of Luna Park in 1903, the opening of the Hippodrome in 1905, the Broadway years from 1905 through 1912, and the showman's concluding ambition, the failed Toyland Grown Up, at the 1915 San Francisco world's fair. Each chapter also is an essay in cultural history. By necessity as well as by design, they examine Thompson's actions and beliefs for what they suggest about the development of a culture of consumption and of new gender identities in and for that commercial culture in the United States in the decades after 1870. The final chapter reflects on the continuous appeal (and fear) of Peter Pan manhood in the years since Thompson's death in 1919 at the age of forty-five; it focuses in particular on boy-men in popular culture in the last two decades of the twentieth century.

The ways in which Thompson's conception of human fulfillment was put to use and the enthusiasm with which many embraced it held profound historical and political importance. Through much of the nineteenth century, the word "emancipation" had expressed the most fervent economic, political, and moral aspirations of dispossessed Americans for a nation of freedom and equality. At the end of that century, Fred Thompson and his fellow entrepreneurs of childhood pictured a new promised land in which men would be liberated from the duties, responsibilities, and toil of adulthood—from any claim, that is, other than what they wanted to do. Their oppression was not that they had so little, but that they had so much and yet still could not have any fun. "We're all only kids grown tall," Thompson frequently declared, "and everything is right with us unless we've got tuberculosis of the heart."[27] However banal, this combination of insight and advice was the essential element of make-believe joining Fred Thompson's identity and his short-lived empire—the boy wonder of Broadway, the toymaker of New York, and the kid of Coney Island.

# TWO

# The Moon for a Plaything

Fred Thompson's Apprenticeship in Play, 1873–1901

IN 1915 a writer for *Sunset* observed that Fred Thompson was not the kind of man who ever paid much attention to the "blessed common fundamental things of life—the plowing and baking and stitching, the establishing of a home." The writer, Frances A. Groff, was right. Thompson loathed the confinement of worrying about tomorrow and of attending to the everyday duties and responsibilities that underwrote the breadwinner ethic of the virtuous middle-class American man. He demanded something more electrifying than the wan comforts of bourgeois domesticity and the dependable wage of a secure job. He wanted thrills, adventure, crowds, applause, noise, laughter, luxury, "all," as Groff put it, "that goes to make up the flame of life." He wanted to live in exotic chambers lined with bamboo harvested in India and illumined by incandescent light softened with shades of elephant hide stretched to the point of translucence. He wanted a Japanese manservant and automobiles that dashed at mile-a-minute speeds and racing yachts that won coveted prizes. Thompson wanted nothing less than the moon for a plaything.

For most of his life Fred Thompson saw nothing flawed, tragic, or even foolish in refusing to acknowledge that his means could never realize the material splendor of his dreams, that he lived in a permanent condition of longing for a moon that was never quite in his reach. On the contrary, to concede that his wishes were unattainable or ill advised would be to surrender his heart to the afflictions of age, disappointment, and limitation. "When he dreams," remarked Groff, "there are no limits to his dreams."[1]

Dreams and desires achieved a new significance in the vocabulary and consciousness of western Europeans and Americans at the turn of the twentieth century. Psychologists and Darwinian naturalists, political economists, folklorists, sociologists, writers, and artists were divorcing their analysis, understanding, and representation of the unconscious forces and motives that drive human behavior from the moral cosmology of Christian theology. Whereas many of the turn-of-the-century students of desire, such as Sigmund Freud and the American novelist Theodore Dreiser, retained grave suspicions about the destructive power or ungovernability of human longings, the architects and advocates of the new culture of consumption, in historian William Leach's words, "took the dread and fear" out of the splendid dreams that the consumer marketplace catered to its public. They "gave life a happy face that would never grow old."[2]

If the emerging urban consumer culture in the United States had an actual happy face smiling over its landscape, it was that of Fred Thompson. The visage of this playful dreamer gradually assumed form and came into focus over the meandering course of the first thirty years of his life, the period before he built Luna Park on Coney Island. Thompson was not born to leisure or to play; just the opposite. He came of age in steel towns from western Pennsylvania to St. Louis, and the expectation was that he, like his father, would find his calling in the promise of the industrial nation. In this respect, he was very much the son of both his father and the commercial culture that nurtured him in his youth. But even as he served his apprenticeship in factories and internalized that culture's myths and promises, he never fully accepted the terms of Gilded Age industry. There had to be something less serious, something with more smiles than the grim rewards of either the punishing conditions of shop-floor labor or the restless mental work of managers and engineers committed to continuous-process manufacturing and increased efficiencies and outputs. The keenest insight he acquired over the course of his apprenticeship, which ranged from steel mills to the gaudy midways of fin de siècle world's fairs, was that he was not alone in his discontents. Other men shared the desire to have more fun. Instead of censuring or repressing this wish, Thompson ultimately exploited it by applying his industrial patrimony to produce a marketable and fantastic form of rebellion against the diminishing rewards of work in an industrializing corporate society. His endorsement of such wishes alienated him from contemporaries who believed social order, wealth, and progress rested on considerations graver than "fun." Although these men may have granted leisure a place in modern life—the rested man, after all, was the productive man—they never meant for leisure to become idleness or to produce nothing more than personal gratification. But Thompson, who apprenticed in work and play, was a new breed of man, one who understood that joy was precisely what mattered in life, and that what a man actually wanted was, in his words, to do "the opposite to the things he HAS to do." Granted, it was childish to wish for the moon, but what, he wondered, was wrong with that?[3]

### Pottering Around

Thompson was born on Halloween in 1873. In the typical stories told about him during the years of his amusement successes, observers such as Groff took pleasure in noting that America's leading showman, this always youthful and impertinent fun-maker with that "certain elfin quality" about him, came into existence on a traditional day of masquerade and misrule. Thompson seemed destined to be a showman. According to Groff, "all his life ... was an unconscious preparation for his ascendancy in the business."[4]

Picking out the influences and histories that made Fred Thompson is a trickier matter than relying on his account of how he rose from ordinary respectability to uncommon grandeur. Thompson's autobiographical voice charts his world-finder role in the early century's revolution in consumer amusements, but his story suppresses how his first twenty-eight years encompassed and reflected the social and economic disruptions and transformations of America's post–Civil War industrial revolution. Halloween in 1873 came at the beginning of the nationwide panic, which, over the next six years, would stretch into the most severe industrial depression of the century. New industrial firms threw hundreds of thousands into unemployment and severely cut the wages of those still working. In Pittsburgh, the wonder "metropolis of the American iron industry" in 1871, the furnaces were stilled as the metals market collapsed and the price per ton plummeted by 50 percent. "Idle men by the scores," according to a contemporary account, "were to be seen on every street, and the city wore a listless and woe-begone look." Across the country men like the young railroad fireman in Terra Haute, Indiana, Eugene Debs, whose job had seemed to assure a middle-class future shielded from the anonymous misery of poverty, were peremptorily thrown out of work. Debs and others like him went "on the tramp" to distant cities in search of work, setting off fears of a nation of "vagabonds."[5]

Railroad companies, like the regional line that fired Debs, were among the first to feel the panic, and they responded with job and wage reductions that challenged the widely held belief in an American nation marching forward behind the banner of free labor, industrial expansion, and material prosperity. Even before another round of severe wage reductions in mid-July 1877 incited the violent confrontations of the Great Railway Strike, the specter of a nation divided by warring workers and capitalists already was provoking fears that the European contagion of class conflict had infected the republic. In the aftermath of the short-lived "uprising," many middle- and working-class Americans, both those sympathetic to the striking workers and those who, with the *New York Tribune*, regarded them as "ignorant rabble with hungry mouths," came to fear for the survival of the republic itself. The future champion of labor Henry Demarest Lloyd, writing from his office at the *Chicago Tribune*, feared the "end of free government" and the "final disintegration of society" into mobs of the desperately poor at war with the armies of the rich. "What made the strike so alarming," historian John L. Thomas observes, "was not only the national scale of the violence, but also the new alignment of forces: workers against railroad managers, artisans and mechanics defending their moral economy against new businessmen, the deserving poor against the filthy rich."[6] Although neither he nor his journalistic biographers ever assigned any importance to these events, Thompson grew up amid and fell heir both to the hopeful expectations inspired by the seemingly limitless productivity of large-scale manufacturing and to the fears generated by the social conflicts sparked by the transformations in industrial work.

In the accounts that made sense of his astonishing appearance on the New York scene in 1903, journalists, like Thompson himself, attributed his development to the particular aspects of the new industrial America symbolized by his father, the engineer. His mother, Martha, was assigned little influence in her son's preparation; her background and opinions were left untold. Virtually nothing is known about her. Given the traditions of biographical writing, it is not surprising that her husband is portrayed as the principal parental actor in her son's drama. Thompson's journalistic biographers, like Thompson the autobiographer, were preoccupied with his public success. The useful or marketable skills, the genius for creation that got him where he was, could have corresponded only to the public, external activities and influence of his father. His mother may have quietly shaped his character, but his father taught him how to do big things.[7]

The spotlight that was cast on the supposed patrimonial foundation of Thompson's personality accentuated the lasting influence that the industrial engineer bequeathed to the future manufacturer of play. The father, Frederic "Casey" Thompson, had immigrated as a boy with his family from England to America, probably in 1850. The Thompson family eventually settled in Cleveland, where it established ties strong enough for Casey to serve in an Ohio infantry division in the Civil War. Although the information is sketchy, it appears that by the early 1870s Casey had become a skilled ironworker who, over the next decade, gradually worked his way off the shop floor and into management. When Fred was born, the family was living in Ironton, Ohio, in the heart of the Hanging Rock iron district across the Ohio River from Kentucky. Casey had moved his family there shortly before his son's birth, but Fred did not grow up in Ironton or any other particular location; rather, he came of age in the industrial archipelago of Gilded Age America. Within a year of his birth the family had moved upriver to Portsmouth, Ohio, where Casey worked the rolling mill at the Burgess Steel and Iron Works. The Thompsons stayed in Portsmouth until 1878 or 1879, then moved to a succession of steel cities—Johnstown, Pennsylvania, the site of the colossal Cambria Iron Works; Chicago; Springfield, Illinois; St. Louis—before settling finally in Nashville, Tennessee, probably in 1888. Even when the family stayed in one place, like St. Louis, the residence served as a home base from which Casey traveled to supervise waterworks projects in Dallas, Houston, and other growing towns in Texas. Why the Thompson family kept moving is unclear. Considering the instability of American industries in these two decades, Casey may well have lost his position in some instances, but it seems more likely that he was continuously pursuing new and better opportunities, cashing in on his managerial expertise to work for higher or more-promising bidders.[8]

Casey Thompson's ambitions may have kept the family almost constantly in motion, but Fred Thompson's childhood actually was no more mobile than that of earlier or contemporary generations of American men. He was an ordinary middle-class white male in the late nineteenth century, confronting the same anxious and hopeful feelings about his prospects that other youths of similar social backgrounds faced. Part of what distinguished him from other mobile Americans was his alienation from the actual or idealized rural hinterland, the moral economy of the pre–Civil War agricultural nation. Thompson was a product of the rapidly growing industrial cities of the late nineteenth century. In autobiographical accounts, he portrayed his mobile adult personality as the incarnation of his itinerant childhood, except that, as he described it, the unsettledness of his youth was an advantage rather than a liability; it gave spark to his personality and zest to his life, which were especially suited to the business of manufacturing pleasure.[9]

In Thompson's view, his youthful rebellions and restlessness were manifestations of the erratic but creative energies of a boy too impatient for the formal limitations and expectations of middle-class childhood in the late nineteenth century. He was continually defying his parents' authority. He especially bristled at the confinement of school, and attempted several times to quit, succeeding finally (in his words, against "parental insistence") in 1887 while living in St. Louis. As Thompson told the story, he did not like school; what he liked was "pottering around the mills." "I had a taste for mechanics, inherited, I suppose, and I liked to be where there was machinery," he recalled in 1905. Even at the ages of thirteen and fourteen the work he substituted for formal education reflected his likes. For a time, he apprenticed under a stained-glass maker; he also worked for Worthington Pump and Machinery, one of the leading American suppliers of massive hydraulic equipment for urban water and sewage systems (and possibly his father's employer). "I was in the office, but got into the shops as often as I could, and picked up more mechanical knowledge." At the time, his preferences were sending him in opposing directions: toward mechanical improvement and systems on one hand, and the sensual pleasures of light and color on the other. In retrospect, as Frances Groff put it, these expe-

28

riences were preparing Thompson later to combine materials and new technologies for producing light, color, and moving water into radiant visions of a new golden age of abundance and pleasure. Yet the choices he exercised also suggest that, as a youth, he acted as though work were not a necessity or an obligation—as was going to school. Work, in Thompson's mind and experience, had to conform to the hedonistic imperative to be fun.[10]

Although Thompson's inclination to hedonism existed in tension with his mechanical habit of mind, it was related to the ambivalence in the attitudes about work and leisure of the northern middle class, which after midcentury was willing to allow a place for leisure and even "play" in the distribution of life's energies. Historian Daniel Rodgers has written that the mechanization of industrial work and the diminution of the skill involved in production, combined with the astounding wealth of goods emanating from modern factories, undermined the middle-class "values of thrift, diligence, and self-discipline" and "ate away at the still older pillars of the nineteenth-century work ethic, the injunctions to useful effort and diligent self-discipline." With increasing frequency, overworked bourgeois men were ordered to balance their labor with leisure, to find, as the *Chautauquan* urged in 1896, "a middle ground between the idler and the man who works himself to death." Yet, as the magazine's command suggests, the theological and secular reform voices sanctioning greater leisure harbored hostilities to any suggestion that pleasure was a moral end in itself. As Rodgers observes, "the predilection to see the moral life as a mustering of the will against the temptations within and the trials without remained the strongest [pillar of the work ethic], the least affected by the industrial transformation." Thompson's calculus of "likes" suggested an alternative connection between work and play in which the thin dividing line of the *Chautauquan* virtually disappeared in the insistence that work, like life, should yield pleasure and profit.[11]

Thompson's breezy memories of his fun-loving childhood attraction to the steel mill and the new processes of metals production did not reflect the experiences of many thousands of American men for whom pouring steel was an everyday matter of life and death. Steelwork rewarded such people with unusually high pay and a sense of proud male solidarity, but it was a violent, exhausting sequence of twelve-hour shifts six days a week under dangerous conditions that often killed or maimed those who labored to make the steel. Thompson surely recognized that neither the communal rewards nor the perils of such work were for him. Neither was he especially concerned with the struggle for control of the industrial workplace. The American steel factories where Casey Thompson managed and his son played were at the center of the conflict in the late nineteenth century over the relative power of labor and capital in the new industrial age. This debate went beyond the politics of union formation and job protection to encompass broader cultural and political questions about "what the Republic should be" in an age of industrial expansion and technological innovation. Industrialists such as Andrew Carnegie insisted that the general good was secured by the free accumulation of wealth. But workingmen, both skilled and unskilled, native born and immigrant, in large factories and smaller workshops, insisted that individual property rights had to be moderated by "an egalitarian moral code" that attended first to the larger community's needs. Their standards identified the dignity of the "honest toiler" as the bulwark that guarded the nation against great concentrations of wealth and power. Although craftworkers such as those in metals manufacturing were an unrepresentative elite, their defense of their autonomy in the workplace and the laboring man's right to a living wage voiced the more general belief among white men in the nineteenth century that the quality of one's work determined the quality of one's "manhood," a word that captured the popular understanding "of dignity, respectability, defiant egalitarianism, and patriarchal male supremacy." The violent conflicts of the Gilded Age between capital and labor were not about the right to private property or the benefits of material comfort; few disputed the truth of these issues. Rather they were about whether modern, industrial America would be dominated by the wage system, the unrestricted accumulation of capital, and the "empirical and cruel law of supply and demand," or be subject to the claims of industrial workers to live comfortably and securely as men.[12]

These questions became momentous and the efforts to answer them increasingly violent in the steel industry during and after the decade of Thompson's birth, when the era's depressions pushed industrialists to eliminate the costly and uncontrollable factor of production: skilled masters of the essential manual techniques of metal production. These men exercised unusual leverage over the mill owners and fiercely guarded against technological or other innovations that would insult their manhood by undermining the priority of their craft. Andrew Carnegie's prized engineer, Alexander Lyman Holley, derided the skills of such workers as "tradition, trial, failure, and guesswork," and committed his energies to liberating the industrial workplace from such primitive forces.[13]

Unlike many skilled industrial workers of his era, Casey Thompson appears not to have possessed a binding loyalty or sense of duty to any particular place or community of workers. Although he may have been guided by an internal work ethic, his itinerancy suggests that his principal allegiance was to the market value of his expertise. Frances Groff, in her 1915 account, described him as "a civil, hydraulic and mechanical engineer," who trained his son in both the techniques and the morality of solving mechanical problems. The starting point for Casey was always the same: "Go to the first principle and work up from it and everything is simple." When "the boy Frederic brought to him a problem, he first had to tell his father the origin, the A, B, C, of it, before the father would explain its complexities. If it was lifting water, the boy had to tell how water was lifted in the primitive by the savages." This approach encompassed more than how to master the rudimentary principles of physics. It also advanced the engineer's "morality of improvement"; that is, the assurance that mechanical improvements to production and the economic advantages that accrued trumped all other conceptions of value. The engineer's obligation to provide the most efficient solution to a problem ensured the greatest outcome in response to the least expenditure of effort. The results could be measured, but quantity was not just a method of weighing value; it constituted value. The engineers' faith was that fulfilling their obligation made the world a better place. Machines, they argued, operated according to universal scientific principles and laws, and their application to problems of production and organization provided rational solutions that were unbiased by the particular claims of interested groups, such as laboring men who were more loyal to their jobs than to getting the job done right. The social critic and historian Lewis Mumford called this way of thinking the "mechanical habit of mind," and Fred Thompson possessed it as fully as the new generation of engineers like his father, who were seeking, through rational management, mechanical innovations, and laboratory analysis, to liberate manufacturing and the pursuit of economic advantage from the backward, "rule of thumb" practices of craftsmen. For people who thought this way, "invention" was not one option but a stern duty. The bequest from Thompson's father went beyond the ABCs of solving problems; it incorporated a set of loyalties, obligations, and faiths that the younger Thompson later identified, celebrated, and exploited, even as he applied them in ways of which his father could not have anticipated or approved. He called this outlook the American "Genius for Industrial Organization."[14]

The many accounts of the meandering course and chance circumstances that took Fred Thompson from the iron furnaces of the Midwest to Coney Island's plaster palaces of amusement do not mention these larger social changes and conflicts. This omission seems worth noting, especially in the case of a man who spent much of his childhood pottering around steel mills, who was the son of an industrial engineer, and who was living in the Chicago vicinity in 1886, when the century's most notorious incident of labor violence, the Haymarket riot, occurred in that city. Despite their absence in his official presentation of self, these events and the conflicts that underlay them defined his habits of mind as much as did his father's devotion to efficiency and time clocks.

Young Fred's insubordination and rebellion against the industrial culture of his father concealed a deeper commitment to the paternal world of interlocking and interchangeable parts, circuits of distribution and control, and systems of organization. The future "toymaker of New York" did not deny the mechanicalized worldview of his father, but directed it toward unexplored markets for pleasure. What drew him to factories was not the shop culture of fraternal solidarity, manly accomplishment, and authority prized by laboring men, or the moral and economic dividends yielded to managers and their employers when expensive workers were supplanted by capital improvements. His attraction was an intensely private fascination with what machines could do. He tended to judge industrial settings in terms of personal tastes and preferences; they were places where he could indulge his penchants, amuse himself, and marvel at the organization of machinery and labor without having to submit himself to their rigor and discipline. He was betwixt and between the shop-floor culture of laboring men and the mechanicalized mentality of managerial middle-class men. What mattered most to him was being amused, and what amused him most were the machines themselves—the presses, blast furnaces, traveling cranes, and trip hammers of a steel plant; Worthington's big hydraulic pumps that could fill or drain a small lake in a matter of minutes. Their magnificent gigantism thrilled him as long as the violent conditions of the industrial shop floor were irrelevant to his welfare and could be softened into a stirring vision of technological organization. In his eyes, to use Lewis Mumford's words, it was the "machine," not the laboring men or the labor of men, that was "the true embodiment of everything that was excellent." Thompson wished to indulge his passion for the manufacturing process while dodging the discipline and confinement of work. Any claims or realities that might diminish or qualify his access to pleasure, whether the expectations of his father, the mutualistic ethic of working men, or the cost concerns of managers and engineers, would hold no authority over him.[15]

### Work That Suited Me

Thompson's youthful rebellions and the worry that his insubordination and indecisiveness apparently caused his family were, in many ways, familiar themes of conflict in the lives of nineteenth-century middle-class American men. Such rebellion had underwritten the vast library of Davy Crockett tales that bourgeois men anxiously consumed. Humorous stories about the autonomy of this unrestrained son of the "fabled frontier" reassured midcentury men that their own youthful rejection of the older economic order of the fathers, with its ties of patrimony, deference, and patronage, was necessary to the sacred task of unfettering the natural order of free-market capitalism. Other recent accounts of youthful male defiance in antebellum America suggest that insubordinate sons, as well as the tales spun about them, could be as hostile to the "market revolution" as the stories about Crockett and others were supportive of it. Yet whether these young men were trying to build a new commercial world or to restore a lost preindustrial one, they were not supposed to wear the coonskin caps of antiauthoritarianism all their lives. At some point they would have to grow up.[16]

The rebelliousness of boys and the unsettled and tumultuous lives of young men could be tolerated so long as such foolishness reflected temporary stages in the individual's progressive advance toward mature, self-restrained manhood. As a rule, Victorian men believed that they were substantively different from, and morally superior to, not just, as one would expect, women and girls, but also boys and male "youth." Boy life, or "culture," as the historian Anthony Rotundo calls it, "was a world of play, a social space where one evaded the duties and restrictions of adult society." The transitional period between boyhood and manhood, which for most lasted from the teens until the mid- to late twenties, was expected to be a period of shifting social allegiances and occupational identities, when a male was neither a playful boy nor a settled man. For the Victorian middle class, manhood was finally measured and valued by the degree to which men moved beyond the "playful, hedonistic, libidinal quality of the boys' world" and the unsteadiness of their youth to the higher and more solid ground of patriarchal authority.[17]

Manliness, then, was not the automatic result of possessing a male body. Boys had male bodies, but they had yet to prove their manhood. Grown men, on the other hand, were no better than or different from boys if they did not or, in the case of the "inferior" races, could not behave like men. Being a man, as this logic suggests, was all about being manly, which was a moral quality, not a physical attribute. A man demonstrated his entitlement to the honor in a number of ways—for instance, by acquiring property and acting with thrifty self-restraint, uncompromising independence, and willful disregard for "effeminate" leisure and luxury. Outside the slave South, the setting in which this honorable "self-made" manhood was both achieved and enacted was the antebellum society of small-scale, entrepreneurial capitalism and partisan politics. There success was equated with self-mastery and measured by the degree to which a man had achieved independence through either business ownership or recognized skill and autonomy in the workplace. In Rotundo's words, men were supposed to be "quiet and sober, for theirs was a life of serious business. They had families to support, reputations to earn, responsibilities to meet. Their world was based on work, not play, and their survival in it depended on patient planning, not spontaneous impulse. To prosper, then, a man had to delay gratification and restrain desire."[18]

In disparaging the whole notion of child's play, Victorian men solidified their own sense of gender entitlement. "Play" described the untamed actions of children and "savages," and "boy" was a racial slur that denied African American men, whether slave or free, their capacity for independent or "self-made" manhood. Citizenship, political participation, property ownership, and market success were the essential components of manly identity in the first seventy years of the nineteenth century. Enfranchised men were expected to exercise their rights in a manner that marked the distinction between the reckless antics of savages and the informed, responsible acts of civilized men. White men had to give up childish behavior as they matured from boyhood to manhood, especially if they aimed to accumulate wealth and earn the respect of others. Many men also felt compelled to exterminate the play impulse in others: in immigrant, working-class men, whose mischief they attacked in Sabbatarian and temperance campaigns, or in Native Americans, whom they regarded as "playful, violent, improvident, wild." If the "childish" communal ways of Indians could not be converted to the manly values of private property and commercial farming, then the Indians could be forcibly removed to make way for a mature civilization. The boundary between work and play, then, was one of the essential ideological dividers in the nineteenth century. Manliness was measured by the degree to which (white) men abandoned or restrained the playful impulses of boys, Indians, or African Americans, and achieved their negation by donning the mantle of duty, responsibility, self-control, and self-ownership. The same logic applied to the republic as a whole. In the words of the midcentury historian Francis Parkman, "Barbarism is to civilization what childhood is to maturity." The (white) man was the nation in microcosm. If he played or failed to grow up, the nation as a whole was at risk.[19]

The ethos of workplace hedonism that Fred Thompson assembled over the last two decades of the nineteenth century indicated that, by the end of the century, the authority of older understandings of boyhood and adulthood and distinctions between play and work were being challenged. In the 1890s, long after the time of Davy Crockett, many males, on the threshold of manhood, had been like the muckraking journalist Ray Stannard Baker, "torn" between what they desired and what they felt it was their manly duty to do. All knew that work "lay at the heart of a man's role; if work was a problem, so was manhood."[20] An insistence that work had to be fun raised just such problems. It amounted to refusing to become a "man" and violated the officially sanctioned expectations about the acceptable route to personal salvation, property ownership, and social and personal responsibility. Yet many men of Thompson's race, class, and age were yearning to experience boyish pleasures that earlier generations had scorned. In the new light, the problems of the contemporary world were its excessive maturity and oppressive seriousness, its hostile resistance to playful, improvident fun.

Why American men like Fred Thompson were trying to be what they had once labored not to be is a complicated issue. Most scholars today argue that broad social and economic changes were weakening the claims of "self-made" manhood and leaving middle-class men fretful about their manhood: the erosion of male autonomy in the industrial and bureaucratic workplace; the new political and cultural authority of immigrant and working-class communities; the penetration of "new women," whether as workers or consumers, into the once exclusively male public worlds of business and politics; and, finally, the emergence of a consumer culture that subverted the ethos of self-control and delayed gratification even as it promised a freedom and fulfillment through consumption that men rarely produced anymore in the workplace or achieved in politics. Underlying these troubles was the rapid decline of self-employment in agriculture and business. In the early nineteenth century, as many as four out of five white men owned their own farms, artisan shops, or businesses. These conditions were experienced in the everyday lives of ordinary white men and helped define "American manhood" in class, age, ethnic, and racial terms. Manliness was the exclusive condition not of males, but of independent, property-owning men. Women and girls were excluded from the category, but so were boys, African-American slaves, and wage-working immigrant men. By 1900, however, independent business ownership was fading in an increasingly corporate capitalist society, and middle-class men typically worked for others rather than for themselves. Even affluent men usually brought home salaries, which disconnected the older indicators of manhood from current social realities. Having a well-paying job and the privileges of purchase that it enabled became, as a matter of necessity, the new signs of manly distinction. Still, many men worried that wealth, ease, and comfort were no substitute for what they imagined as the invigorating, risk-filled lives of earlier generations of men. Elliott J. Gorn, whose history of bare-knuckle boxing in America tracks the growing middle-class fascination with the once despised sports of working-class men, has observed that turn-of-the-century men were beset with an array of hard-to-answer questions. "Where would a sense of maleness come from for the worker who sat at a desk all day? How could one be manly without independence? Where was virility to be found in increasingly faceless bureaucracies? How might clerks or salesmen feel masculine doing 'women's work'? What became of rugged individualism inside intensively rationalized corporations? How could a man be a patriarch when his job kept him away from home for most of his waking hours?"[21]

White middle-class men still valued older ideals of manhood based on property ownership and control of one's labor. But as these goals became more difficult to attain, the men had to reinvent the terms of manhood in order to preserve their sense of themselves as men, which was the basis of their economic, political, and sexual priority. The male body, as opposed to the manly character inside, became the new foundation of manhood. In the process men envied or appropriated qualities as well as social behaviors that once were regarded as subversive of manliness, such as the rough physical energy and conflict of boxing and other working-class male sports. In addition, the once impermeable moral and physical boundary between men and boys began to fade. Middle-class men sought to cultivate and prolong the exuberant and rebellious playfulness of savages and boys. In the new rival, but ascendant, gender culture of "passionate" or "expressive" manhood, controlled, "civilized" standards of behavior seemed to encourage effeminacy and weakness instead of keeping them at bay. Under these conditions, it was men who never stopped playing and resisted "growing up," not those who left childhood behind, who staved off degeneracy and emerged as culture heroes of manliness.[22]

These versions of hypermasculinity and the compensations they offered received cultural sanction from many directions. At the more popular level, the new "boy-man" continuum could be seen in the adult enthusiasm for sports that celebrated the male body, and in the new determination of middle-class men to be the "chums" of their sons in new organizations like the Boy Scouts. The psychologist G. Stanley Hall urged harried and fatigued white men to recharge their manhood by recapitulating the "savage" play of children. Teddy Roosevelt's playacting as frontiersman and "Rough Rider" consciously cultivated the image of the boy-achiever on the athletic playing fields of life. In 1902, the novelist Owen Wister published *The Virginian*, which helped lay the foundations for the twentieth-century veneration of the cowboy. Although the story was typical in defining the frontier as the crucible of the American character, it subverted this convention by describing the "lost" West of the 1870s as a space defined not by the work of self-reliant men, but by the gamboling of cowboys on the vast "playground of young men."[23] Play, while still problematic, was increasingly being encouraged as a necessary antidote to the "overcivilized" condition of middle-class men in a corporate consumer society.

Yet the commercial culture of Peter Pan, which exploited adults' wishes to believe in fairies and their willingness to pay to return to their childhood, capitalized on a different order of fantasy play and fantastic role-playing, one constructed less in opposition to than in friendly support of the world of goods. Studies of the new "passionate" behavior and attitudes of middle-class men have concentrated on the siege mentality of such men and their defensive efforts to compensate for the historical "crisis" of what they experienced as a modernizing and effeminizing corporate society. Although true in many respects, the emphasis placed on the "woes" of such men has obscured the complicated ways in which men such as Thompson endeavored to fashion an authentic masculinity that could meet the challenges and seize the opportunities of the new economy. During his youth, Thompson was as perplexed as other young men of his class and generation who were expected to learn to control their impulses and become responsible men. Yet his peculiar reconciliation of his desire for fun with the dominant culture's duties of work and production pointed to alternative masculine identities, which were more in tune with the ethos of a corporate consumer society.[24]

Thompson's conversion to "Peter Pantheism" began to emerge once his family left the industrializing Midwest and took up residence in the New South of Nashville, Tennessee, a city better known for its commercial and financial capitalism than for its heavy industries. The Thompson family had connections there. Casey's brother, George W. Thompson, was one of the city's leading commercial and residential architects. Casey left industrial engineering for good at this point and, probably with his brother's assistance, went into the stonecutting and construction business. Following that lead, young Fred also "shook the shops," as he put it, and eventually studied architectural drawing in his uncle's office. "I had always, as a kid and later, been fond of drawing, particularly mechanical drawing," Thompson explained, "and in the architect's office I had work that suited me."[25]

What is striking here is not the indecisiveness that attended his becoming a man, but how he worked his way out of the limbo between delayed and instant gratification, boyhood and manhood, pottering around the mills and productive, socially valuable work. Thompson orchestrated these conventional oppositions into an unusual combination, much as he later used colored glass, light, and hydraulic machinery in his amusements to produce delightful entertainments. The work that "suited" him replicated the boyhood joy of drawing. Instead of surrendering childhood pleasures, he had found a way to make them remunerative. Thompson's claims did not deny the importance of work to male identity; on the contrary, he continued to affirm work as the activity that made him a man. Yet he was easing his way out from under older expectations of responsible and controlled manliness and extracting himself as well from the religious and civic obligations that had defined in the nineteenth century what kind of man was needed to preserve the republic. In making his choices, he assigned unusual priority to personal gratification, positing an ethic that men should be guided not by adult expectations but by the boy's wish for fun. Hedonism, instead of the opposite of work, was its most necessary condition. No man could prosper without it.

### Gala Days

Starting at the bottom of the architectural trade, however, was neither fun nor sufficiently remunerative. No line of business or work occupied Thompson's attention for long. The Nashville city directories for the 1890s sketch his erratic search for more-pleasing work and quicker, more-lucrative, or at least more-exciting returns. Between 1889 and 1899 he listed himself in five different guises: salesman, agent in building specialties, draughtsman, agent for an iron works, and, for four of the last five years, artist. Thompson seemed unable to reconcile the inclinations that steered him toward personal enjoyment and artistic expressiveness—stained glass and architecture—with either the middle-class expectation of productive, moneymaking work or the disciplined and organized processes of industrial management. In 1891 he set up his own business brokering building materials, steel, and furniture for local contractors. These, he later claimed, were his "gala days." He "made money hand over fist," as much as fifteen hundred dollars a month, which was an unusually high income for someone not yet twenty years old. Yet the windfall manifested a pattern that he would replicate with brilliant as well as disastrous consequences during his New York years. For if Thompson by inclination was averse to serious business, steady application of energy, and patient planning, he also was an uncommonly prodigal spendthrift. His appetites rapidly outpaced his income. "Didn't drink, or gamble, either," he claimed, no doubt lying, "but there were a lot of lively young fellows at the clubs, and I was one of them." Casey Thompson implored his son to return to architecture in exchange for settling his debts of some four thousand dollars. The youth accepted his father's offer, returned to his uncle's architectural office as a "tracer" or draughtsman, and repaid the loan from his father. Thompson recounted the story of his father's intervention in newspaper and magazine interviews after 1903. Although it emphasized the prodigal son's redemption and the lessons learned from his mistakes, the tale also contributed to the construction of the showman's identity as an irrepressible boy-man who resisted submitting to the joyless duties and restrictions of mature manhood. It also sketched the paternalistic role that Thompson, contemporary journalists, and later historians attributed to his Coney Island business partner, Elmer "Skip" Dundy, who, as the figure of adult authority, reason, and sobriety, supposedly balanced the excesses of the perennial child. This alleged compromise probably was a fiction, but in this and other instances, it suggested that Thompson had found a way to coordinate the adventure of play with the repressive discipline of prudent business activity, exuberant boyish freedom with the steadying hand of management.[26]

However much he liked to draw, Thompson did not remain a tracer for long. He later would boast of his wanderlust and inability to focus on any line of work or to devote himself to any particular vocation. There have been erroneous recent claims that he, like many of the era's most celebrated architects, studied at the renowned École des Beaux Arts in Paris. His off-and-on-again work with his uncle was the extent of his formal architectural education. There was nothing unusual about such meager instruction at a time when "the illiteracy of apprentices trained by half-trained practitioners" still defined most architectural education. But by the 1890s the trend was toward the "progressive" ideal of the professional architect, trained, certified, and licensed according to objective, universal standards. The graduates of the Parisian institute, which the architect Louis Sullivan called the "fountain head of theory," embodied this ideal most famously. Although its influence has been closely identified with the monumental neoclassicism of Gilded Age America, the École actually placed emphasis less on style than on "the student's discovery of the logically correct solution to the architectural problem confronting him." As the historian William Wilson observed, what mattered most was mastery of "the principles of proportion, scale, balanced arrangement of forms, and unity.... The École advocated no particular style, but its emphasis on logic, vigor, and the fine arts favored the classic." Whether by inclination, fortune, or premeditation, Thompson never mastered formal design principles or techniques in the Beaux Arts manner, and he petulantly dismissed and derided what he did not and could not possess. Yet the shallowness of his architectural training, combined with the defensiveness it bred, may also have freed him from too great a concern with correctness. At the same time, the practical experience of illustrating other men's ideas on paper probably honed his mimetic inclinations. He learned to reproduce with facility surface patterns or details and deploy them in combinations that delighted, even if the composition as a whole disregarded functionality and the requirements of formal consistency or logic. Such concerns were beyond him; he was impressed only by the effect of the finished product. Did it win the favor of the masses? Strictly speaking, would they pay to see or enter it?[27]

In this respect, Thompson's inclinations and mimetic skills prepared him well as a commercial artist. The work of such artists, because of their primary concern for what sells, tends toward the tried-and-true. The aversion to innovations, however, can also cause problems—that is, declining novelty in a consumer economy the engines of which run on the new. To keep their products from becoming stale, commercial artists often look to "high" culture for aesthetic themes that they adapt to their own needs. For instance, Thompson's contemporary, the Viennese emigré Joseph Urban (born in 1872), enlivened the American consumer marketplace in the 1910s and 1920s by incorporating the aesthetic vocabulary of European modernism into the display and design of commodities. Thompson, on the other hand, tended to cannibalize the genteel aesthetic of nineteenth-century neoclassicism and the sensual "otherness" of Orientalist stereotypes into the unlikely and avowedly commercial combinations of his amusements. His most important training along these lines began in late 1892 or early 1893, when he tired of the pleasures of Nashville and, like millions of other Americans, was lured to Chicago for the Columbian International Exposition.[28]

Chicago's White City was the most famous and, with a paid attendance of as many as twenty-seven million, the most popular of the many world's fairs held in the United States between 1890 and 1916. Constructed south of the city on Lake Michigan, the fair celebrated Columbus's first voyage of discovery to the New World. What made world's fairs worldly was the participation of foreign nations, which contributed cultural artifacts, from manufactured goods and artistic treasures to examples of their "primitive" peoples, whose villages were reconstructed in the commercial amusement section, or "midway," of the fair. Notwithstanding the appeals to internationalism, the great expositions in Chicago and other American cities were nationalist showcases for the industrial and cultural achievements of the United States. That chauvinism, in turn, was inflected by a booster's emphasis on the leading roles of the host cities' titans of finance, commerce, and industry. In Chicago, for instance, the great merchant Marshall Field and the industrialist George Pullman took leading public roles in staging the fair. Symbols of civilization's achievements—from dynamos to typewriters—were displayed in vast exhibition halls, which actually were fancy sheds framed with wooden or steel beams and done up to look like marble palaces. The marble effect came from a malleable gypsum compound called "staff," which was plastered on the buildings' exteriors, molded, and spray-painted to resemble stone. Staff sculptures and ornaments could be produced in mass quantities, and the skins of buildings fashioned into comparatively inexpensive, although nonetheless impressive, neoclassical monuments, reminiscent while not exactly copies of European masterpieces. The nation's leading architects competed to design the major features of the fairs, which spread out over hundreds of acres of urban space transformed into commodious parkland. The resulting plaster cities splendidly shone forth as the highest expressions of the attainments and apparently unified purposes of modern civilization, and especially of American capitalism's vanguard role in the coming century.[29]

As representations of civilization, fairs obviously had ideological purposes. Looking outward, they demonstrated the racial and material superiority of the West over the (nonwhite) rest of the world. Looking inward, Chicago's White City, like later fairs modeled on its example, was a metaphor for urban life, which business, financial, and cultural elites posed critically against the grimy congestion and disorganized commotion of the industrial city beyond its pristine borders. The ennobling monuments and serene lagoons, the organized management, the hierarchies of taste, and the tractable work force—all showed how a modern, industrial city "might be governed as well as how it might look." Architecture played a central role in this project. The Chicago exposition spectacularly represented an urban reform effort that had been gaining currency since the 1870s and that, after 1900, would be called the "City Beautiful" movement. The influential designers and artists who went to Chicago sought to use their art to restore civic harmony and purpose to the heterogeneous cities of the late nineteenth century. They wished for their art to inculcate a "civic spirit" by inspiring "the individual citizen to embrace higher ideals through a new artistic environment." In their minds, architecture was "a moral and political enterprise" that "reflected and shaped behavior."[30]

## Perfect Cities

Fairs were not just produced; they also had to be consumed, and those who paid their way through the gates had various and often conflicting interests and impressions that did not necessarily defer to the cultural leadership of the wealthy and often educated men and women who planned and built expositions. Thompson, for one, never assigned the Columbian exposition any extraordinary influence in his life. Only nineteen to twenty years old at the time, he worked as a janitor and later a "demonstrator" at one of the industrial exhibits and supplemented his income by stringing articles and sketches for a Chicago newspaper. But beginning with Chicago in 1893, he was involved with every major world's fair in the United States through the Pan-American Exposition in Buffalo in 1901. He became what Frances Groff called an "exposition moth." Thompson never indicated what led him either to the Columbian exposition or to the business of building the temporary plaster edifices common to world's fairgrounds, whether he longed to duplicate the White City's pristine architectural monuments or simply recognized that such rare economies of scale were irresistible opportunities for profit. By the early 1890s he had the elementary skills needed to understand and pursue the work. He knew contractors through his uncle and father and from his own brokerage business, and his brief architectural education had taught him at least the basics of design. But there is no evidence that the direction he followed resulted from any premeditation. He certainly did not approach expositions, initially at least, as a showman in the manner of the Columbian's great impresario, Sol Bloom. As Thompson later explained, he "came in contact with show people" through his newspaper work, "but never thought of it as a business." Nor did he, like Pullman and other genteel sponsors, regard expositions as frozen sermons. When the fair ended, it seems that he moved on to Iowa to work at a steel mill.[31]

Even if Thompson was unwilling to concede the influence of the exposition, the Chicago fair and its imitators affected his outlook, although not as the fair's major designers had intended. There were many reasons why he resisted the White City's genteel charms. The leading architects came from the "burned-over" district of western New York State in the 1830s and 1840s. This region, stocked with immigrants from New England, many of whom made good in the early nineteenth century's commercial revolution in agriculture and business, was at the center of what some historians regard as "the greatest outpouring of religious feeling in Christendom" since the seventeenth century. The revivals of the Second Great Awakening and the sectarian revolution they inspired gave rise to midcentury reform movements that profoundly shaped middle-class culture thereafter. Chicagoans such as Pullman and the innovative retailer Marshall Field were inheritors of the perfectionist evangelical culture of antebellum America. The new evangelists rejected Calvinism's determinist doctrines and asserted the efficacy of the human will in achieving not only salvation but even the perfection of the self. Sin was no longer the persistent stain on the human heart, but the selfish preferences of individuals. The middle-class evangelical culture combined a faith in the personal and social benefits of character reformation with a godly duty to vanquish sin from the visible world. Social reform, productive work, and religious duty were one and the same, and that these endeavors often served the business interests of their adherents provided further evidence of God's favor.[32]

The Chicago that men such as Field and Pullman and, in some cases, their wives built was a "new outpost of the burned-over district." Their assumption was that business enterprise and religious or secular reform activities composed a divinely approved alliance. The great civic institutions of the city—the YMCA, the evangelist Dwight L. Moody's Bible Institute, the University of Chicago—were beneficiaries of the evangelical impulse to bend men's inclinations to the regenerated will, but tailored to the outsized needs of the industrial metropolis. Their faith was that culture, rightly formed, whether as architecture or music or exposition cities, was a principal tool in the building of the modern Jerusalem. Thus a man such as George Pullman, who made one of the era's magnificent fortunes manufacturing luxurious railway passenger cars, could aspire to instill the "simple" values of his rural, evangelical childhood among Chicago's raw and ill-mannered working class through the exemplary environment of his model workers' town, Pullman. His only wish, he said, was to show his workers "that decency, propriety and good manners are not unattainable luxuries for them; that it is not necessary to be loosely or carelessly dressed in order to do good work, to save money, and to raise themselves in the social scale." If followed, these simple rules foretold a future of godliness and modest comfort.[33]

Like millions of others who lived in Chicago or journeyed there in 1893 to see the White City, Fred Thompson did not share this particular evangelical, reformist, or rural background. Younger than Pullman by a full generation, Thompson also was the child of a foreign-born immigrant. Nor was he spurred to reform activity by the evangelical assurance of God's active presence in contemporary culture; as he later put it, the best church was one closed for a picnic. Thompson was alienated from the prudential moral culture of the evangelical middle class, which extolled the personal benefits of gradual accumulation. As an opponent of lotteries had explained in 1828, "That man, who rises gradually into notice from obscurity, and who, by frugality, temperance, and perseverance in business becomes wealthy, is alone the happy man in the enjoyment of his possessions. He feels a complacency and a contentment, which that man knows nothing of, who starts up, at once, like the mushroom, from obscurity, into the ranks of the rich." Thompson's contempt for this outlook was abetted by his skepticism about the personal value of work and by his inclination to equate what he and others should do with what they wanted to do. As his meandering among occupations indicated, he was not inclined to suffer the small, patient steps that rich men such as Pullman promised would yield the proper life of Sunday schools, quiet libraries, savings banks, uplifting theater, and the polite material surroundings of home. What he wanted were luxuries as splendid as Pullman's, only amplified by excitement and thrills. In many ways, he was much closer in spirit to his fellow first-generation American, Sol Bloom, the director of the fair's mile-long avenue of amusements, the Midway Plaisance.[34]

The fair's planners had initially placed the Midway under the direction of the respected Harvard ethnologist Frederic Ward Putnam. His instruction was to produce an educational "Street of All Nations," where fair patrons could observe the primitive ways of uncivilized peoples—American Indians; Dahomey, Javanese, and Samoan natives. Anthropology promised to impose decency on the operation in the eyes of the city's leaders, who were leery of the disreputable types that popular amusements attracted and concerned that commercialism would cheapen the main exposition. But amusement concessionaires, lured by the chance for windfall profits, overran efforts to gloss over raw commercialism and indulgent sensuality. The Midway ended up a mix of "authentic" ethnic villages and carnival fare. The city's "custodians of culture" had to rely on geographical distance and aesthetic distinction to demarcate the divide between arts that wrought improvement in the observer and those that sought merely to amuse. But from the start, the Midway attracted larger and more-enthusiastic crowds than the exposition proper.[35]

The genius of the Midway was Sol Bloom, who once described himself as "an enterprising young man with a knack for making money." He was born in Pekin, Illinois, in 1870 to Polish-Jewish immigrant parents, but moved with his family to San Francisco in 1873, in the midst of the depression. Before he was twenty, and through as much chicanery as pluck, he had amassed a small fortune from running a popular theater. In the late 1880s he cashed in his accounts and went on a world tour that took him no farther than the 1889 Paris world's fair. Acutely aware of his cultural deficiencies, Bloom was determined to stuff his head with the artistic and industrial achievements of Europe's culture capital, but he quickly had his fill of such solemn subjects. Much more "fascinating" were the exotica of colonial Africa and Asia—Bedouin acrobats, Arabian sword-swallowers, and other attractions in the reconstructed Algerian village. Bloom returned to the United States after securing an option on his "favorite among favorites." When he went to Chicago, the Algerians went too.[36]

Bloom was hired to make the Midway a paying proposition, not to reform the metropolis. But when the showman arrived in Chicago, he discovered that the Midway was under the aegis of the Harvard ethnologist. As a result, Bloom actually encouraged the cultural and psychological division of Midway and exposition and did all he could to edge out Putnam, whose reform agenda threatened the only concern of the showmen—making money. For Bloom, culture was valuable only when it generated profits. The fair as Midway and White City thus incorporated rival moral economies. The advocates of each wished for the landslide approval of the attending multitudes, but they divided on whether the market confirmed a preexisting and transcendent morality or actually determined morality itself. As far as Bloom was concerned, something was good if people bought it. As the owner of the fair's most notorious attraction, the *danse du ventre*, performed by a troupe of belly dancers at his Algerian village, he would know. Furthermore, Bloom's moral economy did not need the sanction or sponsorship of the White City. Fifteen years after the Columbian exposition, the amusement park manager John Calvin Brown credited the Chicago Midway with proving a most valuable point: "The segregation of amusements in population centers would be profitable even without the drawing capacity of the main and expensive exposition."[37]

### Bachelor Life

In 1893 and for the rest of the decade, Fred Thompson resisted embracing the lessons Sol Bloom offered. His return to the steel mill in Iowa was only temporary. He used his wages to fund a year of study at a Cincinnati art academy. Thompson still was unable to commit his energies to a career in illustration. Another art student whom he befriended owned an interest in a mine in Mexico and talked him into going south after he finished his instruction. Thompson studied mining engineering for three months in Mexico City, then traveled to a remote mining camp near the Pacific coast, eight days by burro from Guadalajara. Battling the heat, scorpions, bandits, and fever, he effectively built his first city, setting up the mines, constructing roads, and supervising 250 impoverished Mexican laborers. The mines, Thompson claimed, "paid the company big, and I was offered all sorts of good things to stay, but I couldn't stand the climate." He returned to Nashville in 1894.[38]

These vacillations between producing and brokering industrial commodities and fabricating images may have resulted less from indirection than from unease with the implications of all the options. As Thompson assumed from personal experience and from the widely published middle-class critics of modern industrial work, manufacturing labor made drudges of men. On the other hand, he may well have felt that either the "brain work" of industrial management, with its systematizing drive for higher yields, or the solemn life of business was slavery under another name, and would cast him in the image of the sober father who had reined in his fun.[39]

Another problem was Fred Thompson's social standing. In Nashville his family's status and aspirations were solidly white collar. Through most of the 1890s, Casey Thompson and his family, like that of his prominent brother, resided in the prosperous streetcar suburb of Edgefield, a bourgeois enclave of comfortable homes and impressive redbrick churches. Located east of the main business center, across the Cumberland River, Edgefield was home to the New South city's rising merchant and manufacturing elite. For most of that decade, Fred Thompson boarded with his parents, which, alone, did not make him unusual. The percentage of urban middle-class men who remained unmarried well into their twenties or thirties was rising rapidly at the end of the nineteenth century. The largest segment of this male population continued to reside with family or kin, leading lives of semidependence, not fully under parental scrutiny, but not free of it either. Living at home was especially common for middle-class single men and had its advantages: they probably saved money even as "boarders," and it gave them a domestic identity that fended off the common associations of single life in commercial boardinghouses with nomadic roués. Thompson's addresses in Edgefield served as secure home bases from which he ventured out with other "lively young fellows" to attractions in Nashville and later in Chicago, Mexico, and Atlanta. At the same time, however, he lived among striving middle-class people who usually measured a man's worth by his steadiness and achievements at work, and disapproved of "pottering." In neighborhoods like Edgefield, achievement-oriented men took notice when a young man did not settle down to the responsibilities of marriage and family, or when he made money more quickly than was good for him. Unmarried and residing in his parents' home, unable or unwilling to secure a stable position or reputable work identity, incapable of handling his money independently of his father's supervision, traveling around the country, and, eventually, casting his lot with showmen—Thompson was on unsteady ground as a man, especially as he inched toward thirty. At a time when marriage signaled the transition from irresponsible youth to responsible adulthood, he effectively abstained from growing up.[40]

Thompson's bachelor status sheds light on the persistent dilemmas with which he struggled, not just in the 1890s, but even as his boy-man show businesses took off with the opening of Luna Park in 1903. Throughout the nineteenth century, "bachelor" was a label that referred as much to a man's class, race, and outlook on life as to his unmarried status; bachelors were almost invariably white, middle- to upper-class men who chose to delay matrimony. Throughout the 1890s Thompson landed commendable jobs—such as working for his uncle—that held promise for the future and could have built a foundation for reputable adulthood and marriage. But he could not settle into them. Although not wealthy, Thompson did enjoy a good time, and his willingness to pay for it allied him with other well-heeled single men of his day, who rejoiced in their happy-go-lucky freedom from breadwinner responsibilities. For the city man, a journalist wrote in 1888 in the *Forum*, "matrimonial discouragements and bachelor compensations are many. They can have any number of comforts and pleasures outside of wedlock; more, indeed, than they would or should allow themselves within it." Yet free-spending bachelors also stood for immaturity and raised alarms not only in their communities but also among journalists and social scientists, who connected declining marriage rates among native-born whites to the degeneration of the Anglo-Saxon race. For Thompson, being a boy at heart proved to be his greatest advantage and his most troublesome liability. He had his share of fun and eventually made (and lost) a fortune selling it to men like himself. But an air of degeneracy and immaturity, like that which trailed the antics of bachelors, always hung about his identity as a fun-loving spendthrift and his occupation of manufacturing play. Bachelors usually moved on to marriage and adulthood. But even when he did tie the knot at the age of thirty-three, Thompson did not surrender his boyhood. The resulting tension reminded him that, no matter how much money he made and how hard he wished, he would never be fully at ease as both a boy and a man.[41]

Thompson appears to have been no less apprehensive about the insecure prospects of art. Drawing and painting may have seemed freer, more like play than work, but such pursuits rarely rewarded one with independence and wealth. Declaring oneself an artist also evoked associations with self-indulgent effeminacy, an unmanly hedonism and sensuality that may well have alarmed his problem-solving father and left Thompson seeking assurance of his respectability. Such concerns about art were common among bourgeois American men at the end of the nineteenth century. Some of the era's wealthiest men, such as the financier J. Pierpont Morgan, demonstrated their financial power and artistic sensitivities and created public sensations by plundering Europe of its ancient and contemporary masterpieces. But other domestic voices, encouraged by the Darwinian paradigm of conflict and science, called for a revolt against the sentimentality of contemporary art and the "emasculated" artist in American society. Critics targeted the corrupting influence of dime novels on men and parlor dramas on women. Such works, wrote the late-nineteenth-century novelist William Dean Howells, were full of "idle lies about human nature and the social fabric." Untrue to the facts of everyday life, they "tickle our prejudices and lull our judgment" and render "their readers indifferent to 'plodding perseverance and plain industry,' and to 'matter-of-fact poverty and commonplace distress.'" Howells and others called instead for "realism," a literature of "red blood" that would liberate fiction from its parlor captivity.[42]

The opposition between effeminate sentimentalism and manly realism was a construction of the late nineteenth century. For most of the century, the "realism" of a painter such as Thomas Eakins, rather than signaling his artistic muscle, would have been regarded as "incompatible with ideals of high-art painting." Even Chicago's White City, although derided by the modernist architect Louis Sullivan as demonstrating "a naked exhibitionism of charlatanry in the higher feudal and domineering culture," reflected an older notion that rigorous adherence to principles of proportion and balance resulted in vigorous buildings. At the end of the century, artistic ideals were reformulated. In the light of the emerging ideal of passionate masculinity, the manly structures of the past wilted, appearing frilly, overrefined denials of what one contemporary called "the rather rough game of American nineteenth-century life." The new preferences were expressed in Sullivan's tribute to the commercial style of Chicago's Marshall Field wholesale store: "I mean, here is a *man* for you to look at ... a man that lives and breathes, that has red blood; a real man, a manly man; a virile force—broad, vigorous and with a whelm of energy—an entire male."[43]

The novels of Howells, Jack London, Theodore Dreiser, and Henry B. Fuller, and the art of George Bellows, John Sloan, and Frederic Remington, sought, in various ways, to play the new, rougher game of masculinity by claiming to represent the "real" aspects of American life at the end of the century. Fuller's *With the Procession* (1895), like other novels that were set in Chicago in the period and that addressed the businessman as "artist," constructs an argument for the "real" in modern life; it also sketches the conflicts and dilemmas that beset restless men like Fred Thompson. Fuller's story concerns the men of the solid and prosperous Marshall family of Chicago, two of whom prove unsuited to the tooth-and-claw game of the late-nineteenth-century urban "cesspool." The patriarch, the merchant David Marshall, wearily dwells in the past, still the stolid shopkeeper marching off each day as he has for the last forty years, even though the city and its cultural and social leadership have raced past him. The heir to the family business, the youngest son, Truesdale, on the other hand, is a flawless "cosmopolite" recently returned from Europe, where he "dabbled in pigments" in Paris and voice training in Milan. Truesdale, who now sports a "little black mustache" and a "small tuft at the edge of his underlip," is a sensualist who values the pleasures of the artistic life as much as or more than the ideals of art, and the blackmail that arises from his bohemian liaison with a working-class woman finally and actually worries his father to death. Only the older son, the lawyer Roger, "tough and technical and litigious," seems fit for "the grisly wrestling with realities." In the end it is Roger, not the "brilliant and cultured" Truesdale, who best embodies the realist art that Fuller contends to be so true to life. For the patriarch David Marshall, art was an "inexplicable thing" or "a mere surface decoration." For Truesdale, it was the highest pursuit of the "pioneer" he sought to be—"the pioneer of a leisure class." Only Roger understands that life (like art) is not a "paltry affair" but a terrible battle with realities. As Fuller observes, "his was the hand to seize, not to soothe." David Marshall dies (as the book begins) "like the breaking down of a machine whose trustworthiness had been hitherto infallible"; Truesdale liquidates his inheritance and flees the "hideous hubbub" for the Oriental serenity of Japan. Roger alone remains unsentimental, altering his father's will to eliminate a foolish bequest for a college building (a move that his sentimental sister reverses).[44]

Thompson, in his encounters with his father no less than with his polite neighbors, may have felt shadowed, like Truesdale Marshall, by the paternal query, "What have I got for my money?" At the same time, however, he dreaded the fate of Fuller's worn-out shopkeeper, who "seemed completely serious, to have been so always, to have been born half grown up, to have been dowered at the start with too keen a consciousness of the burdens and responsibilities of life.... You imagined him as having been caught early, broken to harness at once, and kept between the shafts ever since." At least in 1895, the expectation that Thompson would produce and work in a manner recognized by his father's generation restrained his rebellion. But neither was he convinced by or attracted to the "grisly wrestling" of hard-boiled realism. For Thompson, ever the hustler, the problem was in finding a way to make the life of pleasure pay off, thus meeting the cultural expectation that his "work" would produce something real and reputable.[45]

## An Exposition Fiend

Thompson made important, although tentative and indirect, steps in resolving these dilemmas upon his departure from Mexico in 1894. Soon after returning to Nashville, he left to bid on construction projects at the 1895 Cotton States and International Exposition in Atlanta. Most of the work had already been awarded by the time he arrived, which left him only a small interest. Afterward he returned to Nashville to work for his uncle and was poised with a partner, a local builder named John J. Dunnavant, to land substantial contracts for the Tennessee Centennial and International Exposition planned for 1897 in that city.[46]

Thompson worked both sides of the cultural divide at the Nashville fair. His uncle's architectural partnership, Thompson and Zwicker, had won the design competition for the centennial's auditorium and transportation and electrical buildings. Fred Thompson's elevations of these projects suggest his polish as an illustrator. But he also designed a number of the fair's major structures, including the Negro Building, where the practical achievements of the "colored race" were officially celebrated (fig. 2.1). The design won the centennial's architectural prize,

Fig. 2.1. Fred Thompson's rendering of the Tennessee Centennial Exposition's Negro Building as a "Moorish" palace was awarded an architectural prize, which convinced him he was an "artist." (*Tennessee State Library and Archives.*)

which enhanced his personal prestige and draw as an architect of exposition buildings and flattered his image of himself: "I concluded I was a real artist." His award-winning design was in the "Moorish" style and demonstrated that, for all his lack of formal education, he could deliver the *effect* that the majority population would buy. The integration of the exterior of the building with proper and "progressive" racial symbols—in this case, African accents—suggests more than Thompson's mastery of racial symbols. His triumph also indicates his uncanny commercial inclinations, his instincts for what historian Chester H. Liebs has called "architecture for speed-reading." Liebs's terminology refers specifically to the roadside architecture of the "car culture" of the 1920s and later, when buildings in the shape of giant dogs or milk bottles operated both as places of business and as road signs. These structures "combined advertising and architecture into an ingenious and unified commercial package" and created "a total synthesis of sign and building—evocative, compelling, and effective in the quest to attract, hold, and sell." Thompson's Moorish palace operated in much the same way. It advertised what was "on sale" inside and the color of its contents as effectively as a billboard; there could be no confusing its exhibits with those in the staff version of the Parthenon, the architectural pride and joy of the Nashville exposition.[47]

Notwithstanding Thompson's artistic and advertising achievement, it was not the ideal city of the exposition that held the most practical and symbolic significance for the nascent showman. Rather, it was the amusement midway, Vanity Fair. The benighted city from the seventeenth-century Puritan text *A Pilgrim's Progress* formed the conceptual center of Thompson's career of building glittering earthly cities of pleasure and desire that claimed to outshine the Celestial City waiting at the end of a pious pilgrimage toward salvation. At this point in his history, Vanity Fair was a tempting byway, much as it was in the story by John Bunyan, rather than his business destination. An unspecified but sizeable portion of his and Dunnavant's construction contracts was made with Vanity Fair's showmen, some of whom had shallower pockets than they pretended. The partners were rudely introduced to the chicanery of show business when they had to accept ownership of the Blue Grotto, an expensive scenic reproduction of the Isle of Capri, in lieu of payment. The grotto was not actually in Vanity Fair, but nestled among trees and flowerbeds on a small island in the fair's lake. It offered "picturesque" views of Mount Vesuvius and an outdoor Italian restaurant where one could "enjoy an ice or cup of coffee" amid lovely surroundings. The amusement "in every detail was artistic," but it failed to attract. "The first thing I did," Thompson later explained, "was to change the name to 'The Caves of Monte Cristo' and put some people in it." Translation: Thompson added, first, a title that linked it to the romantic adventures of the Alexandre Dumas tale. The story was well known in the 1880s and 1890s both as a novel and as a sensational stage show featuring the actor James O'Neill (father of playwright Eugene), who performed the role more than fifty-eight hundred times in theaters across the country. Next, Thompson incorporated a "leg show" highlighting the "Beautiful Ione," the "spirit of the cave" who was wrapped tightly in gauze and miraculously walked on water (actually a sheet of plate glass beneath a film of water). There was little narrative or formal logic here, but no matter; in Thompson's words, the "effect was pretty, the public liked it, and the show managed to live."[48]

By reviving the Blue Grotto with a swashbuckling title and a "leg show," Thompson demonstrated that he knew not only which public he wanted (red-blooded men) and what that public liked (action and "giddy skirt dances"), but also how to play with gender and class. The artistry of the Blue Grotto—pretty "European" scenery, cultivated coffee drinking—marked it as a genteel women's matinee attraction that belonged in the refined atmosphere of the exposition proper. It was an unobjectionable bourgeois recreation, although perhaps, in the language of the time, *overnice* and *overcivilized*. To its soothing ambience of leisurely idleness Thompson added a gloss of uncivilized action, which altered the terms of the attraction's appeal to middle-class women and brought it more in line with what lively young fellows like himself would want. For educated men, the allusion to Dumas injected a hint of the red-blooded "romantic activism" that writers of the era were advocating as a revitalizing antidote to literary parlor dramas. With the spirit of the cave, on the other hand, Thompson, like Sol Bloom before him, was cashing in on the currency of the *danse du ventre*, or "cooch dance," which since 1893 had become a standard attraction in vaudeville. Thompson's "thinly clad girl" offered a different variety of visual pleasure. But unlike Bloom's attraction, she was offered within the exposition city itself. Under cover of a business emergency, Thompson slipped a little "hoochy coochy" onto the main stage of the exposition. His achievement suggests that the cultural boundaries that separated the high-minded from the profane were insecure against the pressure applied by the consumer market economy, the advocates of which were keenly sensitive to the passionate appetites of lively young men. The Beautiful Ione changed the Blue Grotto from an instructive and quiet respite "after the fashion of the outdoor resorts of the Old World" to a titillating show-narrative displaying and exploiting the Orientalized female body.[49]

The Blue Grotto foreshadowed Thompson's efforts on Coney Island and on Broadway to reorient the commercial forms of play to middle-class men's tastes. His more deliberate contribution to the amusement midway, however, was a gigantic electrified teeter-totter, which he and a fellow inventor designed for the fair and patented in 1898. The Giant Seesaw was Thompson's first effort as a toymaker: an object from everyday child-life but magnified on a Brobdingnagian scale (fig. 2.2). The official historian of the fair called it "the nineteenth century evolution of the pine board and the rail fence."[50] The contraption stood seventy-five feet tall at its fulcrum, with a spacious viewing car at each end of the

Fig. 2.2. The Giant Seesaw on the Tennessee Centennial Exposition midway was Fred Thompson's first effort at designing a toy big enough to impress grown-up children. (*Tennessee State Library and Archives.*)

steel arm that stretched eighty feet on either side. As one car loaded passengers on a ground-level platform, the other paused at the crest of its ascent, giving an unprecedented view of the Tennessee city from some 150 feet in the air; once loaded, the arms began shifting, one rising as the other lowered, the entire trip taking about five minutes.[51] No doubt the Giant Seesaw's promoters wanted their device to be for Nashville what George W. G. Ferris's mammoth steel wheel had been to the Columbian exposition, a technological wonder and historical landmark thrillingly and safely uniting machine, amusement, and lucrative return on investment.[52] The Giant Seesaw was not nearly the engineering feat of Chicago's Ferris Wheel, nor did it have the visual appeal of a gargantuan turning wheel. Still, it indicated the antic direction of Thompson's showmanship. In order to view the accomplishments of a mature, progressive civilization, the viewer had to regress to childhood by playing with an exaggerated toy.[53]

Thompson understood the pleasures of gazing at scantily clad women, for spectators no less than for the owner of the show, and was beginning to sense the market value of play. But he still resisted Vanity Fair as either a prudent way to make money or a productive and seemly enterprise. For one, he did not make any money. When the centennial ended, he and Dunnavant found themselves "practically on our uppers." But instead of going back to work with his uncle, Thompson and his partner looked to reverse their losses at the Trans-Mississippi and International Exposition planned for the following summer in Omaha, Nebraska. Thompson, arriving early and almost penniless, showed some of what he had learned (and been subjected to) at Nashville. "All the while I kept up a big money front. Let them think I had stacks of it," he later recalled. The charade worked; he claimed that he and Dunnavant collected large contracts for official state buildings and midway amusements.[54]

But Thompson was not the only one putting up a front. This time he had to repossess the California Gold Mine concession, a complex of shafts and tunnels demonstrating the mining business. "It was really a good, elaborate plant, but nothing in it to thrill," he later reflected. "Of course, it failed." Thompson discarded the didactic theme, renamed it "Heaven and Hell," and filled the subterranean space with skeletons, coffins, and "everything grewsome [sic] and horrible." On top of the building he constructed a celestial auditorium brilliantly illuminated with incandescent lights and outfitted with a stage, on which pranced a troupe of ballerinas (including the Beautiful Ione). Then, when local ministers complained that the show made a mockery of divine judgment, he turned the protest into a publicity bonanza. "I lay back, chuckled and let them boom me." Instead of changing the attraction, he manufactured the illusion of change, advertising widely for a more acceptable title for the show. The stunt worked, his management was swamped with suggestions, and within ten days of its opening, an Omaha newspaper reported, "Heaven and Hell, under its new name of Darkness and Dawn," was "the novelty of the Midway." Or, in Thompsonian language, "the ten cent pieces came pouring in." He and his partner, with these and other profits in hand, left Omaha "winners" when the fair closed at the end of October.[55]

Darkness and Dawn was Thompson's first big-money success, but the change that came over him, he later claimed, exceeded the effects of the windfall he pocketed. In Omaha, he said, he also began considering show business his chosen field and to regard himself as a showman. "I began to be a kind of exposition fiend," he recalled in 1905. "I seemed to look for an exposition every year, so that I could have a great crowd of people and a big rush of business going on around me. The ordinary show business of the theatre and that kind did not appeal to me. I wanted occasions and throngs." His family, he said, "fought bitterly" to change his mind, but with no success. He was intoxicated with the swarms who went to world's fairs. Thompson already was looking ahead to the Pan-American Exposition in Buffalo in 1901, where he planned to introduce himself in a new guise. At the end of the Omaha season, he recalled years later, "I realized that I might be an inventor and constructor of shows. Not dramatic—I never wanted to be an actor—but the other kind [of shows]."[56]

These words hardly constituted a confident declaration of identity. Concerns that the business of amusements and play was an illegitimate occupation for an honorable man dogged Thompson even as he came to make his fortune and construct his identity with shows. Thompson's parents did not have to fight the drift of his interests for him to know there was something shady about a man who dealt in the insubstantiality of illusion, no matter how much money he made in the process. For one, world's fair shows were speculative gambles. Although such shows offered the chance for stunning profits, middle-class Americans knew what happened to men who tried to make money without working for it. Losing was likely, and it wasted wealth that was earned through actual work. Even winning big weakened a man because it made him forget the hard truth that only steady, patient industry produced anything of lasting value.[57]

Thompson's investment in shows raised other concerns besides the ways his moneymaking potentially violated the moral economy of petit bourgeois capitalism. Animosity toward "theatricality" is a long-standing tradition in Western cultures. In this view, theatrical entertainments and theater people by their very natures challenge the authority of established rules and definitions with their alternative enactment of reality. They threaten the integrity of community boundaries and distinctions—between high and low, sacred and profane, young and old, men and women. In the theater, the imperturbability of the status quo is confronted by an imaginative world of shifting illusion, one that "prizes growth, process, exploration, flexibility, variety and versatility of response." The mix of nineteenth-century prejudices for and against theatrical entertainments in the urban United States reflected these enduring hostilities. But middle-class distrust was given its particular inflection by long-standing and deeply ingrained theological and civic republican suspicions about the trickery of the theater, the unmanliness of theatricality, and the pernicious, effeminizing effects that such entertainments had on audiences.[58]

Scholars usually single out sixteenth- and seventeenth-century English and Anglo-American Puritans for their determined opposition to theaters as institutions and theatricality as a social practice, both of which, in their eyes, encouraged hypocrisy and deception, undermined the stability of moral guideposts, and thereby assisted the actual work of the devil. Stage actors were just like Satan, the shrewd illusionist who could convincingly assume any form to lead the unsuspecting down the path of rebellion against God's order. By the nineteenth century in the United States, the Puritan hostility toward theater survived more as a prejudice or a suspicion about the gullibility of audiences and the depravity of actors than as an aspect of a theology-centered belief in the innate depravity and willfully disobedient natures of God's children. The problem was not so much theatricality as it was the kind of people who hung about theaters. In part, older fears of the diabolical essence of theatricality could not survive intact in an increasingly secular, scientific, and, for some, prosperous market culture that saw little harm in healthful recreational leisure as a way of displaying status and of balancing the rational, disciplined work rhythms of a business civilization. At the same time, new evangelical Protestant sects, which paired their denunciation of worldly and degenerate pleasures such as theatergoing with an optimistic conviction that Satan was not the insurmountable foe that he once seemed to be, actually encouraged more-tolerant attitudes toward theater. Perhaps, some thought, the medium was not sinful in itself and, if disciplined, could be a force for social improvement. When the mid-nineteenth century's great evangelical reform texts, T. S. Arthur's temperance tract *Ten Nights in a Barroom* and Harriet Beecher Stowe's *Uncle Tom's Cabin*, were made into popular stage shows, two of the era's most denounced vices—reading for pleasure and theatergoing—were joined in an actual dramatization of the emerging accommodation. It was what one saw and did in the theater, not theatricality itself, that potentially was dangerous.[59]

Although few antebellum evangelical Protestants were willing to defend the theater as a social necessity, by the 1880s many mainstream churches had joined antebellum "liberal" defenders of amusements in urging their comfortable urban parishioners not to turn their backs on the world's pleasures. Theaters would be there no matter what they did; better to reform their content through patronage than leave them to the unrefined influence of the general populace. And besides, are not all people entitled to a little pleasure? Although theatergoing still made the list of vices prepared by evangelical sects such as Methodism in the 1870s, such practices did not seem so dangerous in themselves as they once had, especially when theater managers began catering to middle-class audiences and rid their auditoriums of the unrefined or vicious riffraff that had defined the essence of antebellum commercial amusements. By the end of the nineteenth century, urban and suburban Americans who faithfully attended the mainstream Protestant churches regarded the theater much as they did the world around them—flawed, improvable, and on the upswing. Actors and acting were redeemed in the process. "In most American cities," observes the historian William Leach, "all that remained of a fierce opposition to actors was the conviction that they were *literally* (not theologically) connected with deviance."[60]

Thompson's own deviance with Heaven and Hell, then, had only to be reformed, which was easily accomplished, and the "new," secularized show went on with popular and, one suspects, clerical approval. So when he called himself an "exposition fiend," he certainly did not mean that he was fiendish in the older sense of the term, meaning devilish or demonic. "Fiend" had once been part of the stock vocabulary of moralizing exposés of the "secret life" of early and mid-nineteenth-century cities. Such works claimed to tell the "real" story of the hidden order of wily men who posed as trustworthy citizens, all the better to fleece the honorable and corrupt the innocent. Victorian Americans especially fretted over the fate of the "free-floating" young woman and man in the highly mobile and impersonal market society of the mid-nineteenth century. Such youths who left rural homes for urban opportunities separated themselves from the family or communal ties that traditionally bound them; without such external protections, it was feared, youths were defenseless against the arts of confidence men, seducers, and gamblers.[61]

By the end of the century, the concerns about appearances and confidence in a market culture had virtually vanished from their familiar place in the didactic literature of the urban middle class. By then, men who gambled in stocks and agricultural commodities, or who dealt in impersonations and tricks to create pleasing illusions or fantasies, had become a familiar and largely accepted aspect of American cities and towns. Dealers in illusion found an especially hospitable home in the new institutions of consumption that proliferated in urban America after 1880: department stores, theaters, advertising agencies, restaurants, dance halls, and amusement parks, to name only a few. As experts in the arts of trickery, from department store window dressers to stage managers to designers of commercial amusements, filled the ranks of these businesses in the first third of the twentieth century, they developed a commercial aesthetic that aimed not only to sell goods, but also to reinvent the city as a theatrical landscape of commodities "jumping and dancing with life." Along with theater owners, they struggled to domesticate or camouflage the more subversive aspects of their "tricks of the trade" and became a troubling, if largely accepted, part of the consumer marketplace and twentieth-century life as a whole.[62]

When Thompson called and thought of himself as an "exposition fiend," he probably evoked, in his own mind or that of another, associations not with the master manipulator Satan so much as with the enticements of an urbanizing commercial culture. Many rural and urban Americans resisted the secularizing hegemony of science and the lure of material comfort and sought to preserve traditional suspicions of this world. But, as the great student of American religious beliefs William James explained in *The Varieties of Religious Experience* (1902), a growing conviction within the urban middle class was that "evil is simply a lie" and the world essentially good. This liberal outlook reflected and encouraged the gradual separation of desire—wishing for what you do not or are not allowed to have—from the category of sin, and brought a broad array of mainstream American religious faiths more in line with the secular interests of the new consumer industries. Calvinism alerted believers to their vulnerability to the seductive traps of the visible world. The evangelical Protestants of post–Civil War America, on the other hand, were more upbeat about their salvation, more confident in their ability to resist corruption, and less convinced that an all-powerful sovereign might punish them for their flaws. Like theatergoing, desire—

even obsessive desire—was not necessarily a sinful or dangerous impulse if channeled in the right direction. The new breed of urban merchant and entertainment entrepreneur, in keeping with the relaxed religious attitudes, reinforced these changes by encouraging people to relinquish ancient but foolish suspicions about the corrupting influence of material goods and by directing them toward their commercial version of earthly fulfillment. For growing numbers of Americans, older visions of paradise could not stand up against the picture of the desirable brought to life in "the color of a great city." "Of all the pathetic dreams," wrote the early-twentieth-century novelist Theodore Dreiser, "that which pictures a spiritual salvation elsewhere for one who has failed in his dreams here is the thinnest and the palest, a beggar's dole indeed."[63]

In 1898, Fred Thompson was only beginning to glimpse the possibilities for pleasure and profit in manufacturing amusement, and, at this stage of his development, he paid little attention to the destructive potential of ungovernable "longing" and "desire" that Dreiser wrote into novels such as *Sister Carrie*, *The Financier*, and *The Titan*. Thompson regarded himself as a fiend of the perpetually smiling, good-natured, and well-meaning variety, one irresistibly but benignly drawn to the occasions and throngs of the great city, and an inventor of and dealer in fabrications that harmlessly amused, pleased, and pocketed the dimes of the multitudes. Still, the lightheartedness of his claims could not fully dispel older meanings of words such as *fiend* and *desire*, and these implications continued to cast a shadow over the illusions and tricks he was learning to play on his public.[64]

The expectations associated with the civic republican traditions lent even greater force to Thompson's anxieties. Eighteenth-century republicanism, with its ideal of the enlightened and virtuous male citizen standing guard against the corruption of the commonwealth, had bequeathed to the succeeding century a popular tradition of worry that indulgent, sensual pleasures such as theatergoing softened the manly rectitude on which the new American nation depended for its survival. Much like later evangelical reformers who were concerned about the sinful condition of the nation, Revolutionary-era patriots such as Samuel Adams allowed that a theater could be a "school of morality," but in practice it and similar amusements were more likely to be instruments of effeminacy's "languid train." In the nineteenth century such beliefs fostered a producerist mentality, or labor republicanism, which held that independent and virtuous men were secure in a moral economy that shunned the "artificial tastes" of the luxury-loving few. This outlook was encouraged by a faith that the American economy, with its manly backbone of skilled artisans and freeholding farmers, attended to the general *needs* of all the people, rather than to their *desires*. As such, America was fundamentally different from the Old World economies of Europe, where a debased and hopeless majority labored to produce trifles and luxuries for the rich few. What were theatrical entertainments but manufactured trifles that weakened men with pleasures that were neither real nor necessary? The shining citizens of nineteenth-century labor republicanism were not the eighteenth century's enlightened elite of educated gentlemen, but economically self-sufficient artisans, "peculiarly virtuous men" who were "imbued with the spirit of independence, fellowship, and commonwealth and free from the economic dependence that bred corruption." As the Reverend George W. Bethune told the New York Mercantile Library Association in 1839, in America "the laborer is honorable, the idler infamous." Here "we have no leisure; for the truly virtuous and faithful will find occupation for every moment." The foundation of this "manly achiever" ideal was built out of self-control, self-reliance, and the belief that the full liberty of manhood was achieved through productive work or business ownership.[65]

By the time of the Omaha fair in 1898, small and large American cities were in the midst of a theatrical revolution. Entrepreneurs built hundreds of new houses over the next two decades to market dramatic and spectacular productions that catered to an urban middle class eager for proper theatrical entertainment. Still, theatricality and acting remained troublesome in a culture that traditionally regarded illusion and appearance as the instruments of the unvirtuous. In contrast to the Victorian model of controlled and responsible manhood, an actor produced nothing with his body but pleasure or amusement for people who did nothing with their bodies but watch. With his early education in the conflicts between the hardy brotherhood of steelworkers and the new scientific fraternity of industrial engineers, Thompson was reluctant to commit his own body to "act" in any nonproductive capacity. He made it clear on a number of occasions that he "never wanted to be an actor." As he recalled his only effort in that regard, performing as a monk in Darkness and Dawn, the men in the audience had made him look "ridiculous" in front of a woman who had caught his eye: "It galled me bitterly to have to don the monk's robe and appear before her as a Midway 'spieler' or side-show talker ... as I marched down the center [the audience] commenced to make jesting remarks—all in good fun, but it embarrassed me greatly." The whole incident, in which he produced nothing but *spiel* (which means "play" in German) and huckstering talk, illuminated the persistent tension he felt between authentically masculine work and the effeminizing potential of play. Acting made him look and feel diminished as a man. From that point on, he determined, he would never again be an actor, someone who made a spectacle of himself and produced nothing but pleasure. Instead, he would be "an inventor and constructor of shows."[66]

It was not enough that he made a killing with Darkness and Dawn; he also had to garb himself linguistically with the stage properties of the producer's tools to ward off the stinging suspicion that there was something illegitimate, socially irresponsible, and effeminate about his showmanship. Other middle-class men of his generation, who feared being unmanned by the conditions of modern life, especially the alienating character of bureaucratic corporate work, followed a similar strategy. They took up hobbies such as woodworking, in the newly invented domestic space of basement workshops, to rebuild themselves in the image of preindustrial craftsmen. Thompson's turn of phrase was not just a psychologically compensatory response to his own "crisis of masculinity." Enlisting the image of a leather-aproned artisan, someone who wielded tools and made things of substance, he attempted to lend legitimacy to a despised and derided area of commerce; he was trying to carve out a manly sphere of action within the treacherous field of show business. The lines that Thompson drew between acting in and building shows, diabolical and good-natured fiends, and shows that mocked sacred beliefs and those that merely exploited them were useful and artful fictions. But they nonetheless revealed the balancing act he was trying to perform in pursuing his ambitions and appetites under the critical eyes of enduring middle-class expectations about the behavior of men.[67]

Good-natured fiend or otherwise, Thompson was not ready in 1898 to make amusements his full-time occupation. The Omaha fair had been such a success that its promoters decided to reopen it in 1899. The second year flopped, and many investors, including Thompson's future partner, Skip Dundy, lost their shirts. But Thompson had already taken his money and moved on to New York City, rented a studio apartment there, and enrolled at the Art Students League, one of the leading art academies in the United States. There he studied with several of the most celebrated academic painters and illustrators in the United States—Frederick Dielman, John H. Twachtman, Kenyon Cox, Walter Appleton Clark, and George Bridgman—many of whom were known for their shimmering postimpressionist canvases. In later accounts, he described the move to New York as purposeful and premeditated: "I felt the need of more education." In this respect, he may have been like his show business counterpart, Sol Bloom, who had embarked on his world tour after coming to "a crude realization that if I wanted to get a fuller enjoyment out of my wealth I would have to increase my *capacity for enjoyment* by learning more about the world." Art instruction provided lessons in refinement of craft and taste that may have smoothed some of Thompson's rougher provincial edges, or his insecurities that he was nothing more than a carnival "spieler." But as much as anything else, the Art Students League was an unqualified indulgence on his part, a rejection of his father's injunctions to work steadily and save prudently, which recapitulated earlier (and foreshadowed later) spending sprees that followed periods of intense labor or windfall profit. It also promised to expand his capacity for enjoyment. Thompson, ever the spendthrift, could not bear to hoard his money; the very thought of reinvesting his profits in another year in Omaha was absurd. This particular fling in New York did not ruin him financially, although the color of the city itself provided a glimpse of more-thrilling pleasures yet to be had. New York was anything but the commonplace past for Thompson, and the excitement of the city's throngs, as well as the alienation he must have felt as a stranger there, aroused visions of a paradise more dazzling and outlandish than the heaven that waited at the end of the journey from hell in Omaha.[68]

### The Great Secret of Aërial Flight

Even as he was polishing his technique at the Art Students League, Thompson had his eyes on the 1901 Pan-American Exposition in Buffalo, which promised to be the most grandiose world's fair since Chicago. Like the leading men who designed other such events, its planners envisioned a "colossal university" whose palatial Spanish Renaissance buildings would affirm the leadership of the United States in the

COURT OF THE FOUNTAINS AND ELECTRIC TOWER

Fig. 2.3. The Electric Tower was the most imposing architectural symbol of the progress of American civilization at the 1901 Pan-American Exposition in Buffalo. (*Billy Rose Theatre Collection, The New York Public Library for the Performing Arts, Astor, Lenox and Tilden Foundations.*)

common cause of the new century's "civilization." Within the city itself were to be collected "the best object lessons the Western Hemisphere can produce," molded into "a curriculum far more comprehensive than that of any established institution," and deployed for the instruction and improvement of the "people." As the story went, the Pan-American would "illustrate progress during the century just closed," but it also would look forward to the new century and "lay a strong and enduring foundation for international, commercial and social unity in the world." Furthering the earnest instructional theme, the Buffalo planners had selected John M. Carrère, the architect of the New York Public Library, to design the general scheme of the 350-acre exposition city and to supervise the architectural luminaries who executed the actual buildings (fig. 2.3). In the view of one intoxicated fairgoer, the whole resembled "a great

exotic orchid, with the [monumental Electric] Tower for a stamen."
Beauty aside, national uplift and racial progress were central themes and
American colonial expansion a component of the political agenda of the
fair's promoters. The architectural and chromatic scheme of the Pan-
American enacted an allegory of modern civilization's indebtedness to
and dependence on the United States.[69]

Notwithstanding the calculated interests of Buffalo's racial and business elites, the Pan-American hardly succeeded in winning new adherents to its agenda. For one, scarcely any "people" showed up for their
lessons. Attendance fell far below official expectations of more than
twenty million. Buffalo's leading men may have controlled the high-
minded and ennobling symbols of their fair city, but no one to speak of
paid to see their show. By the end of July the colossal university was an
even bigger flop, a Beaux Arts ghost town on weekdays and scarcely any
more animated on weekends. What people were paying to see were the
new ideas that were stirring along the amusement midway. While the
exposition's monuments preached sermons on social uplift, progress
for "backward" races, and the serious business of universal peace and
colonial expansion, the midway, according to the guidebook written by
Richard H. Barry, offered a "jumble of fantastic architecture" that
clashed with the harmonious unity of the exposition's legitimate structures "like a gilded shoulder on the polished mahogany frame of a plate
glass mirror."[70]

Although the Buffalo midway seemed to be freewheeling commercialism run amok, the unifying imprint of "the Kid," as Thompson's fellow showmen called him, overrode its apparent diversity. When he
arrived in Buffalo in the spring of 1900 to bid for contracts and concessions, Thompson was twenty-six years old. Although he had not won
any architectural prizes since Nashville, he had proved his mettle as a
show builder and designer, as a master of publicity, and as a savant of
the vagaries of entertaining the masses. In both his previous ventures
he had invigorated dying amusements by injecting them with action,
sexual appeal, and impressive mechanical illusions. Thompson later
claimed that with this reputation he and his partner Dunnavant were
able to collect more than a million dollars in construction contracts for
the Buffalo fair, an amount exceeding 10 percent of its publicized aggregate cost. Even if this figure was exaggerated, Thompson emerged in
the process as the principal architect of the Pan-American midway, the

designer of all but five of its attractions; in effect, he was the amusement counterpart to John M. Carrère.[71]

Unlike the architect of the great Forty-second Street library, Thompson constructed a story not of civilized progress but of boyish play. The first principles of his premeditated allegory were outlined in August 1900 in a statement that, although issued by the exposition's publicity office, almost certainly was written by "the Kid." The release managed to praise the noble aspirations of the exposition while dismissing their relevance to the "average visitor." "We may find infinite instruction," it said, "and a high and holy satisfaction in viewing the products of the soil which tell of the natural resources of this or that country or state, or the products of the loom or mill or other manufactory which speak of man's industry and the activity of his hand and brain." The "average" person described by this release had a precise gender. He was not interested in looking at warehouses of industrial machinery and canned goods. What he actually wanted were pleasures that would "satisfy that craving with which he is possessed for something wonderful and startling and absolutely new."[72] By inclination as well as from his experiences in Nashville and Omaha, Thompson knew that ordinary men like himself were stirred by visions that excited their cravings rather than by object lessons that reminded them of their assumed needs and prescribed duties. Whereas the imposing architecture of the exposition city admonished people to better themselves—"Speak to the Earth and It Shall Teach Thee," urged the inscription on one building—Thompson knew that such lessons and calls to duty would not sell.[73] Like other average men, whom he imagined as fun-loving free-spenders like himself, he rebelled against the workaday and compulsory; he longed for something that a man would find alien, startling, and wondrously new. The resulting midway, according to Richard Barry, was all about the "longing for a whimsical return to boyishness and buncombe ... that lies deep seated in all natures." It "is the most gigantic, the most complex, the most costly and the most exacting plaything yet devised for modern man."[74] Thompson oriented the purposes of his fair around the particular desires of men.

One night, the story goes, during his art student days in New York, Thompson was worrying over an idea for his Omaha gold mine, Darkness and Dawn, when a vision came to him. In his many retellings of this moment of insight, the story signified not just the planning of a profitable amusement device but his genesis as a showman and the first step in the revolution of modern amusements. He was trying to invent a sensational effect for transporting pilgrims across a fiery abyss when he saw an airship streaking through the sky. "As I solved the mechanical problem it struck me that this was an idea for a show in itself, independent of the other, and I immediately thought, 'Where will I take the airship?' And then it occurred to me, 'To the moon.'" Before he went to bed that night he had sketched out something new, a participatory narrative of escape to a startling world of exotic, sensual, and material pleasure. With the three-dimensional depth of the stereopticon—that fixture of the Victorian parlor—the scenic apparatuses and dramatic action of the theatrical stage, the mystique of futuristic technology, the authority of pseudoscience, and the allure of an exotic, Orientalized fantasy, A Trip to the Moon would be his most famous and profitable amusement and the foundational fantasy of his investment in the commercial culture of Peter Pan.[75]

Historians have described A Trip to the Moon as a "dramatic" or "fantasy cyclorama," but such comparisons do not do justice to its elaborate construction or dramatic action. Although the undertaking was large and complicated (the building itself occupied thirty-four thousand square feet), its component technologies were not unusually advanced. The moonship was "a green and white cigar shaped thing, the size of a small lake steamer with a great cabin in the middle" and three fan-shaped canvas wings that flapped on either side (fig. 2.4). Thompson produced the apparent passage across time and space with an array of clever scenic tricks. The floor beneath the ship was painted to represent the distant ground below, so passengers had the sense that they already were high in the air when they boarded. Passengers entered at one end of the ship, where the scenery depicted an aerial view of the fair, and once the flight ended, exited at the opposite end, where the scenery was that of the principality of the Man in the Moon. Once the flight began, the orchestrated manipulation of scenic screens, which surrounded the ship and were painted to represent clouds, Earth, and the Moon, prompted the sensation of rising, forward, and descending movement. (The experience was much like the disorienting impression of forward movement one gets today when sitting in a stationary airliner, awaiting departure from the gate as a neighboring jet backs away.) Colored lights and stereopticons created visual effects such as lightning during flight.

Fig. 2.4. For the price of fifty cents, the moonship *Luna* took passengers past the city of Buffalo, over the roaring waters of Niagara Falls, then straight to the Moon. (*Buffalo and Erie County Historical Society.*)

The ship itself was suspended by guy wires from a central pole, which gave it the buoyant movement of a boat at dock; it seemed to be floating in the air, and rocked as passengers boarded and swayed with the movement of the flight. A hidden buzzer duplicated the sound of the wind, and fans concealed inside the ship simulated forward movement by blowing air on passengers' faces.[76]

After paying their dimes, voyagers gathered in a darkened auditorium, where a guide from the Aërial Navigation Company explained "in pregnant phrases" the "great secret of anti-gravitation and aerial flight" and "the extraordinary nature of the adventure on which they are embarking." The pseudoscientific lecture may have been an important element in establishing the plausibility of the illusion. The science fiction writer H. G. Wells contended that pseudoscience was essential to his fantasies because turn-of-the-century readers no longer accepted the credibility of magic. Instead "of the usual interview with the devil or a magician," Wells made "ingenious use of scientific patter" to establish the authority of his fantasy. With the proper magical mood ingeniously established, the audience saw the moonship *Luna* descending through starry space toward Earth. Julian Hawthorne, writing about the ride in *Cosmopolitan*, expected at this point to watch a conventional stage show on the "various chapters of the journey," and was surprised when the guide ordered the members of the audience to participate in the drama. After filing through a narrow passageway, they took their seats on the moonship. "Slowly," wrote the guidebook author Barry, the *Luna* "gathers a long undulating motion." The exposition grounds recede, Buffalo becomes a "sprawling" mass of blinking lights, and the "roar" of Niagara is heard as the ship passes over it. The Earth becomes a "great globe," then "a ball, then a mere speck and finally sinks from sight." The ship rushes through a storm, and as the clouds pass, the "moon is seen to sink across the line of sight from above and a seared countenance, the face of the Man in the Moon is plainly visible. Rocks and lava pilings, stained red and yellow and green as though by fire and decomposition, are just ahead." The ship slows, turns, and lands in "a yawning hole in the moon's side, the crater of an extinct volcano."[77]

On the Moon, Thompson constructed a topsy-turvy world in which the "normal" in appearance and scale was disturbed. A group of "midget" Selenites greeted the voyagers with "queer twitterings" and hors d'oeuvres of green cheese and led them down a long avenue of "illuminated foliage of fantastic trees and toadstool growths," past a row of lunar stores (with show windows displaying the riches of the lunar civilization) and the "Moon Calf—Avenging Spirit of the Moon," to the palace of the Man in the Moon (fig. 2.5). Passing the sentry of giants patrolling the gates, the voyagers took their seats in the cavernous throne room, where they were surrounded by "huge jewels and masses of gold and weird vistas and abysses." Here they were treated to a regal entertainment of moon maids dancing amid spewing fountains and dazzling incandescent lights. Then the guide led them back "into the familiar daylight of the Midway."[78]

Of course, A Trip to the Moon—with its plaster façade, its pseudoscientific lecture, the flimsiness of its props, the tricks of its theatrical trade—was an obvious hoax. After all, its patron spirit was the Moon

Fig. 2.5. On the lunar surface, tiny, gibbering Selenites, Moon maidens, and giants prepared voyagers for the regal pleasures offered by the Man in the Moon. (*Buffalo and Erie County Historical Society.*)

Calf, or fool. Nor was it original. Jules Verne had published *A Voyage to the Moon* in 1865, and Wells's own story, "The First Men in the Moon," had been serialized in *Cosmopolitan* in the months before the Buffalo fair. Still, by all accounts, Thompson's Trip was one of the sensations, if not *the* sensation, of the entire exposition. There were reports of motion sickness and fainting, and a correspondent for *Cosmopolitan* left with a woman who "expressed alarm and could not be convinced by her friends or the attendants that the air-ship ... was stationary." According to Barry, men placed wagers on whether the ship actually left the ground. The sure winner, though, was Thompson, who later claimed he "cleaned up" five times his original investment and continued to rake in the dimes over the next decade with the same illusion at Coney Island. Anyone who later embarked on Disneyland's 1955 fantasy Rocket to the Moon or rode E.T.'s flying bicycle at the Universal Studios Orlando theme park experienced a sensation that Thompson brought to market in 1901.[79]

The Trip was au courant in a number of other ways that suggest reasons for its popularity. For one, its tricks and iconography exploited the new technologies of incandescent lighting. With the proximity of Niagara Falls and the recent completion of the first hydroelectric plant there, electrical current was one of the exposition's main attractions. American expositions used electrical lighting to stage narratives of material abundance and civilized progress. They illuminated not just buildings but "dream landscapes" that dramatized for visitors the Western world's rapid ascent from savagery to civilization and projected a vision of the electrified future. But whereas the Buffalo fair underlined the industrial applications of electricity, Thompson's Trip to the Moon constructed a parallel narrative of journeying from the dark present into an electrically illuminated future of ease and play. His destination was in tune with the marvels of a consumer-oriented economy, although it still complemented the productive wheels of industry and the "high and holy" attractions on display in the exposition palaces.[80]

The narrative of A Trip to the Moon had less in common with either literary predecessors or the Exposition's material rendering of Western industrial civilization than it did with contemporary examinations or evocations of strange and enticing new worlds that explored (or appealed to) the nonrational cravings that possessed "average" people. Such works as L. Frank Baum's *Wonderful Wizard of Oz*, Sigmund Freud's *Interpretation of Dreams*, and Thorstein Veblen's *Theory of the Leisure Class*, all of which appeared between 1899 and 1901, reflected a heightened cultural awareness of the unconscious forces, drives, and motives underlying human behavior. These works appeared at a crucial moment in the long historical transition of the West away from its religious and agrarian past to a secular, scientific, industrial, urban, and consumer culture.[81]

Through much of the nineteenth century, this transition had left many of the most privileged and powerful bourgeois Western Europeans and Americans acutely dissatisfied with a world that seemed unreal, inauthentic, and coldly distanced from human needs. Although they tended to be the ones who had benefited most from the new industrial culture, such men longed to escape the pervasive hold of what the turn-of-the-century Viennese writer Robert Musil called the "wooden yardstick of rationality."[82] For solace or refuge, many followed the path taken by the feckless aesthete Truesdale Marshall, to the timeless, mysterious "Orient" of China, Japan, Turkey, or Arabia. The experience of the Orient, whether literally through travel or imaginatively through art, literature, or interior decoration, immersed them in an "exotic" world that had resisted or escaped modernity by virtue of its chronological and geographical distance from the contemporary West.[83] Such antimodernist musings about and overseas adventures among non-Western "others" occurred simultaneously with Americans' completion of the conquest of their continent and the rapid turning abroad—to Pacific and Caribbean islands, Central and South America—to bring new territories and benighted nonwhite people under the civilizing dominion of the United States. The literary critic Edward Said, in his influential book *Orientalism*, has argued that Europeans' images and stereotypes of the mysterious East underwrote French and English imperialism, justifying the conquest of decadent, inferior peoples.[84] In the United States, the rival images of noble and needy savage—one enviably free of civilization's restraints, the other desperate and despicable proof of Western superiority and beneficence—did not so much contradict as complement each other. Even the most sympathetic Americans, such as the Chicago reformer Jane Addams, who spent most of her lifetime working in that city's impoverished and exploited immigrant wards, assumed the political authority to choose what among primitive peoples was valuable and warranted preserving and what could use the hot-water application of "contact with a better class of Americans."[85] The "exotics" or "primitives," in other words, offered both refuge and resource to groups with the political power and cultural authority to accept or reject, claim or exploit them.

Expansionism and escapism played prominently in the architecture and exhibits of the Buffalo exposition, although they were cast in the friendly terms of "pan-American" harmony and the mutual interests of nations of the Western Hemisphere. The midway's authentic ethnological villages of non-Western "savages" and "others" addressed such serious topics in more-popular forms. But all of these shows, it seems, were poorly attended. It was Thompson's twenty-minute-long rendering of these themes that grabbed people's attention and, even at twice the price of its rivals, played to capacity virtually every half-hour that the fair was open. His illusion commercialized the transition from an agrarian and religious age to a secular and scientific one with humor and optimism. At a time when many Americans were engaged in remaking distant lands and peoples in their own image, A Trip to the Moon implicitly poked fun at the popular enthusiasm for or against overseas expansion; only a Moon Calf could take its colonial dreams seriously. Less of a joke, it seems, was the way the illusion appealed to an antimodernist longing for an exotic and very modern escape from the naysaying restraints of Western and Christian convention. Although he built a Buffalo version of Darkness and Dawn, Thompson's energies were focused on the *Luna* enterprise. The ship's ascent from the darkened city of Buffalo to the resplendent kingdom of the Man in the Moon may have retraced the familiar path to salvation caricatured in Darkness and Dawn, but in its new incarnation the voyage was thoroughly secularized, and paradise relocated from heaven to the heavens. To get there, a man had only to believe that fun was a worthy salvation in itself.[86]

The *Luna* journey capitalized on another aspect of contemporary Orientalism, the urban bourgeoisie's fascination with the prospects of space travel and extraterrestrial life. Such timeless speculations had achieved the legitimacy of scientific investigation in Europe and America after 1877, when the Italian astronomer Giovanni Virginio Schiaparelli discovered "canals" on the surface of Mars. The report ignited decades of debate about the existence and character of *human* life on that planet. As the great popularizer of Martian studies, the Frenchman Camille Flammarion, asserted in his influential work *La Planète Mars* (1892), "The actual conditions on Mars are such that it would be wrong to deny that it could be inhabited by human species whose intelligence and methods of action could be far superior to our own." Earth's moon received its own share of speculative attention. There was Wells's story, and in the 1890s a popular "illustrated lecture" called "A Trip to the Moon" attracted audiences in New York. Although it appears no claims were made for life on the Moon, the lecturer used glass slides, scenic drops, colored lights, and a large plaster moon to produce close-up views of the Earth and of the Moon, giving spectators the sensation that they actually were only two to three miles above the lunar surface. Regardless of whether Thompson's Trip was more or less fraudulent than this lecture, it exploited the same curiosity about and longing for what Flammarion called "other worlds."[87]

The taste for extraterrestrial pleasures also was encouraged by the new spiritualist and "mind-cure" faiths to which prophets, mediums, occultists, swamis, and other varieties of mystic were converting what some contemporaries regarded as alarming numbers of urban, middle-class Europeans and Americans during the last half of the nineteenth century. Séances, meditation, rapping and spinning tables, spectral visions, crystal balls, and fortune-tellers—such practices and aspects of "Spiritism," a European observer wrote in 1885, were "threatening to become a public calamity, to which every government has to direct its attention." Governments paid little heed, but psychologists in Europe and America—William James, Sigmund Freud, G. Stanley Hall, to name only a few—devoted countless hours to searching out and observing mediums for what their hysterics revealed about the unconscious reaches of the mind.[88]

In the United States, spiritualism was never an organized movement but an inclusive name for a diverse array of popular "mind-cure" sects, many of which exist still today: Christian Science, New Thought, and theosophy, for example. Their spiritual roots were in the antebellum disestablishment and sectarian revolt against traditional Protestant authority and doctrines, the Christian "liberalism" of Universalism and Unitarianism, and the radical dissent of feminist supporters of the "Free Love" movement, Swedenborgianism, and transcendentalism. But they also reflected and responded to the growing sentiment at the end of the century among "progressive," urban, middle-class men and, especially, women that traditional Christian beliefs were irrationally cruel and inhumane, irreconcilable with modern scientific discoveries, and primitively patriarchal. Some, such as Mary Baker Eddy's Christian Science, claimed authority in the Bible, but others, such as theosophy, were enemies of Christianity in any form and flourished instead by advocating an unsystematic mix of Eastern religious thought and scientific theories of nuclear physics and evolution. At the core of many of these diverse faiths was what William James called the "gospel of healthy-mindedness," which conceives "good as the essential and universal aspect of being, [and] deliberately excludes evil from its field of vision." The proselytes of healthy-minded faiths insisted that traditional Christian notions of sin, guilt, sacrifice, and redemption were wrong-headed and harmful limitations on human potential. God, they contended, was not a judgmental father telling people what to do, but an invigorating and nurturing divine force that, if embraced, opened all believers to their inner divinity and a life in this world of limitless "spiritual sunshine," joy, and bliss. As the influential Hindu swami Vivekenanda told Americans, "We are really gods, not sinners. We must not beg for salvation but demand it as our spiritual birthright."[89]

Many late-nineteenth-century feminists in Europe and America embraced theosophy, the organizational arm of the charismatic mystic Madame Helene Blavatsky, and other spiritualist groups that dismissed the authority of God the Father and enlisted the higher powers of spirit mediums, who usually were women. The ways in which bourgeois Americans and western Europeans understood women's natures—that they were innately passive, intuitive, and disposed to maternal benevolence—may have disqualified them from cultural or political authority in a rational, scientific, business culture. But these gendered conceptions qualified them exclusively for leadership in many of the spiritualist religions, which asserted new dimensions of female power and authority. Women's inborn spirituality gave them privileged access to higher, or "occult," truths that men's rationality missed. Through the trance-inspired visions of female mediums, past earthly worlds as well as new extraterrestrial ones were resurrected or discovered. These worlds were unimaginably and sumptuously rich. They often were guided by female divine forces and lacked the conventions and rules that limited American women's actions in the late nineteenth century. Blavatsky assembled a cult around Isis, the queen of ancient Egypt. In spiritualism the solidity of the body itself no longer seemed dependable or necessary. "In the seances at the fin de siècle," writes historian Sonu Shamdasani, "women became men and men became women. There was no limit to who one could be or to how many."[90]

Spiritualism also undermined masculinist economic norms. Mind cure's embrace of the material world in the here and now, its renunciation of sin, repression, and the patriarchal Christian God, and its insistence that misery was merely a state of mind also sanctioned the new mentality, practices, and desires encouraged by the emerging urban consumer marketplace, which was challenging the priority of the older masculine order of self-denial, obligation to duty, and productive work. The popular culture of mind cure, with its "ready-made consumer mentality," was integrated into many aspects of late-nineteenth-century urban American culture, from the bromides of the influential advertising sloganeer Elbert Hubbard to the bland prescription to be "glad" in

Eleanor Porter's famous 1912 children's book, *Pollyanna*, and the emerging culture industry of positive thinking in the 1920s. Mind-cure or healthy-minded theologies authorized and sanctified the "uninspected wish"; they validated the heart's desire and freed it from centuries of Protestant theological restraint. These religions found ready adherents among a new generation of tired businessmen and alienated women, whose affluence was no compensation for the lack of power or the deficiency of startling wonder they felt in their everyday lives. Stifling boredom and drab surroundings were the complaints not of the working men who labored on the shop floors of steel mills, but of ordinary middle-class men like Thompson, who knew the fatigue he described and the impatience with injunctions, religious or otherwise, to accept one's lot with forbearance. In Thompson's otherworldly lunar paradise, a man could break away, for a few minutes, from the suffocating and solemn limitations of everyday life.[91]

The vision of soaring in a winged vessel in A Trip to the Moon came to Thompson around the same time that the Swiss psychologist Théodore Flournoy was publishing *From India to the Planet Mars*, his widely read analysis of the "great somnambulistic romances" of a young Geneva medium, Élise-Catherine Müller, whom he disguised under the pseudonym Hélène Smith. Flournoy's richly detailed narrative account of her trances made Müller internationally famous at the turn of the century, and not just among her fellow spiritualists, or psychologists like the author. The translator of the 1900 English-language edition, Daniel B. Vermilye, justified the project by citing "the widespread and increasing interest" in Britain and America "in the phenomena exhibited by its heroine—an interest which marks a new era in the progress of human knowledge." What made Müller heroic were the recoveries of her highly colored past adventures as the fifteenth-century Hindu princess Simadini and as the eighteenth-century French queen Marie Antoinette. But Müller's most sensational mental journeys were to the contemporary planet Mars, where she befriended its exotically beautiful and yellow-tinted people, acquired their language, beheld amazing flying-machines, and luxuriated in a peach-colored world of red-brick soil, blue-pink lakes, and "beautiful birds of many-colored plumage flying and singing around her." Flournoy concluded that Müller's dreams of a past and current Martian "existence more brilliant than her own" were Orientalized inversions of "the modest environment" of her everyday life. She was the daughter of a merchant and worked as a salesclerk in a retail shop, but in her trances she flew away from "the realities of life" and the "fundamental feeling of imprisonment in a too paltry sphere" that "crushed and bruised" her. "Thence came these visions," writes Flournoy, "always warm, luminous, highly colored, exotic, bizarre; and these brilliant apparitions, superbly dressed, in which her antipathy for her insipid and unpleasant surroundings betrays itself, her weariness of ordinary, commonplace people, her disgust for prosaic occupations, for vulgar and disagreeable things, for the narrow house, the dirty streets, the cold winters, and the gray sky." Flournoy determined that Müller's exuberantly imagined Martian "romance" was not real, but a "supremely childish, puerile" projection of an unconscious wish, the product of a "former, infantine, less evolved state of [her] individuality, which has again come to light, renewed its life, and once more become active." Müller, in other words, was engaged in a form of creative play, which in later trances would take her on similar adventures in the other worlds of Uranus and the Earth's moon.[92]

There is no evidence that Thompson ever read Flournoy's book, although it would be surprising if he did not know of the heroine Hélène Smith, whose exploits were widely discussed in European and American newspapers. But unlike Flournoy, Thompson did not regard wishes like those of Hélène as expressions of a necessarily troubled and repressed person who longed childishly and impossibly for a more highly colored life. If such wishes were childish, in Thompson's mind there was nothing wrong with them. Nor did he suggest that the dissatisfactions and antipathies of the average man could be alleviated through political, religious, or cultural renewal, as radicals such as Henry Demarest Lloyd and Eugene Debs and evangelists such as Dwight L. Moody were urging working- and middle-class Americans at the time. The only problem he identified was particular to the showman's condition: how to turn these unrestrained and uninspected wishes into turnstiled amusements. A Trip to the Moon was, to be sure, a lot of silly business, but Thompson's illusion also was a commercial version of Müller's child's wish to sail out of a drab and colorless existence and into a luminous world of strange and exotic possibilities. As the guidebook author Barry observed of the Buffalo attraction, with A Trip to the Moon the "prodigal promise which every father makes to his child that he shall have the moon for a plaything is now possible of realization."[93]

### An Exposition Is Not a Serious Thing

For Thompson it was not enough that he was doing land-office business marketing impossible wishes; he insisted impertinently that the exposition as a whole should sell such otherworldly dreams. For the first three months of the fair, attendance had not remotely approached the numbers the promoters had anticipated. Although merely an embarrassment to the city's leading citizens, the empty streets were experienced painfully along the Midway. Bankruptcy was likely for the entire amusement zone, not for just a few of its concessions. Desperate, the Midway entrepreneurs turned to an ambitious and irreverent plan offered by Thompson. He proposed to operate the entire exposition as a show by staging a "Midway Day," when for one day "nothing but fun and frolic should exist throughout the open spaces of the exposition." The advertising and promotion of the fair would be turned over to the showmen, the uplifting curriculum of the "colossal university" shelved, and the carnivalesque improprieties of the Midway allowed to rule the domain. "From the very first we have objected to the Exposition taking itself so seriously," Thompson explained. "An exposition is not, nor should it be, a serious thing. Amusement should predominate. It should be billed like a circus." The fair's managers were not amused or pleased, especially when he asserted that the exposition was a failure "because there was not a showman" among its executives. When he tried to explain "the value of a laugh," the "distinguished committee" peremptorily rejected his proposal and countered that the Pan-American was, first and foremost, "a colossal educational institution instructive of the best of the arts and trades and sciences." Undeterred, Thompson appealed to the president of the exposition, the prominent lawyer John G. Milburn, who overruled his board. Midway Day was scheduled for the first Saturday in August.[94]

With little more than a week to prepare, Thompson organized the plastering of broadsides throughout much of the northeastern United States. Full-page newspaper advertisements released a torrent of alliterative hyperbole: "Marvels for the Millions ... A Sorrow Breaker! ... Mirth for the Masses." According to the official count, 106,315 passed through the gates on Midway Day, surpassing previous crowd records. The fair's management was caught completely unprepared; railroads leading to Buffalo and the entrance gates to the park were overwhelmed by the swarms of fairgoers.[95]

"It was like a page torn from the history of ancient Rome," exclaimed the *Buffalo Courier*, "a mixture of barbarism, dazzling, lavish, weird, crowned by the glory of civilization." This was exactly as Thompson wanted his spectacle described. Although it was billed as a carnivalesque release from restraints, Midway Day was precisely prepared and timed to prevent a still or unplanned moment from occurring: parades, pageants, circus performances; ten thousand homing pigeons liberated "to carry to all the world and the rest of mankind the greetings of the Pan-American Exposition"; human cannonballs and a marriage ceremony in a balloon two thousand feet above the fairgrounds; a finale of eight hundred dancers on an open-air stage. Thompson used the magnificent buildings as background scenery or stage properties for the actual performances. The daredevil Cameroni slid by his teeth down a rope from the top of the Electric Tower to the sports stadium, where a crowd of twenty-five thousand awaited. The diver Matt Gay leaped from the tower's colonnade into the Grand Canal below. Each stunt mocked the iconographic significance of the tower as an object of wonder and awe, valuable in and of itself. No aspect of the exposition was sacred, nothing so serious that it could not be ridiculed or exploited. "For once," the *Courier* crowed, "the Pan-American Exposition lost its identity and became the Midway, all Midway and nothing but Midway."[96]

Afterward some of the distinguished committee credited the mass appeal of Midway Day's entertainments for its unprecedented success and blamed the highbrow tone of earlier advertising for the Pan-American's summertime lethargy. "There has been enough periodical advertising," declared fair chairman John N. Scatcherd. "Intelligent thinking people have had their fill of descriptions.... What is necessary now is to reach the class that attends an exposition for the fun and amusement there is in it." In other words, mirth for the masses had won the argument, a lesson that Thompson repeated for the fair's management: "Ther[e] is no dignity in a crowd. Therefore, the dignified Exposition will not be favored with crowds. Get down to the level of the masses. Provide what they want and provide it liberally." He implored the management to make every day "a special day" by converting the exposition into a permanent carnival, a Mardi Gras on Lake Erie, "boomed" coast to coast with millions of colorful posters. "Keep it up ceaselessly. Startle the public with the spectacular features offered."[97]

Mardi Gras did not go to Buffalo, although the fortunes of the Midway showmen and the fair as a whole did improve, and thanks not only to the boost encouraged by Midway Day. Leon Czolgosz, the reputed anarchist, contributed more than his share when he assassinated President William McKinley at the exposition's Temple of Music on 6 September 1901. The startling news of the president's murder was boomed in newspapers from coast to coast. In the two months following the assassination, almost two million people went to the Pan-American.[98]

For all its fanfare, Midway Day was, as much as anything else, a brilliant fit of childish pique on the part of Fred Thompson. Every broadside and publicity release, every premeditated stunt that turned the exposition into a well-regulated playground, dramatized his resentment at being rebuffed and belittled by the illustrious men who, for all their achievements as captains of industry and finance, idly watched as the Pan-American went up in what *Billboard* magazine called a "glorious blaze of financial failure." "The Pan-American has arranged a beautiful stage setting," Thompson explained in the aftermath of his big day. "The spectators admire the setting and then wait in vain for the stage performance." Seriousness of purpose had no cash value with the crowd, and consumer choice was the only source of validation Thompson took seriously.[99]

As Thompson told this story—and he did, time and time again, in the decade of his New York successes—the day the showmen took over the exposition was the moment when the meandering course of his life assumed a certain direction and the future emerged clearly in his mind's eye. His great discovery was that his most dishonorable tendencies and impulses—how he hated to sit still, his dread of regularity and grudge toward rules, his resentment of authority (especially in the form of older men), the way the words "duty" and "responsibility" grated on his ears, his appetite for dazzling excitement and pleasure, his fondness for spending money, his conviction that life should be about fun and frolic—were not necessarily liabilities or moral flaws in a "land of desire." They could be assets, instruments of pleasure *and* profit instead of traps on the highway to achievement. Midway Day proved that the "crowds" were with him. They did not want to be instructed or improved; they wanted it "liberally" affirmed that what they *should* do was what they *wanted* to do. As he later explained, "It was the success of [Midway] day and the resentment I felt towards the architects for their treatment of the Midway that started me thinking about building an exposition of my own." When he was in charge, showmen like himself no longer would be held in contempt, tucked away on "some long street in a back yard" like a "side show to be more or less ashamed of." They would be the show.[100]

Lessons along these lines had been around at least since 1893, when Sol Bloom's Midway proved vastly more popular than the ennobling fare of Chicago's White City. Yet Midway Day did more than recite an earlier day's lessons; it emboldened Thompson to picture another kind of "perfect city" for the twentieth century. Five years after the event, he recalled standing "at the entrance of the Pan-American Exposition the morning after 'Midway Day,' and, looking over its classical architecture" he saw a future in which palaces of amusement, not "immense exposition buildings filled with canned goods, preserved meats, etc.," would predominate. "I saw Luna Park complete, no definite style of architecture being in my mind, a number of palaces in free Renaissance, well proportioned and balanced, the skyline broken with countless towers and minarets, the whole thing a rather Oriental dream." This vision outlined a "plausible fiction" about the possibilities of life in the new metropolitan world. But unlike the great world's fairs that it caricatured, Thompson would teach people the subjects they wanted to learn: how to play and have fun.[101]

When he decided to take his toys and build his own exposition, Fred Thompson was defining and acting out the promise of the commercial culture of Peter Pan. With the close of the Buffalo fair and, in important ways, the nineteenth century, Thompson had contrived a strategy for catering to the disappointments of middle-class men such as he, who longed for an existence more brilliant than the modest circumstances of their everyday lives. He possessed a commodity form of amusement in the model of A Trip to the Moon and a supportive personality of an exuberantly youthful man making money by inventing and building playthings for the masses. All he lacked was a suitable venue, a large enough theater in which to dramatize the pleasures and possibilities of play.

# THREE

# Life Is Only a Merry-Go-Round

Luna Park, 1903–13

O N a chilly, wet afternoon in mid-May 1905, when Coney Island's main attractions threw their gates open for the new
summer season, a writer for the *New York Sun* witnessed the
"edifying spectacle" of "a young man in a brown suit and a flat topped
felt hat" acting as though he hadn't a care in the world as he made the
rounds at Luna Park, the island's most famous and popular amusement
park. One moment he was parading Luna's avenues of plaster palaces
on the back of an elephant; another, he was coasting in a flat-bottomed
boat down the steep water-slide of the Shoot-the-Chutes, plunging into
the cold lagoon, a young woman clutched in either arm; later, he was ca-
reering through the curves and "breath snatching dips" of the scenic
railway. As it turned out, the young man who was out for "a little fun"
that day was the designer, part owner, and manager of Luna Park, Fred
Thompson. But as his frolic was designed to show, the profit was not in
coldly factoring costs against revenues; the payoff came from being a
part of the show. In the *Sun*'s words, he was "Frederic Thompson, capitalist, amusement inventor and perennial small boy."[1]

Throughout his eleven seasons at Luna Park, the image of Fred
Thompson as the fun-loving boy-capitalist on a spree was as much a feature of the park as its exaggerated "Oriental" architecture or the Shoot-

the-Chutes. Thompson staged his performances to show that Luna Park was built by and for a new kind of man, one who would accept no less than all the fun to which he was entitled. Thompson, then, was largely indistinguishable from the Coney Island resort that he named for the continuously mutating moon: a radiant reflection of energy, never the same or in the same place from one moment to the next, the very representation of capricious and insatiable desire. Above all, he said, his park meant unceasing variety and change, "movement, movement, movement everywhere."[2] What was true of Luna Park would be true of Thompson; he was what he sold.

The fantasy of a Never Land free of obligations, where men could relive their childhoods, ride on elephants, and play with any toy they liked, was Luna's governing narrative, the story that Thompson used to explain his amusement park, his vision of the good life, and how he had come to be the man he was. Although Luna's pictorial attractions, scenic railways, and sensational reenactments of topical floods and conflagrations expanded in many ways on "Victorian ways of seeing and experiencing,"[3] its construction as a marketplace of play and effortless abundance plotted the coordinates of a new cultural outlook that placed the park and its inventor at the center of twentieth-century consumer capitalism in the United States. With Luna Park no less than with himself, he encouraged and represented new ways of imagining pleasure and fulfillment for middle-class men in such a world, dismissing older apprehensions about the personal and social dangers of immaturity, material luxury, and self-indulgence. This outlook defined maturity and seriousness as afflictions, and cheerfulness as the elixir of modern life; and it underlay virtually every aspect of his plaster-and-lath metropolis of play and pleasure, from its Orientalist skyline of domes and minarets to the blaring bands that perpetually paraded through its streets to the "edifying spectacle" of the light-hearted proprietor swooping down the Chutes. Luna's architecture, amusements, and proprietor played important roles in furthering this market culture, but their specific contributions were to the particular pattern of meanings that composed the commercial culture of Peter Pan. Luna was one of the most influential—and, in all probability, the most popular—of the broad array of institutions whose designers and supporters enlisted or claimed for themselves the fantasy of unending childhood to define their particular enterprises.

Thompson encouraged "people," presumably all men and women, to seek foolish gratification in his marketplace. But the usual context of his remarks—the pronouns he used, the problems and anxieties he identified, the wishes he assigned to his clientele, the atmosphere he touted, the kind of play he marketed, the role he assumed of the boy who never grew up—plotted a more exclusive field of vision. Thompson left Buffalo in late 1901 convinced that Americans in general, but especially those men like himself—white, middle class, worked to death—burned with dissatisfaction and longing. There was little new about this insight into what Alexis de Tocqueville in the 1830s called the "permanent agitation" and "slight but troublesome restlessness" that continuously stirred within American men.[4] What marked Thompson as different from previous generations of inconsolable men was that he did not hold out political action, the promise of private property or personal wealth, or preparation for the New Jerusalem as the hope for a better future. Rather, he staked his investment on the premise that American men wished not to care more but to care less, not to work harder or to be richer, but to have more fun. They longed, in his words, to return to a time when "play was everything; when responsibility had never been dreamed of;... when we decided from personal experience what games we liked best."[5] Luna would be their—and his—playground.

### From Buffalo to Surf Avenue

In Buffalo, Thompson had allied himself with a new partner, Elmer "Skip" Dundy, an Omaha rival who had outmaneuvered him in winning the Pan-American concession for Thompson's big success in 1898, Darkness and Dawn. Out of necessity, the two laid aside differences and developed an apparently symbiotic relationship that lasted until Dundy's death in early 1907. Their partnership was built on a peculiar fiction. Dundy, although himself an inveterate gambler and notorious roué on the city's pleasure circuit, publicly played the adult role of the quietly reliable businessman in the partnership; rarely was he quoted on any aspect of the partnership's ventures. Thompson made all the noise and hogged the attention; he made sure no one doubted that he was the one with imagination, the dreamer, the boy-man of the two.[6]

The veteran showman George C. Tilyou, who had met Thompson in Buffalo, lured him to Coney Island (or "Coney," as it was popularly known) over Dundy's resistance. To that point, Tilyou had been the is-

land's most successful amusement entrepreneur and had built up a lucrative following of working- and lower-middle-class New Yorkers for
his large complex of amusements, Steeplechase Park, which had
opened in 1897. Tilyou knew a winner when he saw one, and he wanted
A Trip to the Moon for his park. By January 1902 construction was underway on a Steeplechase version of the *Luna* voyage.[7]

Dundy's initial reluctance to invest in Coney is not surprising. In
1902 it bore little resemblance to the mass markets of affluent middle-
class consumers at world's fairs. Coney was not truly an island, but a
slip of sand and marsh ambiguously separated from the southernmost
promontory of Brooklyn by a small creek that once had flowed uninterrupted from Gravesend to Sheepshead Bay. Its principal natural attraction since the end of the Civil War had been the stretch of sandy
shoreline that runs nearly four miles from Sheepshead Bay on the east
to the Lower Bay near the narrow entrance to the harbors of New York
City and New Jersey on the west. Although it was located some ten
miles south of the vital center of Manhattan—Fourteenth Street and
Union Square—by 1902 Coney Island no longer was isolated from
greater New York City but well integrated into the metropolitan area.
The expansion of regular surface rail and steamship service made a
summer outing to escape the city heat a crowded, sweaty, inconvenient,
but comparatively inexpensive and coveted treat for millions living in
the densely populated neighborhoods of lower Manhattan and Brooklyn.[8] On summer weekends and any night of the week, electric trolleys
laden with passengers, "heads protruding from windows like pins from
a cushion," snaked through "the vegetable gardens and fireflies of the
Borough of Brooklyn," before depositing their human cargo at the end
of the line (fig. 3.1). Querulous middle-class observers who described
the curious spectacle for polite magazines tended only to see the "tight-
packed horde, odorous with sweat" slouching toward Coney on hot
summer days, or to state their amusement at the island's "spectacle of
poverty in spangles," the young women preening in last year's hats.
But, as Catharine Brody recalled in 1928 about her childhood, it was
"an altogether different matter to go to the Island from a tenement-
house." The parks themselves were "expensive treats ... and accordingly
prized and enjoyed. The beach itself was the place for a long-awaited
holiday."[9]

If nature had been the island's principal attraction in the nineteenth

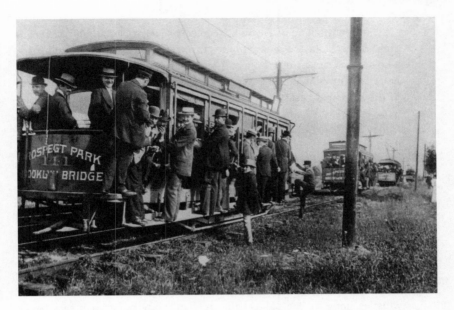

Fig. 3.1. Although genteel observers complained of the malodorous "tight-packed horde" that jammed trolleys to Coney Island, especially on holiday weekends, the men shown here around 1915 appear not to mind the accommodations. (*Neg. No. 48353, ©Collection of The New-York Historical Society.*)

century, it was the synthetic Coney Island of "fun" that lured metropolitan residents in the early twentieth century. By 1902 the island had been arranged into three identifiable areas, each with a particular reputation for commercial recreation. Wealthy merchants, politicians, and entertainment figures and their families—the rising middle-class elite—strutted at the eastern end of the island, at the exclusive and luxurious hotels along Manhattan Beach. The young Theodore Dreiser, who first visited there in 1894, remembered Manhattan Beach as an entrancing fairyland that "held and contained all summer long all that was best and most leisurely and pleasure-loving in New York's great middle class of that day."[10] Less prosperous middle-class patrons stopped just west of there on Brighton Beach, with its popularly priced hotels and outdoor concerts. At the island's far western end, the sporting male crowd of all classes gathered for "rougher" masculine attractions of spirited drinking, prostitution, gambling, brawls, prizefights, and horse racing.

The Coney Island of Tilyou's Steeplechase Park was situated between these respectable and racy extremes in West Brighton, by the late 1890s a boisterous cluster of public bathhouses, saloons, beer gardens, dance halls, mammoth restaurants, and penny arcades jammed on either side of the principal east-west thoroughfare of Surf Avenue and called the "Bowery." Even before the era of the great parks, West Brighton, or Coney as it was called, was the island's focal point, attracting three hundred thousand to five hundred thousand working women and men and (if they had them) their children to its rollicking entertainments and breezy beaches, especially on hot summer Sundays.[11] By 1909 the number of summer visitors had grown to twenty million.[12] West Brighton's amusements catered to the "cultural style" of working-class New Yorkers, rather than to the polite tastes of the Manhattan Beach set.[13] "There is one thing at Coney Island that you can get for nothing," observed the playwright Elmer Blaney Harris in 1908, "and that is Noise.... Bands, orchestras, pianos, at war with gramophones, hand-organs, calliopes; overhead, a roar of wheels in a deathlock with shrieks and screams; whistles, gongs, rifles all busy; the smell of candy, popcorn, meats, beer, tobacco, blended with the odor of the crowd redolent now and then of patchouli; a streaming river of people arched over by electric signs—this is the Bowery at Coney Island."[14]

Although far from the sexual and gambling subculture of the far western end's Norton Point, West Brighton's unrefined joys and odors marked it as unsuitable for respectable, middle-class people, particularly women. It regularly provoked the wrath of ministers and reformers outraged by the illicit pleasure economy that prospered there. Coney, the Episcopal bishop of Long Island sermonized late in 1902, is a "modern Tiberius," "a place where [Satan] invites young men and young women to come and lose their souls by drink and debauchery."[15] The minister may not have recognized it, but a moral and economic transformation actually had begun in West Brighton in the 1890s, with the construction of the large, enclosed amusements, Paul Boyton's Sea Lion Park in 1896 and Tilyou's Steeplechase Park the following year. Boyton's park centered on the popular Shoot-the-Chutes, and Tilyou's was named for its most famous ride, a mechanical horse race that circled the park. As important as their rides, however, was the showmen's idea to set their collections of amusements inside fences, which defined their geographical identity and supposedly kept out Coney's notorious undesirables—

roughnecks and prostitutes—while enabling management to charge a ten-cent entry fee.[16]

Still, in 1902, as the bishop's comments indicate, Coney Island labored under a reputation for moral darkness; it was seen as a haven for swindlers, pickpockets, confidence men, and flesh-peddlers. Or, as Thompson self-servingly asserted in 1907, the pre-Luna Coney "was a byword for all that was vulgar, vicious and deplorable. It was the epitome of human nature at its worst seeking its amusement. Its pleasures were those no self-respecting man or woman could possibly enjoy."[17] In many ways, he was right. Although Steeplechase and the beaches lured more women and children to Coney at the end of the century, the island in 1902 remained divided by both class and sex, with the rough social life of men, particularly working-class men, shadowing West Brighton and that of proper middle-class women and their families shining brightly at Brighton and Manhattan Beaches.[18] Thompson and Dundy had to reform both the class and the gender identities of the West Brighton amusement economy if they were to attract the same audience—the great decent middle class—that they had in Buffalo or Omaha, where the atmosphere on the midway was, for the most part, inoffensive and the patrons not necessarily segregated by gender. Expelling the sex trade (or, rather, claiming to do so) was the first step in establishing the mythology of Luna Park as a free and easy nursery for grown-up children.

## The Heart of Coney Island

Thompson and his partner made a killing in their one season at Steeplechase and began looking for "a larger field on Coney Island."[19] They leased Boyton's failing Sea Lion Park, a narrow, twenty-two-acre strip of sand on the landward side of Surf Avenue. (Another sixteen acres would be added in 1904.)[20] Fewer than three months after Steeplechase had closed, the *Brooklyn Daily Eagle* reported five hundred men were transforming the shabby park and had almost completed the building for A Trip to the Moon. "Our plans may seem venturesome and ambitious," Thompson told the newspaper, "but they have been carefully conceived and matured, and, make or break, they will be carried out to the letter. We have unbounded faith in the future of Coney Island and are risking a fortune in this enterprise."[21]

The illustrations accompanying the *Eagle* article indicated the experiment in store: a sparkling Electric Tower rising two hundred feet from a shimmering reflecting lagoon; an imposing Court of Honor with monumental buildings, towers, pinnacles, and arcades. The array of attractions Thompson promised exceeded any previously offered at Coney, although Luna, with notable exceptions, relied on world's fair standards, from scenic "novelties" like the River Styx and the Grand Canyon to Eskimo and other ethnic villages.[22] In its layout Luna copied the Beaux Arts arrangement established by previous world's fairs: an elongated reflecting pool flanked by monumental architecture and balanced at either end by a towering structure. In the case of Luna, the Chutes spilled into one end of the lagoon, while the Electric Tower stood at the opposite end, fountains spewing at its base. Although Luna's unified aesthetic blatantly and deliberately deferred to past world's fairs, the showman repudiated the fairs' dignified antagonism toward buying and spending. At Luna, the Orientalist air of it all marked the palatial structures as houses or bazaars of amusement, not improvement. Everything was for sale.

In the manner of Midway Day, Thompson and Dundy orchestrated the premiere with military precision, booming it throughout the metropolitan area with exuberant posters and press releases. At the moment of the opening on 16 May 1903, when the outlines of Luna's buildings were sketched against the early evening gloom by two hundred thousand or more incandescent lights, Luna seemed an extravagantly luxurious world in comparison with the warren of beer halls and attractions on the Bowery or even at Steeplechase Park, which was Surf Avenue cleaned up and enclosed by a fence. The carefully engineered stunt reenacted the spectacular chiaroscuro of A Trip to the Moon and Darkness and Dawn but on a greater scale. Five hand-carved Roman chariots stood at the entrance on Surf Avenue, beneath a massive arch blazing with electric lights and proclaiming "The Heart of Coney Island ... Thompson and Dundy." The chariots were box offices; each was occupied by a "beautiful young woman in evening attire and wearing a red picture hat." Waiting inside were "a long line of uniformed men like an army of elevated railway ticket choppers" and costumed barkers extolling the wonders of the "Electric City by the Sea." Luna was a combination circus, dime museum, and exposition midway; it had a dance hall, a monkey theater, an outdoor circus, Venetian canals, and a nurs-

ery of premature babies warming in glass-enclosed incubators, overseen by licensed nurses and doctors. On opening night, Cameroni
reprised his Pan-American stunt, coasting from the top of the Electric
Tower by his teeth. A Trip to the Moon premiered in a building nearly
twice the size of Buffalo's; adjoining it were the scenic illusions 20,000
Leagues under the Sea to the North Pole and War of Worlds. Luna Park,
concluded the *Eagle*, "covers the field of amusement almost as completely as the St. Louis fair will cover that of industries."[23]

Luna's construction as an architectural "Oriental dream," as Thompson had described it, marked it as the first "theme" park and an epochal
event in the history of American amusements. The resort attracted extraordinary, if not amazing, crowds from its first night, when as many
as 60,000 pushed into the new park. Over the Fourth of July holiday
that first year, attendance records were established when 142,000 entered the park on Saturday and 103,000 on Sunday.[24] Thompson's publicity men reported that 5,000,000 paid to enter the gates in 1906. The
numbers had to be exaggerated (Thompson would not have been much
of a showman if they were not), but the crush of people was no ballyhoo,
and it lent credibility to their bragging that the first summer's receipts
paid off the million dollars they claimed to have spent building Luna.[25]
By the end of the decade even the grave *New York Times* expressed the
island's allure in vaudevillian voice: Coney had gotten so crowded, "who
ever goes" there "nowadays except everybody?"[26]

The business of Luna Park was a fairly straightforward matter. Like
its predecessors on the island, Luna was a fenced-in collection of independent concessions, which usually paid a lease fee and a percentage of
their gross revenue to the park's owners. Thompson and Dundy owned
only a few attractions, such as A Trip to the Moon and 20,000 Leagues,
which often paid quite well. But the real money was in Luna Park's
gates. With admission set at ten cents, millions of dimes rolled in every
summer and all of them went into the pockets of the partners and their
investors.[27] The only tax on their fortunes was a rainy day. Where
Thompson and Dundy got the money to finance the enterprise remains
something of a mystery. Luna's viability was proved beyond a doubt in
the matter of a single summer month in 1903, although prior to that
May night the venture was nothing short of a gamble. Unknown as they
were, Thompson and Dundy alone could not have financed a project of
this scope. The loudly advertised cost of the park, one million dollars,

was certainly an outlandish fabrication. (If Luna had cost a million, surely Thompson would have doubled the figure.) The silent partner appears to have been the maverick industrialist John W. Gates, nicknamed "Bet-a-Million Gates" for his reckless personal and business behavior, which newspapers at the time covered in detail. Although there is little other than anecdotal evidence to connect him with Luna Park, Gates's crucial backing of Thompson and Dundy in the Hippodrome venture makes it likely that he was behind the Coney Island investment.[28]

Whether four million or two million entered their gates during any one summer, everyone could see that Thompson and Dundy had a bonanza in Luna Park. In Thompson's version of how he and his partner struck it rich, Coney Island prior to the summer of 1903 was "the greatest show grounds in the world without a showman on it."[29] This claim was Thompsonian bluster, although it was true that no one at Coney had baited the audience he had in mind or used his instruments of attraction. Since the mid-nineteenth century, theater owners in New York and other American cities had sought to make their establishments more respectable by controlling the content of performances, hushing rowdy audiences, diminishing alcohol consumption, and making it more difficult to pursue the illicit pleasures of the "third tier," the gallery where prostitutes and their male consorts mingled. From the beginning the disciplining of theatrical amusements promised to broaden audiences in the name of artistic and public service, but the actual effect was to narrow the patronage, removing working-class men to make way for genteel, middle-class men and, especially, women, who in growing numbers were frequenting the urban retail establishments near which theater owners consciously positioned their houses. This transformation was especially noticeable in vaudeville. Its roots were in the ill-famed "concert saloons," which, in the middle-class Victorian imagination, were the vicious haunts of working-class men, prostitutes, and drunks. Tony Pastor, the inventor of "refined vaudeville," became the dominant vaudeville showman in the 1880s and 1890s in New York by moving his theaters to more-fashionable neighborhoods and toning down the raciness of the entertainments, all in the name of welcoming middle-class women and even their children into his audiences. B. F. Keith and Edward Albee carried the process even further in the 1890s and early 1900s, promoting the "respectable thrills" of "family vaudeville." Thompson borrowed his reformist vocabulary from these theatrical predecessors.[30]

Although he readily took their money, Thompson was not interested in catering to recent immigrants or to the women and men who worked in the city's factories and sweatshops. They already went to Coney when they could. Nor did he take aim at the carriage trade, whose pockets were deep but numbers small; throngs were what he needed. The audience he targeted, in other words, looked like him, the New York counterpart to world's fair crowds. Some were petit bourgeois entrepreneurs, but the big money was in two rapidly emerging sectors of the city's population. The more important was the new and growing employee class of white-collar clerks, salesmen, and salaried managers who staffed or supervised the offices of New York's government, legal, financial, retail, and service economy, or hustled the goods and services of the urban marketplace locally or on the road. This class formed the critical foundation of the city's new commercial amusement economy, and it was Thompson's bread and butter.[31] The other target was the itinerant cohort of this class: domestic tourists who, after 1890, flocked to New York, either on business or expressly for pleasure. Luna and Coney Island were tourist destinations.[32]

Vast numbers of young, poorly paid working women also went to Coney's parks, usually with female friends or even on their own. Transportation was a bargain, but with little expendable cash, such women often had to rely on the eager men they met there to "treat" them to the rest, knowing that favors would be expected in return (fig. 3.2). Such women had their own motives, agendas, and resources in this uneven exchange relationship, which gained them access to Coney's cheap amusements even as it exposed their economic vulnerability. Some idea of the new sexual economy of treating at the cleaned-up Coney Island was suggested by the playwright Elmer Blaney Harris's description of his first outing to the "city of lath and burlap." While walking on the beach, Harris was "fascinated" by "a little maid" who, while beneath his station, was nonetheless irresistible in her wet "translucent" bath-dress. A chance encounter later proved that "Dora" had had her eyes on him as well. She accepted his invitation to show him the island and proved every bit his match, slipping in and out of his control, playing the "star performer" on the rides, and giving him "but the tips of her fingers" as they danced at the Luna Park pavilion. Harris wanted to move closer, but she "succeeded in making me feel that I was in no wise necessary, merely useful as an escort." She confirmed his impression when, in ex-

Fig. 3.2. Fred Thompson vowed to reform Coney Island's longstanding reputation as a haven from respectability where, as this postcard shows, men were free to behave like animals in hot pursuit of pleasure. (*Neg. No. 73940, ©Collection of The New-York Historical Society.*)

change for the treats, she kissed him on the cheek and disappeared into the crowd, returning to the "harness" of her job as a barbershop manicurist.[33] The widespread practice of men "treating" women (and women "treating" men) in this fashion underscores why Thompson believed the spending power of white-collar men made his coffers ring. Although far from wealthy, such men had the surplus time, wealth, and energy to purchase pleasure, and if they had no wives (or did not wish to bring them along), they knew they could find willing partners among the strangers in the crowd.[34] When Harris bankrolled Dora's frolic, or the white-collar functionaries Bert and Johnny treated a pair of working "wrens" to the island's attractions in King Vidor's 1928 silent movie, *The Crowd*, they acted out Thompson's assertion that men were willing to pay to get women to play with them.[35]

Thompson had reasons beyond the practical for wanting the audience as well as the bounds of respectability to be as broad as possible at Luna. The showman himself had no intention of abandoning gentility altogether and becoming a byword for all that was vulgar and vicious. As

Reginald Kauffman wrote in 1909, Thompson and Dundy were determined from the outset "to establish a large amusement park with 'Respectability' written large over its gateway."[36] As they liked to advertise, Luna was "The Place for Your Mother, Your Wife, Your Daughter and Your Sister."[37] Yet neither was he willing to shoot the Chutes empty-armed, forgoing the large part of the fun of "Summer Amusement." Thompson was a young bachelor, wandering far from home, and probably well schooled in the bohemian pleasures of the city's nightlife; but he carried in his heart, as the ad suggests, his mother's injunction to behave. Like other unmarried middle-class men of his era, he had to negotiate the rival expectations of genteel domesticity and motherly suasion on one hand, and the need to forge his manhood in the antidomestic world of "rough" or carnal pleasures on the other. Luna incorporated the bachelor's strategy of mediation. Thompson tried to make his amusements respectable without being prissy, suggestively fun without crossing over into raciness.[38]

For a man who was what he sold, this balancing act was a private and public enterprise that required careful maneuvering and propagandizing about himself and his amusement park. To convince skeptics that pleasure and fun could be "decent" and that the desires that Luna encouraged were mostly sunshine and smiles, he strategically displaced immorality and depraved sensuality onto social abstractions, such as the rowdies, ruffians, and prostitutes who supposedly were nabbed in the filters of Luna's gates. Thompson boasted in the middle-class women's magazine *Everybody's* that he "soundly thrashed" the first "rowdy" who trespassed on Luna's grounds and ended the problem once and for all by reminding him that Luna was a place for "his mother and sister," not to mention the magazine's readers. At the same time, he encouraged the playful, carefree, if indiscriminate, mixing of women and men. There was nothing indecorous about this kind of fun so long as the frolicking people were, in his words, "pure and good," by which he meant middle class.[39]

## The Crying Need for Novelty

Word of the partners' achievement quickly spread beyond New York as people in and out of the amusement business witnessed Luna's crowds, or at least reports of them, with amazed envy. In the fall of 1903, an alliance of businessmen and politicians broke ground for Dreamland on the seaside of Surf Avenue and promised to eclipse Luna in every way.[40] The following autumn another group announced plans to build a "perfect reproduction" of Niagara Falls spilling into the ocean at Manhattan Beach. Unlike Dreamland, but like so many others, it never came to be.[41] Still, in the three years after Luna's first season, imitators of Thompson's venture appeared in small and large cities across the country and eventually around the world. The typical investors, especially in smaller cities, were street railway lines. Such firms already were heavily invested in equipment that lay idle on summer weekends, when business ordinarily was slow; they also possessed the capital to construct parks in outlying areas of cities, which allowed them to ring up revenues with park admission fees (ten cents) and trolley fares (twenty-five cents).[42] "The result," the amusement entrepreneur John Calvin Brown noted in 1908, "has been that every progressive and optimistic promoter has not only called most of the cities of 50,000 inhabitants population centers, but has, in his optimism, permitted himself to advise the construction of a superfluous number of amusement parks in each actual population center."[43] By 1905, when the new and short-lived magazine *Midway* published a three-page listing of amusement parks, Illinois had thirty-seven and Ohio more than seventy. Scattered across America were at least four Dreamlands, five Luna Parks, two Manhattan Beaches, four White Cities, seventeen Electric Parks, five Sans Souci parks, four Wonderlands, and one Fairyland.[44] The new vaudeville weekly *Variety* estimated in 1906 that there were four hundred amusement parks in the United States and ran a weekly column on park news that closely followed the doings of Thompson and Dundy.[45] In 1908 a writer in *Show World* asserted, with justification, that Luna had "set the pace for every other modern amusement park in the world."[46] Few were as impressive or as heavily patronized as Luna, but, as the names of the parks suggest, when developers followed Thompson's lead, they also manufactured the purported qualities of his amusements, the strategies for representing and selling play to adult consumers.[47] They built worlds *sans souci*.

They also constructed worlds sans variety. The entrepreneurial energies that Luna unleashed aimed to copy the tried-and-true outline of Thompson's original pleasure formula: "white and shining places" of Orientalized towers and palaces ringing a body of water, glaringly profuse electrical "outline" lighting, and attractions that incorporated thrills, illusions of exotic places, ethnic villages, and reproductions of "disaster" or "destruction" (the eruption of Mount Vesuvius or the Battle for Port Arthur).[48] There was little actual incentive for investors in any part of the United States to alter the basic outline of the Thompsonian form itself. Why risk tampering with the proven product? Most markets were local, and parks appeared unique even if they were not; in any event, the Luna Parks in Pittsburgh or Scranton, Pennsylvania, had the special cachet of the big-city original. Once the convention was established, imitations of Luna and Dreamland were stamped out and distributed across the country with factory-like precision.[49] Edward C. Boyce, one of the forces behind Chicago's White City amusement park (1905), took the process to its logical conclusion—vertical integration. "I design, erect and operate Amusement Resorts," Boyce claimed in his 1905 catalogue, *Modern Amusement Parks*. He would provide plans and superintend construction or "build under contract," organizing corporations, furnishing capital, and supplying amusement devices. "I know how to build at a minimum cost.... Alterations and delays play havoc with cost and occasion much loss of business." Such was the underlying logic of Wonderland; the process of organizing and manufacturing a "municipality of fun" was easily rationalized and industrialized.[50]

The crowded avenues at the Coney Island parks after 1903 also set would-be inventors to work dreaming up new or unusual thrills. The "great tidal wave of human ingenuity" that had flooded the United States Patent Office with applications for new inventions in the thirty years following the Civil War had occasionally leaked into the field of amusement inventions.[51] Showmen such as George Tilyou had been active in the 1890s, but only two or three patents were classified each year in the category of amusement devices until after 1901, when the widely publicized popularity of Steeplechase, Luna, and Dreamland appears to have stimulated a surge of inventiveness. Although there were no amusement patents granted in 1901, there were fourteen in 1902, and twenty-one in 1903, including Thompson's A Trip to the Moon and 20,000 Leagues under the Sea.[52] The figure peaked at sixty in 1907, declining gradually thereafter.[53]

The zeal to tap into the market for amusement devices reflected an assumption, especially common among amusement entrepreneurs, that people are involuntarily attracted to originality and novelty and tire

Fig. 3.3. Coney Island showmen were always on the alert for fresh ideas that combined novelty and, if possible, peril—such as sending Luna Park's elephants plunging down a water slide. (*Theatre Collection, Museum of the City of New York.*)

quickly of the same old fare. "Novelty!" observed one student of Coney showmanship, is the customer's neverending "cry—give us something new or you don't get our money!"[54] Thompson agreed: "The life of your average summer device is ephemeral—an hour in the scheme of days."[55] No appeal is lasting, said Dreamland's Samuel Gumpertz. "The only way to make an old show go is to hang out a new sign—and that won't work more than one time with the audience."[56] Aaron Jones, "the Napoleon of Chicago amusements" and an officer of Chicago's White City, predicted in early 1908 that there "is $1,000,000 waiting for the inventor of a distinct novelty for a summer amusement park." The problem, according to Jones, was inventing novelty: "I don't mean a variation of a 'ride' or an elaboration of the illusion idea; the device that will prove successful must be totally foreign from anything now in use. There is a crying need for novelties among amusement parks."[57] A variation on the usual spectacles, such as sending elephants instead of people "a-sliding" down a water chute into the Luna lagoon (fig. 3.3), was a quick fix, but, as one writer observed, such thrills soon grow stale, "so the feats must each year be more and more dangerous to excite the interest of the spectators. How far the cultivation of this appetite will go no one can foretell."[58] Novelty, as Jones and Thompson knew, was not so easily invented, no matter how great the incentive; many of the patents claimed improvements on existing amusement technologies rather than wholly new conceptions. But the search continued. Both Luna and Dreamland ran contests for new ideas as promotional gimmicks; the public responded enthusiastically but with little innovation. Dreamland, for instance, was swamped with suggestions of a mountain storm and a falling elevator, both of which already were staple amusements.[59]

The unending and even desperate search for and staging of "Novelty!" by such showmen was central to the way Thompson and other architects of the emerging consumer marketplace understood themselves and their potential customers. In part, they were guided by and exploited the long-standing belief that the American nation was a land of perpetual renewal and rebirth, a view so well entrenched that the novelist Henry James named the eponymous icon of *The American* (1877) Christopher Newman.[60] Although for some Americans the zest for innovation and new experiences was part of a more profound inquiry into human existence, for many the celebration of youth and newness and the faith that Americans alone were excepted from the shackles of history justified an indifference or even radical malevolence toward all that was "old," especially inherited claims—customs, habits, "sin," even contractual obligations—that stood in the way of "progressive change."[61] Thus President Andrew Jackson, defending the Indian Removal Act in 1830, could find solace; although such actions violated treaties and threatened to annihilate whole tribes of Native Americans, "true philanthropy reconciles the mind to ... the extinction of one generation to make room for another" in the name of progress.[62] By the end of the nineteenth century, when some, like James, still cast a cold, ironic eye on such "new" thinking, commercial capitalism had reinvented and reinvigorated the "cult of the new," proclaiming the power of fashion and style—instead of newly vacated lands to the west—to renew existence and erase the dull record of the past and present. "Innovation" came to mean the production of an endless series of new and improved commodities. Fashion merchandising, in league with the new urban department stores, advertising agencies, and design colleges, institutionalized and industrialized the unending generation of newness after 1890.

The massive expansion of the garment industry in New York and other American cities and the integration of national and international transportation and communications systems enabled this development. The economist Simon Nelson Patten, the most ardent academic defender of the new commercial world at the turn of the century, saw the promise of the future in such progressive eradication of "traditional restraints on consumption, all taboos against luxury." We must, he insisted, eliminate any "repressive moral agency" that enforces allegiance to the "old" instead of "a firm adhesion to the new."[63] Luna, as well as its many imitators, was arrayed to dismantle the behavioral restraint of "discipline and penalty" that, in Patten's words, "depresses men" and confines them to "the dark side of the street."[64]

Yet Luna Park was not just about releasing men from outmoded allegiances; it also was about tapping into the wish to consume novelty itself and encouraging different obligations. Recently the historical sociologist Colin Campbell has argued that the quest for the "new" is deeply ingrained in modern Western culture. Only in modern industrial societies have innovation and novelty risen to the level of moral obligations. Preindustrial peoples regarded the universe (as well as the individuals who inhabited it) as closed, fixed, and final, not as an open-ended supply of infinite possibilities. Peasants lived in a local world of limitations and finite supply. A "self-seeking" person who acted as if that world should be altered to fit her or his desires—as opposed to the other way around—placed the "self" above the customary ways of the community and blasphemed the divine order of things. In such a "closed" worldview, incompleteness was unimaginable, and the novel and upstart were feared or punished instead of venerated. The modern consumer society's "endlessly changeable pattern of consumption," writes Campbell, "is impossible for the [premodern] individual to contemplate, or for the society as it is constituted to tolerate."[65]

The central hallmark that distinguishes modern industrial consumer societies from traditional preindustrial societies is the insatiable desire for change. Crucial to these distinctions has been the historical shift in the meaning of "hedonism." Pleasure seeking in modern societies differs fundamentally from that in premodern societies. Traditional hedonism directed itself toward the sensory pleasures generated or the discomforts alleviated by the known attributes of objects. For instance, a person desired food that had relieved hunger and yielded gustatory pleasure in the past; as often with children even today, unknown or unusual foods provoked apprehension or disgust. Modern hedonism, on the other hand, starts with the emotional longings of individuals for unfamiliar objects or experiences that appear to correspond to their dreams of pleasure. Whereas traditional hedonists value the properties that objects already have exhibited and remember pleasures of old, modern hedonists regard the past as a record of disappointments. They are pleased and guided most by the imaginative anticipation of tasty delights yet unknown. The modern "is continually withdrawing from reality as fast as he encounters it" and daydreaming about future possibilities for pleasure, the next attraction down the line.[66]

Colin Campbell, then, is less concerned with the "real" (as opposed to the advertised) properties of goods or of the actual experiences, pleasurable or otherwise, that consumers derive from the purchase or use of them. The most potent driving force behind consumption, he argues, is neither satisfaction nor pleasure, but the dissatisfaction and disappointment that inevitably arise because a product cannot possibly live up to what the consumer "daydreamed" it would deliver. This is why novelty is so important. The new sustains the hope that the dismal record of past disappointments can be erased by future fulfillments. "The fact that a so-called 'new' product may not, in reality, offer anything resembling either additional utility or a novel experience is largely irrelevant ... [because] the 'real' nature of products is of little consequence compared with what it is possible for consumers to believe about them." Modern hedonists are insatiable because "all real consumption is a disillusioning experience." Consumers may get the object they wanted, but they never get the pleasure of which they dreamed.[67]

For Campbell, the engines that power the perpetual longing of modern consumerism are not the image factories of Madison Avenue or the conspicuously enviable behaviors of the rich and famous. Rather, the engine room is in the heads of modern people, and the force impelling consumption is the rich array of self-pleasing fantasies and daydreams that consumers themselves concoct. Advertisers, he argues, cannot convert satisfaction into dissatisfaction because there is no satisfaction in the first place. What gets "manipulated," he argues, are the messages of goods, not the consumers or their wants. Campbell directs our attention to the symbolic meanings that producers, through advertising and other instruments, attach to goods so that they can win a role in the "pleasurable dramas" that consumers imagine. Dissatisfaction and "enjoyable discomfort" are the modern condition. Consumer capitalism merely— or rather, especially—capitalizes on that condition.[68]

### Grown-up Children

The architectural, aesthetic, engineering, and merchandising conventions at Luna Park and later enterprises were the instruments Thompson used to compose pleasurable dramas that excited and took advantage of his patrons' discomforts and feelings of shortcoming. In part, his amusements responded to prevalent anxieties and longings, but they did more than just react to existing wishes. They also produced particular meanings, identities, and obligations—a new cultural style that was in tune with and reinforced the ethos of consumer capitalism. Thompson began with his tirelessly repeated bromide that adults, in reality, are children, and amusement parks their toys, although rendered on a scale that appeals to the enlarged expectations of adulthood.[69] His efforts to exhume and then exploit the buried child-spirit in his customers dated back at least to the 1897 Tennessee centennial and the Giant Seesaw, and they increased in complexity and interest with each succeeding venture. As banal as it sounded even then, the theory that adults long to regress to childhood inspired new commodities and merchandising strategies that were anything but drab. This market culture of Peter Pan urged all people to view its offerings with the credulous, acquisitive eyes of a child, not the wary eyes of an adult. Entrepreneurs of play such as Thompson reassured themselves, no less than their customers, that their suspicions of marketplace trickery and of a shifting environment of theatrical surfaces were not only without foundation, but foolish. People had only to adjust their outlook and relax their defenses. At Coney Island, Thompson explained in 1907, enlisting the vocabulary of *Peter Pan*, "we are not dealing with New Yorkers as they are in New York, but with big children who have come to fairyland and want the fairies to make them laugh and show them strange things." At Luna, New Yorkers could be and believe what they wished.[70]

Thompson's strategy of the "eternal child" had a long lineage; reflections on childhood dated back, in the modern period at least, to John Locke's writings on psychology and education in the late seventeenth century. In the nineteenth century, Romantic educators, artists, and poets, many of them influenced by Jean-Jacques Rousseau's *Emile*, venerated the instinctual child and the aesthetic resource of play.[71] "Man," wrote the poet Friedrich Schiller, "plays only when he is in the full sense of the word a man, and *he is only wholly Man when he is playing*." This call to play, issued in the midst of rapid industrial and political transformation and growth of a money economy, also contained a critical edge of dissent that reflected the Romantics' sense of cultural fragmentation and alienation in contemporary Europe.[72]

By the time Thompson opened his playground for grown-ups in 1903, reform-minded American men and some women still were turning to play to address the problems of an industrializing, urban society. Many were trained in the new scientific theories of sociology, psychology, anthropology, and education, and had turned play into a professional reform tool. The new play authorities tended to mix evolutionary science with less empirical assertions that endowed childhood with an importance that arose from either its innocence or its primitive energy.[73] The glow surrounding child-life was one aspect of the social and economic changes caused by the nineteenth-century market revolution, which moved production out of homes and into workshops, offices, and factories, and fundamentally altered the social role of the family. Most obviously, the rapid decline of the family-based labor system diminished the need for children's labor. The new child-centered home more often sheltered them from work, giving at least the middle-class child a life of extraordinary leisure to play. The size of American families declined by half over the century, and even more so for the urban bourgeoisie, which was concerned about the high costs of equipping and educating children for their grown-up roles. Sternly disciplining and training children to work for adults gradually gave way to lovingly nurturing and preparing them to be adults. In addition, after 1890, middle-class reformers campaigned effectively for child-labor laws and compulsory school-attendance laws, which further shielded working-class children from work settings.[74]

Although middle-class Americans celebrated children's liberation from older forms of restraint and adversity as evidence of national progress, these changes also worried a broad array of scientists and reformers, who led the movement to organize and direct the play activities of American children, revising pedagogy, instituting new youth activities such as Boy Scouts and Camp Fire Girls, and constructing urban parks and playgrounds. Among the most influential of the play theorists was the psychologist G. Stanley Hall, one of America's pioneers in scientific child study. Hall's special anxiety was the modern "boy," which, for him, had a more specific reference than the word implied. Hall was convinced that the comforts of modernity had vitiated the core of America's racial and cultural leadership—educated, middle-class white men. Parents—especially mothers—enfeebled children from birth by telling them to restrain their passions, to soften their emotions, and to delay all manner of sensual gratification. Civilization was thus bequeathing to the nation an effeminized generation of nervous, overintellectualized men ill equipped to lead or govern. In "our day and civilization," Hall observed with asperity, "the hot life of feeling is remote and decadent. Culture represses, and intellect saps its root. The very word passion is becoming obsolete," leaving men with "refined sensibilities" but "parched and bankrupt" hearts. Hall was no enemy of civilization or of intellectual achievement and ambition. On the contrary, the problem was how to retain the benefits of progress without diminishing the virility needed to protect it. The problem of weak men, he determined, was actually a boy problem. Hall's recapitulation theory of psychology held that each modern Western white child, in developing to adulthood, relives the evolutionary history of the human species from primitive savagery to advanced civilization. Such children literally were miniature primitives bearing the ontological stamp of their racial ancestors. The key was to encourage the tendencies of the little male savage (boys, not girls, interested Hall), directing them in constructive channels such as sports and rough games, instead of mollycoddling them with "that rot they teach ... about the little raindrop fairies with their buckets washing down the windows." By cultivating savagery, parents and teachers inoculated future men against the effeminizing demands and restraints of civilized adult life. "We shall go back to reading the old, bloody stories to children, and children will like to hear them because they are healthy little savages."[75]

Hall's theories and injunctions to let boys be managed primitives existed in uneasy tension with a generation of Progressive Era play theorists who were concerned principally with taming the savagery of unassimilated, deracinated immigrant boys, who were destined for the low-wage labor force. These theorists especially lamented how the conditions of modern cities—cramped living spaces, unskilled labor, overextended or absentee parents, and schools overconcerned with rote learning—contributed to the general physical, mental, and moral decline of the child. They based their hopes for the future of the republic on "constructive play." The leaders of the Playground Association of America, founded in 1906, borrowed selectively from Hall and other theorists of child development to formulate play programs to mold urban children for a free life in a democratic, urban mass society. The "Play Progressives" tended to regard urban life as unwholesome, artificial, and constantly changing, especially when poor children had so much time free from adult regulation. What would become of a nation whose children grew up unsupervised in densely crowded and unhealthy cities, seething with vicious commercial entertainments that profited, as the reformer Jane Addams put it, from children's "invincible love of pleasure"? Public dance halls were especially notorious in this regard. Addams regarded them as "a sorry substitute for the old dances on the village green in which all of the older people of the village participated." Only proper and properly supervised play—group games, team sports, cooperative pageants, and plays—could replace what the discipline of the village green, apprenticeship in skilled trades, or the rigors of advancing the frontier had indoctrinated in earlier generations. Even as reformers celebrated the creative freedom and power of play, they were trying to find a scientifically based, rational system for imposing order on a fluid and unsupervised urban environment. "Directed" play would mold children into responsible, self-restrained adults, who could fit into an integrated urban industrial society.[76]

While playground reformers focused on urban disorder and the "needs" of poor children, growing numbers of middle-class parents, in a moderate response to the concerns that Hall articulated, enlisted their children in organized sports, Boy Scouts, or Camp Fire Girls, to give them a taste of old-fashioned adversity. Many also turned to the advice of child and play experts to help them supervise and manage the household play of their children, often with the assistance of "educational toys." The anticommercialism of these toys, called "tools" for learning or constructive play, reflected bourgeois Americans' sentimental distaste for pecuniary exchange. Parents armed themselves with simple block sets or sturdy dolls to immunize their children against the fantastic claims and enticements of the consumer marketplace. Middle-class children were admonished to "outgrow fantasy, not to celebrate it," and to play-build their characters for a rational adulthood. Whereas the inner-city playground movement pushed values suited to the semi- or unskilled labor needs of industrial capitalism, play with educational toys in suburban or affluent urban settings was supposed to cultivate wise managers for that labor force.[77]

In one sense, all of these reformers and theorists were, like Fred Thompson, entrepreneurs of childhood. Whether they were molding children to be industrial laborers or managers, they advanced the culturewide effort to exploit the potential of play for national unity and efficiency, industrial progress, personal profit, or all three, in the first two decades of the twentieth century. Even the play experts, who were suspicious of amusement as an end in itself and cautioned against giving children too many toys or merely pleasing them, paradoxically fostered a marketplace role for the child and parent as consumers of high-end "tools" of play.[78] The theorists and reformers were influential contributors to the discourse on play and the commodity markets for children, in both inner-city ethnic and middle-class suburban neighborhoods. However, these Progressive Era voices were meek in comparison to the extravagant claims for play and personal fulfillment issuing from the consumer marketplace and backed by unprecedented sources of capital. Thompson's closest ally in the turn-of-the-century play movement was the booming domestic toy industry, which overwhelmed reformers' claims to be the stewards of America's children. During Luna's first decade, the new generation of American toymakers, urban merchants, and catalogue houses dramatically expanded the array of playthings pitched to children and their parents. Accounts of Thompson's enterprises often appeared in the pages of the industry trade journals, which recognized and claimed him as their fellow toymaker.

Before 1890, manufactured toys were a rare and expensive commodity in American stores and homes, even among the well-to-do, who regarded them as a luxury, not a necessity.[79] The major supplier of playthings in this country was Germany, where craft traditions organized by toy merchants and brokers dominated especially the lines of dolls and mechanical playthings. R. H. Macy in New York and John Wanamaker in Philadelphia sold toys in the 1880s, but they were ahead of their contemporaries until the decade after 1900, when large urban department stores across the country greatly expanded Christmas toy merchandising. After 1910, the year-round, permanent toy department became the standard in large-scale retailing. From that point, the great urban stores, although they accounted for a minority share of toy sales, nevertheless dominated the industry, developing the principal merchandising strategies and techniques—in effect inventing both the child consumer and the toy department, an oasis of play and delight for selling toys to children of all ages.[80]

Although it initially lagged behind domestic retailers, the American toy industry began its revolution around 1905 as consumer demand for toys soared. The extraordinary growth of the domestic industry resulted from the combined forces of new mass manufacturing techniques, the "visible hand" of marketing and tariff protection, and the impact of the Great War, which cut off German suppliers during the economic boom times of the war years. American toymakers were handed a protected, monopoly environment at a time when many Americans had cash and, with inflation running high, ample incentive to spend it. What followed, in the words of one toy man, was "a great revolution of the *toy* industry." The output of fifty-five leading manufacturers nearly tripled from 1913 to 1919, from $5.5 million to nearly $16 million. The fourteen domestic doll factories that labored in the shadow of their German superiors in 1913 grew to ten times that number in 1919.[81] Retail growth was equally spectacular during that period. By 1915 nearly seven acres of floor space in Chicago's eight leading department stores were selling $2 million in toys annually. In Christmas 1919 the American toy appetite seemed unlimited, with record toy sales reported by retailers. "We have never experienced anything like it," said R. C. Gibson, the buyer for Marshall Field, where a hundred clerks worked year-round in the toy department. Nor was the revolution restricted to the massive urban stores or the largest cities. The buyer for a Huntingdon, West Virginia, store claimed that his sales had grown from $12,000 in 1912 to $200,000 in 1919. "The American appetite for toys is insatiable," a leading wholesaler happily declared in 1923. In all, the industry grew 1,300 percent in the two decades after 1905, producing more than $58 million worth of toys in 1925. The trade journal *Playthings*, which had started with 20 pages in 1903—the same year as Luna Park—published its largest issue (514 pages) that year.[82]

When Thompson averred that "what grown men most want is to be transformed into children,"[83] he imagined the toy-buying, joy-seeking boy celebrated by the toy industry, not the boy-worker of progressive educators. Thompson never referred to play with the vocabulary of organized and supervised group games and pageants. For him, playing was not a collective social ritual in which an individual was connected and submitted to a larger whole and made to feel, as Jane Addams wished, the "fellowship as well as the pleasures" of structured and harmonious group activity and identity.[84] It was just this sort of submission that he longed to escape. He refused or was unable to think of communities or mutualities except in terms of audiences—that is, universal mass markets of common desires that brought people together as consumers. He had nothing but contempt for the invisible hand of the village green. "New desires," he said, demanded amusements "quicker and steeper and more joyously terrifying all the time."[85] For the showman, reclaiming the essential child inside the adult freed a grown man to indulge in the personal pleasures of spending. Thompson's boy-man resembled the "little people" described in 1913 in *Toys and Novelties*, a toy industry trade journal. The writer maintained that children "are the real 'spenders,'" because, unlike adults, they have "no barriers to climb, no scruples to overcome. The child does not stop to ponder over the 'matter of needless expense,' and the cost of goods." "And better still," he added, "the little folks are the easiest of all customers to influence."[86]

Thompson's ideal boy-man was similarly uninhibited by barriers and scruples, subject only to his privately intense dissatisfactions and whims. The showman was not catering to the usual abstractions that contemporaries posed against the shifting and uncertain terrain of the volatile urban market society: the republican ideal of the imperturbable, civic-minded citizen, or the rational, utility-maximizing economic man, or the bourgeois "ideal of unified, controlled, sincere selfhood."[87] He encouraged a different order of abstraction, one that was not fixed or permanent but in continuous flux. "Their tendencies are constantly changing," Thompson wrote in 1910. "These grown-up children want new toys all the time.... Each season the grown children become more insatiable. They are thrill-hungry. They ask a new thought; they demand a new laugh; they clamor for a new sensation." Out of necessity, a showman becomes "a hunter for ideas, a stalker for suggestions ... a sort of humanized sponge for ideas, ideas, ideas for those millions of insatiable ones."[88] Such an unanchored, infinitely desiring self encompassed the endlessly dissatisfied qualities of the modern hedonist described by Colin Campbell. It also was cast in the image of Thompson himself, dashing from the elephant's back to the scenic railway to the Chutes, guided by no compass other than the lingering dissatisfaction of the last thrill, the not quite sufficient joy of the present laugh, the hopeful hunger for the next sensation.

Thompson's insistence that needs were not fixed, stable, or satiable, but unnecessarily straitjacketed by custom and habit, provoked the wrath of a number of critics who were committed to the moral universe of controlled, sincere selfhood and outraged by Luna's shifting and shifty landscape. Nothing at Coney was "genuine" or believable but the courage needed to shoot the Chutes, the writer Robert Wilson Neal asserted in a typical complaint. The rest was a moral "waste land" of makeshift firetraps overseen by "faker and spieler." Coney had no substance or essence; the whole island reeked "with the deception of a newer vulgarity and cheap make-believe."[89] Indignation like that of Neal was fully justified. With its antic, Orientalized skyline, its swarming populace of amusement seekers, its shifting exhibition of commercial pleasures, its "swirling," "tortuous," and "very quickly moving" thrill rides, Luna was designed to sell and celebrate the very characteristics of modern urban life that made observers like Neal recoil. Often they expressed their disgust in a gendered terminology. G. Stanley Hall, for instance, fretted for a nation of citified, effeminate men, and denounced metropolitan life for occupying boys with subjects that, because "mainly in motion and therefore transient," left them unfit for modern virile manhood.[90] The specter of a treacherous effeminacy haunted these expressions of concern. What kind of man was attracted to such meretricious and flimsy fare?

An unscrupulous and hard-to-please child-man like Thompson, of course. The showman represented a new kind of heroic figure who embodied the consuming personality ideally suited to the needs of both the demand and supply sides of consumer capitalism. Such men beheld the world as he did:

> We are young, and being young we want to be made to laugh, no
> matter how foolish is the method by which you do it; we are young
> and we believe everything, therefore do the most impossible things
> and we will pretend to believe them and applaud; we are poor ...
> make us forget that there are luxuries and perhaps necessities
> beyond our means—stir us so that we will remember the hours that

we are spending with you for months to come; we are tired and
weary and overworked—don't add to our burdens, lighten them by
your most fantastic and foolish endeavors.[91]

This passage clearly states the outlook or consciousness of the commercial culture of Peter Pan. Beyond glorifying play, Luna Park challenged
the moral economy of the nineteenth century by shifting the normative
focus of male adult life from property ownership and civic responsibility
back to the days before time clocks, bosses, wives, and children.

Other insightful historical analyses have shown that the commercial
amusements at Coney Island accelerated both the decline of "a genteel
middle-class cultural hegemony" and "the rise of a heterosocial culture
that owed its form in part to the structure of working-class social life."[92]
But Thompson's construction of his marketplace of play for the amuse-
ment-seeker as an insatiable child who wants new toys all the time also
underscored Luna Park's central importance as both a producer and a
reflection of a new cultural outlook. In part, Luna was an early and dazzling distillation of the way in which businessmen were reconceptualiz-
ing human personality and the morality of exploitation to fit the
interests and instruments of industrial and consumer capitalism.
Thompson, who both rejoiced and panicked at the thought of millions
of insatiable consumers, unfixed by either custom or supply and demand, expressed how businessmen were coming to regard markets in
general as dynamic and manageable. From the nineteenth and into the
early twentieth century, the dominant "block universe" model of economic thinking treated human needs and markets as finite and satiable.[93] But by 1910, Thompson was joined by manufacturers and
retailers who were beginning to recognize, from practical experience,
that limitations were artificial and arbitrary, and markets potentially as
open-ended and insatiable as people themselves. New products, as
Thompson well knew, instead of meeting existing demand, created new
needs, new demands for new sensations. Twentieth-century mass mar-
keters, rather than limiting themselves to the "expressed demand" for
their products, have energetically used planned strategies of production,
distribution, and promotion to make and develop products and markets
even where the desire for them did not exist.[94] The historian William
Leach has argued that the dominant concept of self shaping the moral
universe of twentieth-century consumer America "is that of a demand-

ing child, susceptible to outbursts of both primal rage and primal yearn-ing." That juvenile self had its earliest, most intense and smiling ex-pression in the figure of the thrill-hungry, unappeasable boy-man Fred Thompson, and its most popular representation in his Coney Island playground for the masses.[95]

## Toy-Lands Elaborated by Adult Hands

All of Luna's major "toys"—its architecture, the mind-jarring rides, the reenactments of bloody historical events or urban disasters, the blind-ing brilliance of its electrical lighting—dramatized the showman's pre-tense of childish nonchalance and impertinence in the face of externally imposed rules. The plasticity of its physical environment of play, for in-stance, blithely dismissed the relevance of architectural or design con-ventions. Architecture, like anything else for Thompson, was a matter of surfaces. "Theatrically speaking," he said, it "is nothing more nor less than scenery." The architecture of world's fair exposition halls, churches, and courthouses invariably was, in his opinion, severe, bal-anced, symmetrical, linear, angular, heavy, solid, traditional, and per-manent. These buildings expressed prohibitive authority and immovable values and truths impervious to human wishes. They com-posed stern architectural sermons enforcing limitations on wants and boding a life of unremitting, pleasureless labor and self-denial. "Straight lines," he told the readers of *Architectural Review*, "are as hard and serious as baccalaureate sermons."[96] In comparison to the cramped, arid, bankrupt imagination of what he contemptuously la-beled the "T-square-triangle fellow," who allowed tradition and history to constrain his conception of what was architecturally possible, his own childishly creative dreams pictured an altogether different world of visual wonder and delight. "What architect designed the buildings of Fairyland—of Picture-Book Land? None. He was an artist who knew nothing of T-squares and triangles, or one who cleverly disguised his knowledge. Amusement-parks and expositions are nothing more than Fairy Picture-Books—Toy-Lands elaborated by adult hands."[97] The showman delighted in juxtaposing the inviting fluidity and warm sen-suality of his metropolis with the hard inflexibility of conventional ar-chitecture for a mass audience. Luna structures elevated the temporal, fabricated, and personal over universal, timeless, and divine concepts immune to particular wishes. The plaster-and-lath construction was the cheapest and least durable method of building his amusements, but it was the only appropriate material for a structure the usefulness of which was by definition ephemeral, uncertain, and theatrical, and the appearance of which had "to appeal to the child-imagination in sight as well as feeling."[98] "You see," he explained, "I have built Luna Park on a definite architectural plan. As it is a place of amusement, I have eliminated all classic, conventional forms in its structure, and taken a sort of free Renaissance and Oriental type for my model, using spires and minarets wherever I could; in order to get the festive, joyous effect to be derived always from the graceful lines given in this style of architecture."[99] Thompson conceptually aligned himself with other boy-men of his generation who represented the emerging commercial culture, such as the artist Maxfield Parrish, who was known as the Peter Pan of illustrators because of his joyful, whimsical renderings of stories and nursery rhymes that underscored the warmth and magic of childhood; or Winsor McCay, who stocked "Slumberland" with architecture reminiscent of that at the Coney Island parks.[100] Amusement buildings, according to Thompson, should affirm and encourage personal enjoyment and spending in the present moment instead of reminding people of tomorrow.

Thompson would have people think that Luna was a radical departure from all prevailing norms, a step out of history. Yet the references to historical models suggest the degree to which he actually exploited orthodox and well-understood inversions of Western hierarchies. As an "Oriental dream," Luna did not eliminate convention; it substituted the convention of Eastern sensuality and release from materiality for representations of imperturbable Western rectitude and rationality. The completion of the park was a spectacular culmination of more than a century of Western dreams of the East as both repellently and alluringly "irrational, depraved (fallen), childlike, 'different.'" The literary scholar Edward Said has argued in his influential study *Orientalism* that scholarship, literature, and art in eighteenth- and nineteenth-century Europe (and, to a lesser extent, America) defined the weakness and backwardness of these ancient civilizations and thereby laid the ideological groundwork—psychological as well as political—for Western imperial domination of vast regions of Asia and Africa. At the same time, many Europeans and Americans betrayed an intense discomfort with the "rationality" of the West and an envy of the very characteristics that made the Orient inferior to the Occident. The midcentury painting *The Slave Market* by the French artist Jean-Léon Gérôme invited such mixed reactions. The image is rendered as a detached, closely detailed, and dreamlike glimpse at a timeless Near Eastern scene. A disrobed and light-skinned female, flanked by a male seller and buyer (suggestively probing her mouth with two stiff fingers), glows luminously at the center of the shadowy slave market. With little subtlety, it exposes the arrant sexuality and savagery of flesh-peddling even as it exposes the viewer to a fantastic deal she or he should not want to witness. In this example of the Orientalist's art, the distance between civilized Us and savage Them seems clear and even safe; she, the "victim," does not look us, the viewers, in the eye. Even without the spectator being directly implicated by the gaze of the slave, the picture still invites the spectator, whether male or female, to assess both the transaction and the objected being transacted and to consider the pleasures at stake. Such carefully negotiated scenes could stimulate interest and outrage—"lip-licking and tongue-clicking"—at the same time.[101]

No doubt there was an imperial dimension to Thompson's Oriental dream at Coney Island, but the markets he sought to penetrate and the dissatisfactions and longings he sought to exploit were located closer to home. Luna, with its minarets, pinnacles, and surface aversion to right angles, incorporated this alternative value system in a way that was peculiar only for its size and intensity. Similar yearnings were apparent in the Orientalist aspects of such religious movements as Free Thought and theosophy (the rise of which coincided with the British occupation of Egypt after 1882) and colored the fantasies of other planetary worlds such as Mars and Uranus. The exotic settings and fantasies of *The Arabian Nights* were among the most popular tropes employed by retailers and manufacturers in the first thirty years of the twentieth century to lend animation and nonmaterial, mysterious allure to styles of clothing and domestic furnishings, fashion pageants and window displays, and other commodities.[102] Luna Park and A Trip to the Moon were the vanguard of the tidal wave of Orientalism that swept through American commercial culture after 1900. They demonstrated the profits of teaming the American genius for industrial organization with the proclivities of the eternally childlike East for luxurious fantasy and indulgent pleasure. Running within the Progressive Era's search for order was an equally ardent, determined, and orderly search for disorder. The beauty as well as the cash value of Thompson's Orientalism lay in the way it fostered an amusement environment that was simultaneously naughty and nice, erotically suggestive but apparently as clean as a whistle, a place where a man could let go without completely letting go of himself. In September 1902 the *Brooklyn Daily Eagle* saw the moral reforms in store for Coney and yet applauded efforts to preserve the "life and spirit and noise" of the island's carnival.[103]

In addition, the way in which Thompson used Orientalism shows that, as much as he claimed to be a child of his day, his buildings actually incorporated a long-standing Victorian faith in the power of architectural environments to determine behavior and affect character. Good houses, Victorians thought, *made* good people, and vice versa. Rather than overthrowing the "associational functionalism" of nineteenth-century design, Thompson altered the desired outcome, using Victorian means to achieve modern ends—not good and prudent, but playful, spending people.[104] "It is marvelous what you can do in the way of arousing human emotions by the use that you make, architecturally, of simple lines," Thompson told a newspaper reporter in 1906.[105] In both its conception and its appearance, Luna's architecture stood in opposition to the antitheatrical everyday world of solidity and permanence.

In Thompson's opinion, his rides also engaged adults in a dramatic reenactment of their lost juvenile primitivism. Most of the mechanical devices designed for speed and movement at Luna derived from Thompson's archetype of aggressive or action-oriented boys' play. A frequently cited example was the popular Shoot-the-Chutes; its inventor had been inspired by watching boys skip stones across a pond.[106] Thompson favored rides, illusions, and elaborations of boys' play that duplicated the curves of his architecture and fostered the antic sensation of release from self-restraint, such as the Mountain Torrent, which descended, as a magazine writer described it, in a "winding and devious" pattern instead of in a trustworthy straight line.[107] Thompson's popular Helter Skelter required customers to take an "automatic stairway to the top of a high tower," from which they slalomed down troughs of slick rattan, which plunged in a bouncing, snaking descent before depositing them onto a soft mattress, usually amid a crowd of spectators (fig. 3.4).[108] Two of Luna's most popular mechanical rides—the Tickler and the Virginia Reel—dispatched carloads of passengers careening down a

Fig. 3.4. Movement was everywhere on Luna Park's narrow avenues, from the milling crowds pepped up by brass bands to the "automatic stairway" continuously transporting patrons to the Helter Skelter slide. (*Neg. No. 59458, © Collection of The New-York Historical Society.*)

serpentine route, spinning on casters and ricocheting abruptly off obstacles or each other. With the Tickler, Elmer Blaney Harris remembered in particular, "unless the neck is kept rigid one's head may be snapped from one's shoulders." He and Dora each lost their grip, and ended up on "the bottom of the car, submerged under a plump young lady who held her mouth to keep her teeth in." The idea for Witching Waves, which opened at Luna in 1908, came from watching men at work (not children at play) in a steel-rolling mill. The undulating sheets of metal grabbed the attention of Theophilus Van Kannel, the ingenious inventor of the revolving door, who turned this industrial inspiration into play. Successive segments of a flexible steel floor simultaneously moved up and down, mimicking the ocean's waves and gently propelling riders in wheeled boats over the rolling surface.[109]

As his reliance on Orientalist themes would suggest, Thompson's dramatic spectacles also exploited darker desires. Thompson believed

Fig. 3.5. Fire and Sword, Luna Park's detailed reproduction of a bloody battle in the Balkan War of 1912, encouraged the desire to see, hear, and feel the action in violent spectacle. (*Brooklyn Collection, Brooklyn Public Library.*)

that, like children, adults enjoyed viewing (or vicariously experiencing) "the anxieties of others." The scene of a shipwreck or the aftermath of a train accident, he said, yielded "active pleasure," although his consumer was no longer satisfied solely by the "appeal to the eye." Now, he said, the customer demanded to "hear the boat crash or the train fall apart" or to feel "the sensation of going down some dizzy incline."[110] Some of his spectacles, such as an urban tenement fire (Fire and Flames) or the fall of the Turkish city Adrianople in the "first Balkan War" of 1912–13 (Fire and Sword), were performed in an outsized, although conventional theatrical setting (fig. 3.5). Others, such as the undersea trips to the North Pole, allowed spectators to participate in the sensation, as in A Trip to the Moon.[111] In 1907, for instance, the illusion Night and Morning exploited the respectable nineteenth-century belief that people who actually were in a state of "catalepsy" or trance often were mistaken for dead and accidentally buried alive.[112] Edgar Allan Poe was one of the great popularizers of this "all-absorbing but ... too entirely horrible" theme. It appears in several of his stories, including "The Premature Burial" (1844), in which the narrator argues from personal experience that "a vast number of such interments have actually taken place."[113] Luna's victims began their untimely inhumation by entering a large, dark, oblong room shaped like a coffin. Through the glass ceiling they could see the drooping boughs of weeping willows and a "profusion" of consoling flowers. As the journey began, the coffin trembled and tilted and the world above receded as the room seemed to sink "into the under-world to the accompaniment of strange and weird noises, voices utter[ing] farewells, shrieks and wails. Then the lid is closed and you hear the thud of gravel and earth." The illusion continued with a tour of hell and a concluding resurrection.[114]

Poe's apprehensions suggest the faultiness of Thompson's chronology, which named his steep terrors as the successors to the humbler village amusements. Both the sexual subtext of his thrills and the participatory nightmare of attractions such as Night and Morning link Luna's play to the rich American tradition of sensationalism. The new press freedoms of the early nineteenth century combined with improvements in print technology and book distribution to foster a "sensational" literary culture of salacious and often pornographic crime stories and criminal biographies, racy exposés of the urban netherworld, and wildly thrilling newspaper accounts of public outrages. For the first time, argues literary historian David Reynolds, the "hunger" for sensationalism "could be [and was] fed easily on a mass scale."[115] In much the same way, the growing populations of urban centers and new sources of capital investment at the end of the century joined with technological developments in distributing people (street railways and steamships), power (electricity and electrical light), and information (mass-circulation urban newspapers, color printing, billboards, glossy magazines, inexpensive telegraphy) to encourage the emergence of Coney Island's sensational amusement economy. The audience and amusements at Tilyou's Steeplechase Park were the most closely linked to the ribald economy of midcentury penny newspapers, "third-tier" pleasures, minstrelsy, and burlesque entertainments. The voyeurism of features such as Tilyou's Blow-hole Theater, where a lecherous dwarf teased and directed women into a room where stiff jets of air shot from the floor and exposed their legs and undergarments for an audience of onlookers, verged on the indecent end of the middle-class behavioral spectrum. In doing so, it playfully evoked the visual titillation that had been part of New York City's brazenly visible sexual economy of street prostitution and bawdy houses for most of the nineteenth century, but which had been less openly on display since the systematic antivice crusades of the 1890s.[116] Tilyou's funhouse entertainments bridged the old and new sexual economy and subculture.

Thompson, because he targeted a mass middle-class audience of women and men, sought to distance Luna from the old sexual economy; women who exposed their legs and beyond on the Human Toboggan were supposed to be behaving like children. But he remained committed to the economic rationality of antebellum literary sensationalism. Writers from George Lippard to Edgar Allan Poe knew that Americans devoured stories like the one Poe satirized in "How to Write a Blackwood Article," in which a "gentleman ... got baked in an oven, and came out alive and well, although certainly done to a turn."[117] Although Poe might apologize to his editor for being "on the verge of bad-taste" in a story such as "Berenicë" (in which a man unwittingly vivisects the teeth of his apparently dead wife), he recognized his indebtedness to the hacks he poked fun at, and knew, too, that these "sensations" were "invariably sought after with avidity" by himself as well as his readers.[118] "We thrill," he confessed in the 1840s, "with the most intense of 'pleasurable pain'" to the detailed and grisly accounts of plagues, earthquakes, and massacres.[119] Poe's first-person narratives in tales such as "Berenicë" and "The Fall of the House of Usher" intensely and horrifyingly rendered such voyeuristic thrills for the reader.

Without referencing Poe or other sensationalist writers, Fred Thompson also had confidence in the market for pleasurable pain, which he called the "inborn hungering for terror." No doubt Thompson's burlap-and-plaster thrills were closer to the crude productions of the Blackwood authors that Poe made fun of than to the artful executions of writers of the American Renaissance such as Hawthorne, Melville, and Poe. But Thompson also saw himself as these writers had believed themselves to be—pitted against what Poe called the "stilted dulness," "ponderosity," and "excessively tasteful" gentility of elite quarterlies and their quiet and polite audiences.[120] If he wanted a mass audience, Thompson, like Poe and his contemporaries, had to attend first to the "sensations." "Your average person," Thompson averred, "does not want a conception to be suggested to him. He wants a conception to dazzle, to stun him, to hit him on the head like the crack of doom."[121] There being little space for irony at Luna Park, Thompson actually staged an attraction called the Crack of Doom, which reconstructed the pleasurably painful sights and sounds of a western mining town swept away by a mountain tidal wave that "drowns the panic cries of the ... terror-smitten [sic]" residents. "The thing is hideously convincing," wrote one delighted observer.[122]

### The Cellar Door of Childhood

The Luna Park that Fred Thompson built to hook into the appetites of "those millions of insatiable ones" was a flickering theatrical world endlessly metamorphosing like the grown-up children inhabiting it. Recent scholars and chroniclers of popular amusements have tended to discuss Luna Park as though it was the same in 1912 as in 1903, obscuring the essential dynamism of the enterprise.[123] "You see," the showman said in a 1906 interview conducted inside a plaster volcanic crater at Luna Park, "this being the moon, it is always changing."[124] After opening in 1903, Luna underwent major changes or renovations in 1906, 1908, and 1912. Much of the 1904 addition was devoted to the Indian Durbar, with three hundred natives and dozens of camels and elephants; it flopped and was torn down after one season.[125] With each season new decorative features and amusements replaced some of the previous year's shows or were expanded for the sake of surplus and variety. "Wherever there was a chance to put up a tower or a minaret to break the line of any roof or expanse I have stuck one on to please the eye," Thompson told the *New York Herald* in 1906. He boasted to the *New York Times* that Luna possessed "1,221 towers, minarets, and domes—a great increase over" 1905, which was as it should be.[126] "A stationary Luna Park," he explained, "would be an anomaly, you know."[127] In Thompson's world, waste—too much of a good thing—was an essential virtue.

The equation of Luna Park with "lunar change" provided a rich synthesis of the way the resort combined artifice with nature, the quest for novelty with premodern myth, systematic, managed technology with the improprieties of carnivalesque dreams of plenty. Contradiction, ambiguity, disequilibrium, and instability were the standard bill of fare. The organization of consumer capitalism, as with Luna Park, was fundamentally rational, geared to the methodical production and smooth distribution of goods, a disciplined labor force, and, eventually, the strategic creation of new markets for profits. At Luna, Thompson orchestrated electrical, water, and human-labor power to drive the park's spectacles, illusions, rides, and spirit of festivity. His descriptions, which suggested an enormous, well-oiled machine that "manufactured" amusement, outlined a network of interlocking enterprises from Coney Island to Broadway and beyond.[128] At the Luna Park Scenic Studios on the grounds, for instance, 150 carpenters, electricians, scene painters, and property men worked full time assembling his many theatrical ventures.[129] All of this was stage scenery; also important was manufacturing the drama of amusement, the qualities of gaiety, festivity, and childish spontaneity, which, Thompson maintained, almost never are "spontaneous." "If the wheels are all properly adjusted and the cogs meet rightly there will be comparatively little cause of complaint.... All winter long Mr. Dundy and myself devote every spare minute we can find to the perfecting of this organization."[130] These comments recall his engineer father's imperturbable "mechanical habit of mind."

But Thompson's flawless factory manufactured and celebrated an impulsiveness, wasteful excess, and prodigal spending that nineteenth-century businessmen like his father believed were incompatible with economic productivity, not to mention social order. At Luna he spoke simultaneously in two voices, one imperiously demanding new toys all the time, the other coolly issuing instructions to the system. He was like contemporary advertisers, whose ad copy and images conjured "destabilizing cultural tendencies" with saturnalian visions of the unbounded pleasures and possibilities that would come with the purchase of goods. At the same time, however, advertising men and women had to channel and structure the desired effects of their efforts—consumer demand—according to the planned, rational, and profitable movement of goods.[131]

Luna Park may have been the most concise, visibly dazzling, and popular representation of the enduring tension in modern consumer capitalist societies between "dreams of excess and methodical self-control."[132] Thompson imagined Luna Park jammed with people and ordered to indulge in pleasure, spending, and self-creation rather than deference to externally imposed authority. He organized his system to produce an exotic, if hygienic, replica of the pluralistic, agitated, anxious, mutating metropolis. His vision of summer amusement as "movement, movement, movement everywhere," imagined Luna as the very picture of un-moored selves amid subjects mainly in motion and transient.[133] Only fools, like those who made the error of musing on Luna's famous "ec-centric" statue, searched the park for leisured contemplation, lasting pleasures, or lingering personal attachments. The stone figure of a boy atop a classical pedestal and an inviting bench in front of it resembled statuary found at world's fairs or in genteel urban parks. Taking a seat, however, tripped a lever, which tilted the statue forward as if it were falling on the observer.[134] Everything at Luna was ephemeral, unstable, insincere, or insufficient in itself, including the pleasure of the moment.

Thompson's fashioning of his resort as a seductively animated ma-chine, mutable, varied, and growing with each successive season, also suggests how he used, or played with, gender at Coney Island. The his-tory of the word "luna" can be traced back to an ancient Indo-European root signifying light or brightness. In Western usage, lunar light has usually referred to the reflected, nocturnal, and, by definition, artificial luminescence of the Moon rather than the original Apollonian radiance of the Sun. Forever waxing or waning, raising or lowering the tides, the feminine Moon's transformation, process, and representation tradition-ally have been posed against masculine permanence, completeness, and substantiality.[135] Luna, its name as well as its curvaceous and ever changing architecture implied, was an exotically effeminate, Oriental-ized city of consumption, as different as possible from the ordinary workaday lives of middle-class men, yet finely, although respectably, at-tuned to their stereotyped erotic expectations.

These aspects of the park repeated and capitalized on what Victoria de Grazia describes as the enduring propensity in Western capitalist so-cieties to "feminize the realm of consumption" in opposition to the masculine realm of production. The equation is founded not on the so-cial role of women as consumers, but rather on the imaginative as-sumption that anyone who consumes, regardless of sex, is effeminate. In the mid-eighteenth century, the social theorist Adam Smith tried to adjust these gendered distinctions to the new, miraculous productivity of industrializing Europe. "When Smith imagined the benefits to soci-ety of consumption," observes de Grazia, "it was in terms of the sound wants of industrious craftsmen and frugal peasants, as opposed to the frippery of foppish hangers-on at court or femininized male servants." Thus he was perplexed to discover that industrial ingenuity was misdirected to produce goods "fitter for playthings of children than the serious pursuits of men."[136] In 1785, Samuel Adams, fretting about the future of the new American republic, relied on the same gender polarities in reviling Boston's Sans Souci Club, whose dancing and card playing constituted an effeminacy "so totally repugnant to virtue, as in its very name (*Sans Souci*, or *free and easy*) to banish the idea by throwing aside every necessary restraint." If these men were dismayed by contemporary developments, imagine their reaction to the rash of Sans Souci resorts that opened in the wake of Luna Park's success.[137]

Thompson imagined the dangers to the republic in different terms—the particular gripes of middle-class men like him. The problem, as he saw it, was simple: the "average man lives very largely the creature of conventions, the tragic victim of set and settled circumstances. Custom and habit force him to take life solemnly."[138] As was the solution: he told men to follow his lead, to free themselves from their straitjackets of custom and habit, especially their foolish reluctance to spend money. Luna was located just beyond the land of sober duty. Thompson never meant that a man should not work to make money. No one, contemporaries remarked, threw himself into his work as enthusiastically or made money in so splendid a fashion as Fred Thompson. The showman merely insisted that he was no less a man for enjoying his pecuniary rewards, for purchasing the pleasures that he could afford or, more important, that he wanted. "My idea," he explained modestly, "was that of every showman—to erect a park where people would laugh, enjoy themselves, and would spend money while being amused."[139]

Anyone with a dime could take A Trip to the Moon, and women always were a welcome and large part of the crowd at Luna Park, but Thompson's toys really were for boys like him. The play he described suggests that behind his smiling, boyish face were a childhood *and* adulthood marked by severe loneliness and isolation as well as by deeply divided, if not misogynistic, feelings toward actual women. In all his pronouncements on the subjects, Thompson never referred directly to parents or to relationships with other children or adults. Childhood, which, for him, was always a metaphor for adulthood, was a period of existential alienation, when the child was not integrated with others but exiled to a dark unknown—the "cellar door of childhood." "You remember," he wrote in 1910, they opened that little door and there was blackness there. They closed it on you and you trembled, trembled deliciously. You wondered what would happen if they forgot about you. You shivered for a little while there in the black—and then you issued forth again with a strange exultancy. Your little nerves had cried to be thrilled— and they were thrilled. Henceforth, you regarded that little cellar door with a strange reverence, a joyous fear. And it was a versatile thing, too, because when the thrill of the dark wore off you could slide down its slippery surface and that was another thrill—a thrill that never ceases.

That "little door" and the "mystery, the thrill, the glamorous uncertainty" behind it, claimed Thompson, were the "protoplasmic germ" of all summer amusements.[140]

A visitor to Luna's avenues would have recognized these terrors—the childhood fear of the dark, the mystery of death, the brutality older children inflict on younger ones, the lure of forbidden excitements—from their many incarnations there. But the "pleasurable dramas" of play described here seem anything but simply "pure and good" or even respectable: a little door positioned in the house's lower region, a forced entry into the frightful but erotically charged blackness behind it, alarm contending with delight at the thought of being enclosed forever, entering and exiting, "reverence," "fear," the furtive stimulation of slippery surfaces, and, at the climax of it all, the issuance of the "germ" of play. Ambiguity hardly seems the word to describe what is at work in this definition of amusement.

From one perspective, the overheated prose may have reflected other concerns in Thompson's life when it was published in 1910 in the middle-class magazine *Metropolitan*. The article came out around the same time that the city's newspapers began printing accounts of the serious troubles in his amusement empire and in his marriage to the stage star Mabel Taliaferro. The hostility of the article about the insatiability of desire and the hunger for terror at the heart of universal child's play hinted at Thompson's own growing desperation and panic, and signaled that he may have been collapsing under the weight of his business and marital failings.[141] At the same time, though, the "cellar" theme was nothing new in 1910; it had been around since the dimes first began rolling in at Omaha and Buffalo, when the fiend for crowds, the pleasure-loving artist, and the entrepreneurial hustler were just being integrated in the guise of "the Kid" showman. Certainly Thompson would have denied that his attractions suggested, metaphorically or otherwise, the experience of heterosexual intercourse or, perhaps worse, the "private vice" of masturbation. What would indulging in those pleasures have implied about a man, his wife, mother, and sister? And yet, as commentators from the early to the late twentieth century have shown, treating and other forms of illicit sexual fun were a necessary part of the attraction of commercial amusements such as Coney Island parks, dance halls, cabarets, and late-night restaurants.[142] Calling amusements child's play and stationing a policeman at the edge of the dance floor did not alter the reality: the swarming crowds, the tightly packed dancers, and the scenic railway tunnels, which, as one visitor put it, seemed each year to grow "longer and darker," enabled and encouraged people to touch and hold each other with as little reserve as they wished or dared.[143]

Beyond the new opportunities that Luna offered for intimate liaisons, the germ theory of play draws attention to the highly heterosexualized character of the park's amusement fantasies. As Thompson explained in the *Metropolitan* article, "the American Girl and Summer Amusement ... are so very inextricably interwoven."[144] He was not exaggerating. In the boy-man's world of Luna Park, the "Girl" was actually built into the amusement superstructure, inspiring the voluptuousness of the skyline and serving as the figurative cellar doorway to a man's delight. Still, the language raised ugly implications about the kind of American Girl who would serve in this capacity: was she a willing participant, or was she forced, like the reluctant boy, to play her part behind the door? Was she contracted to introduce the nervous initiate into the prerogatives of manhood? One suspects that the passage referred to all of these possibilities and more, and would have registered, although perhaps unconsciously, with other men of Thompson's race, class, and status. Even if the essential meaning cannot be determined, the sexually charged imagery betrays the masculinized sensuality of Thompson's venture. His claim to screen indecency and impropriety from the array of temptations sold at Luna was opportunistic and genuinely self-delusional.

Rather than indicating the relaxing of sexual prohibitions and the emergence of a new expressive hedonism at the turn of the century, Luna incorporated into its architecture and thrills the confusion arising from the marked changes in middle-class sex roles and gender identities at the turn of the century, a period when, as historian George Chauncey has put it, both male homosexuality *and* heterosexuality were invented. For most of the nineteenth century, sexual prowess or "style" had been one way for a man to demonstrate his manliness. The emphasis on style is important. How a man had sexual relations reflected more on his manliness than did the sex of his partner. Among working-class New York men in particular, as Chauncey has shown, it was ordinary and acceptable for a man to have sexual relations with another man as long as his partner was womanly in bearing. Playing the aggressive or "masculine" role—penetrating, rather than being penetrated, for instance—proved his virility, even if his partner was male. Yet sexual aggression was only one of the constellation of conventions that were to be observed. Using entrepreneurial abilities and achieving success, mastering a skilled occupation, exercising the political franchise, commanding (rather than being commanded by) others at work, building, raising, and providing for a family—all were equally or more important in establishing a man's standing in the eyes of other men. Moreover, for bourgeois men, entrepreneurial potency had seemed to require the self-regulation of sexual energy; the male sensualist risked ruining himself, his family, and his business by wasting vital resources that were better spent accumulating wealth and property. Victorian male sexuality, then, was a balancing act of self-expression and self-control.[145]

As the decline of the petit bourgeois economy and the growth of corporate capitalism at the end of the century made the older standards of independent manhood harder to achieve, the significance of sexuality rose in relation, for instance, to that of being one's own boss, which hardly any man seemed to be anymore. A revitalized and less fettered erotic appetite, which was expressed exclusively as a desire for women and accompanied by an undeviating absence of desire for men, supplied "a new, more positive way to demonstrate their manhood." The importance of the scorned symbols of nineteenth-century unmanliness—propertyless men, shiftless nonwhites, immature boys—thus diminished in relation to a commanding new figure of unmanliness, the "homosexual." Middle-class ideals of manhood increasingly centered on a single, seemingly unambiguous issue: the sex of the partners, rather than the style of the sex between them. A man who engaged in any sexual intimacy with other males was not just guilty of a homosexual act, but implicated as a "fairy." In other words, he was no longer a "man." Yet the new "heterosexual and heterosocial imperatives," to use Chauncey's words, provoked as much anxiety as reassurance.[146] From one angle, the renunciation of male intimacy occurred at a time when middle-class men were, more than ever, admiring the muscular bodies of such working-class heroes as cowboys, prizefighters, athletes, and sailors. From another, the new focus on heterosexual sex emerged just as middle-class definitions of womanhood were changing to include erotic desires. In the new marital ideal, a man had sex not just to reproduce, but to please himself *and* his wife. "Acknowledging the existence of female sexuality," observes historian Christina Simmons, "called for a more vigorous male sexuality in response. Lack of the necessary vigor might hint of homosexuality."[147] A virile man, then, was obliged to succeed not just at the office; he also had to prove himself erotically in the conjugal bedroom. A lack of enthusiasm or achievement in either venue could raise disturbing implications. From this view, the new sexual and performance standards for bourgeois men might come across, not as liberation, but as oppression under another name.[148]

Luna Park was one of the early century's more impressive stages on which to pursue the uncertain returns on the new imperatives for mixed-sex recreation, providing an affordable and practical opportunity for a man to demonstrate his way with women. Such opportunities seemed to meet with few obstacles. Mixed in the milling crowds, women as well as men could escape the governance of family and neighbors who might otherwise caution against or regulate their liaisons. As Dora the manicurist explained to her playwright admirer, "I s'pose there's thousands of men in this crowd I'd like, but—well, most of 'em—you know how it is—always the third rail—see?" The reference to the subway's dangerously electrified extra rail showed that she regarded the attentions of strange men with caution, but welcomed them nonetheless. Dora was unescorted by choice, not "because I have to be, or because I like it."[149]

And yet, for all of the sexual mixing, innuendo, and displaced desire built into Luna Park, the very idea that to walk through the gates was to regress to a lost childhood proposed an alternative itinerary of escapist fantasy. The marked sensual aspect of Luna was interwoven with a countervailing daydream, of becoming a little boy again and flying back to a pre- or asexual childhood. Such was the beauty of Luna's inconsistencies. The boy whom Thompson idealized brimmed with fun and good spirits and relished the Chutes because it was like coasting down a coal chute or being skipped across a pond like a stone. It was a relatively harmless way of defying the "most potent enemies" of their own little world that middle-class boys cultivated in the nineteenth century—fathers who loaded them down with chores to do and mothers who implanted a guilt-triggering "voice of conscience" in their sons' hearts.[150] Thompson's boy was the prepubescent and, for that matter, pre-Freudian child. The presumed good nature of such a child and of his yearning to dwell in a Never Land of like-minded boys exposed a desire, perhaps equal in strength to the erotic attraction of the little door, to flee a particular aspect of adulthood—the demands, liabilities, and contingencies of the new male heterosexuality.

This regressive dimension of Luna was related to the more general reevaluation of boyhood at the turn of the twentieth century, although it was different in important ways from the impulses that gave rise to the Boy Scout movement. Men in nineteenth-century America had little regard for either boys or play. Boys could not own or accumulate property, and property was the foundation of independence, the basic distinction between white childhood and white manhood. Boys, whether enslaved to whites, apprenticed to a trade, or sheltered from care in the bourgeois home, were marked by their dependence and their subordination to grown-up authority. If white, they were men in waiting; if not, they were locked in a condition of permanent and despised racial childhood.[151] But with widespread social changes at the turn of the century, especially the dramatic decline of business ownership and self-employment in urban economies, white boyhood itself took on a new appeal. Boys might not own property, but most men did not own their own businesses anymore. Boys might be dependent on others for what they needed, but so were men in the new corporate economy, and at least boys were not handicapped by jobs, wives, and children. Boys might not be entitled to the prerogatives of adult sexuality, but neither did they have to account for their performance or answer to another person's erotic expectations. What boys could do was play and have fun. In comparison to grown men, they seemed completely unfettered, which was why, as Thompson understood it, men wanted to go to Never Land.[152]

Even with the expanded opportunities for heterosexual play that the Orientalized playland of Luna offered, Thompson's park was a defiantly asexual oasis of escape from carnality. It is easy enough to see that centering pleasures on the "American Girl" and telling men to stop being foolish penny-pinchers subverted long-standing middle-class rules of economic and social behavior and reinforced the heterosocial and heterosexual imperative. But these injunctions were inseparable from Luna's other invitation—to flee the obligations and encumbrances of the new sexual and social expectations, and to enter a boy-man's world of carefree fun and unrestricted adventure.[153] Acting on sexual desire was (and is) as much an imperative as a prerogative of adult men, another chore on the list of obligations for which they would be held accountable. Thompson sketched out a place where men could briefly elude the archenemies of hedonism, the interwoven economic and sexual pressures to perform and to succeed.[154] In this prepubescent world for grown-up boys, men could frolic to their heart's content, blow their cash with ease, thumb their noses at propriety, forget their families and the claims of women, and believe in fairies with little risk of being mistaken for them.[155]

Temporarily turning the world upside down was what Coney Island's popular thrills were supposed to do. Rides like the Chutes or the Tickler, which tossed and buffeted its passengers like so many "shuttlecocks," overwhelmed people, underscoring just how little control they had and making them laugh at themselves.[156] There was no escaping the conclusion that, even with a girl in either arm, a man braving the Mountain Torrent or riding the Tickler was hardly the master of his craft. The real operators were behind the scenes and worked for the park, and the customer was as likely as not to end up at the bottom, rather than the top, of the heap at the conclusion of the ride. What mastery he possessed came from buying the ticket, and even that was a shaky foundation for authority, as Dora showed her harried escort. John Kasson, in his landmark study of Coney Island, has argued that such rides "allowed customers the exhilaration of whirlwind activity without physical exertion, of thrilling drama without imaginative effort." No matter how scary the rides, as signs explained, there was "No Danger Whatever."[157] From this perspective, the ultimate outcome of whatever relief Luna offered from industrial discipline and routine was not actual liberation, but a renewed submission to managerial hierarchies.[158] The conclusion about Luna's usefulness to the dominant social class is reasonable, although it overlooks another potential dimension of that service. After

Fig. 3.6. Even critics unmoved by Luna Park in daylight were stirred by the hundreds of thousands of electrical lights that sketched the edges of its features after dark. (*Gottscho-Schleisner Collection, Museum of the City of New York.*)

all, Thompson marketed his amusements not to oppressed factory operatives so much as to the overworked, excessively sober, peevish representatives of the new managerial class. The watchful eye overseeing the fun may have been an essential element of Luna's fantasy appeal as a sanctuary from the immense pressures on men to be self-reliant men, to perform and to succeed in everyday life.[59]

### Why Is That?

By all accounts, Luna's most sensational enactment of the "cellar door" occurred at twilight when its incandescent lamps were lit, igniting, in the words of the theater critic and playwright Channing Pollock, "a thing never to be forgotten" (fig. 3.6). Luna's lighting dramatized the tensions at work in Thompson's pleasure resort. In its very profusion, the lighting scheme was engineered to be playfully and wastefully extravagant, to broadcast the liberating festivity abounding at Luna. As Pollock put it,

"Bejeweled with glittering bulbs, iridescent and glowing, the place seemed a burning mirage, twisting itself into fantastic shapes that whirled and spun and teetered bewilderingly."[160] But illumination also acted as an order-bringing police authority, reassuring patrons that there were no shadows, bewildering or otherwise, in which vice could hide.[161]

Thompson and Dundy claimed to have 250,000 or more incandescent bulbs outlining their structures and illuminating the interiors on opening night, not to mention the power demands of the scenic illusions and rides. Early promotions of the park called it an "Electric City by the Sea" or an "Electric Eden,"[162] and underscored how the "old," pre-Luna Coney was a "dim and dismal place" of sexual license and crime, feared by decent, respectable people.[163] In such before-and-after descriptions, Thompson drew on deeply ingrained cultural associations of nighttime with femininity. Nightfall traditionally has been viewed as "chaos, the realm of dreams," and the antonym of the solid, rational, masculine world of daylight.[164] The trick for Thompson was in constructing the delicious thrill of the dark cellar door, maneuvering between these mythic extremes, disciplining the saturnalian world of darkness—for which Coney was already notorious—without nullifying its associations with festivity and play.

On one hand, then, illumination played a significant public-relations role in creating the impression that Luna was a safe and welcome environment for respectable women. The Brooklyn Edison Company, which supplied Luna's power, credited its current with transforming "the entire moral and material character" of Coney. "Under its benign rays the possibilities of crime are reduced to a minimum and its searching gleam finds out the perverted and the false and mercilessly exposes it.... The flimsiness and crudity, the vileness and the vice ... have been succeeded by an elaborate stability and a decent regard for the amenities of civilized existence."[165] In the view of Brooklyn Edison, light had, with searing efficiency, routed the vicious, meretricious, and fraudulent from the benighted Coney of the pre-Luna period and created a "substantial, brilliant and artistic" new world.[166] Thompson's well-worn bromide that only decency pays also testified to the moral, sanitizing force of incandescent light. "In the glare of the thousands of electric bulbs," Thompson claimed, Coney Island "was ashamed of its sordidness" and reformed itself where public officials and preachers had for decades failed.[167]

As important as this police function was to the new image of Coney

Island, the actual deployment of lighting at Luna attracted mythic or premodern associations with saturnalia and festivity that both offset and worked in partnership with the island's enlightened order. Between 1890 and 1910 the use of electrical lighting in public spaces and for community or national celebrations grew in both degree and extravagance with the invention and manufacture of comparatively inexpensive incandescent lamps, plus further advances in developing powerful concentrated sources of light.[168] But the meanings assigned to this illumination exceeded the practical application of lighting technology to eliminate darkened public streets and parks. In spite of its instrumental purposes, industrial organization, and rational design, even artificial lighting can produce an ecstatic feeling of liberation from restraints.[169] For a number of scientists and intellectuals of this period, electrical illumination stirred such mythic associations and deeply felt emotions of contending longings, fears, and wishes. Lighting technologies were named for pagan deities: for example, the Mercury vapor and the Mazda lamps. Luna Park's lighting scheme provoked similar associations with non-Christian festivity. A number of contemporaries observed or claimed they had experienced an exhilarating release from the bonds of quotidian existence when they beheld the nocturnal transfiguration of the flimsy park into an alluring image of fire, death, and desire, a radiant and, by most accounts, irresistible picture of festivity that people would pay to experience.[170]

Electricity, Thompson frankly stated in 1905, is the showman's "best friend." "Almost anything is possible now in the way of stage illusion by utilizing electric force and light. It has been a magic power for stage directors."[171] Thompson's fellowship with this magic began in earnest at the Victorian world's fairs, which, starting with Chicago, were the principal showcases of new uses of electrical and hydraulic power, especially in the production of incandescent illumination. The growing power and importance of the United States were reflected in the expanding and intensifying uses of energy. Incandescent lighting was not just invented by an American; it was America's story.[172] The promoters of American expositions used spectacular lighting "to create narratives of abundance and progress." They illuminated not just buildings but a dream landscape that embodied progress, dazzling spectators with a vision of how the United States had rapidly evolved from savagery to the pinnacle of civilization.[173] The chief narrator at each of the world's fairs in which

Thompson participated was Thomas Edison's pupil Luther Stieringer. Unlike his pragmatic teacher, Stieringer was most stirred by the aesthetics of illumination. According to an admiring contemporary, Stieringer was a "creative artist, compelled by a keen sense of beauty."[174] From Chicago to Buffalo, Stieringer's aims steadily shifted away from providing light to creating "artistic results" with illumination; "not lighting," but "light-painting." At the Pan-American, for instance, he tucked "mere glow-worm" incandescents in recesses along the architectural lines of the buildings, creating "great glowing masses of chiaroscuro ... music not quite frozen." Each night, spectators beheld in awed silence "the triumph of the new principle, the deliverance of the eye from the bondage of glare." The "problem" with incandescent lighting, for Stieringer's admirer and others, was its piercing, cold, hard glare, which only superficially corresponded to the glowing warmth of the candle. Bare electrical light, according to this view, operates with such scientific efficiency that it shuts down the eye to all but its concentrated energy, stripping objects of their substantiality.[175] Although Luna's practice of outlining buildings with unfrosted or shaded bulbs was comparatively cheap to plan and administer, Matthew Luckiesh, a contemporary physicist at General Electric's Nela Research Laboratory, observed that the "effect was almost wholly that of light, for the glare from the visible lamps obscured the buildings or other objects."[176]

The most famous critics venturing to Coney after 1903 addressed the ambiguities of electrical lighting, especially the confusion it generated about surfaces and substances, appearances and realities, desires stimulated and disappointed. The Russian radical Maxim Gorky, who visited in 1906, initially was swept away by the "magic picture of a flaming city" of "miraculous castles, palaces, and temples."[177] James G. Huneker, a conservative American critic, in the early 1910s also was momentarily thrilled by the nighttime "city of flame" burning enticingly but dangerously, like a candle.[178] As historians often have noted, Gorky and Huneker concluded that Coney was a political and cultural problem. At the heart of both observers' judgment was their shared fear of the sham world created there, yet when both critics turned to judge Coney, they inadvertently paid tribute to Thompson's skills. Gorky called the "magic and fantastic" city a "cheap, hastily constructed toyhouse for the amusement of children."[179] Huneker was even more direct: "Everything is the reflection of a cracked mirror held in the hand of the clever showman, who, knowing us as children of a larger growth, compounds his mess, bizarre and ridiculous, accordingly."[180] Gorky and Huneker condemned Coney's brilliance for the very properties that Thompson found most useful and marketable—it turned men into children.

Thompson could see only the friendly, smiling faces in the shadowless light of his nocturnal playground. Where others sought the delicate shadings of music not quite frozen, Thompson engineered disconcerting blare and heat. By 1909 Luna burned more than a million lights.[181] Where Luther Stieringer had delivered the troubled eye from the bondage of glare, Thompson restored the unsettling brilliance of the unshaded lamp. His lighting designs were unsubtle, to say the least, and, like his architecture, were determined by his preference for action and fascination instead of contemplation and contentment. He did not want his audience responding to his attractions with "How beautiful!" but in audible confusion with "Why is that?" or "What is that?"[182]

### A Carnival of Plenty

By combining his curvilinear, theatrical architecture with the new science and progressive narrative of incandescent lighting, Thompson engineered a peculiarly American fairy tale in material form, of a city glistening with electrical brilliance on the far edge of the dismal metropolis of work and responsibility. Thompson meant for Luna Park to provide the adventurous sensation of being rescued and liberated from a temporal world of darkness and transported to a sparkling city of light—the dramatic plot of A Trip to the Moon universalized in the domain of the amusement park. This particular version of commercial mythmaking, so prevalent in the consumer institutions of the time, was potently expressed in the Carnival of Plenty, the theme of the island's Mardi Gras festival in 1906. Three years earlier, Coney entrepreneurs had adopted the Mardi Gras promotional scheme that Thompson had peddled to Pan-American officials after the initial success of Midway Day. They designated 1903 as the "Year of Progress, One," referring to the "reign of new things" that Luna Park's first season had established.

Although the permanent residents of the island were almost universally Catholic, Coney's end-of-season festival was thoroughly secular. The "avowed purpose" of the Surf Avenue parades, as the *Brooklyn Daily Eagle* reported, "was merely to stir up interest so that the Coney Island season would last well into October." In this respect alone, the celebration proved effective; each year, according to newspaper accounts, the crowds were larger, by 1906 numbering in the hundreds of thousands on each of the six nights of Mardi Gras.[183] To attract such crowds the showmen dressed their parade in a carnivalesque imagery of allegory, myth, and fantasy to dramatize the progress of commercial amusements. The Coney Mardi Gras was yet another example of commercial enterprises using the "irrationalist and animist countertendencies" of premodern festivity to stir up consumption.[184] Like the festivals held in Catholic cultures, the Coney celebration bid farewell to a particular season, but the island's fête altered the traditional relation to the agrarian calendar to fit the new industrial order. Rather than signaling the season of renunciation, fasting, and renewal with the arrival of spring and a long season of replenishing labor, the Surf Avenue version occurred at the end of the summer—its season of excess and pleasure—before the onset of the cold, playless days of fall and winter. On one hand, Coney's Mardi Gras confirms the pattern of rationalization that scholars have frequently noted in the development of modern industrial processes and market exchange, which tends to sever the intimate connections between preindustrial customs of labor and consumption and the agricultural or liturgical calendar. Industrial work was seasonless and timeless, as demanding in winter or after sundown as it was in summer or after dawn.[185]

But the Coney Island festival also shows how new consumer institutions such as the summer parks, which still were clearly demarcated by place and season, appropriated liturgical traditions to conjure up markets. The Mardi Gras used managerial techniques and new technologies to dramatize grotesque pictures of excessive appetite and release from social control, all of which complemented the instrumental purpose of adding a week to the business cycle. Although Thompson was not identified as the designer, the 1906 Carnival of Plenty acted out Luna's underlying themes of play, pleasure, and plenitude. Attended by brass bands and automobiles, "Prince Plenty" and "Queen Prospera" led a mile-long assortment of electrically illuminated and animated floats, each of which performed one of the carnal appetites to which Coney's businesses appealed. The "laughing girls perched upon huge wine glasses and mammoth bottles" told the story of "Plenty of Wine"; the Man in the Moon and his court attendants composed "Plenty of Moonlight"; women dressed as greenbacks represented "Plenty of Money"; enormous cackling heads dramatized "Plenty of Laughing." Other floats dramatized "Plenty" of fish, smoke, meat, vegetables, sunshine, amusement, and bathing, followed by "illustrated tableaux of nursery rhymes" and a "great industrial parade."[186] The "unrivalled pictures" of the sensual paradise of Plenty and Prospera made fun of the "work-obsessed visions of modern capitalism and socialism." They did so by depicting Coney exactly as Fred Thompson wished it to be seen: as a marvelous showcase of goods appealing to and encouraging dissatisfaction, and tying "the longing for luxury, [and] for a life of ease in a land beyond toil,"[187] to what Thompson called the "most typically American Institutions"— "the Genius for Industrial Organization, the American Girl and Summer Amusement."[188]

In 1906 Thompson himself seemed to feast on plenty. That year he announced a range of plans that effectively would have extended the reach of his Coney Island playground to encompass the whole city. In addition to Luna, his mammoth Hippodrome theater, and schemes for a vaudeville empire, Thompson announced a project that harked back to his earliest ventures on the midway of the Nashville world's fair; his new "uptown wonderland" would be called "Vanity Fair."[189] Thompson and Dundy leased land at Fort George, a location that overlooked the Harlem River in the farthest northwest reaches of Manhattan. Nearly a half-century before Walt Disney, Thompson envisioned a Magic Kingdom: a pleasure resort operating year-round and featuring architecture and amusements organized around a single narrative theme. "We thought we had exceeded the limit when Luna Park was completed, but our Harlem plans will amaze New Yorkers," he boasted.[190]

With Vanity Fair, Thompson proposed to redraw the spiritual road map that the seventeenth-century English Puritan John Bunyan had handed down to more than two centuries of American readers of *The Pilgrim's Progress*. Since its publication in 1678, Bunyan's tale of the pilgrim Christian, who abandoned the City of Destruction to seek the salvation of the Celestial City, and of his trials, ordeals, adventures, and glorious triumph, had been one of the most widely read books in the English language. Thompson must have known the book well, but he had no intention of offering New Yorkers pious instruction in the ways of Christian salvation. Rather, he proposed to reproduce the marketplace of earthly delights and pleasures in the Town of Vanity, in which, according to Bunyan, "are all such merchandise sold, as houses, lands, trades, places, honours, preferments, titles, countries, kingdoms, lusts, pleasures, and delights of all sorts."[191] Although Thompson's exact plans have been lost, that he saw in this description a model for an unprecedented amusement venture in itself demonstrates how his amusements built on a spiritual heritage shared by Protestant Americans, while simultaneously subverting and rerouting its religious message to affirm, rather than to discount, the ultimate meaning of the world of goods.

Generations of American readers regarded Bunyan's book not simply as an allegorical homily but as a masterfully crafted tale of adventure as thrilling to the Puritan reader of the late seventeenth century in the Old and New Worlds as later secular narratives were to more-liberal religious readers.[192] Until the Civil War, America remained a "Bunyan-saturated" culture. At a time when books were still a rare possession even in prosperous homes, *The Pilgrim's Progress* usually occupied a treasured position next to the Bible in Protestant households, especially for children.[193] "O charming story! dear delightful book!" exclaimed Bronson Alcott, recalling his childhood joy in reading *Pilgrim's Progress*. For Alcott, the Romantic student of childhood and the founder of the utopian Fruitlands community in 1843, it was the thrill of Christian's adventurous quest, not his piety, that absorbed him. The very thought of the book, he wrote, "unites me with childhood, and seems to chronicle my Identity. How I was rapt in it! How gladly did I seat myself, after the day's labours on the farm, in the chimney niche, with the tallow candle in my hand, and pore over its enchanting pages until late in the night!"[194] Alcott's enchantment was a strikingly pagan but, for a transcendentalist dissenter, typically Romantic reaction to a Protestant text founded on the Calvinist precepts of human depravity and the predetermined course of divine election. The conversion wrought in him by Christian's example was not the conviction of his own sinfulness and the inscrutability of salvation. If anything, his memories manifest a comfort and ease that suggests an antebellum recasting of Christian's warning that one must leave the present life in order to reach the Holy City into the perfectionist strategies for creating a Kingdom of Heaven on earth.[195]

As the Alcott example demonstrates, the meaning of Bunyan's tale for American readers was never confined to its original Puritan context. Fred Thompson was merely the latest of many Americans in the nineteenth century who enlisted the tale for their own purposes. The pleasantly resurfaced road to salvation depicted in Nathaniel Hawthorne's 1843 story "The Celestial Railroad" abused the buoyant optimism of antebellum reformers and utopians such as Alcott.[196] Post–Civil War American women were likely to have read of *Pilgrim's Progress* in *Little Women*, the popular novel published in 1868 by Alcott's daughter. Through her fiction, Louisa May Alcott passed along her childhood of reading and acting out *Pilgrim's Progress*, although the journey no longer took the shape of a perilous quest for salvation. The March daughters turn the pilgrimage into a game that helps them understand the sacrifice and ultimate meaning of the war that has taken their father to the battlefront. "What fun it was," remembers daughter Jo, "especially ... passing through the Valley where the hobgoblins were!" And her mother replies: "We are never too old for this, my dear, because it is a play we are playing all the time in one way or another. Our burdens are here, our road is before us, and the longing for goodness and happiness is the guide that leads us through many troubles and mistakes to the peace which is a true Celestial City."[197]

By 1900, America was less saturated with Bunyan readers, but the commercial culture developing in American cities still showed the continuing power of his work in American life. Modern middle-class men were less likely to be seeking forgiveness from their sins and the kingdom beyond the grave than relief from everyday difficulties and responsibilities and access to a life of ease in a land beyond toil. Such, at least, was the message of *A Pilgrim's Progress by Mister Bunion*, the pseudonymous creation of the cartoonist Winsor McCay, which the *New York Herald* introduced in June 1905. McCay illustrated the comically futile efforts of Mister Bunion to rid himself of his "burden," a "cursed valise" loaded, not with sin, but with "dull care" and as painful to bear as the eponymous toe ailment. "I can get a lot of fun out of it," McCay predicted to his editor. Mister Bunion "will always be looking for 'Glad Avenue' and will have occasional visits to Easy Street, but his burden will stick to him and I will have him try to burn it, bury it, and throw it in the sea, blow it up, advertise it for sale or give away, get it run over by trains, hit by autos, and hundreds of things he will try to do to get rid of it but can't."[198] Another popular inversion of Bunyan's allegory was L. Frank Baum's *Wonderful Wizard of Oz*. William Leach has uncovered the Bunyanesque elements of Dorothy's pilgrimage from Kansas, her own City of Destruction, to the Emerald City of Oz: from her silver shoes to the Emerald City, which, "studded everywhere with sparkling emeralds," was comparable to Bunyan's "extremely glorious" Celestial City, "builded of pearls and precious stones."[199] Baum's appropriation amounted to more than dotting a literary work with familiar markings. He rerouted the pilgrimage into "an optimistic, affirmative vision of America that reinforced the priorities and values of the new industrial order."[200]

Some scholars have viewed *The Wizard of Oz* as a satirical allegory aimed at contemporary Populist politicians at the end of the nineteenth century,[201] but Leach has shown that Baum actually cared little for these matters. His passion was for the world of goods. Baum's various occupations as theatrical producer, dry-goods merchant, display designer, fairy-tale writer, and playwright revealed, rather than a fragmented personality, a brilliantly imaginative fascination and passion for the urban marketplace developing in such major cities as Chicago and New York. Born in 1856, Baum followed a desultory career as an impresario, then merchant, until, in Chicago in 1897, he started the first magazine devoted solely to window display. He urged window dressers to construct pleasing, living pictures full of color and action. In 1900, the same year as *The Wonderful Wizard of Oz*, he published *The Art of Decorating Show Windows and Dry Goods Interiors*, the first book on the subject, and one widely valued among urban retailers. Baum permanently left merchandising to write children's fiction that same year. But the integration of his imagination into the urban marketplace and the new art of displaying goods cannot be separated from his literary fairy tales. Baum's stories abound with the glimmering lights and fantastic animations and transformations that entrepreneurs were rushing to employ in selling in department stores, restaurants, hotels, theaters, and, two years later, Luna Park. "I have no shame in acknowledging that I [like my readers] ... am also a child," Baum wrote in 1900; "for since I can remember my eyes have always grown big at tales of the marvellous."[202] Baum in effect urged display men to use their windows to stimulate the marvel and fascination that he linked to his childishness and to make consumers' eyes grow big, like his, with the desire for possession. According to Leach, Baum's fairy tales, with their amazing metamorphoses and transformations, their glittering landscapes of jeweled lights and outsized flora, "reflect the polymorphous nature of the commodity market and of the new urban world in which the market took its grandest expression."[203]

The revision and marketing of traditional fairy tales with smiling surfaces was a major project of Peter Pans such as Baum and Thompson. Baum's book, like the plans for Vanity Fair, demonstrates how the grown-up boys reoriented the longing for spiritual deliverance to the secular desire for material fulfillment. The child's wish to be pleased and delivered from painful instruction should be a lifelong condition. Baum explained that he wrote his book not to teach "morality" but "solely to please children of today. It aspires to being a modernized fairy tale, in which the wonderment and joy are retained and the heartaches and nightmares are left out."[204] It is likely that New York's toymaker had a similar aim in mind. Vanity Fair probably would have travestied Bunyan's tale, rewarding its patrons with a radiant show of gilded chorus girls dancing and singing amid fountains, waterfalls, and colored lights. The message would have been the same as that of Luna Park: liberation was in play, salvation in this world, and pleasure in spending. Designs, plans, and preliminary financing were completed during late 1905 and early 1906, but little came of the project. There were many factors, but the most important may have been municipal politics and the decision not to extend the subway within reach of Thompson's site. His pilgrims were stranded without a celestial railway.[205]

### When You Are Dead, You Are Dead a Long While

Fred Thompson spent twelve seasons at Coney Island, nine of them presiding as Prince Plenty of Luna Park. In April 1912 his creditors put an end to his boyish spending spree, in much the same way that his father had intervened twenty years earlier when Thompson had spent himself into a corner in Nashville. His father took away his toys and made him go back to work as a menial architectural tracer to settle his debts. The new owners and managers of Luna kept him on in the figurehead capacity of "managing architect" at what was, for him, the paltry salary of a hundred dollars a week.[206]

This affront, as well as his personal bankruptcy and the dispossession of Luna, diminished neither his impertinence nor the significance of what he had accomplished. From his travels in the United States, Europe, Asia, and Africa, he must have known that he had invented the modern amusement park—what we today regard as a "theme park"— and that "Luna Parks" were being built in cities around the globe, from Harrisburg, Pennsylvania, to Buenos Aires to Melbourne. At a time when American manufacturers focused on building and supplying domestic markets, Thompson's intellectual property—his Oriental dream of a plaster fairy-tale city, a playground for grown-up boys and girls, an electric city by the sea—was perhaps the nation's most dazzling cultural export.

Only fifty years earlier, Europeans, whether for or against political reform, had conventionally regarded America as the seedbed of republican principles, "Liberty, Equality, and Fraternity," which, if planted abroad, would subvert the traditional social order of privilege, deference, submission, and hierarchy. By the time of Luna's first decade, Thompson and others like him were trying to revise the notion of manly republican citizenship and to reorient its hopes for liberty to the cultural offerings of the consumer marketplace. Earlier generations of American men had envisioned a prosperous, independent citizenry freed from the historical contingencies of sin, inequality, and propertylessness. Many had fought or rebelled, like the African-American abolitionist Frederick Douglass, to escape the perpetual childhood of enslavement and to achieve the full rights of manly adulthood. Thompson's Luna Park shows how the entrepreneurs of consumer capitalism encouraged and exploited the relocation of the traditional coordinates of middle-class manhood from the religious and civic obligations of the nineteenth century to what one historian has called the "shifting ensemble of cultural and material commodities" that were distributed and promoted by the consumer marketplace in the twentieth.[207] Thompson also imagined liberating a nation of great "throngs" of enslaved men, but the emancipation he offered was from "dull care," the customs and habits that made them take life solemnly, and other onerous aspects of adulthood. Whereas the oppressed of the past had fought to be men, his tyrannized generation of middle-class men would pay to be boys.

Evidence of his audacity and of his achievement is suggested by a small sign that appeared on a ticket kiosk outside one of Luna's attractions in 1912 or 1913. It announced: "Frederic Thompson's Life Is Only a Merry-Go-Round." The inscription was a minuscule feature in the sensationaly Orientalized surroundings of the park, but its insight went to the heart of Thompson's amusement enterprise. As a practical matter, it alluded to a musical number from Thompson's 1910 Broadway revue *Girlies*, which had been notorious for its liberal "display of lingerie and limb." The sign was meant to direct patrons to one of the park's newer attractions, a house of mirrors called the Bunny Hug. As any young New Yorker would have known, the "bunny hug" was a ragtime dance step, the kind that middle-class reformers denounced for exposing single, unprotected women to the brazen embraces of predatory men. An amusement code-named in this manner at least implied opportunities for risqué fun.

As aphorism, however, the inscription and the show tune to which it referred integrated the Bunny Hug's version of fun with the ethos and larger promise of the plaster paradise surrounding it. Here the framework of consuming manhood was fully displayed. "Cheer up and smile," went the song's chorus, "For when you are dead, you are dead a long while."

> If life isn't all that you'd like it to be,
> Remember this motto and take it from me:
>
> "Life is only a merry go round
> The more I go round, the more I have found,
> When a man is dead and he's stuck in the ground,
> The merry-go-round'll go round and round."[208]

There can be little doubt that Thompson himself was the author of the impertinent reflection on his life, which fused his identity with the perennial children's amusement. "Cheer up and smile" was his creed. From the moment he and Skip Dundy opened the resort in 1903, he had promoted the metropolis of play and pleasure as the one place on earth where life was all that a man would want it to be. This promise, rendered in the totality of the park's architecture, spectacular lighting, scenic illusions, and mechanical amusements, was predicated on the primary importance of pleasure as an end in itself. Relieved of the religious and civic duties that dominated nineteenth-century American culture, the vision of a better world to come has been recast as an amusement for children that goes "round and round." The song and the inscription expressed the ethos of Peter Pan culture and of the new boy-man who could represent and exploit its possibilities. Thompson built Luna for those who wanted a "little fun" before the "long while" set in. American men would be fools to wish for anything more or to strive for anything less.

# FOUR

# New York's Gigantic Toy

The Hippodrome, 1902–6

I N December 1904, a recent innovation in electrical billboard advertising called the "talking sign" appeared high above Brooklyn's most crowded shopping district. In successive flashes of incandescent typescript, the sign heralded a new era: "New York Hippodrome ... Entertainment for the Masses ... Management Thompson & Dundy ... Now Building Open Jan 1905." The "Mason Monogram," as it was named after its inventor, was typical of Fred Thompson's attention-grabbing promotional style. It had movement, action, originality, and incandescent brilliance, and it never stopped barking its message. What the sign delivered, though, was not just information—what, when, and where. Itself a kind of advertising plaything, the Mason Monogram also broadcast a promise that anyone familiar with nearby Luna Park would have recognized.[1]

The Hippodrome was the largest theater in the world when it opened in 1905 on a block-long stretch of Sixth Avenue between Forty-third and Forty-fourth Streets in Manhattan. It was ideally suited to this tight integration of location, method, message, and product. Thompson designed his mammoth novelty as a great showplace for the millions of New Yorkers who frequented the city's department stores, who filled his coffers at Luna Park, and who, in his mind, had thus far been priced out of

Fig. 4.1. New Yorkers were "hugely pleased" with Thompson and Dundy's Hippo-drome, which consumed an entire block of Sixth Avenue between 43rd and 44th Streets. It is shown here during its inaugural 1905 season. (*Neg. No. 59202, ©Collection of The New-York Historical Society.*)

the "best" Broadway theaters. Thompson knew what he was doing in putting a conspicuous and unusual talking sign at the center of Brooklyn's bustling retail shopping district. "We are coming to the age of the department store in theatricals," he announced in 1904, tying his amusement venture to the revolution in corporate retailing that was transforming cities across the country.[2] Thompson intended the Hippo-drome to be more than just a theater for all the people. He designed it as a kind of permanent world's fair exhibition palace, which would show-case a new sense of common purpose and possibility for urban Americans and move fun from the edge to the center of the metropolis. The "talking sign" sketched the outlines of a "gigantic toy" for the over-worked, play-starved people of the city. "And," a local newspaper re-ported, "New York was hugely pleased" (fig. 4.1).[3]

Luna Park gets all the attention when Thompson is remembered today, but in the early twentieth century, as one astute contemporary observed, it was "the Hippodrome that caused these mere boys to be regarded with open wonder. When inaugurated, the entire enterprise was so wholly beyond anything New Yorkers had ever known, that it really took a year to reach a gait." By that point, Thompson and Dundy had lost control of the theater and moved on to other ventures. But what they had built during their short fourteen-month proprietorship—the imposing figure of the toymaker Thompson no less than the gigantic toy of a theater—endured as potent symbols of the commercial culture of Peter Pan. As at Luna Park, management used the language of Never Land to connect and shape the theater's varied components—electrical circuitry, roof trusses, hydraulic lifts, herds of elephants, and throngs of chorus girls—into illustrated lectures on the felicity and necessity of play. From one perspective, Thompson's memorable productions, *A Yankee Circus on Mars* and *A Society Circus*, were little more than enlarged variety entertainments concocted out of spectacle, pantomime, vaudeville, circus, operetta, ballet, and musical comedy. But the meanings of the shows exceeded the tally of the loosely connected details. Compressed into the service of Peter Pan culture, they composed sugared sermons for adults, child's fare promising grown-up relief from the generalized fatigue and melancholy of the day.[4]

Even more than Luna Park, the Hippodrome—or Hip, as it was called—demonstrated the power of new commercial institutions and sources of capital to colonize new markets for pleasure, even those that poked fun at the rationality, repression, and discipline of modern business. But rather than undermining the Hippodrome's viability or rendering it a self-defeating operation, this tension enlivened its appeal, especially for the grown-up boys of American business like Fred Thompson, who thrilled at the thought and sight of machine-powered pleasures, such as a legion of "leggy" chorus girls entwined with circuits of incandescent lights and sparkling like the Mason Monogram. The Hippodrome productions were not simply spectacles or hodgepodge collections of variety entertainments, but stunning commercial myth-making. Thompson was a skilled merchandiser of escape, but he offered the Hippodrome not so much as an evasion of modernity as its possible fulfillment: the powerful mechanisms of American industry and the delightful abundance of a consumer Never Land brought together by youthful entrepreneurs and fashioned as marvelous, dream-like entertainments for a democratic audience of millions.

## The Age of the Department Store in Theatricals

Fred Thompson was not the first American showman to propose building a gigantic hippodrome. P. T. Barnum in 1874 had operated a "Roman" hippodrome between Twenty-sixth and Twenty-seventh Streets in Manhattan. The arena held eight thousand spectators in a grandstand arrangement of seating, which wrapped around an elongated oval performance space. Barnum's extravaganzas "mingled peril with magnificence" and heraldic opulence with the thrill of chariot races and Wild West violence, but as a rule, they were European or British imports, not domestic productions.[5]

Even Barnum's elaborate productions paled in comparison with the audacious ambitions of the Spectatorium, a magnificent permanent theater seating ten thousand that the nineteenth-century dramatist Steele MacKaye envisioned for the 1893 Columbian exposition in Chicago.[6] MacKaye had grown up among the social elite of Brooklyn and Manhattan. Much like Thompson, he rebelled against the business civilization of his father and went into the business of entertainment. He had a genius for theater and stage design and helped introduce the revolutionary "method" style of acting to the United States. But beneath his theatrical garb MacKaye remained committed to the social and moral universe of his father; he just proposed different tools for ordering the unruly nation, substituting the theater for the church. "Our faith in prayers is waning," he explained, "our faith in performances is strengthening."[7] His career as playwright, acting instructor, and stage designer culminated, in his mind, in his effort to fulfill the "divine duty" of building a great national theater and school of drama reflecting his spiritual devotion to "Art" and his radical ideas for redefining drama.

MacKaye did not plan to break completely from the entertainment basis of Barnum's productions, only "to uplift" audiences as he amused them. He envisioned an art for the masses and diagnosed many of the social evils on which the designer of Luna Park would later build his amusement empire. But MacKaye's ambition attracted the financial backing of Chicago's leading industrialists and bankers because it operated in concert with the ideological aims of the fair's designers and investors. Drama, according to MacKaye, offered spiritual sustenance to an impoverished age, revealing "the real worth of life" to those whose own existence was "benumbed by overwork" or "deadened by the poisonous sweets of luxury."[8] More profoundly, it would provide a basis for unity and order in a secularizing, heterogeneous nation. The entertainment that MacKaye planned for his "temple"—*The World Finder*, or the story of Christopher Columbus—was heroic material for contemplation and spiritual harmony. In form and action, the proposed show was not so different from extravaganzas staged by Barnum and other spectacle designers; its agenda of restoring order and stability to a disharmonious nation was what put MacKaye's faith in performances in concert "with the imperial self-image" of the City Beautiful.[9]

No culture would ever be unified by *The World Finder*. Construction of the Spectatorium progressed no further than its looming steel skeleton when the panic of 1893 frightened away its financial support. Fred Thompson must have been familiar with the failed enterprise from his own involvement in the Columbian exposition. Considering Thompson's ambitions in the early 1890s, it seems likely that he was stirred by the cultural and artistic pretensions of the Spectatorium. In many respects the lives of the "toymaker of New York" and the "world finder" ran on parallel tracks, although separated by a generation. Thompson's later rhetoric bears a remarkable resemblance to MacKaye's messianic pronouncements. The builder of the Hippodrome may well have shared some of MacKaye's lofty sentiments early in his life. But by 1904, when he had begun his theater, he proposed unifying American culture on a different basis than stories of human struggle and achievement. Pleasure, as he put it, was a noble end in itself.

The word "hippodrome" usually refers to the ancient Roman and Greek arenas for horse and chariot races, although the more immediate predecessors to the New York venture were "hippodramas," dramatic (even Shakespearean) productions that incorporated and showcased spectacular equestrian skills and stunts.[10] Such shows flourished on indoor and outdoor stages in London and Paris in the first half of the nineteenth century. Horses were less important to Thompson's productions than were the nineteenth-century traditions of melodrama, farce, spectacle, circus, and pantomime, in particular those imported to the United States from Europe, where they had been produced by the Kiralfy brothers, Bolossy and Imre, and at London's Drury Lane theater. In their

overheated emphasis on pictorial splendor, magical mechanical transformations, multitudes of luxuriously caparisoned chorus girls, and
kaleidoscopic lighting effects, the Hippodrome shows restaged many of
the scenic wonders that had been accomplished on a smaller scale or
with less extravagant mechanical illusions in other settings, such as London's annual Christmas pantomimes.[11]

Thompson did not just copy such European forms, however. He domesticated them, adapting them to the world of American consumer
capitalism. When viewed as a whole—with its organization as a mammoth mechanical toy, its preaching of the necessary joy of play—
Thompson's temple of entertainment aimed, like MacKaye's, for
nothing less than the "education and inspiration of the masses." But the
glimmering productions delivered there proposed to convince Americans that the real worth of life was in the abundant and luxurious sweets
of the marketplace.

Building a hippodrome in the heart of Manhattan apparently had occurred to Thompson even before he and Dundy decided to build Luna
Park. New York, and especially Manhattan, appealed to Thompson because of the concentrated throngs of comparatively affluent middle-
class men and women and the city's highly developed and integrated
urban transportation system. When Thompson moved to New York
from Buffalo in 1901, he found that the city's high-end "legitimate" or
dramatic theaters had hardly altered the appeal of their entertainments
or expanded the foundation of their audience over the last decade of the
nineteenth century. Vaudeville was expanding its markets, but the dramatic theaters still catered to the carriage trade to the exclusion of the
mass middle-class audience that had grown up around them. "I was astounded at the conditions as they existed," Thompson explained shortly
after construction began on the Hippodrome. "Here was a city with millions of people in its confines, and not one amusement resort which appealed to more than 25 per cent of them at the very outside." Thompson
claimed that he and Dundy tried as early as 1901 to put a hippodrome at
Seventh Avenue and Thirty-ninth Street in Manhattan but had to retreat
because of opposition from neighborhood residents. In the alternative
they concentrated on Coney Island, but the audience Thompson was
trying to attract was the same, whether at Luna or the Hippodrome.[12]

In Thompson's mind, theatrical entertainment had to be liberated in
the manner of modern urban retailing. The showman knew what he

was doing in linking the Hippodrome with the great department stores at the turn of the century, whose meaning and historical importance were readily apparent to the rapidly growing population of retail customers and workers, especially the women who were discovering new public roles either as shoppers or as store buyers and clerks. The concept of the department store provided Thompson with an organizational model as well as a class setting and democratic vocabulary of public service for his theater. Urban retailing was increasingly dominated at the turn of the century by huge corporate retail firms headed by aggressive merchants who sold an unprecedented array of luxuries, necessities, and services from all over the world. Such stores appeared even in small American cities. In whatever setting, they were "symbolic of the very essence of the consumer revolution" at the turn of the century.[13]

In part, the rapid ascent to dominance of urban merchandising reflected two indivisible structural changes in the American industrial economy: the extraordinary growth in agricultural and industrial production, stimulated by new technologies and continuous-process manufacturing techniques; and the dominance of the corporate form of business organization, which amassed unprecedented sources of capital. Retailing, which once had been the province of limited partnerships or independent merchants, was revolutionized by the new volume of goods and the new supplies of capital that enabled merchants to build mass markets. In terms of size and volume of sales and activity, R. H. Macy in New York and Marshall Field in Chicago, to mention two obvious from many possible examples, became recognized features of urban life and architecture by the first decade of the twentieth century.[14] "Picture to yourself then," wrote H. Gordon Selfridge, a mastermind of Chicago's Marshall Field Company and founder of Selfridges department store in London, "an enormous building or perhaps a group of superb buildings designed with the highest quality of the architect's skill and planned down to the minutest detail by those who are masters of the details of the business itself.... These buildings measure their floor area by the acre and twenty, thirty, or even forty acres of floor space—or even two million square feet—are not extraordinary.... Bigness alone is nothing, but bigness filled with the activity that does everything continually better means much."[15]

Doing things better, for Selfridge and his retailing contemporaries, meant more than organizing and managing a large enterprise. Just as

important, stores had to picture "the desirable" for middle-class customers increasingly attuned to an enticing spectacle. Theodore
Dreiser's depiction of his desire-driven heroine, Sister Carrie, who finds
each counter she passed in the stores of Chicago "a show place of dazzling interest and attraction," suggests how the new stores turned retailing into theater. (Carrie herself goes on to become an accomplished
actress.)[16] Merchants developed innovative advertising and merchandising schemes as well as a roster of free services available to all customers
to attract the consuming middle-class millions and to promote shopping as an important, progressive aspect of contemporary life. Retail entrepreneurs located their stores at the confluence of the new urban
mass-transportation systems. Service became the pervasive slogan of
urban retailing. "The chief profit a wise man makes on his sales is not in
dollars and cents but in serving his customers," the great merchant
John Wanamaker wrote in 1918. This ethos encouraged a "certain heady
democracy" in stores where the city's wealthiest and humblest walked
the same aisles even if they could not buy the same goods. But more
than anything else, department stores were defined by their middle-
classness, in terms of the material comfort and styles of life they marketed and of the base of customers they enticed through their doors.
Such shoppers came to regard service as their entitlement, and the new
breed of corporate merchants flattered their authority and demands—
"Give the lady what she wants," was Field's creed—because the merchants believed their private profits depended on this public service.[17]

Thompson's effort to expand the potential audience for theatrical productions and to redefine the ethos of theatrical entertainment in the progressive, public-spirited vocabulary of the modern corporation and
department store was not altogether new. Much like the project of re-
forming Coney Island, the Hippodrome's claims to democratize and purify theatrical entertainments were distinguished more by the scale of
the laundering than by the cleansing itself; the Hip's reform agenda was
part of the larger process of gentrifying the theater that had begun in the
mid-nineteenth century.[18] But whereas at Coney Island Thompson
sought to *elevate* a notoriously unrefined form of amusement, at the Hippodrome he aimed to *redistribute* the luxuries concentrated at the tony
top of the entertainment marketplace. He would cater, through the Hippodrome's expanded seating capacity, low ticket prices, and varied show-
bill, to the millions in the middle, who could not afford, or felt demeaned

by, the aristocratic atmosphere of what he pilloried as the high-priced entertainments of the exclusive legitimate theaters on Broadway. Thompson counted as many as three million "nice, respectable, intelligent" New Yorkers who never attended the cheaper vaudeville and "cannot afford to pay $2 for an orchestra seat in a fancy Broadway theatre among a lot of overdressed people." "They feel as though their clothes were not good enough, and so they stay at home. They have too much self respect to go up in the gallery and too much intelligence to go to the cheap theatres. Those are the patrons we are after, the masses, and our motto will be to give them the best possible show for the least possible money." Hippodrome tickets ranged from twenty-five cents to a dollar.[19]

Thompson claimed that the Hippodrome had democratized theater-going in the same way that department stores had democratized shopping; the rich as well as the humble could mingle at the Hippodrome as they could at no other Broadway theater. In truth, Thompson wanted to tap the urban constituency of middle-class consumers who had been frequenting "refined vaudeville" since the 1880s and who daily filled the city's department stores.[20] After 1915 these audiences would fuel the proliferation of motion-picture houses in American cities.[21] The world's fairs and especially Luna Park had shown Thompson and his partner Dundy that great fortunes could be made from collecting millions of dimes and nickels. The Hippodrome, to duplicate this formula, would demand unrelenting full houses attracted by its inexpensive tickets to offset the enormous price of producing theatrical luxury for what *Broadway* magazine called "the great outstanding masses."[22]

To attract these throngs, Thompson had to fashion an entertainment that flattered the middle-class taste for and expectation of material luxury, unstinting service, and managerial efficiency and system. Thompson consciously designed the Hippodrome, even more than Luna Park, to incorporate the middle-class dream of a world relieved of drudgery, restored to harmony, and filled with play through the techniques and mechanical habits of the modern managerial mind. The Hip's energetic mixture of incongruous attractions created a form of amusement that was varied, lively, nonlinear, affirming rather than prescriptive, and abundantly available.

Thompson assured the Broadway establishment that the Hippodrome would be as good for them as it was for the outstanding masses. His Hippodrome would "impart the theater habit" to millions with "slim purses" who either had lost interest in drama because of the high prices or never had it in the first place. A new audience for theater would emerge and spread into rival houses just as, the partners claimed, Luna Park had expanded the patronage and leavened the moral quality of all of Coney Island's amusements. The magazines and newspapers of New York generally praised the partners for this progressive innovation. "This great building fills a long-felt want," *Broadway* magazine reported. "Its prices are for the public. Its vast proportions make its appeal for patronage thoroughly sincere and honest. The plan of amusement is of that human sort that makes the whole world kin." Another magazine identified the important links among the Hippodrome, Progressive politics, and Theodore Roosevelt's presidential slogan, calling it a "square deal" in safety, comfort, price, and value. "And not least of its attractions are the civility and courtesy which replace the usual contemptuous and boorish treatment the theatre-goer encounters in other places of amusement." The comparison underscores an unexpected but significant intersection of Thompson's commercial frivolity and the campaign of some Progressives such as Roosevelt and Walter Lippmann to defend the potential rationality and social benefits of the new corporate order. A superb building, planned to the highest degree, the Hippodrome was not overweening bigness, but Progressive bigness that did everything continually better and attended to the wants of the masses rather than to the demands of the elite or lowly few. Many Progressives were ambivalent at best about the frivolousness and waste of the "mass culture" represented by such institutions as the Hippodrome and Luna Park. Appearances notwithstanding, the Hippodrome did not overturn or rebel against the Progressive order so much as seek to realize the potential for rational organization and management in the field of commercial play. As stated by Thompson and Dundy's publicity department, the Hippodrome offered a "revel of recreation at rational rates."[23]

Because the Hippodrome was an unprecedented venture in middle-class amusement, New Yorkers had difficulty placing it in relation to existing theaters and urban institutions. Broadway impresarios were neither impressed nor reassured by Thompson's proclamations. With fifty-two hundred seats, and matinee and evening performances six days a week, the Hippodrome would be seeking a potential audience in excess of sixty thousand weekly. Oscar Hammerstein, who was planning his Manhattan Opera House at the same time, condescendingly equated the Hippodrome with the annual visits of the circus and predicted that "theatres will suffer immensely ... for at least the first six weeks," before conditions returned to normal. Thompson and Dundy suspected A. L. Erlanger and Marc Klaw of the Theatre Syndicate of waging secret warfare to delay the project through the city's Building Department, which challenged the Hippodrome's construction features. The allegations are not surprising because the Syndicate, which held a near monopoly on theatrical productions in America, was generally despised during a time of antitrust sentiments. In addition, one of Klaw and Erlanger's contributions to American theatrical life was the importation of spectacular London pantomimes, with which presumably the Hippodrome would directly compete. The allegations probably were fabricated. The Syndicate had more-reliable methods of responding to Thompson's populist approach; in typical monopoly fashion, it announced a drop in ticket prices.[24] Rumors also were published of a pending "circus war." Thompson, who had publicized conflicts with clergymen and business and civic leaders to promote his world's fair ventures, "boomed" the injustice of the "Circus Trust." He was ready, he proclaimed in January 1905, "to wage a merry war on our three ringed opponents." The conflicts with the circus and the legitimate theaters indicate that Thompson had conceived of an amusement that bridged the distance between elitist and popular forms of entertainment.[25] Regardless of his opponent, Thompson could draw on Progressive rhetoric to distinguish the universal benefits and rational rates of his big business against the narrow-minded, particularistic interests of the Syndicate and circus monopolies.

### Brokers in Beauty

Thompson and Dundy advertised the total cost of the Hippodrome, the Sixth Avenue property, and its stage entertainment as $3,500,000. Luna Park had been a munificent benefactor during its first two seasons, but hardly to the extent necessary to finance a project of this size. John W. "Bet-a-Million" Gates emerged as the big money behind Thompson and Dundy at the Hippodrome as he probably had been at Luna Park. Born the son of a feckless Illinois farmer in 1855, Gates was one of the most outrageous industrialists and speculators at the turn of the century. A born showman and confidence man, he delighted in generating public attention with his crude, belching manners and voracious appetites for financial risk, rich food and drink, and, especially, gambling. He had won his first fortune in the near homicidal competition among barbed-wire manufacturers for the great western markets in the 1870s and 1880s. He later expanded into steel manufacturing, oil, and real estate. His greater public notoriety, however, came from his reputation for dropping a million dollars in a marathon poker game, or thousands wagering on raindrops dribbling down train windows. Among the country's leading industrialists, on the other hand, he was known as a skilled and truculent monopolist and stock manipulator; his unrefined manners, aggressive dealing, and compulsive gambling earned him the undying enmity of such commercial, financial, and industrial titans as Marshall Field, Andrew Carnegie, and, above all, the fastidious Episcopalian John Pierpont Morgan. Gates remained on the periphery of the industrial elite of Chicago and New York, preferring the company of mavericks who, like himself, had risen from nothing to millions. He was almost destined to ally himself with Thompson and Dundy for numerous reasons. Both showmen, for instance, were notorious gamblers, and Thompson was a precedent-defying renegade in the city's amusements. But a fundamental rationality ran beneath the rebelliousness of all three as they sought to colonize whole new territories of the city with the logic of capitalist investment. The partners' amusement ventures would attract and delight someone like Gates because they promised to make millions while parodying and challenging the cultural authority of New York's genteel financial leadership.[26]

The United States Realty Company, of which Gates was a principal investor, owned the Sixth Avenue property where the Hippodrome was built, and for all intents and purposes, the theater itself. In mid-September Thompson and Dundy borrowed nine hundred thousand dollars from the New York Security and Trust Company—an institution closely tied to U.S. Realty—and shortly afterward it was announced that Gates would be president of the Hippodrome Company. Aside from Dundy, all of the company's directors also were on the board of U.S. Realty, including Harry S. Black, who was president of the realty company. Black was a Canadian who had married the daughter of George A. Fuller, one of the leading American builders of skyscrapers and major public buildings. The Fuller Construction Company was later absorbed by U.S. Realty, creating a formidable alliance, which, as it turned out, provided the real estate, financing, and contractors to build the Hippodrome. From the beginning, then, Thompson and Dundy's hold on the Hippodrome was tenuous and subordinate to the investment interests of their backers, who were powerful real-estate developers and financiers, masters of vertical corporate and industrial integration, not impresarios or playful boy-men. Having comparatively little money themselves, Thompson and Dundy triumphed by convincing these businessmen of the viability of their formula of amusement as a money-making investment. With Luna Park piling up dimes, the potential of the theater must have seemed a low-risk gamble.[27]

The Hippodrome certainly was big business, but it also was a gigantic machine of illusion, which systematically organized an unprecedented collection of human labor and technology to manufacture fantastic entertainments. Observers well beyond the immediate Broadway community recognized its significance. Expansively detailed and laudatory accounts of the Hippodrome's construction and stage effects appeared in many of the technical magazines on engineering, illumination, electricity, and architecture. These articles, like those appearing in middle-class magazines and daily newspapers, presented lavishly detailed descriptions of the building, from how many bricks covered the theater (six million) to how many feet of copper wiring (110,000) were used in connecting the Hippodrome's twenty-five thousand incandescent lights. It was an age fascinated with human and technological quantifiation. It also was an age of industrial integration, in which an amusement venture drew on and stimulated innovations across a broad territory of American manufacturing, from incandescent lighting and electrical-power generation to mass transportation to industrial engineering and architecture. In the case of the Hippodrome, the tributes from these sources and the seemingly endless lists of measurements underscored Thompson's ability to marshal hundreds of thousands of minute parts, details, and people into a system that responded efficiently and willingly to his commands. The Hippodrome was not just big; it was controlled, organized, and mechanicalized bigness, arrayed, the advertisements claimed, solely to please and enchant the great middle-class masses.[28]

When completed, the Hippodrome squatted—eighty-nine feet high in front and about two hundred feet long and wide—along a full block of one of the city's principal north-south thoroughfares. Like a sleight of hand, it had risen from an empty lot behind the Sixth Avenue elevated railroad to completion in ten months. Sabbatarian protests against Sunday construction and other objections to Thompson's promise of round-the-clock labor had spoiled plans for a Christmas opening, but the debut on 12 April 1905 still was a remarkable feat given the size of the project and its cost. It also was testimony to what Thompson had learned during his world's fair days.[29]

With its brick façade and terra-cotta trimmings and decoration, the Hippodrome appeared to be a conventional, although massive, masonry structure. The front mixed classical motifs with overstated Thompsonian fancy. Tall Corinthian porticos with fluted columns flanked a central Roman arch with an impressive elephant-head keystone. Towers at the corners cradled huge skeletal orbs, outlined with incandescent lights. The final product was of an unprecedented size and scale for a theater, but the solidity was an illusion akin to the architectural tricks of the Chicago and Buffalo expositions. The Hippodrome actually was a cavernous shed, like a world's fair exhibition palace, covered with brick and mortar, rather than plaster, to disguise the modern steel framework that did the real structural work. The steel wall columns braced massive roof trusses, which spanned the breadth of the building and created an expansive interior space. The trusses were described as the largest ever used in the United States, although the idea was little different from the staff-covered warehouses of world's fairs.[30] The seating ascended in three steps from the orchestra pit, with most in the balcony and gallery. This tiered effect left the auditorium open for the most part, which accentuated its enormity. An immense dome, more than a hundred feet in diameter and manifesting no means of support except for the pillars at each corner, appeared to hover above it all. It, too, was an illusion. The dome actually was suspended from the invisible trusses, and the four pillars were made of plaster.[31]

It was no illusion that the Hippodrome, as the *New York Clipper* observed, was "a place of magnificent distances," but Thompson's theater was not big solely for the sake of being the largest theater in the world.[32] One of the showman's favorite amusement tricks at Luna Park was the antic alteration of scale and perspective, which momentarily disturbed the viewer's sense of his or her own size and identity. Thompson acutely comprehended the psychological effect of a shifting architectural environment. Architecture, in his opinion, affected its inhabitant's sense of self even more readily than the theatrical entertainments offered on the

Fig. 4.2. Beholding the vastness of the audience was itself one of the Hippodrome's most impressive and even bewildering attractions—an awe-inspiring vision, as one observer put it, that makes a person "tremble and shrink." (*Theatre Collection, Museum of the City of New York.*)

stage. The Hippodrome's "associational functionalism" shocked the spectator with its hugeness even as it impressed heavily on the viewers their own relative smallness.[33] The critic from the *New York Tribune*, after considering "the hugeness and brilliancy of the entertainment," confessed that he was "bound to express little but admiration, almost untempered admiration, for mere bulk is always impressive, not to say unsettling, to the mind." Other commentators noted the effect of entering the auditorium and gazing out into the distance for the first time. *Billboard*'s correspondent recalled, "you tremble and shrink before a mountain-wave of human faces that threatens to overwhe[l]m you. It is a vision that awes" (fig. 4.2). The Hippodrome incorporated Thompson's fiendish passion for occasions and throngs, in which ordinary egos shrank before and within the crowd. The *New York Herald* reported the bewilderment of a well-known comedian upon his introduction to the

Hippodrome's stage. "Why, I'd be lost here," he protested. "It would be like trying to act in a ten acre lot." The *New York Tribune* critic confirmed the comedian's fears. Solo voices, spoken dialogue, and tunes were dissipated in the cavernous theater; only the amassed voices of the enormous choruses were able to overcome the breadth of the stage and auditorium. By design, the Hippodrome was a visual rather than an aural thrill. For the Hip's stage director, according to R. H. Burnside, who later served in that capacity, "the fact he had always upper-most in his mind was its immensity. He *had* to think on such a scale." Burnside said the Hippodrome's elephants "never ceased to be a wonder to the audience" because they appeared so small on the stage and thus "emphasized the immense proportions." Even the elephants were awed by its scale.[34]

Wonder, astonishment, fascination, awe, bewilderment—Thompson's theater and its entertainments were organized and deployed to stimulate these reactions from his audiences. The Hippodrome's productions mixed popular songs and circus and vaudeville acts with opulent stage settings, grand opera, avant-garde ballet, and Luna Park lighting, mechanical effects, and illusions. The configuration of the stage—fifty feet deep, nearly two hundred wide—and the magnitude and comprehensiveness of the productions presented problems of coordination of movement, color, perspective, mechanics, actors, and animals that were unusual in the American theater. Others, such as the Kiralfy brothers, had staged massive outdoor spectacles at several American world's fairs, but no one had done so in a theater and on this scale. Thompson combed Europe and North America for "experts"—one writer called them "broker[s] in beauty"—to translate his extravagant ideas into material form on the Hippodrome stage. The crew gathered reflects the diverse sources assembling the commercial culture in America at this time as well as the plasticity of aesthetic boundaries in the marketplace of pleasure. Thompson's lieutenants did not fit easily into rigid definitions of high and low culture, art divorced from the pecuniary motives of the marketplace and art in the service of commercial interests. They tended to move in all spheres, and the result of their association at the Hippodrome was unusually eclectic. At the same time, the Hip's aesthetic linked it to ventures in other areas of commercial culture.[35]

The ballet master, Vincenzo Romeo, had choreographed the dance in spectacles imported from Europe such as *Bluebeard* and *Ali Baba*. The composer Manuel Klein, who had at least one Broadway musical to his credit, was the principal conductor and composer and promised the Hippodrome would have an orchestra, not a circus band: "People like blare all right, but they like something else, too. They like light and shade and delicate effects." The stage manager, Edward Temple, had directed grand opera for the Grau-Savage Grand Opera Company as well as productions for Klaw and Erlanger. Luna Park's Hugh Thomas and Edward Carrigan built the lighting and stage properties. Claude Hagen, who had invented the famous stage effects for the chariot race in *Ben Hur*, was hired to design the stage, although he and Thompson and Dundy fell out before the project was completed. Hagen had directed Luna Park's outdoor disaster spectacle, Fire and Flames, in 1903 and would go on to design the elitist New Theatre's revolving stage as well as to direct and manage other Coney Island summer shows. The equestrian corps was under the veteran circus trainer Frank Melville.[36]

The most important figures emerging from Thompson's worldwide search were the costume designer, Alfredo Edel, and the scenic designer, Arthur Voegtlin. Thompson claimed to have seen Edel's work in Paris, although it is likely that he had witnessed the Kiralfy spectacle, *America*, in 1893 at the Columbian exposition; it had been Edel's only prior costume work in the United States. The *New York Times* credited Edel with creating costumes for more than three hundred spectacles, operas, and burlesques. His work had appeared in Verdi's later operas, *Otello* and *Simon Boccanegra*, and in productions at the Comédie Française. The divas Melba and Eames had worn his gowns. "In his line no man in Europe has a higher reputation or more successes to his credit," according to the *Times*. His specialty was "stage beauty en masse," coordinating the color and texture of a stage tableau composed of hundreds of chorus girls. "Of course," he said, "my work takes me most into that realm of theatric art where the stage is crowded with people, especially with pretty girls in many-colored, brilliant garments of various sorts and designs." In terms of size, the Hippodrome premiere was "one of the largest undertakings" of his exemplary career. "I am designing costumes for a stage that will hold 400 people at a time," he told the *Times*. "I am in the position of the artist who has to paint a big picture with a small brush. The result will be impressionistic."[37]

The scenic designer, Arthur Voegtlin, had been reared in the atmosphere of nineteenth-century spectacle theater and artistic realism. His father, William Voegtlin, had been a leading scenic designer of the late nineteenth century, but the son (like Thompson) wanted most to be an artist. "Art stung me very badly early in life; in fact, I never quite recovered," he revealed in a 1912 interview. "I wanted to paint pictures, and nothing could stop me, even the admonition of my eminent father." After studying landscape painting for several years, he was forced by poverty into an apprenticeship with his father. He later undertook an independent career, gaining a reputation for staging lavishly detailed realistic scenery. When the Madison Square Garden arena was transformed into a circuit of piazzas and canals for "Venice in New York" in 1903, Voegtlin designed and managed the reconstruction of the Italian city. Thompson employed his services for outdoor spectacles at Luna Park, including The Great Train Robbery, for which Voegtlin wrote the script and designed the scenery. As with Thompson, the press portrayed Voegtlin as a visionary artist and inspired dreamer. He claimed that he had never visited any of the exotic settings he duplicated on a vast scale of realism on the Hippodrome and other stages. "These pictures simply come to me," Voegtlin explained to the *New York Times*, which summarized his creative process: "He plans his spectacles from the sweep of a skyline to the scarf on a native's shoulder, apparently out of nothing.... He opens his eyes for the vision, and it comes. And perhaps the most astounding of all the aspects of this curious mode of creation is the fact that the vision comes timed to a minute, spaced to an inch, and colored to an overtone."[38]

The carefully calibrated extravagance of the Hippodrome's big pictures reveals how the many vectors of urban consumer culture converged in the "gigantic toy." The theater's brokers were well aware of the strategies of display and enticement being developed by new market institutions. For instance, Voegtlin, after leaving the Hippodrome, produced elaborate fashion and commercial spectacles in the late 1910s and early 1920s before finally moving on to Hollywood.[39] Charles De Soria, the chief electrician, was even more illustrative of the Hip's symbiotic alliance with the urban consumer economy. De Soria designed one of the more celebrated scenes in the second major Hippodrome production, A Society Circus, in 1906. Two stage lovers sat in the cusp of an anthropomorphic crescent moon. As they serenaded each other, the moon went through its various phases, changing facial expressions each time a stage cloud rolled in front of it; the transformations delighted audiences. That same year Murray's Italian Gardens also engaged De Soria to design its lighting effects. Murray's was the latest of a growing number of lavishly decorated restaurants that had opened in the city since the 1890s and catered, like the Hippodrome, to the growing demand for urban nightlife, especially hungry theater crowds.[40] The restaurant was pure gustatory theater. As the *Illuminating Engineer* reported, "all the artificial appeal to the senses that could be commanded by an apparently reckless expenditure of time, money, and ingenuity" had been mobilized to stage it as the verdant courtyard of a Mediterranean villa. De Soria was a key figure in the production. Among his tricks: the ceiling was riddled with "small star-shaped openings" behind which electric lights were "alternately lighted and extinguished, giving the appearance of twinkling stars." The clouds shifting across this theatrical sky replicated the moon illusion from *A Society Circus*. Three-dimensional effects were added to the dining room's murals with additional theatrical lighting tricks of the trade. De Soria's spectacle reflected the recognition among restaurateurs that audiences for food expected theater. Like department stores and theaters, reported the magazine, restaurants were becoming "veritable show places, often patronized, and rightly so, for what is to be seen quite as much as for what is to be eaten."[41]

### Dollars and Dynamos

De Soria's well-lit restaurant, with fountains trickling and a ceiling alive with motion, also dramatized the obsession with animation and movement that was expressed in Luna Park's attractions and architecture and in so many other ways in early-twentieth-century commercial culture. Thompson's stage director, Edward Temple, explained the Hip's aspirations this way: "We have sought for constant change, unceasing action, never-halting movement."[42] People could sit down at the Hippodrome, but they could never be at rest. The most important instrument and medium that Thompson used to express and deliver this continuous-process entertainment was electrical current. Electricity, said Thompson, was the "best friend" of the Hippodrome, its animating spirit, providing the power for the most menial as well as the spectacular effects. "Give me dynamos," he boasted, "and I can make dividends."[43]

Thompson and his lieutenants were convinced that anything less than lively was dead. The value and power of the talking sign, for instance, was in its integration of technological novelty, show- and sales-manship. As La Rue Vredenburgh of Boston's Edison Illuminating Company stated its case in 1905, the talking sign's appeal lies in its "versatility and attractiveness, enabling the user to present such various and extended arguments that it should prove a profitable investment."[44] Thompson's attraction to the Mason Monogram paralleled his fascination with the publicity value of wireless communication and other modern novelties that "spoke" to the masses and, it was presumed, distributed information persuasively, personally, and with less effort than print advertising. The connection between the two means of communication and Thompson's championing of them underscores how civic and business leaders transformed the meaning of "public" city streets and squares from shared property to "vehicles" for private interests to transmit information about products to market constituencies.[45] Thompson sensed the advertising possibilities of "wireless" publicity. For instance, on opening night of his Broadway thriller *Via Wireless* in 1908, which centered on the use of that technology, Thompson collaborated with the United Wireless Telephone Company to send telegrams to every guest in a hundred New York hotels, informing them that a "wireless message" awaited them at the Liberty Theatre; the playhouse was mobbed by people fooled by the stunt.[46]

The cost of advertising on Broadway eliminated the possibility of an expensive talking sign. As a result, Thompson and Dundy substituted assertion for persuasion. Thompson located his major billboards at the junctions of major transportation lines that were also the locations of important department stores catering to the middle-class shopper. The principal sign on Broadway—shouting "HIPPODROME" in garish red lights—appeared atop a five-story building at Herald Square. The *Illuminating Engineer* called it "one of the most conspicuous signs in the city" because it boomed its message in a setting "surrounded on the sides and overshadowed by" Macy's, one of the largest retail stores in the world. Throngs of middle-class shoppers, not to mention thousands of store workers, entered it daily.[47]

Farther north, the block-long front of the theater itself was configured as an electrified signboard that "threw a fire and glare of electric illumination for miles." Pedestrians, street traffic, and, most important, passengers on the Sixth Avenue elevated line could not avoid seeing "Hippodrome," which was spelled out seven times on the façade, each sign using hundreds of lamps. The showmen traced the name of the production in lights, outlined the edges of the building, and ignited the balls surmounting each corner with incandescents. On opening night, the effect was an unprecedented and dazzling advertisement. As the critic Alan Dale approached the theater on the elevated, "a tumult of sudden light hit you on the eyeballs.... If you were blind you would feel the heat of the grandiose display, and if you were deaf you would inhale the vivacity of its appeal." The exterior lighting of the Hippodrome, as nighttime photographs indicate, duplicated the transfiguring effect of Luna Park's lighting; the heaviness of the theater dissolved behind its brilliant skeleton of incandescent lamps. Thompson had brought the electrical ballyhoo of Luna Park to the heart of theatrical New York.[48]

A similar brilliance was used in the stage lighting. New York Edison provided the bulk of the theater's electrical load, practically all of which was used in the production of *The Court of the Golden Fountains* during the Hippodrome's second season. "There are over 4,000 central station[s] in the United States," the *Illuminating Engineer* reported, and "the maximum output of a majority of these stations is less than the amount of current used on the Hippodrome stage."[49] Electricity warmed the greasepaint and curling irons for the hundreds of chorus girls; the wardrobe department used electric irons to press costumes; electric carriage calls operated at either side of the theater; carpenters heated their glue with electricity—not to mention the electrification of the fire-extinguishing system, heating and cooling thermostats, water pumps, exhaust fans, and "no end of telephones and electric signals and all sorts of such things." Thompson's electricians devised an unusual system of duplicate switches to cope with the orchestration of many different circuits in the stage lighting. It allowed thousands of lamps to be extinguished, then immediately relit in a new configuration, which produced startling effects that constantly changed with the unceasing action of the production.[50]

Virtually all of the actual mechanical power systems of the Hippodrome were concealed, out of the view of the audience, in its basement. There was no attempt to make the actual technology aesthetically pleasing, as often was the case in nineteenth-century adorations of the machine.[51] The technological specifications may have been publicly disclosed, but only the effects were seen; the aesthetic value was in the transformations and transportations that unseen machines enacted on the stage. Four hydraulic lifts, manufactured by the Otis Elevator Company, were stationed beneath the main stage, and additional lifts were located beneath the stage's apron, which protruded into the auditorium beyond the proscenium arch. These powerful mechanisms produced stunning stage effects. Lowering the apron disclosed a massive water tank, which was used to create a river or lake onstage. The stage lift, on the other hand, could enact a levitation midscene. In *The Court of the Golden Fountains*, a cast of four hundred was raised, quietly and apparently without effort, eight feet above the rest of the stage. The *Engineering Record* could not contain its enthusiasm for Thompson's "mechanical triumph of high order." What startled the *Record*, which ordinarily covered innovations in bridge construction and manufacturing, was how Thompson had adapted the machinery of industry to the production of amusement. "The undertaking," it wrote, "is in all respects one of the boldest ever attempted along mechanical lines."[52]

Fred Thompson's devotion to the functional rationality of modern industry went beyond pottering with its machines. The Hippodrome showed that beneath his boyish, fun-loving grin, Thompson was very much the systematizing son of his engineering father. However eccentric, he was a worthy successor to the great rationalizers and reorganizers of the industrial workplace in the late nineteenth century, such as Alexander Lyman Holley, the designer of Andrew Carnegie's fully integrated Edgar Thomson Steel Works (1877). Holley was a brilliant designer of plants in which managerial operations and oversight, labor, machinery, buildings, and the supporting supply and transportation facilities were thoroughly and harmoniously integrated. He designed the Thomson works from the ground up to ensure the regular and continuous processing of materials into finished manufactured goods from the suppliers of raw materials all the way to the consumer. This design, in particular, incorporated a kind of industrial aesthetic. Whereas older plants that had grown over time were marked by a catch-as-catch-can layout of buildings, railroad spurs, and roadways, the Thomson "plan"—a circuit of buildings wired together by the gentle, "easy curves" of railroad lines binding the site together and linking it to both suppliers and markets—was determined by the unifying principle of continuous flow.[53] Holley insisted that mass production was as much about the distribution of materials into, within, and out of the factory as it was about the labor of making things. All aspects of production had to submit to the priority of commodity flow.

Even though he preferred play to work, and playgrounds like Luna Park to industrial shop floors, Fred Thompson was as devoted to continuous-flow processing as industrial designers like Holley. This outlook was part of a much larger social and cultural transformation in the United States as growing numbers of businessmen endeavored to eliminate all physical, temporal, and cultural obstacles to the smooth supply of commodities.[54] Whether in terms of the audience, the performance, the production of stage effects, or the management of the enterprise, Thompson conceived of his theater as an orderly channeling of fluid materials. The Hippodrome was "a great Distributing House," to borrow H. Gordon Selfridge's description of the modern department store.[55]

The showman designed the Hippodrome for the rapid, frictionless movement of people, animals, and stage properties. The theater's mass-transportation system consisted of broad semicircular passageways, running roughly parallel on each of the building's five levels. In the auditorium, the principal seating areas emptied in the rear onto wide thoroughfares leading to exits at either side of the building. In the basement, a horseshoe-shaped runway began at either side of the apron stage and descended beneath the orchestra seats to connect stage right with stage left out of the audience's view. Arranged along this broad highway were stables and storage areas for stage equipment. The arrangement allowed immediate access to animals and properties, which then swiftly flowed on and off the stage. The passageway also facilitated creating the illusion of an infinite profusion of animals and actors. For instance, a cavalry charge leading from stage right to stage left circled beneath the audience and reemerged stage right, appearing as an unceasing flow.[56]

The organizational imperative also governed the management of people. To administer "so complicated a human mechanism as the Hippodrome," one observer noted, Thompson employed a modern managerial arrangement of departments—engineering, carpentry, stage management, choreography, costumes, illumination, electricity, scene design, music—each governed by one "broker in beauty," answerable only to him. As Thompson imagined it, the Hippodrome was a consanguineous machine: "We have no friction. We work together like a big family."[57] Edward Temple, the stage manager, was in charge of the "discipline" onstage and the presentation of Thompson's grandly imagined stage picture. Critics marveled at the synchronized order of the choruses and ballets, which sometimes numbered as many as four hundred young women: "The lines of advancing figures look something like the busy threads of a shuttle which are being woven into some fanciful design, sometimes like the filaments of a spider's thread, sometimes like the ripples on the shore as the waves advance and retreat."[58] The Hippodrome initiated a novel form of scenery changing between scenes: the actual mechanics and system of moving the stage materiel were enacted as part of the performance. In *A Yankee Circus* "a smooth-faced boy in a velveteen suit and top boots" barked commands to his troop of stagehands, costumed in white and conventionally referred to as the "Hippodrome scene shifting army." These men, operating with the exactness of a military tattoo, marched properties off and onto the stage in view of the audience. "It was a show in itself to see the way the white uniformed army ... flew at their task and whisked things out of the way," the *New York Sun* reported. Thompson further filled in the gaps between scenes with circus performances, eliminating any pause in action or movement, ensuring that each scene merged seamlessly into the next.[59]

A number of writers expanded the organizational metaphor from the structure and layout of the theater to the actual composition of the audience. The Hippodrome, by virtue of its size and economical prices, seemed a microcosm of the community at large. "The Hippodrome is a city in itself," reported the *New York World*. The *Sun* and the *Times* offered the theater as a unique example of an American consumer's democracy. "There were millionaires in it," reported the *Sun*. "There were ragged fellows who possibly had come by the quarter which let them into the top gallery by questionable methods. There were men of every walk of life—and there were women of every variety of age, beauty and costume." The Hippodrome, it seemed, was America's national and nationalizing theater, serving a revel of regal recreation to a harmonious and democratic audience.[60]

As a whole, then, the Hippodrome arose in the imagination of Thompson, his brokers, and his middle-class commentators as the modern perfection of flow, its ductwork coiling smoothly within the boxlike structure of the theater, incessantly filling and emptying the stage and auditorium, harmonizing the diverse interests and concerns of New

Yorkers with its pleasurable pictures. As at Luna Park, he had eliminated interludes of monotony by channeling his compulsive preoccupation with commodity flow and economies of scale into the manufacturing and distribution of fantasy and illusion for the "great outstanding masses." Thompson was far from unique in imposing a system on the production of commercial amusements; men such as A. L. Erlanger and B. F. Keith already had revolutionized the production of, respectively, legitimate drama and vaudeville by rationalizing and gaining control over the bookings of plays and acts.[61] Thompson's innovation was in making the invisible system of the show register thrillingly on his audience's senses. As one backstage visitor to the Hip's point of production observed, the "most surprising fact of all ... is the perfect system, the quiet that reigns here" behind the stage. A columnist writing five years later noted, without irony, the importance of system and organization to the Hip's stage fantasies: "The fact is what mortal man has accomplished behind the Hippodrome scenes, by drill and system, is as wonderful as anything that the most fanciful dreamers of fiction have imagined." The writer could have added industrial engineers such as Alexander Holley to the list of those impressed. Bureaucracy had never looked better.[62]

## The Test of Supreme Commercial Genius

True to this spirit, Thompson's productions at the Hippodrome as well as his later Broadway ventures were *built*, not written, a distinction that managed to evoke conflicting images of the tool-laden preindustrial craftsman, the mechanized industrial shop floor, and the modern corporate manager. For instance, he designed his first Hippodrome production, *A Yankee Circus on Mars*, much as he had his Trip to the Moon; he already knew where the circus troupe would go before he had a reason for it to go there.[63] For his 1907 theatrical smash, *Brewster's Millions*, Thompson had manufactured the entire play—stage effects, advertising, scenery, stage manager, and star—before the actual script was written.[64] A more revealing example of what Thompson meant by "building" plays was *Via Wireless* (1908–9). Briefly, the plot involved a competition between a hero and a villain for the control of a new and advanced naval gun and the heart of a virtuous woman. The action peaks aboard a foundering yacht in a raging ocean storm; only the efforts of a courageous wireless operator on a nearby steamship save them from going down. During the scene the audience saw only the frenzied work of the steamship operator as he used his wireless to guide rescuers to the sinking yacht. Audiences and critics thrilled at the scenic spectacle of "a heaving, rolling vessel, of booming thunder, flashing lightning, flying clouds and of the big odds against puny man in grappling with destroying elements."[65] In other words, the real attraction of *Via Wireless* was not its melodramatic plot, but its scenic effects. One critic astutely called it a "creation rather than a play."[66]

But Thompson's publicity man, Glenmore Davis, insisted that the play *was* still the thing, only in the twentieth century "it is seldom written. It is generally built." Davis outlined the showman's system in an article published in *Success* magazine in 1909. The text of the play was enough during Shakespeare's time, but today playwrights "depend on a property-man, a costumer, a wig-maker, a scenic-artist, a carpenter, an electrician, a stage-director, a press-agent, a booking agent, and somebody with a lot of ideas. They are the men behind the playwright. They are absolutely indispensable to the success of any play produced to-day."[67]

From Thompson's perspective, staging a Broadway production was no different from administering his or any other big "Distribution House." Although representing Thompson, Davis was speaking in the larger voice of defenders of the new corporate economy. As the merchant Selfridge explained, the "man of business of the twentieth century" knows "that one man cannot do it all, and that anyone who attempts to hold within his two hands all the threads of a great business of the present day fails to achieve the greatest success." The "ability, therefore, to organize, to breathe into others that fire of enthusiasm, that quality of judgment, that spirit of progress, has long been considered by thinking men of commerce as the final and greatest of all qualities, the test of supreme commercial genius."[68] The Shakespeares of the twentieth century, in other words, had to be modern corporate managers who understood, as the financier George W. Perkins explained in 1908, the "all-permeating principle of the universe" and the divine law of the modern corporation—organization.[69]

*Via Wireless* incorporated the rival mystiques of managerialism and producerism that inflected Thompson's billion-dollar grin. Davis describes the preproduction planning and manufacturing of the play, arguing that it required a charismatic "Man with the Ideas," who possessed an integrated vision of the fragmented process, to oversee, command, and integrate the "ten thousand details [that] went to make up the complete picture." The "lack of any one might have spoiled all the rest. Every one had to think hard and work fast and the Man with the Ideas had to supervise everything." The first action in the play was set in a location drawn from Thompson's youth—a fully operating, realistically detailed blast furnace of a gigantic steel mill. The showman had long believed that "to represent the casting of a big six-inch gun with realistic effects on the stage would make the public sit up and take notice." To achieve documentary realism, Thompson took his brokers to the Midvale Steel Works near Philadelphia, where "each man became intimately acquainted with the things he must duplicate," especially the "atmosphere" of "hard, masculine, grimy work—mechanical work which soils hands, faces, and trousers." The process was concluded in three weeks at Thompson's play "factory," the Luna Park Scenic Studios, which another writer called "probably the most extensive establishment of the kind in the world." When the play premiered in Washington, D.C., according to Davis, "so carefully had Mr. Thompson worked out his plans that everything—play, players, and thirty thousand dollars' worth of intricate scenery—dove-tailed together with such nicety that the first-night onlookers must have thought they had been associated for weeks and even months."[70]

As the wireless stunt described above demonstrated, the planning and construction did not end with building the play. The audience had to be built, too. In Washington, Thompson made certain the president, Theodore Roosevelt, was in the audience to give his approval. Around the time of the show's run in Philadelphia, the newspapers reported that a wireless operator aboard the steamer *Republic* had performed a rescue remarkably similar to that in *Via Wireless*. Thompson rushed to hire the operator, Jack Binns, to appear on the stage during the production; the sensational stunt brought attention to Thompson's perspicacity as a manufacturer of publicity no less than to the play. Binns later became a fixture of Thompson productions, starring as the operator in the play and in the Luna Park version of the show.[71]

As in the Hippodrome productions, the built environment of *Via Wireless* involved Thompson's zeal for industrial organization, the resources of planning, expertise, technology, strictly rehearsed human labor, and ideas brought together under his "precise and enthusiastic direction" to produce fascination and wonder. Here were the contradictions at the center of all of Thompson's projects: organized liberation, premeditated fantasy, planned pleasure, the premodern craftsman and the modern corporate manager, the mechanical habit of mind and the boyish spirit of play. An unnoticed coincidence was that the Midvale works, which posed for the foundry scene, had been the laboratory in the 1880s for the time and motion studies that formed the basis of Frederick Winslow Taylor's scientific management principles for achieving "a fair day's work." Taylor insisted that only scientific study by efficiency-minded experts could determine the best way to perform any industrial task. Taylor would not become a celebrity until 1910 and afterward, when Progressives such as the lawyer Louis D. Brandeis championed his efficiency methods as tools for social and cultural reform and revitalization, and it is unlikely that either Thompson or his publicity man Davis knew of him. Yet the showmen were no less committed to Taylor's and other Progressives' value structure of organization, system, and "a greater national efficiency," although in the service of play, not work.[72]

Contemporary observers apparently did not feel that discipline, system, and drill, the essential qualities of mechanical perfection that allowed for mass production in the first place, might at some level contradict or limit the conceptualization of dreams or fantasies on the Hippodrome stage. The stage pictures were so gorgeous; the scale of the entertainment so prodigious; the availability and price of a ticket so egalitarian: what possibly was there to oppose in either the method or the message of New York's dazzling new toy? In terms of social and productive efficiency and flow, it rivaled the "machinery of distribution" outlined in *Looking Backward* (1888), Edward Bellamy's utopian novel about the harmonious city of Boston in the year 2000. It also foreshadowed the Highland Park plant where Henry Ford manufactured the Model T after 1909. But Ford imagined his automobile as a utilitarian tool for the delight of the common man, and *Looking Backward* had achieved its social perfection through universal instruction in "obedience, subordination, and devotion to duty." The Hippodrome claimed to plot a different route to fulfillment and social order, one that avoided both usefulness and submission.[73] Still, we are left with the image of the Hippodrome's sparkling choruses, decorated in Edel's otherworldly costumes, shifting in machinelike precision in the formation of "stage beauty en masse." Which more fittingly described them—the rhythmic lapping of waves on the shore, the filaments of a spider's web, or some glimmering fabric woven by a machine? The very confusion of this imagery suggests the ways in which the Hippodrome, like most of Thompson's amusement projects, destabilized boundaries between the artificial and the natural, production and consumption, control and release.[74] The tensions among the authority and domination of industrial production, the rationality and control of the machine, the power of Thompson's imagination, and the liberating fantasy of theatrical illusion existed at the center of most of the showman's contributions to the commercial culture of Peter Pan. The building, like the productions on its stage, laid claim to bringing pleasure and freedom to the masses through the precise management of technology, human labor, and ideas.

### Everybody Must Be Happy

Thompson's organized hyperbole, steadily manufactured since he had announced his project the previous summer, reached a climax in the first week of April 1905 as the Hippodrome's publicists blanketed the metropolitan area with advertisements, news stories, and circus-style posters. "Doubtless there never was in the history of the world a place of amusement or attraction that was so thoroughly, systematically, and consistently advertised," *Billboard* reported. The week before the Wednesday opening, a full-page announcement appeared in the *New York Times* headlining "The National Theatre." More than an advertisement, it was a messianic manifesto proclaiming a new age of democratic amusement in America: "New York's permanent new amusement institution, the Hippodrome, is the largest, safest, costliest playhouse in the world and first, single and independent of its kind. America's only real representative amusement institution. Representing a triumphant alliance of capital, experience and genius and an outlay of $3,500,000. Its equal nowhere in the world. Ushering in a glorious new era in amusement history and framed for the tastes and pleasure of the whole people." Thompson and Dundy proclaimed a superhuman break with history, "dispossessing the by-gone old age of theatrical routine and circus monotony with stirring progress and rousing reform, breaking free in method, style and price of performance and different and distinct from every other playhouse in construction, equipment and conduct."[75]

The Hippodrome opened with two productions, *A Yankee Circus on Mars* and *Andersonville: A Story of Wilson's Raiders*. Several of the city's newspapers treated the premiere as front-page news with exclamatory headlines. "Bigness was in the air," one paper reported. "Men told each other that this was the biggest hippodrome in the world. 'Big' men sat in the boxes." The *New York Herald* concluded that the Hippodrome had "satisfied the national craving for something that shall be the biggest and most imposing in its dimensions." Everything this opening night "was to be on Brobdingnagian proportions."[76]

From the moment of its announcement, the Hip's novelty and size were integrated with its association with play. This massive citadel out of the Arabian Nights with its Corinthian porticos and stunning incandescent billboards was, in the words of a number of newspapers, a big "toy." "The subway's nose is out of joint," noted one New York paper; "the town has a newer toy." Writers called the theater a "playground" and a "pleasure palace." The Hippodrome was Thompson and Dundy's "new, gigantic toy. It was also New-York's new toy," another paper reported. Thompson succeeded in fusing the Hip's identity with an adult version of childhood, play, and playthings, all of which remained indelible and central facets of the theater long after the Thompson and Dundy proprietorship ended and until the theater was torn down in 1939.[77]

The idea of play as a resource for personal or even cultural revitalization or recreation, as discussed in the previous chapter, had been in the air throughout the nineteenth century, especially as urban, middle-class American men sought to define a proper and constructive use for the expanding moments of the day when they were not making money. The Hippodrome's toy identity was related to this discussion and to the sentimentalization and sacralization of middle-class childhood. The rush to identify and celebrate the Hippodrome as a gigantic toy for adults reflected this ascendant toy consciousness, a familiarity with and fondness for children's playthings and an indulgent nod toward what seemed the naturally irresistible appeal of such trifling material pleasures. Like Luna Park, the town's newest toy was geared to fun and pleasure as ends in themselves. It was closely allied with the sensational growth after 1900 of domestic demand for manufactured playthings and the soaring awareness among members of the urban and suburban middle class of their children's desire *and* need for such commodities, whether as tools for learning or as pleasures in themselves.

Thompson had no interest in toys as tools for learning, but he did believe he had something to teach audiences. His first Hippodrome lecture along these lines was *A Yankee Circus on Mars*. The spectacle expanded on the winning formula of Thompson's original amusement fantasy, A Trip to the Moon. As in the case of the popular illusion, Thompson began with movement from this world to another. "I've made so many trips to the moon at Luna Park," he explained shortly before the premiere, "that a trip to Mars seemed the most natural thing in the world, or, rather, out of it. The only thing that bothered me was finding an excuse for taking a circus there." Given such comments, *A Yankee Circus on Mars* appears to have been concocted as a practical excuse for the circus performances rather than as a narrative incorporating such entertainments. In any event, there is no telling if audiences even recognized the plot, although it was outlined in detail in the program. Acknowledging the ambiguities of audience reception and the ad hoc character of the production, there still can be little doubt that the show, with its dancing girls, circus performances, and automobile-driving elephants, disclosed and encouraged the showman's view of the world. Thompson discovered a reason to go to Mars when he read a newspaper report that a well-known circus company was bankrupt and scheduled for auction. The larger meaning was not lost on the showman. On opening night as many as six thousand New Yorkers were given a revitalizing dramatic tonic of play, in which the fun-loving King Borealis of Mars rescues a bankrupt New England circus from the earthbound enemies of pleasure.[78]

The curtain rose to reveal a small but fully appointed tent circus in performance in Jayboro, Vermont, before a crowd of hicks, rubes, and children.[79] The ballyhoo of the freak-show spieler promises all manner of delights to the locals, a "combination of fairyland, paradise, Fourth of July, happy hunting ground, Thanksgiving, Christmas, summer resort, and Washington's birthday all rolled into one." But there is trouble in paradise: the company is in arrears and a group of disgruntled workers—the Fat Lady, the Wild Man of Borneo, and others—want to strike for unpaid wages. The Tattooed Man quiets the unrest, but conditions deteriorate further when the local sheriff arrives to auction off the assets. Then from out of the sky a gleaming airship arrives and from it emerges a messenger dispatched by King Borealis of Mars to bring a Yankee circus to entertain his pleasure-loving planet. The emissary set-

Fig. 4.3. An ensemble of three hundred Martians proclaimed the wonders of their merry planet—"We work and ... call it play!"—in this scene from *A Yankee Circus on Mars* (1905). (*Billy Rose Theatre Collection, The New York Public Library for the Performing Arts, Astor, Lenox and Tilden Foundations.*)

tles the circus's debts and gathers the members of the troupe to deliver them from the hostility of Yankee land to Mars, where the strange people have not forgotten how to play.[80]

On Mars the "barbaric splendors" of the Elysian Gardens slowly emerge out of the "moonlight shadows." In the background two gilded dragons, fifty feet tall, form a reptilian arch for the anticipated performance. The royal astronomer paces the vast stage, searching the sky for the spaceship. Then a chorus of Martians, garbed in Edel's fantastic costumes, marches on stage "in groups of thirties and forties, each one more glittering in peacock hues of its robes and equipments than the one before"—royal guards, Amazon guards, councilors, aristocrats "with nothing at all to do!" Elephants motor onstage, wearing goggles and driving automobiles hauling the Milkmaids of Mars. The ensemble, numbering some three hundred in all, joins in a chorus: "We work and we sing a song / We call it play!" (fig. 4.3).[81]

The airship whirs in from above the stage, hits the floor, and explodes, knocking the monarch of Mars, King Borealis, from his throne and into a romantic tangle with the Saucy Soubrette of the circus, Au-

Fig. 4.4. In his Hippodrome shows, Thompson mixed circus blare and otherworldly specta-cle with loftier fare, such as the "Dance of the Hours" from Amilcare Ponchielli's opera *La Gioconda*, which was the finale of *A Yankee Circus*. (*Theatre Collection, Museum of the City of New York.*)

rora. If she will be his Aurora, he tells her, he will be her Borealis. A waltzing incandescent love song follows with the glimmering opales-cence of the northern lights cast against the backdrop.[82] The army of scene-shifters arrives onstage, the Yankee circus performs, and then comes the Martian finale, the "Dance of the Hours" from Ponchielli's *La Gioconda*, with 150 young women dressed in costumes representing morning, day, evening, and night, and different lighting effects for each hour. "It was breathless," the *New York Sun* recounted, "the shifting ten-der beauty of it; it was unearthly." The ballet and chorus "fairly made the crowd go mad with the intoxication of sound and sight" (fig. 4.4).[83] An intermission followed the rapturous finale, giving the audience a rest before the Civil War romance, *Andersonville*. In the conclusion, the Hippodrome water tank became the setting for the battle at Rooky Ford, with Union and Confederate cavalry and infantry charging across the stage river.[84] There was plenty of praise for the *Andersonville* scenes, but the impression that lingered from the first evening among critics and in newspaper accounts was the dramatization of adult play, relocated from the earthbound culture of toil to a distant pleasure-loving planet.

The next season Thompson and Dundy presented another double bill: *A Society Circus* and *The Court of the Golden Fountains*. This time the theme was all play, with the fun-starved land transferred to Bohemia, where the suffering aristocrat was Lady Volumnia, a woman whose millions bring her only "misery untold." Orientalist gypsies replaced Martians as the countercultural "other" of hedonism, but again the message was aimed at the audience of "fools" who lived amid the delights of American life and derived so little joy from their privilege. Lady Volumnia is introduced to the joys of spending by a gypsy, who convinces her to sponsor a circus performance with her miserable fortune, a gesture that restores gaiety to the village and to her barren life. With high and low in love (he seduces her, too) and abundance and play reconciled and united in marriage, the entire Hippodrome company erupted in the rapturous song, "Everybody Must Be Happy."[85]

If the audience refused this injunction, it was not because it was left wanting for sensation. For the final scene, Thompson and his beauty brokers assembled virtually all of the electrical and illuminating power of the Hippodrome as well as the entire main stage and water tank into an aquatic and incandescent tableau called *The Court of the Golden Fountains* (fig. 4.5). As the curtain rose, the entire lighting capacity of the Hippodrome began dimly to illuminate the scene, gradually ascending to full power. In the background, hundreds of costumed wedding guests and gilded extras were arrayed on terraces, which, in the midst of the scene, were elevated eight feet above stage level. In the foreground, a golden ship, outlined with lights and decorated with tiers of costumed chorus girls, lay moored in the Hippodrome lake. Gigantic shells encrusted with incandescent lights sheltered chorus girls holding strings of glowing pearls—actually, circuits of round incandescent lamps. As the curtain rose, mussels parted to reveal the female mollusk within. Thrones of electrified bulrushes surrounded the boat, each holding a chorus girl in a bower of cattails. Chorus-girl caryatids appeared to hold up the fountains, which "spouted forth what looked like liquid flames in all colors of the rainbow." Live swans navigated among incandescent lily pads. "When this curtain revealed the climax," the *New York Times* reported, "the audience sat hushed for a moment, and then burst into applause that made what had been given before seem tame." The stage

Fig. 4.5. *The Court of the Golden Fountains* finale of *A Society Circus* was excessive even by Thompsonian standards, using all of the Hippodrome's electrical, hydraulic, and lighting power in one seven-minute burst of brilliance. (*Billy Rose Theatre Collection, The New York Public Library for the Performing Arts, Astor, Lenox and Tilden Foundations.*)

picture was all Fred Thompson—the "American Girl" electrified, animated, and displayed as an object lesson on the felicities of spending. It was subtle as the crack of doom and so brilliantly lit, one suspects that electrical lights throughout Manhattan may have dimmed for the seven minutes that the Hippodrome was the brightest and happiest spot on the planet.[86]

### A Boy Who Has Never Grown Up

The Hip's shows, the "palace" itself, the impresario—all joined in an integrated performance of the showy pleasures and personal profits of the emerging commercial culture. As children's fare served up for adults, the Hip's *Circus* productions were part of the broad and rapid migration of children's fantasy literature from page to adult stage. This movement began with the unexpected popularity of the 1902 musical extravaganza version of L. Frank Baum's therapeutic text of consumption, *The Won-*

*derful Wizard of Oz*. After premiering in Chicago, the glimmering, kaleidoscopic animation of the child Dorothy's adventure in the Land of Oz moved to New York in January 1903 and played an astonishing 293 performances at the new Majestic Theatre. The show made stars of its original cast, especially the vaudeville blackface comedian Fred Stone, who played the Scarecrow part, and spread its mind-cure message of uncontainable happiness during four more years of touring the United States.[87] The musical comedy also inspired a host of kindred theatrical productions: *Babes in Toyland, The Land of Nod, It Happened in Nordland*, and *The Toymaker of Nuremberg*, to name only a handful. Childhood, as producers quickly discerned from the popularity of the *Wizard*, presented a profitable new source of stage material that was easily modified for adult consumption (which usually meant injecting vaudeville-style humor and battalions of chorus girls) and well suited to spectacularization.[88]

All of these shows exploited the appeal of childhood, of the power of wishes, and of delight in the world of material splendor, but the production and the figure that best underscored these themes and provided a name to the urge never to grow up was J. M. Barrie's eccentric *Peter Pan*, which began its long New York run in November 1905, a month before Thompson's *Society Circus* opened. In contemporary discussions, Maude Adams, the actor who supposedly inspired Barrie, seemed to embody Peter's resistance to the corruption of age.[89] She, too, had never actually grown up. Her private secretary Louise Boynton wrote in the *Century* in 1906 that Adams possessed "the soul of an artist and the heart of a child." The *Los Angeles Examiner* described her as "a latter-day Ariel, the offspring of an elf and an angel, knowing all about the sordidness of humanity, but not of it."[90] On stage, according to one biographer, Adams was "radiant as the golden dust on the butterfly's wings ... elfish, diaphanous, analysis-defying, mysterious, almost weirdly winsome."[91] Following this theme, Americans throughout the twentieth century have insisted on the play's fundamental purity and welcomed it as a tonic for what ails the modern nation, especially the culture's excessive materialism. No doubt, the convention of portraying Peter with a female actor—from Maude Adams to, recently, the Olympic gymnast Cathy Rigby—has contributed to the antimodern image of innocence, drawing on the cultural stereotypes that identify what would ordinarily be troubling in a boy (lack of worldly ambition, permanent infantilism, and asexuality) with girls. There is a gendered consistency in the two representations that would not work, for instance, if Peter's adolescent counterpart, the girl Wendy, were played by a male actor. When Peter has been played in a notable production by a man, such as Robin Williams in the film *Hook* (1991), he is a fallen Peter Pan, who has lost his original innocence.[92]

Since its original American production, Peter Pan's charm has been his (her) invigorating imperviousness to corruption. Warnings to the producer Charles Frohman and to Adams to stay away from such "fragile" fare, and the initial "perplexity" of audiences, were cited as certain signs of turn-of-the-century America's jadedness.[93] But Adams immediately saw the magic in the play, and the result, as the gravely serious *Theatre Magazine* declared, was "an epic of childish joy and fancy ... the apotheosis of youth and all its high-colored fictions."[94] According to Boynton, it was as if a new "religion of Peter Pantheism" full of "joy and innocence, freshness of morning, the buoyant, creative, up-building energy of life at the springtime" swept over New York during the first season. Peter's charm was his immunity to cynicism; he knew "nothing of the injustice of the world ... nothing of its ugliness and vice, ... [or] the problems created by passion and greed and cruelty." His was simply an irresistible "child's voice calling to the other children to come and play. And they came, children of all ages, and all conditions; poor, neglected children; rich, over-cultivated children; old, tired children, and listened and laughed and were young."[95] An "artist" anonymously quoted in the *New York Times* explained that *Peter Pan* reminds men of "the time when the universe was but our playground, humanity our playthings, everything gifted with a fairy animation and fairy ears to listen to schemes for mighty deeds and with a fairy power to perfect them."[96] Otheman Stevens, in the *Los Angeles Examiner*, praised Peter for restoring him to the sweet embrace of his mother's arms by showing "us our dead child selves, innocent, clean and sweet."[97] There were naysayers, such as the newspaper critic Alan Dale, who called *Peter Pan* "drivel" and found Adams too old for the part. A critic for the *New York Evening Telegraph* injected another note of realism, arguing that no one was "less fitted ... to play the part of a boy who didn't want to grow up and be President" than Maude Adams, "the most ambitious woman on the American stage to-day."[98] As for such dissenters from the more general acclaim, wrote the *Theatre* critic, "Pity them! They could never have been young themselves. They were born old with all their teeth cut."[99]

Regardless of Barrie's intentions, *Peter Pan*'s perceived advocacy of guileless, eternal youth and play was embraced like other affirmative fairy tales and stories of the era, notably *The Wonderful Wizard of Oz* and *Pollyanna* (1912). It became a kind of morality tale or fable of abundance for middle-class Americans living in twentieth-century commercial culture, with a mind-cure recipe for happiness: a little fairy dust in the eyes will restore the laughter, joy, and "up-building energy." This message emerged in harmony, rather than in radical conflict, with consumer capitalism, providing less a fundamental alternative to cold-hearted materialism than a strategy for warming it up and making it more fun. Barrie's drama provided a metaphorical name for what already was emerging as a leitmotif of the new commercial age in the United States—that having fun and playing are essential to a man's life.

Fred Thompson's life and his publicly assumed role of the enterprising dreamer seemed to have been scripted from Barrie's play. This characterization was far from unique for the era. The men who, like Fred Thompson, were most actively engaged in inventing the new world of goods were assiduous promoters of their roles as a new breed of adventurous, history-defying entrepreneurs. In his paean to the progressive might of the commercial imagination, *The Romance of Commerce*, H. Gordon Selfridge expresses supercilious impatience with the plodding work ethic of such nineteenth-century inspirational writers as Samuel Smiles. Thrift, industry, sobriety, saving, and the other chestnuts of wisdom composing the work ethic, according to Selfridge, were "good but not very exciting precepts," "cautious rather than imaginative." What the twentieth century needed was to loosen the "springs of imagination" with a new generation of "great merchant-adventurers who fearlessly" will lead the progress of commerce: "Imagination urges us on. It is the yeast of progress. It pictures the desirable. It is like the architect's plan, while judgment and effort follow and build. No great thing was ever accomplished by the world's greatest men or greatest merchants without imagination."[100] Thompson's imagination alone, then, did not set him apart from his contemporaries; it was the source, or, rather, the boyish body, of his ideas that distinguished him as a man of the twentieth century.

Although the showman had not reached his thirty-first birthday when he launched the construction of the Hippodrome, the source of his status as a boy wonder of New York went beyond his numerical age. The development of Thompson's imagination, as contemporary observers figured it, had been prematurely arrested, leaving him in a magical middle ground where he was neither child nor man but a marvelous combination of the two. Here was a grown man who was responsible for millions of dollars in commercial investments, yet who refused to raise the curtain on opening night until his mother had taken her seat in the audience.[101] Chroniclers of his accomplishments unquestioningly attributed his extraordinary success to his boyishness. Those who know Thompson, according to one newspaper writer, "are familiar with a peculiarly faraway infantile smile which comes over him sometimes when he is sitting alone. Mr. Dundy, who finances Mr. Thompson's dreams, has said that he is always made nervous by that smile." Other writers noted his "boyish way" of laughing, or his "soft voiced, pink cheeked, lazy moving" collegiate youthfulness and insouciance. The audacity to build the Hippodrome seemed to flow from the unconsciousness of youth. "Only a young man, and ahead of his time at that, could have conceived and carried out such an enterprise," observed circus veteran W. W. Cole. The popular novelist and journalist Samuel Merwin, who was the most determined student of Thompson's career, described him as "a boy who has never grown up."

> He is a sort of everyday Peter Pan who has lived to carry out absolutely his boyish dreams. No grown man could conceivably have done what he has done, for your grown man would have known at the start that it was impossible. His executive ability and physical and mental stamina are those of maturity; his dreams and his courage are wholly the dreams and the courage of youth. The combined result is one of the rarest and one of the finest things in the world. Apparently the only danger in his path is the danger that some day he may suddenly grow up.

"If this should happen," observed Merwin, Thompson "will be lost. It is sheer, sublime boldness that has carried him thus far; it is sheer boldness that must carry him through.[102]

For Merwin the Lost Boys of the new century were the superannuated, dyspeptic men who had lost touch with the dreaming, daring boys inside. Thompson the "everyday Peter Pan" provided a new model for manly success in American life by enlivening the rationality of the mature managerial capitalist with the instinct, generosity, imagination, audacity, and instinct for fun of the eternal boy. During the winter and spring of 1906, both of New York's Peter Pans, the one on the Empire Theatre stage and the other one at the Hippodrome, seemed to respond to a longing among urban Americans to return to a lost Never Land of childhood. Like a primitive or child, he had little sense of history, as contemporaries were fond of pointing out. He was constantly making over himself as well as the world around him, claiming to defy all precedents, limitations, qualifications, and doubts. Thompson "never stops to think whether a thing can be done or not," the *New York Sun* observed. "Nobody ever did such a thing before? ... So much the better; originality pays."[103] "His enthusiasm is irresistible," wrote Merwin. "He sweeps you out of yourself. He makes you see visions. With him you ignore the tremendous difficulties in the way of molding men and women and materials into dream-pictures."[104] Thompson's imagination was particularly suited to a commercial culture that appealed to the consumer's vision through the rapidly expanding use of mechanically reproduced images in advertising, magazines, newspapers, and, soon, moving pictures.

Thompson prototypically captured the youthful spirit of vitality and "high-level consumption" that were later celebrated in the screen and off-screen lives of Douglas Fairbanks and Mary Pickford in the late 1910s and 1920s.[105] The showman constructed—and publicized—his bachelor's apartment in Manhattan in the same spirit of theatricality and fabrication of the self. For his home, he converted a stable next door to the Algonquin Hotel and across Forty-fourth Street from his giant theater into an Orientalist wonderland, a combination Luna Park and Hippodrome. The living room of this "masculine enclave" was lined with carved paneling removed from a castle in Baden-Baden and illuminated indirectly by seventy incandescents and one arc light. "The effect," reported the *New York Morning Telegraph*, "is a subdued radiance." A jungle motif prevailed in the dining room, which was lined in bamboo from India and decorated with Indian embroideries and altar cloths. The chandelier was made of translucent elephant hide. A dumbwaiter connected the dining room to the Algonquin's kitchen. In the library, books were hidden behind special panels that flipped around to reveal

Fig. 4.6. Luna Park and his theatrical successes enabled Fred Thompson to purchase the ultimate toys for grown-up boys— racing and pleasure yachts. Here he commands the helm of the *Shamrock* and, it seems, his wife Mabel Taliaferro, whose head is superimposed on the wheel. (*Billy Rose Theatre Collection, The New York Public Library for the Performing Arts, Astor, Lenox and Tilden Foundations.*)

his collection at the touch of a switch. Throughout the house were elephants, Thompson's favored charm, "in every nook and corner in every size but life size, in gold, silver, bronze, jade and wood."[106]

Like his productions, Thompson seemed to thrive on incessant movement. The riches gleaned from his ventures enabled him to purchase or lease the era's ultimate adult toys, yachts (fig. 4.6). Newspapers reported that his crews won yacht races, that he kept memberships at numerous yacht clubs, and that he entertained Broadway stars and producers as well as the financiers whose favors he sought aboard his boat. Yachts and oceangoing liners, with their alluring speed and luxury, were a favorite melodramatic plot device in Thompson's stage and amusement park productions, appearing in realistic scale.[107] In preparation for the Hippodrome openings, the showman ransacked Europe and northern Africa for circus acts and novelties. In the process, he set and publicized a record pace for intercontinental travel, sailing from New York to England and back in sixteen days. On another scouting trip, he raced from Boston to Gibraltar to interior Morocco, then turned northward to Spain, Paris, and Berlin, across the channel to London, then back to New York, all within a month. Thompson liked to ship his favorite "mile-a-minute" automobile to Europe so he could tour the Continent at his accustomed speed. He and Dundy kept three cars in a garage beneath their Luna Park office because, he explained, "when we need one we need it as a man needs a pistol in Texas."[108]

Thompson dispatched the road companies of his theatrical productions at record-setting and attention-getting speeds across the eastern United States. In 1909 he arranged with the Marconi company to transform his train's barbershop into a wireless station so that it could stay in continuous communication with wireless outposts as it attempted to set a speed record from Buffalo to Chicago. The gimmick combined his passions for speed, communication, and publicity, and, according to the *New York Morning Telegraph*, "was perhaps the most celebrated railroad train ever organized." The paper had already reported that, "spurred by necessity as well as by demands of his temperament for speed and activity," Thompson had "enmeshed his enterprises in and around New York in a network of wireless telegraphy." Even Thompson's wife, Mabel Taliaferro, the star of Thompson's popular play *Polly of the Circus*, was enmeshed in his zeal for promotion. A newspaper reported that her car, the "Pollymobile," was equipped for "light housekeeping," including electric lights and a mobile wireless outfit "installed at great expense." When Taliaferro fell ill while on tour in Chicago, Thompson, with the help of the New York Central Railroad, made a record-breaking dash to Chicago from New York; the newspapers duly recorded the mission of mercy. No relationship or incident was immune to the showman's publicity mill, which distributed the news in releases called *Frederic Thompson's Mile-a-Minute Specials*.[109]

With all of these purchases and stunts, Thompson, like Peter Pan, seemed to crow, "I'm youth—eternal youth! ... I'm joy, joy, joy!"[110] In building his image, he publicized his inability to squeeze a penny. Newspapers portrayed him, not as a wastrel, but as a public-spirited spendthrift, distributing the commodities of play and happiness instead of hoarding his money. "He doesn't care for money itself," Thompson's assistant, Harry Kline, explained. "It is just made to be spent in doing something else." As Merwin observed of the Hippodrome, "There is no spirit, in this house, of an employer who is merely working against the day when he shall have money enough to withdraw to his yacht." He fêted his employees, hosted newspaper delivery boys and entertained metropolitan newspaper executives at Luna Park, and organized an endless succession of circus parades to announce the opening of his various productions. He gave both the Hippodrome and Luna Park over for a day to raise money for victims of the San Francisco earthquake. He was infamous for entertaining all of Broadway on his yacht; he gave A. L. Erlanger a jewel-studded, solid-gold key when he served as the official opener of Luna Park. He was an endless advertiser and self-promoter and demonstrated almost no desire to store away his income; he displayed instead a wish to be known as the Santa Claus of New York. All of these gestures underscored his identification with that vital anticommercial commercial icon invented in 1820s New York.[111] Much as Santa's magical delivery of presents disguised the commercial exchange that preceded—and enabled—generous gift giving in the bourgeois household, Thompson's generosity obscured his fundamental entrepreneurialism and complicity with and reliance on the not-so-smiling worlds of industrial, finance, and consumer capitalism.[112] The pleasures that he purchased and advertised were expressions and extensions of the good cheer, joy, and gaiety that he demonstrated in the conduct of his daily life. "How can a fellow succeed as a showman?" Thompson responded to an inquiry. The "way not to fail is to be cheerful. Nobody can succeed with a 'grouch.' Good spirits and success go hand in hand."[113] The *Spot Light* confirmed his popularity in 1908 when it called him "the best liked chap in New York to-day."[114]

### Distributing Wonderland

Giddy with their own brilliance, Thompson and his partner were swept up in visions of empire—Yankee circuses, if not on Mars, then across the United States and Europe. Thompson's entrepreneurial aspirations, his obsession with the unceasing movement and frictionless flow of mass production and distribution, exceeded the internal organization and system of a single amusement project like the Hippodrome.

The showmen never intended for their great enterprises of adult play to be solitary ventures in mass amusement. Even before the Hippodrome had demonstrated its apparent ability to attract packed houses and generate mountainous revenues, Thompson had announced his intention "to build and control a chain of amusement resorts all over the United States," in effect using his New York operations as both prototypes and production hubs from which to build and then supply a national or even international distribution network of entertainment for the masses. At various times during his reign in New York, Thompson proposed large-scale amusements for a half-dozen locations, including Rochester, New York, and Atlantic City. As the new Pennsylvania Station rose toward completion in 1908, the showman could not resist proposing a "permanent world's fair" for the roof of this major new transportation complex, a proposal it appears railroad executives did not pursue. In 1907, Gates and other well-heeled capitalists were identified as backers of an insular Luna Park for the Seine, "to give Paris and the continent their first taste of American outdoor amusements along the lines of Luna Park." In January 1906, *Variety* reported the imminent construction of a Thompson park, in partnership with the New York Central railway, for suburban Westchester County, "which will tap the country from Harlem to Tarrytown."[115]

Thompson and Dundy also dreamed of breaking into vaudeville, which they never were able to do.[116] A circuit of hippodromes, which the New York theater would feed with spectacular productions, seemed more likely. Four months before the first theater had opened, Thompson told the *New York Herald* that he and Dundy expected "to get a chain of theatres or hippodromes around the country where our big acts can be exhibited." At this early date, the circuit plan reflected necessity more than greed. Not yet knowing whether the original production costs could be offset through the revenues collected at the Hippodrome's box office, Thompson fully expected that he would have to rely on the same system then operating in the legitimate theater; that is, depending on long tours through the provinces for the profits of plays originally produced on Broadway at a loss. "It costs too much to put [the Hippodrome productions] on for just a few weeks in New York," he told the *Herald*.[117] After its long season in New York, *A Yankee Circus* went on tour in Chicago, Philadelphia, and Boston, the only cities with stages remotely large enough for the production, but even these were inadequate. Reports abounded of a circuit of Thompson and Dundy Hippodromes, and various locations were identified: Chicago, New Orleans, Montreal, Indianapolis. Thompson returned from Europe in February 1906 with plans to erect a duplicate of his Sixth Avenue house in London at a cost of two million dollars. London, he said, is "the only city where our shows can be produced for any sort of run." By the end of the following March, excavation work was reported underway and acts were being booked for the first season.[118] European amusement parks, London Hippodromes, national circuits of circuses and variety acts—Thompson's entrepreneurial reveries in all of these cases exceeded his grasp.[119]

All of these projects, viewed together, illustrate Thompson's efforts to devise both a factory process for manufacturing amusement and a national distribution system that would efficiently merchandise his commodities as it simultaneously and limitlessly expanded the markets for his entertainments. In this respect, he was adding his own peculiar gloss to systems that already had been introduced in vaudeville and "legitimate" theater. The problem that confounded Thompson most consistently was that of distribution. He had neither the self-disciplined personality suited to manage such a task nor the sound backing of institutional capital. The adventure for Thompson was not in implementing or managing, but in conceiving the vision of magnificent stage productions flowing throughout the land in a complementary system of entertainments, each drawing on the resources of the others. The closest he came to realizing this system was his Luna Park Scenic Studios, where he built the sets and properties for his Coney and Broadway productions between 1906 and 1912. The rest remained a dream.

With his belief in the audience's insatiable hunger for ever larger thrills and more-spectacular illusions, Thompson, unlike the financiers who in effect owned his theatrical house, considered costs of secondary importance in realizing the stage pictures that appeared in his head. The article written by Samuel Merwin suggests the delirious panic that inspired Thompson's efforts to picture the desirable. "They tell me I've reached the end of my rope," he told Merwin early in 1906. "But they're wrong. I'm going to beat it!"[120] The successor to *A Society Circus* was an arctic aquatic ballet of sixty or more trained polar bears diving into the Hippodrome's stage tank. *Variety* reported that the sets alone were projected to cost fifty thousand dollars, and the bears an additional seventy-five thousand.[121]

By the time Merwin published his account of the polar bear revue in July 1906, Gates and his fellow powers at U.S. Realty had removed Thompson and Dundy from the show. The new weekly *Variety* paid close attention to the conflict between the impresarios and the financiers, which first came to wide public notice early in the winter of 1906. The initial sensation of the Hippodrome had appeared to confirm Thompson and Dundy's hyperbolic self-promotion of their own unique foresight and genius. At the celebration of the theater's first anniversary in April 1906, the partners gloated in reporting that they had entertained three million people during the previous twelve months and collected gross receipts of two million dollars.[122] The string of mighty Hippodromes seemed a certainty.

The first shock came during the run of *A Society Circus*, when attendance unexpectedly declined and profits correspondingly dwindled. *Variety* reported that the show still was averaging weekly profits of twenty-five thousand dollars, but Gates and his fellow investors demanded an increase in ticket prices and a reduction in expenses; Thompson refused. The board simply waited for him to leave the country in January 1906 and immediately imposed a price increase from $1.50 to $2.00 for the highest-priced tickets.[123] Thompson was vindicated when attendance fell and the original prices had to be restored.[124] On the matter of expenses, *Variety* restated Thompson's firm "belief that to cheapen the performance will result in a severe loss of patronage," and that he would "not be restrained in the spectacular productions through a limit placed on expenditures." Gates, the paper added, already was interviewing replacements.[125]

In the final analysis, the conflict involved more than just balancing costs and revenues; Gates et al. were insisting that Thompson temper his extravagance and consider the price of his enthusiasms—demands that must have reminded him of his father's admonitory voice. He was an unrepentant spendthrift whose "whole souled style" of amusement, as *Variety* put it, alienated even the capricious gambler "Bet-a-Million" Gates.[126] With the impresarios and the owners unappeasably at odds, U.S. Realty tendered the theater to more-experienced and businesslike promoters. Lee and J. J. Shubert, perhaps the most brilliant show businessmen of their era, in partnership with the impresarios Max Anderson and Henry M. Ziegler, took over the Hippodrome in the summer of 1906 and ushered Thompson and Dundy out the door. The "triumphant alliance of capital, experience and genius" had fallen apart scarcely a year after it had formed.[127]

Although Thompson controlled the Hippodrome for only fourteen months, his proprietorship of the theater fixed his place in contemporary American culture. This was no mere showman, but "the best liked chap" in town, and why not? Like his theater, he seemed to embody the dazzling possibilities of modern life and the pleasures of spending. He was like the dancing Milkmaids of Mars, who sang while they worked and called it "play." The glimmering public manifestations of his imagination mirrored a private self that was no less extravagant in its appetites. All of his charms were defined by their sheer excessiveness, whether in terms of heedlessly spending money on expensive dramatic playthings for his audience or lavishly indulging his passion for speed, movement, and theatricality. New York had the excitements of Luna Park and the Hippodrome by virtue of this "whole souled style" of play.

Yet the character whom his publicity staff promoted to the public as a good-natured and beneficial spendthrift, living a life of innocence and smiles, also suppressed manifestations of his appetites that were less pleasing to the eye. Just as Luna Park's "cellar door" capitalized on an imagined childhood that concealed, even as it exploited, the violence of his hunger for terror, Thompson lived in blithe denial of the destructive potential of his desires. The showman may have been able to isolate the festivity of play inside the walls of the amusement park or theater, but in his own life, the line separating acceptable and forbidden intoxicants and indulgences was indistinguishable. The tense nervousness of Thompson's demeanor was apparent to anyone who saw him. "I'll admit that I feel the strain, and get nervous, but I keep at it," he told a reporter in 1905, adding that he did not drink or gamble.[128] But others have told a different story. Later chroniclers of the history of Coney Island have passed along anecdotal stories that Thompson kept ten thousand dollars in gold in his pocket and spent "the coins as though they were hot," or that he tipped the captain of his yacht thirty-eight thousand dollars for setting a record pace. An incessant smoker, he was never seen without a cigar in his hand, and several interviewers reported his habit of nervously shuffling silver dollars in his pocket. Neither was he the teetotaler that he claimed. Thompson was notorious among Broadway insiders for his alcoholic binges. It is likely that his drinking was both an aspect and a cause of the eventual collapse of his fortune and health after 1910. Although he relished being the child who always got what he wanted and the Man with the Ideas who was master of every detail, including himself, both identities were roles he played. Other signs—the lavish tips, the seventy-five-thousand-dollar polar bear folly, the alcoholic sprees—showed that Thompson was in control neither of his enterprises nor of himself.[129]

Even without Fred Thompson, the Hippodrome endured and, for another decade or so, actually thrived, proving that New York's "Mammoth Pleasure Palace" was, as Thompson had intended, a permanent and flourishing aspect of the commercial culture of Peter Pan. Under the artistic leadership of R. H. Burnside and, later, Charles Dillingham, the Hippodrome would continue to demonstrate its mythmaking potential, its productions staving off the claustrophobic limitations of age and the confinements of modernity by marshalling the modern technologies of industrial production and the systematic organization of scientific management to the service of the imagination.[130] By translating the child world of playthings and fantasy literature into the new commodity forms of a mass consumer culture, Thompson and his successors seemed to have fulfilled the incandescent promise of luxurious "Entertainment for the Masses." The Hippodrome pledged to transport its audience to luminous, faraway worlds of play. As with Thompson's original amusement sensation, A Trip to the Moon, it was an imaginary journey that was emancipating even as it was concocted out of electrical circuits, canvas, colored lights, and paint.

# FIVE

# Millionaires and Monsters

## Melodramas of Consumption, 1906–12

URING an unusual pause in his frenzied two years with the New York Hippodrome, Fred Thompson found time to read *Brewster's Millions*. The hit novel published by George Barr McCutcheon in 1902 follows one helter-skelter year in the life of Monty Brewster, a sober, well-liked, hard-working chap who receives a startling surprise shortly after learning he has inherited a million dollars from his grandfather: if he spends every penny of the money within a year and keeps his intentions and motivations secret, he will inherit his uncle's even greater fortune of seven million dollars. Brewster accepts the challenge, and for twelve months turns the world upside down laying waste to his million. Good investments are bad, and vice versa. His friends' considerate interventions on his behalf and concern for his financial and mental well-being hinder him at every turn. For Brewster, extravagance and prodigality are virtues, frugality and economy ruinous. His lavish entertainments and expensive gifts unnerve his friends. When he crowns his prodigality with a round-the-world voyage on a magnificent yacht, his friends climb aboard fearing their benefactor has lost his mind. In a final deus ex machina, the yacht is nearly wrecked in a violent Mediterranean storm and Brewster has to pay fifty thousand dollars in salvage, which fortunately depletes his account at the last possible moment.[1]

McCutcheon's comic novel of the consummate spendthrift captivated Thompson, who determined to make it Thompson and Dundy's first production for the Broadway stage.[2] Thompson may have lost control of the Hippodrome by this point and with it the power to scorch theatergoers' eyes with incandescent fantasies like *The Court of the Golden Fountains*. But he was still Peter Pan at heart and undiminished as a Coney Island showman. Thompson brought plays to Broadway after 1906 that were dramatic adaptations of Luna Park attractions and operated on his amusement credo that thrills "must get quicker and steeper and more joyously terrifying all the time if they are to succeed."[3] His productions, with few exceptions, were variations on melodrama, the nineteenth century's favorite form of theater. Thompson sent his Broadway heroes and heroines along rocky journeys through unexpected perils and misfortunes and subjected them to near-misses and fortuitous benefactions that rivaled the excitements of Luna Park's Shooting the White Horse Rapids. The stage versions of his "cellar door of childhood" exposed Thompson's reliance on thrills in all of his commercial amusements and his indebtedness to the commercial amusement culture of the nineteenth century. Yet, as with his other attractions, Thompson used conventions such as melodrama to explore and define new, peculiarly twentieth-century problems and meanings.

Thompson's most popular productions—*Brewster's Millions, Little Nemo, Polly of the Circus, A Fool There Was, The Spendthrift*—were melodramas of consumption, which he made "more joyously terrifying" by depicting the perils and delights of play and spending in the amusement vocabulary of Luna Park. Exuberant in some instances, terrifying in others, but always didactic, his shows were especially attentive to the unease of middle-class men as they encountered and explored the unfamiliar landscape of desire. Again and again the word "fool" was enlisted to register his heroes' (as well as his own) confusion—they were fools to resist pleasure, fools to indulge in it, fools to let their appetites consume them. In other words, Thompson, through his melodramas of consumption, tried to contain the new market culture's divergent imperatives—to make money and to spend it, to work and to play—and to chart a path that enabled men to recognize and to exploit the opportunities that the world of goods offered. All of these productions integrated the starkly drawn extremes of melodrama with the dazzling toys of spectacular realism; gender was the most important instrument he used to plot this course. Thompson deployed two kinds of heroes—one a jovial consuming man, the other a ferocious consuming woman—to mark the route to the future. The man, naturally, resembled himself, a hale and hearty spender like Monty Brewster, whom he sent navigating through the attractions of a modern-day Vanity Fair. The other type was the hideous inversion of the first, a woman of uncontrolled or unlimited appetites, who embodied the anxieties and concerns that Thompson and his play-builders shared with other middle-class men who were beginning to explore the meaning of abundance, consumption, and life in Never Land. These two figures and their rival consuming adventures, rather than being at odds with each other, worked like the separate melodic lines of musical counterpoint—they were different, but harmonically compatible. These figures ran on parallel, complementary tracks that formed a kind of double helix, the genetic outcome of which was a New Man: loosened from the producerist constraints of the previous century, boyish at heart and open to pleasure, his persistent unease with luxury and consumption safely displaced onto an "other" of monstrous desire, the all-consuming woman.

### The Theatre Syndicate

Thompson and his partner Dundy no more were capable of venturing as upstarts into the field of Broadway's legitimate theater than they had been able to finance the Hippodrome with the mountain of dimes they collected at Luna Park. It was almost inevitable that the partners would ally themselves with the Theatre Syndicate once they had been supplanted at the Hippodrome by the Syndicate's much smaller, but bitter, rivals, the brothers Lee and J. J. Shubert.

Although it owned no theaters itself, the Syndicate was the preeminent power in American drama in the first decade of the twentieth century. It had arrived at this uncontested monopoly position quite rapidly after organizing in 1896 as a partnership of formerly independent theatrical booking agents and impresarios, the most important of which was the agency of Marc Klaw and A. L. Erlanger, or Klaw and Erlanger. Under the leadership of Erlanger, a master at booking, scheduling, and routing theatrical entertainments, the Syndicate wielded virtually unchallenged authority. It decided what shows would play where, when, and for how long, and, because it controlled those decisions, it wielded enormous influence in determining what would be produced in the first place.

The Syndicate's ascent to monopoly status resulted from its systematizing the distribution of theatrical entertainment. The rapid expansion and consolidation of interregional railroad lines and national telegraph networks in post–Civil War America enabled touring theatrical companies, often showcasing a star performer, to displace the hold of local repertory companies in smaller cities and towns. Although these developments opened smaller markets to regular professional theatrical entertainment, which may or may not have been better than what the patrons were accustomed to, they also made possible consolidated and centralized control of the theatrical business. The profits of dramatic productions at the turn of the century depended almost exclusively on the revenues a play or musical comedy generated during road tours through the American provinces. Most plays originated in the Broadway theatrical establishment, but few ended their New York runs in the plus column. "It may safely be said," the *Chicago Tribune* reported in 1900, "that not one play in twenty of those produced in New York, whatever its kind, leaves that city with one cent on the profit side of the ledger of its business manager. The managers do not, as a rule, hope to make money there." Losses were tolerated because a New York opening was considered essential in order to generate large audiences on the road, which in turn would offset the initial production expenses and losses and put the company in the black. The principals forming the Theatre Syndicate held major metropolitan theaters across the country. Klaw and Erlanger, for instance, owned the New Amsterdam and Liberty Theaters on Forty-second Street west of Broadway, where Thompson's post-Hippodrome productions regularly premiered. But the Syndicate itself did not own theaters; it achieved its monopoly and revenues by controlling bookings, which in effect gave it power over hundreds of theaters across the United States without ever having to own or lease the actual buildings. Its revenues were taken as percentages of a theater's gross receipts and year-end profits, not from the profits of the plays themselves. Estimates of the number of its theaters in 1904 ranged from 330 to 500; at its height the Syndicate probably controlled more than 700 coast to coast. A large urban theater could be cut off from major plays even if the Syndicate did not control them. The trust could manipulate the tour of a play by barring it from the Syndicate's minor theaters strung along the route between major cities. Maverick theater owners who tried to maintain their independence would find their stages empty while rivals allied with the Syndicate played to full houses. Kept from offsetting transportation as well as fixed costs with one-night stands, a producer would be unable to leave New York until either he or the independents in Chicago or New Orleans had succumbed to the Syndicate. In order to gain access to a theater, a producer, playwright, or actor had to operate through the Syndicate; and a theater owner, to bring the Syndicate's plays to his stage, had to open his house exclusively to Syndicate productions. "So," wrote the theater historian Alfred L. Bernheim, "cleverly manipulating these two factors—the production and the theatre—against each other, the Syndicate began to climb to ascendancy," the lofty and unrivaled point at which it stood when Thompson and Dundy agreed to stage their productions exclusively through the Syndicate circuit.[4]

The alliance belied any lingering pretense that Thompson was the populist playmaker for the "great middle class" of white-collar clerks and petit bourgeois entrepreneurs, and forced a division in his operations, with Luna Park reserved for the dimes of the masses and his theatrical productions for wealthier patrons able to pay the steep prices of legitimate Broadway theaters. Following the route he took with the Hippodrome, Thompson struck a bargain with the most powerful business organization in the history of the American theater, which allied him with a new source of capital: Klaw and Erlanger. After his experience at the Hippodrome, he must have realized the tenuousness of his position within the Syndicate, but so long as his productions filled the theaters, there was no necessary contradiction between his extravagant sermons on play and the profit imperative of the organization in which he operated.

### The Peter Pans of Stageland

The audiences for Thompson's Broadway productions may have been more affluent than his Hippodrome or Luna Park crowds, but the substance of his amusements remained much the same—melodramas of consumption. Melodrama had spread from France to the United States by the early 1800s, and it became the most popular dramatic form of the nineteenth century. Shakespeare may have been the most popular playwright in America, the national bard in the imagination of many natives, but Americans liked best his melodramatic history plays.[5] By the 1850s, virtually all dramatic productions in the United States, whether they originated abroad or domestically, reflected the influence of melodrama. The organized maelstrom of furious storms, bloody conflagrations, narrow escapes, fortuitous meetings, misunderstood communications, peerless heroes, angelic heroines, and diabolical villains, which one writer has called the "melodramatic vision," was ideally suited to the emerging evangelical culture of antebellum America. Evil and terror were constant threats in shows such as *The Drunkard* and *Uncle Tom's Cabin*, but their starkly one-dimensional stage representatives always lost out in the end to "the holy cause of innocence," proving that pure women and virtuous men will always prevail and that despair and pessimism were alien to the American experience.[6] As Peter Brooks argued in his influential 1976 study, *The Melodramatic Imagination*, the "heightened and hyperbolic" emotional drama of the form, with its "pure and polar concepts of darkness and light, salvation and damnation," may provoke anxious tension and sympathetic tears, but it also reassures us of an underlying or "occult" moral order that transcends and ultimately triumphs over the emotional spills and chills on the stage.[7]

Critical guardians of the theater, from the early nineteenth century to the present day, have derided the "melodramatic imagination" as unsophisticated, anti-intellectual pandering to popular emotions, "a synonym for cheap and nasty thrills" and the antonym to superior forms of stage realism or tragedy. Melodrama audiences are not introspective or self-critical, according to the conventional wisdom; they go, as Henry James observed in a *Nation* review in 1875, "to look and listen, to laugh and cry—not to think."[8] The contempt for melodrama echoed the criticism heaped on other suspect forms of popular amusement, such as the amusement park.[9] Such condescension has characterized melodrama's audiences as passive, undiscriminating, reactive rather than active consumers—in other words, as effeminate, a critical judgment only partially attributable to its enduring attraction to actual women. The correspondence is not surprising, considering the similarity in the emotional thrill and pleasure of tension and release provided by amusement rides and stage melodrama and in the demotic profile of the audiences that crowded the cheap theatrical houses and amusement parks in the years before the triumph of moving pictures. Melodrama, or "Mellowdrammer," as the writer and playwright Porter Emerson Browne pronounced it in *Everybody's* magazine in 1909, "is the primary form of entertainment with the Other Half. In every city of any importance it has several homes. All smell equally bad and contain much the same sort of people and exactly the same sort of piece."[10]

In his guide to melodrama Browne assumed the guise of Jacob Riis to lead his bourgeois readers on a tour of the theatrical life of the Other Half. He explains how to get there—"Get aboard a trolley"—how to address the box office, avoid fights with fellow patrons, eavesdrop on the masses, and dress for the occasion: "a pair of light trousers, striped shirt, tan shoes, red necktie, and flat-rimmed 'dip' will be found quite *de rigueur*."[11] Producing melodrama for the masses was not a difficult matter, according to Browne, if one knew the correct ingredients for the unvarying recipe, which he provided in detail for a bored audience of readers who had "gone stale" on the usual theatrical fare of opera, problem drama, and vaudeville. But Browne's condescending tour of the theatrical slums was ironic, for it was meant to awaken his readers to a lost part of their modern selves. The tour is begun as an antidote to urban ennui issuing from the overcivilized life in which all the sophisticated forms of "amusement have ceased to enthrall." Browne recommends melodrama as a refreshing change in the "amusemential diet," but not simply because it departs from the usual. The point, rather, is to witness the way the audience "eats" melodrama. "It's real to them; as real as is life itself—and sometimes even more real than life itself." Audiences at melodramas, Browne explains, "are the children of the theatre—the Peter Pans of stageland." Melodrama, according to his reasoning, offers the same revitalizing stimulus that Fred Thompson claimed for his amusements; it allows the overcivilized spectator to revisit and enjoy again the simple imaginative pleasures of childhood. "But away down in our hearts, don't we, now, honestly wish that we could get out of a dramatic offering one thousandth part of the amusement and excitement and entertainment that these do. Don't we envy them, just a little, that infinite capacity for enjoyment that is theirs? I do," he concludes.[12]

Porter Emerson Browne would have to be considered one of the most important practitioners of melodrama, in 1909 if not in the twentieth century as a whole, although not in the smelly working-class theaters of lower Manhattan. His landmark "mellowdrammer," *A Fool There Was*, which opened that season under Fred Thompson's sponsorship and stage direction, has since been an enduring aspect of American popular culture. Like so many other critics of melodrama since it rose to dominance in the early nineteenth century, Browne conventionally associated its appeal—the "nick of time" plot twists and turns and the "polarized excesses" of its spotless heroines, stalwart heroes, and depraved villains—with immaturity and childhood. Early on, nineteenth-century critics dismissed such productions as "childish geegaws," or, in the words of the *Boston Weekly Magazine*, "mere sugar plums of show" for the "full-grown babies of the town."[13] More recently, critics have faulted novelists (Henry James among them) who are notable for their use of melodramatic techniques for having tendencies "by no means those of the adult."[14] Likewise, David Grimsted, in his 1968 study of the early nineteenth-century stage, *Melodrama Unveiled*, contends that the form established a "fairy tale" world of impossibility.[15] Other theatrical historians and critics in the twentieth century have employed the notion of melodrama as child's fare or even play to describe the progressive march of American drama from mere Victorian amusement to twentieth-century realism and a "theatre of truth." The dominant historiography has Whiggishly posited a kind of life-cycle narrative: a nineteenth-century stage of infantile melodramatic excess, a Gilded Age adolescence when American playwrights "approached maturity, achieved wholeness, attained seriousness," and a mature adulthood of theatrical realism fulfilled by Eugene O'Neill, especially in his *Long Day's Journey into Night* in 1940.[16] In all these cases, as Peter Brooks has suggested, the indulgence of childish melodrama has been posed against the adult's "repression, sacrifice of the pleasure principle, and a refusal to live beyond the ordinary."[17] If, as these formulations suggest, there is something essentially childish about the consumer demand for melodrama, it is no wonder the boy-man Fred Thompson would uncritically champion the thrills of this Luna Park form of drama.

Browne was mistaken both in localizing melodrama to the Other Half of New York and in infantilizing and feminizing the working-class audience as the beguiled objects of the stage spectacle, easily mistaking illusion for reality. Even in the supposed adolescent period of American theater, stage managers (we would call them directors today) such as Augustin Daly and David Belasco kept melodrama thriving in Broadway's toniest theaters.[18] One also suspects that, as much as they may have longed for it, melodrama's audiences, whether immigrants or urbane sophisticates like Porter Emerson Browne, knew that the orderly disorder of the melodrama existed only in the theater. What distinguished Browne from the usual denouncers and allied him with the toymaker of New York was the playwright's antimodernist, middle-class envy of the credulous "children of the theatre," the unrepressed "capacity for enjoyment" of the unwashed Peter Pans of stageland. He, too, wanted to escape the ordinary and to experience uncomplicated pleasures; he wanted to be a boy who had not grown up. Melodrama, as he and Fred Thompson practiced it, was the *new* amusemential diet, the helter-skelter thrills of Luna Park cooked up for the real Peter Pans of stageland, the grown-up middle-class boys of today.

### Could You Help Me Spend a Million?

Compared to the usual tearjerkers, *Brewster's Millions* was an indulgence ideally suited to the new century and the tastes of the Peter Pans of stageland. The book's author, George Barr McCutcheon, was born in Lafayette, Indiana, in 1866 and was well schooled in melodrama by his respectable, although eccentric, middle-class family, which was notable for its love of theater and even actors. George started as a journalist but turned exclusively to fiction soon after the publication of *Graustark: The Story of a Love behind a Throne*, his first novel and the blockbuster of 1901. Graustark is an imaginary Alpine principality difficult to find even on fictional maps. The book set McCutcheon's reputation as a kind of buoyant Henry James with its cheerful melodramatic narratives of amiable American playboys slipping into and out of trouble in moss-covered but essentially shadowless Old World castles before carrying the day and marrying elusive princesses. At the time of his death in 1928, the *New York Times* indulgently allowed that he brought "innocent happiness" to untold numbers of "college boys, kitchen maids, and daughters of millionaires."[19]

*Brewster's Millions*, published under a pseudonym in 1902, was among McCutcheon's more winsome novelistic gewgaws for the grown-up boy and girl readers described by the *Times*. Over the course of its life, according to his biographers, the book sold more than five million copies, a remarkable feat considering that McCutcheon wrote it in a matter of weeks.[20] In many ways *Brewster's Millions* was Graustark relocated to the congenial palaces of New York, but with the same play-ful antics of princely rich young men. The story was built partly with the elements of farce—comically improbable circumstances, exaggerated for the sake of laughter—although it conspicuously lacks the absurdity, horseplay, and coarse humor typical of the genre. The major architec-ture, rather, was melodrama.[21] True to the convention, the action dis-closes the operation of the "moral occult" of melodrama; in Manhattan as in the Alps, the invisible nobility of character, not the markings of birth or wealth, matters most of all. For instance, once Monty survives his trials and prevails, it is not the shallow heiress Barbara Drew but the sisterly and truly noble Peggy Gray, a woman of modest circumstances, who wins his heart and proves that Monty, rich or poor, is still the rock-solid man he always was.

It is not hard to decipher why Fred Thompson found *Brewster's Mil-lions* irresistible. The fabulously rich presented marvelous scenic possi-bilities. The luxurious yacht filled with suave New Yorkers and perilously tossed without a rudder in a fierce Mediterranean storm became, in his hands, one of the more hair-raising stage spectacles of the era.[22] But on another level, the novel's narrative must have flattered the showman, reading almost like biography. Brewster was a typical melodramatic hero, without pretension, kind and good at heart with a stalwart devotion to the protection of female virtue. But he was also a pleasure-giving spendthrift, shedding thousands of dollars more carelessly than ordinary Americans spent pennies. A benefactor of unearned riches, Brewster neither squirrels away his wealth nor follows the shrewd financial advice of his apparently sober friends. Instead, like Thompson, he lavishes his money on the new adult toys and pleasures of turn-of-the-century urban America: mile-a-minute automobiles, expensive furnishings, a yacht, and feasts for his friends, all of whom eventually come to doubt his san-ity. There is no conventional villain or embodiment of evil in this melo-drama; the antagonist is a society that resists his prodigality, scorns his generosity, conspires against his designs, and insists that he adhere to an older model of rational behavior that would preserve his wealth. Monty courageously marches onward and proclaims that, despite the world's misgivings and warnings to hoard his money, spending generates plea-sure and even greater abundance. The hostility that Monty's largesse and free-spending ways provoke among his awestruck friends and associates must have hit home with Thompson, whose earliest efforts to turn every

day into a money-making holiday made him feel like Brewster, "an out-
cast, a pariah, a hated object." The scope, the rationality, and the fun of
Monty's "reckless extravagance" rendered Thompson's own entrepreneurial sprees in stirring prose form.[23]

*Brewster's Millions* was no more realistic than Luna's *Trip to the
Moon*, but in its own way, it was just as electrifying. Monty's squandering of one fortune to win another, McCutcheon states throughout the
book, is a kind of dream, a "fairy-tale" adventure in "Wonderland." (In
the stage production, after his grandfather's death leaves him a rich
man, Monty proclaims, in *Peter Pan* fashion, "I do believe in Fairies. I
do—I do—I do.")[24] The spectator could envy Monty's dilemma and participate in the Never-Landish fantasy of wasting a million dollars without ever worrying that she or he would face a remotely similar problem.
"To witness this performance," according to a Chicago critic, "is like injecting the wine of life into the veins of a man dying from ennui, like a
glass of sparkling water to the wayfarer in the sunbaked desert.... [T]he
farce ... will drive away the blues."[25] Thompson seemed to offer Brewster as he did himself, as a hero for an optimistic age just beginning in
America. "The effort has been wholly to amuse, and incidentally, to uplift, by offering a good wholesome play," he assured audiences.[26] *Brewster's Millions* premiered in December 1906 at the New Amsterdam
Theatre and was an unqualified hit.[27]

Since its 1902 publication, *Brewster's Millions* has almost never been
out of circulation in the United States, whether as book, stage show, or
movie. The uplifting drama of watching an ordinary American lay waste
to a fortune and suffer the rejection of his friends and community even
as he generously shares his lucre has continually found a favorable audience in the United States. In addition to the 1906–7 stage show,
which toured the United States and Europe, and which Thompson's
publicists humbly called "the most enormously successful play of the
century," there have been at least five American (and two British) film
versions, the first in 1914 and the most recent in 1985, with the African-
American comedian Richard Pryor in the title role. As the latest movie
suggests, producers have experimented with the plot by using different
kinds of actors: from the trim original, Edward Abeles, in the 1914 version, to Fatty Arbuckle in 1921 (one of his last roles before the scandal
that ruined his career), the petite starlet Bebe Daniels (as *Polly* Brewster)
in 1926, the British actor Jack Buchanan in 1935, and Jack Benny in a

1937 radio play. In all its variations, though, the story has purported to teach the same sentimental and prudential lesson. The hero is thoroughly tortured by the "hard labor" of spending the original inheritance and derives little pleasure from the effort. Audiences learn that money actually matters less than more-enduring nonpecuniary values of personal loyalty and honor.[28]

But the fun of the show was in the way it mixed these cautionary bromides with the pleasurable pain and thrill of watching Monty spend a million. The splendor of his prodigality, the impetuous risk and magnificent reward of the big gamble overwhelmed the conventional lesson of character over material wealth. In part, Brewster's Millions belonged to the nineteenth-century literary tradition of "immoral reform," the authors of which unwittingly betrayed a fascination with the erotic sins they denounced.[29] A publicity brochure for the original Broadway show tantalizingly asked: "Would you like to know how to spend $1,000,000 in a year?"[30] The brochure enlisted the audience's aid, while another promotional pamphlet was issued in the form of a checkbook containing Monty's record of waste.[31] What made Brewster's Millions "mirth-provoking entertainment," as Thompson's publicity called it, was the vicarious thrill and anxiety of spending.[32] Brewster's Millions, as the New York Morning Telegraph headlined it, was "Rattling Good" fun.[33]

Brewster's Millions was then and remained a twentieth-century "fable of abundance," and Monty, with the one exception in 1926, a kind of modern everyman, exploring, celebrating, and showing how to enjoy the carnival of plenty as Thompson and other middle-class men like him experienced it. In the most lighthearted manner, Brewster's Millions treats two aspects of modern market behavior that have troubled middle-class American men since the early nineteenth century: the morality of spending and the morality of gambling. It neatly compresses into a rollicking spree more than a century of fears about the subversive danger that material wealth and uncontrolled consumption pose to the solid male citizenry of the republic.[34] Despite all appearances, Brewster's "mad race in pursuit of poverty" leaves the world no worse off, and himself considerably better off, than before. At the end of it all, even the executor of his uncle's estate, the taskmaster who oversees his spree, commends his "business sagacity" and asks Brewster for "some lessons in spending money."[35]

The story, as the compliment indicates, also endorses the hero's mad speculative gamble and puts a smiling face on the greed that motivates it. Gambling was a deeply troublesome and highly subjective category of behavior for the nineteenth-century northern bourgeoisie. Strictly defined, gambling violated the moral precepts of producerism, which regarded honest labor as the first cause of social value. Gamblers threatened to destabilize this moral order, on one hand by encouraging "false hopes for quick [and easy] profits," and on the other by "transforming economic matters into the stuff of play." Winners made wealth without actually working for it and gave nothing in exchange; losers wasted wealth they had labored to produce. These presumptions put the businessmen who were the stewards and beneficiaries of the market revolution in a defensive position. They had to justify the naturalness and socially beneficial character of their own speculative behavior and money making activities while also embodying and endorsing the prudential model of risk-averse calculation and steady accumulation. They suppressed the apparent contradiction by imagining a distinction between the rational and productive character of certain kinds of speculation and the irrational and destructive passions that motivated other people to risk all on a slim chance.[36]

By the end of the nineteenth century, middle-class attitudes were slowly changing with the emergence of large-scale industrial and finance capitalism. Such changes can be seen in the responses to the Populist revolt of the 1890s. Angry farmers, who were bankrupted by falling prices, charged that commodities-exchange brokers were no better than irresponsible gamblers who cheated the real producers by speculating in and manipulating prices, rather than dealing in actual agricultural goods. Brokers such as the members of the Chicago Board of Trade deftly fended off such complaints by leading a campaign against the wildly speculative activities of "bucket shops," the small-time and often fly-by-night operations that took bets on commodities prices. By displacing allegations of immoral chicanery onto the bucket shops, the major brokers "painted themselves as guardians of legitimate commodities markets, as solid citizens who constructed the markets that made the transfer of produce possible." Thus a man who speculated via the Chicago Board of Trade actually made wealth; a man betting via bucket shops was throwing his money away. The first was a "producer" with honorable profits to show for his effort; the second a vicious "gambler" who also got what he deserved.[37]

Fig. 5.1. With firm grip and determined jaw, Monty Brewster (on the right) announces he will "take that contract!" and wager his fortune in an all-or-nothing gamble to win seven million dollars in this scene from *Brewster's Millions*. (*Billy Rose Theatre Collection, The New York Public Library for the Performing Arts, Astor, Lenox and Tilden Foundations.*)

The story of the daring gambler and big spender Monty Brewster hit the shelves and the New Amsterdam stage amidst these historical transformations in what qualified as "producerist" behavior, which shifted the high-stakes wagering of big-market investors to the moral center of the corporate economy. In part, Brewster's story addressed and sanctioned this transformation, but it spoke most directly to men who were fascinated by or envious of the reckless individualism of risk. Many salaried white-collar men were fretting that comfort and job security in a corporate society had undermined the solidity and compromised the risk, danger, and zest that, they imagined, had once characterized American men's lives.[38] *Brewster's Millions* put Monty in their place by making his "manliness" the central issue at stake in his venture. The antidote to ennui and a life that has ceased to enthrall is in the gamble, the play of the game, as much as in the money itself. Monty is introduced as a man whom men "took to ... because he was a good sportsman, a man among men, ... [with] a decent respect for himself and no great aversion

to work." In the novel (unlike the play), the original million initially depresses him because it comes freighted with the memory of his "grim
old dictator" grandfather and his stern "business training" in judicious
money management, which forestalls any use of the fortune besides
prudent investment. It is only when Monty decides to spend it all that
"zest" returns to his life. "Wouldn't you exchange a million for seven
millions?" he rhetorically asks a lawyer, who admits the "sagacity" of the
gamble and commends his "nerve" (fig. 5.1). For his part, Monty is revitalized by the gamble, although temporarily. After a year of free-wheel-
ing consumption, the appeal of Monty's reliable, solid character has
dissolved in the eyes of friends as well as strangers. "A year ago," he
complains near the end of his adventure, "I was called a man," but "today they are stripping me of every claim to that distinction. The world
says I am a fool, a dolt, almost a criminal—but no one believes I am a
man."[39]

Despite his critics and self-doubts, Monty seems as manly as he ever
was. *Brewster's Millions* does not argue for uncontrolled spending without purpose, or gambling without good reason. Brewster's impulsive
prodigality is actually a manly way to make money and have fun in a
speculative economy, a fundamentally rational means to even greater
ends. As much as Brewster turns the world upside down, flaunting his
defiance of thrift and self-control, he actually is a virtuous speculator. In
the end his character is undiminished, as solid as ever.

McCutcheon's message, like that of the stage adaptation, was finally
mixed, which may account for its enduring applicability and appeal for
the rest of the century. *Brewster's Millions* presents a fragmented and unstable commentary on the pursuit of pleasure and the virtue of spending and speculating in the twentieth century. Neither the book nor
Thompson's show endorsed resting contentedly in childishness; they
insisted that the fun of spending had to be contained by an overall system of rational values. Uncontrolled spending without purpose was potentially destructive, but equally so was the irrational hoarding of
wealth. At Luna Park, the showman maintained that the reconstruction
of childhood was temporary, a necessary antidote to the adult life of
work. *Brewster's Millions* contains a similar message about the felicity of
pleasure, advocating a cautious liberation of desire rather than its complete repression; pleasure, it seems, must be controlled, although not to
the extent of barring it entirely or giving it full rein.

In most respects Monty was the nightmarish inversion of the bourgeois "ideal of unified, controlled, sincere selfhood," a man who made a farce of the nineteenth-century dream of a rational economy of just rewards for honest effort.[40] The noble "girl" may choose him near the end of the gamble when he *appears* to be broke, reassuring audiences that authentic love is no respecter of persons. But Monty is not really bound for the poorhouse. This confidence, like all the others, is part of the larger venture, a shell game on the scale of an incorporated America. His gestures of warm hospitality are coldly calculated to return a profit; his pose of humble simplicity is an art of seduction.[41] Yet, on Broadway as in the novel, he appears to be as free of shadows as the halls of Graustark. Monty was a hero for a new era of "commercialized hospitality," or corporate service, in which department store magnates and Coney Island impresarios insisted that their private profits were a function of servicing the public's needs. His self-interested manipulations and deceptions were friendly, not mean-spirited; everyone got something delightful from his tunnel-visioned pursuit of profit. His venture was playing on a grandly boyish scale, but also it was playacting.[42]

Monty was not so much a thoroughly drawn and unified literary character as a charming cultural scarecrow pieced together from the enduring and perplexing contradictions of twentieth-century consumer capitalism's need for profit and service, acquisitiveness and asceticism, control and liberation, work and play, managed men and men who played the games they liked best. He is the stalwart suitor attentive to the vulnerability of women's virtue, the nit-picking accountant who "thoughtfully and religiously calculated his expenses" at the end of every day, the heedless wastrel in a "mad race in pursuit of poverty," and the honorable gambler turning one million into seven before the critical eyes of doubting New Yorkers. What may have been the most troubling aspect of Brewster's entrepreneurial venture may also have been its most enchanting appeal: the artifice of his labor produced nothing but seven times the original million, and a lot of fun along the way. In the end the hero prevails and restores his manly standing as a sagacious businessman, thanks to a providential storm at sea, an act of God that makes sense of the venture and underscores the "moral occult" of spending, gambling, and windfall profits in the new century. Everything, Monty comes to see, is "ruled by a wise Providence."[43]

## A Land of Childhood Fancies

Safe landings like these were possible only in the world of melodrama. Scarcely a month after *Brewster's Millions* opened to great acclaim in New York, Skip Dundy died unexpectedly, orphaning the boy-man of Broadway. In the aftermath Thompson "declared that his own success had gone with him [Dundy] since he would now be obliged to take over responsibility of financial detail and could no longer leave his mind free to receive new ideas."[44] Although subsequent observers have uncritically repeated this observation, the pessimism exaggerates Dundy's demise as a turning point, especially given Dundy's own record of financial recklessness as well as the partners' notorious misfires at Luna Park (the Indian Durbar, for instance) and at the Hippodrome.[45] Still, Dundy's death must have been a blow to Thompson, leaving him alone to manage an ever-widening array of commitments while alerting him that even eternally boyish men will die. But there was hardly any reason for him or others to predict that alone he would accomplish any less than he had with Dundy beside (or over) him.[46] *Brewster's Millions* had only just begun its munificent run, Luna was minting dimes, and future theatrical successes awaited Thompson. The greater shadow looming over Thompson's commercial playground was the financial panic of 1907. The period of the panic, which was part of an international credit crisis that lasted into 1909, encompassed the years of Thompson's most ambitious Broadway ventures. It cut into attendance at theaters and amusement parks, and undoubtedly squeezed his revenues, even for his more popular attractions.[47] Yet even as prominent banking houses in Europe and America were closing their doors, Thompson was moving ahead at mile-a-minute speeds, planning more investments in reckless extravagance, more sermons on play.

The most unrestrained was *Little Nemo*, which was based on Winsor McCay's "funny paper" feature, *Little Nemo in Slumberland*, and which debuted in October 1908 at Klaw and Erlanger's New Amsterdam Theatre. *Little Nemo* was one of the most expensive and financially disastrous productions in that era of American theatrical history. Although not the first newspaper feature to appear on Broadway, *Nemo* was unlike any other cartoon of its time, as admirers then and since have observed. In the words of the artist Maurice Sendak, *Nemo* was "much more than a comic strip.... [It was an] elaborate and audacious fantasy," a surrealistic subversion of bourgeois conventions of form and narrative.[48] With its colorful visual appeal and childhood themes, it appeared ideally suited to Thompsonian spectacle, which was oriented more toward dazzling tableaux than toward plot or character development. In the spring of 1907 Thompson and Klaw and Erlanger fended off the new owners of the Hippodrome to secure the stage rights, and several months later announced that the artistry of their *Nemo* would make theatrical history.[49]

The claims of advancing the frontiers of American theater were mostly bombast. The producers actually were embarking on a rational, tested, and risk-averse venture in commercial marketing. As historian Ian Gordon has shown, the "funny paper" features that emerged between 1890 and 1910, such as *Little Nemo* and Richard Outcault's *Buster Brown*, were among "the first widely consumed commodities produced by the emerging mass entertainment industry." During this period, powerful newspaper owners such as William Randolph Hearst were consolidating and centralizing control over the production and distribution of newspapers in New York City. The "funny papers," which the Hearst papers and others so successfully developed as circulation boosters, were important tools in this process, but they also were expensive to produce. To offset the costs and generate profits, Hearst led the way in forging national syndicates for distributing such features as *Buster Brown* and the *Katzenjammer Kids*. By 1908, the year *Little Nemo* debuted on Broadway, rural and urban "Americans across the country could open their [Sunday] newspapers and read the same strips," among them McCay's feature, which was syndicated by the *New York Herald*. At a time when Americans encountered or recognized few nationally marketed commodities, virtually everyone knew who was in the "funny papers."[50]

With *Little Nemo*, then, Klaw and Erlanger and Thompson employed a calculated strategy of tying in to an existing national market for a brand-name product. The local popularity of the *Herald* feature assured demand for the Broadway production at the Theatre Syndicate's premier venue. The national syndication of *Little Nemo* promised brand recognition once the show was put on the road in the profit-generating phase of commercial theatrical production. In staging *Little Nemo*, the producers consciously followed a marketing formula recently proved by Richard Outcault's *Buster Brown*. That comic strip's theatrical version, which featured the twenty-something midget Master Gabriel as the impudent Buster, had already appeared in Europe and spawned three touring companies in the United States before it began a successful run in New York in 1904–5. The stage show exploited, reinforced, and expanded Buster's appeal as a nationally syndicated newspaper feature, a brand-name commodity, and an advertising icon already famously associated with shoes.[51] The producers' decision to hire Gabriel to play Nemo was testament as much to their determination to replicate the marketing formula of *Buster Brown* as to their casting acuity. *Little Nemo* was a sure winner, and, in typical Broadway fashion, Marc Klaw boasted that the firm would spend the astronomical sum of one hundred thousand dollars on the production. Nemo, said Klaw, "that young dreamer of most gorgeous, grotesque and delightful dreams, has given us the opportunity we have been waiting for."[52]

When completed, *Little Nemo* reflected a uniquely creative, although hardly accidental, collaboration of five entrepreneurs of childhood, an almost surreal alliance of capital and daydreams tied in to a national market for fantasy. McCay was famous for exploiting his juvenile imagination. A. L. Erlanger, the architect of the Theatre Syndicate and overseer of the production, had for several years imported such London spectacles as *Alice in Wonderland* and *Mother Goose* to America. Thompson, who was charged with equipping dreamland according to a standard of authentic reverie, practiced little if any economy in designing "the endless multiplicity" of expensive and elaborate scenes.[53] In his hands, *Little Nemo* became a condensed Luna Park for the stage. Shortly before the Philadelphia opening, newspapers reported that three hundred people were frantically working "day and night to properly equip Little Nemo and his company with suitable paraphernalia for their appearance." In the end, Thompson's outsized plaything accounted for a large, if not the greatest, part of the production and operating expenses.[54]

As Thompson prepared the pictures of dreamland, another boyish man, Victor Herbert, was composing its melodies in the solitude of "Joyland," his retreat at Lake Placid. Herbert was born in Dublin in 1849, the grandson of the Irish Romantic poet Samuel Lover, and grew up in Germany, where he was musically educated in the late Romanticism of Liszt and Wagner. In 1886 he immigrated to the United States and embarked on an ambitious career in solo performances, composing, and conducting, nourished by the rich musical culture of the German immigrant community in New York. Over the next thirty years, he operated in the zone joining high and popular culture, constructing an audience that embraced the great "middle classes" that Thompson targeted at the Hippodrome. He wrote orchestral and chamber works for the cello as well as melodies for the Ziegfeld Follies. He commanded the Pittsburgh Symphony Orchestra and Gilmore's Twenty-second Regiment Band (the principal competitor of John Philip Sousa). His ensembles appeared in vaudeville houses, symphony halls, the Hippodrome, world's fairs, and amusement parks. He achieved his greatest fame with his comic operettas and Broadway musicals: *Babes in Toyland* in 1903; *Babette*, which launched the grand-opera star Fritzi Scheff to fame in comic opera; and the hit comedies *The Red Mill* and *The Lady of the Slipper* (Cinderella).[55] The newspapers and magazines that reported on *Little Nemo* depicted Herbert, like Thompson and McCay, as someone preternaturally sympathetic to children, which already was demonstrated by the enduring music of *Babes in Toyland*. The newspapers said that Herbert was "as enthusiastic as a boy over the new task set for him." The librettist Harry B. Smith praised Herbert's "keen appreciation for the moods of childhood." For Herbert, the challenge was in composing music that conveyed the spirit of dreams and childhood in a musical language for adults. "It's all in Dreamland, you know, and that gives great scope for effects, the writing of which appeals to me immensely."[56]

The last of the entrepreneurs of childhood to join the show was Master Gabriel. Early on, Marc Klaw had announced the search for a child actor to play Nemo, "a boy with red corpuscles in his veins," yet "clean, pure and rare as a four-leaf clover." "If treated otherwise Nemo's reputation would be tarnished hopelessly. One night of vulgarity, and it would come to an end."[57] Unable to find a child who combined old-fashioned bourgeois respectability with the red-blooded energy that was the envy of the new passionate manhood, they turned to an adult actor who could contain these rival imperatives, the well-known impersonator of Buster Brown. Born Gabriel Weigel in New York, Gabriel had grown up in Rhode Island and entered show business at the age of twelve. In 1904–5 *Buster Brown* propelled him out of the vaudeville circuit and into legitimate theater. Combined with the popularity of Outcault's cartoon, the show initiated a Buster Brown craze in merchandising, with picture books, dolls, apparel, accessories, cards, and novelties. An advertisement for Buster Brown Shoes in September 1908 claimed that Buster and his dog Tige had entertained "over a million visitors" to Atlantic City during the previous two months.[58]

Whether as Buster or as Nemo, Gabriel's miniature frame managed to encompass the competing models of refined and passionate manhood that Klaw outlined for the juvenile lead. In a sense, Gabriel followed the path of other famous American midgets who had made their way in the theater. The most celebrated was P. T. Barnum's General Tom Thumb, who rose to international fame in the mid-nineteenth century, in the words of historian Neil Harris, as "the perfect man-child, the perpetual boy, appealing to all ages and conditions." Tom Thumb generated his comedy by mixing the stature of a child with "the fantastic costumes, posturings, and impersonations" of a powerful, full-sized adult. He was a child posing as an adult, "mock[ing] the pretensions of the mighty." Tom Thumb was not seen as monstrous, writes Harris, but as an "oddity" perfectly suited to entertain an optimistic antebellum society convinced of nature's benevolence.[59]

Gabriel never came close to achieving the notoriety of Tom Thumb, but he also was a different kind of man-child. For one, he had a reputation that dispelled the aura of middle-class respectability that Barnum constructed around his star. Gabriel was neither a juvenile at heart nor a stranger to pleasure, as the *Philadelphia Telegraph* noted in 1906:

> The contrast between the little man's mature conversation and his personal appearance is almost uncanny. He has the delicate and perfectly formed limbs and body of a child of 8, and his face is innocent of whiskers, despite his 23 years. To hear this cherub sit and talk about the gayeties of Broadway or the spice of New Orleans or the wickedness of 'Frisco as one cognizant of the world, the flesh and the devil, is a trifle confusing and disturbing. It's all right if you close your eyes, but it seems all wrong with this apparent infant in view.[60]

As both lusty rake and rosy-cheeked cherub, Gabriel could imagine and represent the full range of pleasures inside the cellar door of childhood.

Arriving on stage during the reign of grown-up boys like Fred Thompson, Gabriel also performed some of the most important complexities and contradictions within the emerging culture of Peter Pan. His depiction of boyhood did not travesty politics or power in the manner of Tom

213

Fig. 5.2. As these scenes from *Little Nemo* show, Master Gabriel, although a seasoned actor in his mid-twenties, was literally a boy-man who could pass for eight years old. (*Billy Rose Theatre Collection, The New York Public Library for the Performing Arts, Astor, Lenox and Tilden Foundations.*)

Thumb's ironic manhood. Thumb looked like a child but played the role of a grown man. Gabriel usually dressed in the fanciful costumes of boys, not men, and playacted what he looked like. He so resembled a child that in publicity photographs for the production, he looked just like McCay's son, the actual model for Little Nemo.[61] His roles turned the world upside down by grasping power with infantile hands, making grown men look foolish in the bargain while suggesting the advantages that boys had over men. In *Buster Brown*, for instance, Gabriel's child character steals the authority of his rich father, who has been weakened by superfluous wealth, and restores order to the family and community by leading the successful campaign to elect his sister's industrious and virtuous fiancé mayor of the town.[62] In *Little Nemo*, Gabriel played the child-dreamer who restores vitality and youth to the aging King Morpheus. His roles enacted a rebelliousness, freedom, and longing for something more that rubbed against the limitations of middle-class manhood. He made fun of grown-ups who worried that their power returned so little pleasure and feared the risks of unbounded desire.

Gabriel himself claimed to be such a man. According to the newspapers, he, too, had forgotten how to play. So to prepare himself for the role, he haunted the city's parks and playgrounds to study real children. "I never quite enjoyed the happiness of childhood that comes to other children," he explained. "I began to be grown up so awfully early." Gabriel tailored his Nemo to be a redemptive representation of actual child life, accurate in the detail of its emotions and desires and an instructive model in play. "I've tried in all of them to get the actions of a real little boy, so that every mother and father in the audience will recognize it as being what Billy or Harry does at home in just such humors." He wanted his Nemo to be "just like a thousand other little boys who go to bed to dream of what grown-ups [would] give half of their lives to see again, the visions of Slumberland" (fig. 5.2). Getting to be Nemo restored his youth.[63] Or at least it enabled him to pretend to be a man whose youth had been restored by rediscovering how to play. This was one of the essential fictions of Peter Pan culture, which sold visions of the "land of childhood fancies" that endorsed boyish play while domesticating and disguising the carnal possibilities of 'Frisco and the French Quarter; Peter Pan had red blood clean and pure.[64]

*Little Nemo* had its pre-Broadway opening in Philadelphia on 28 September 1908, with Thompson's "visions of Slumberland" arrayed across the stage. It was, as Winsor McCay summarized for the *New York Morning Telegraph*, "Victor Herbert's masterpiece,... and Frederic Thompson's wildest fancies."[65] As in Thompson's Hippodrome productions, the plot was swamped by the welter of scenic wonders, but the message was there: recovered childhood and play are antidotes to the ennui and exhaustion of modern men "a-working hard all day." It was reinforced by the song lyrics, with their persistent references to toys, dolls, and fairy-tale characters, by scenes of amusement parks, playgrounds, playrooms, dancing teddy bears, and circus animals, and by the action of the plot, a narrative quest for a reinvigorating playmate and the restoration of youth to an aging adult. As *Theatre* observed, "It is 'Peter Pan' all over again, but 'Peter Pan' with the accompaniment of stirring and tuneful music, capital songs, glittering pageants, graceful ballets and clever fooling."[66]

## His Miniature Wife

In the two years that saw *Brewster's Millions* win the jackpot and *Little Nemo* almost singlehandedly lose it, Thompson played the role of reckless spendthrift as if he were a grown-up babe in toyland. His character was cast in sharper relief, with a new shade of immaturity and publicity, in December 1906. The month before, when *Brewster's Millions* was just about to open, Thompson attended a performance of Robert Browning's *Pippa Passes*. Reciting the poetic lines of the happy peasant girl was Mabel Taliaferro, a nineteen-year-old actor who by this point had been on the American stage for sixteen years. At once childlike and pretentiously serious, Taliaferro (pronounced Tolliver) instantly captured his attention and within weeks the veteran player of children and fairies had eloped with the everyday Peter Pan of New York.[67]

The marriage of Fred Thompson and Mabel Taliaferro promised to indulge, flatter, and promote the showman's boy-man image as cunningly as his Hippodrome productions and garage full of toys. Taliaferro's faylike personality—"that vague something," as one newspaper put it, "which reaches out across the footlights and touches the center of sentiment beneath every waist or waist coat"—seemed ready-made for Thompson, who, as her husband and manager, virtually cast her as his "girl wife."[68] Dashing about town in the fully equipped Pollymobile that he purchased for her or being rescued after his well-publicized cross-country dash to her side, Taliaferro had an assigned role in the spectacle of their marriage, with sweetness its major key. All the productions in which he cast her—especially *Polly of the Circus*, *Cinderella*, and *Springtime*—exploited her delicacy and presexual childishness (fig. 5.3). "Mr. Thompson likes me best in sweet, dainty ingénue rôles," Taliaferro stated in a 1908 interview. When prodded to reveal the roles she preferred, she replied, "Do you know ... I was speaking of that very thing to Fred—er—Mr. Thompson, only this morning? We agreed exactly." The writer named the couple "The Fredthompsons."[69]

Like her husband, Taliaferro was a grown-up child whose notoriety and definition of self were linked to her young age and to the childlike qualities and roles she enacted. Critics frequently compared her to Peter Pan's impersonator, Maude Adams. "I am a great believer in youth," Taliaferro declared in 1908. "I think that it is one of the greatest assets that one can possess."[70] Her first dramatic line, delivered at age three in the popular melodrama *Blue Jeans*, was "Mamma, do you think Santa

FREDERIC THOMPSON PRESENTS

MABEL TALIAFERRO
AND
POLLY OF THE CIRCUS
BY MARGARET MAYO
ONE YEAR AT THE LIBERTY THEATF.E.N.Y.

Fig. 5.3. Even with whip in hand, Mabel Taliaferro appears to be all doe-eyed soulfulness and girlish delicacy in this poster for *Polly of the Circus*. (*Billy Rose Theatre Collection, The New York Public Library for the Performing Arts, Astor, Lenox and Tilden Foundations.*)

Claus will come to-night?" In a sense, she never stopped asking and hoping. Her acting persona was built on the sentimentalized child's wish for warm indulgence: Little Eva in *Uncle Tom's Cabin*; the "careworn, sweet-natured little house mother" in *The Children of the Ghetto*; Ermyngarde in *The Little Princess*; the fairy in Yeats's poetic drama *The Land of Heart's Desire*; *Cinderella*, her first major motion-picture role; and many others. Contemporary critics varied in their assessment of her acting abilities, especially as she grew older, but no one denied her trademark combination of sweet, elfin charm with mature, womanly soulfulness. Her voice, observed a critic in 1901, "is a curious mixture of the child's and the woman's, sweet and melodious without the penetrating shrillness of youth." In 1904 another described her as a "wistful little bundle" with a "pathetic little smile and childish face [that] are inspiratious." Slight of stature—by one account, she weighed eighty-five pounds—and self-consciously serious, Taliaferro combined frailty with power, instinct with intellect, innocence with knowledge, independence with vulnerability, publicity with domesticity. She was little girl and New Woman.[71]

Taliaferro's New Womanhood was underwritten by her publicity and resistance to domestication. As a turn-of-the-century social phenomenon, the "New Women" referred to several generations of working-class women who labored outside the home and of middle-class women who put careers before marriage to men. The earliest such women, who were slightly older than Fred Thompson, were notable for abstaining from husbands. Often college educated, many directed their energies toward mothering the troubled, urbanizing nation; their "bad" counterpart was the prostitute who abjured family altogether for a life of pure sexual appetite. In the early twentieth century these categories of newness were revised in response to changes in the urban economy. Some middle-class observers regarded New Women as a distinctly working-class phenomenon, the second-generation offspring of recent European immigrants who labored outside the home, especially as manufacturing operatives and retail shopgirls. In the "Fourteenth Street" paintings of John Sloan or contemporary psychiatric investigations of "hypersexual" women, the working "girl" and her often unembarrassed pursuit of commercial and sexual pleasures represented the new and disturbing social autonomy of urban women, especially the directness and openness with which they appropriated and acted on the male prerogative of sexual pleasure.[72] Such women were neither pure in the conventional sense nor prostitutes, which made their behavior so difficult to categorize except as "new." Other critics targeted middle-class or college-educated women who, as Anna A. Rogers wrote in the *Atlantic Monthly*, shunned the work for which nature designed them—"the dignified *duty* of wedlock" and self-abnegating service to husband and family—for "the worship of the brazen calf of Self." Rogers's article, "Why American Marriages Fail," contended that egoism was to be expected and desired in a man, who could channel selfishness into socially beneficial "hard work." But when a woman gloried "in the assertion of her 'persistent self,'" she unfit herself for marriage and subjected her unsuspecting husband to the "devouring" appetites of her childish ego. Whether they married or not, these "new" New Women neglected family for "self."[73] As these examples suggest, middle-class women and men commonly regarded the New Woman's violation of gender expectations as cause and symptom of the disturbing dynamism and disorder of contemporary urban society. Her rejection of motherhood for power and pleasure, even more than her rejection of husbands, encapsulated all that had gone wrong in the modern world. She was, writes historian Carroll Smith-Rosenberg, "a condensed symbol of disorder and rebellion."[74]

The very ambiguity and instability of Taliaferro's identity marked her as a New Woman. Taliaferro was no little girl, but a professional and nearly lifelong actor who had grown up in the public world of the turn-of-the-century theater. Her mother had been an actor and mistress of wardrobe at the Cincinnati Opera House. Her younger sister Edith, a "saucy little brunette," played harder-edged children's roles, such as the title character in *Rebecca of Sunnybrook Farm*. By the age of thirteen, Mabel was earning seventy-five dollars a week. When leading roles began arriving in 1904, she felt "emancipated!" from "child parts!"[75] But she continued to be cast in child-woman roles, perhaps the most demanding of which was that opposite Fred Thompson. Taliaferro, as constructed for public and private consumption, was a historical compromise: an "autonomous professional [woman] in a non-domestic world" and a child-woman whose pathetic eyes and physical frailty signified her essential vulnerability and dependence.[76] She managed to live and perform both roles, however confusing or contradictory they were.

Once *Pippa Passes* closed, Thompson and Taliaferro, boy-man and girl-woman, eloped after a fairy-tale engagement of two weeks. As the couple embarked on a four-month automobile tour of Europe, newspapers announced that his wife would retire from the stage. The absence was short-lived. Soon after their return, the couple began traveling with Ringling Brothers' Circus to prepare for *Polly of the Circus*, in which Taliaferro would play the title role.[77] *Polly*, as critics noted, was a small-scale Hippodrome production, but its depiction of an amusement-loving man tormented by a larger world, hopelessly grown-up and hostile to fun, also made it the thematic kin of *A Yankee Circus*. In the words of Thompson's publicity men, *Polly* was "a three ring circus with a sermon"—on play—"thrown in."[78]

Taliaferro played a rough-edged equestrienne whose unrefined manners and circus argot disguise her true femininity. After her circus inexplicably pitches its tent next to the church of a small-minded village, the outraged locals plead with the parson to get rid of the menace. But the Reverend John Douglass covertly savors such pleasures, remembering the childhood delight of circuses. When several circus hands arrive at the parsonage bearing the motionless form of Polly, who has been injured during her performance, Douglass takes her in and nurtures her for the next year, healing her injuries and improving her elocution. In exchange, Polly shows him the circus's familial bonds and love and her inner beauty. The minister and the frail equestrienne are falling in love, but Polly, concerned that she has shamed her protector, rejoins the circus. The parson thinks his little patient prefers the big tent to him. The troupe eventually returns to town. Polly, distracted by unfulfilled love, again falls from her horse. This time Douglass is waiting there for her. A final tableau shows the embracing couple watching the circus wagons trail off into the distance.[79]

The show opened about a month after the couple's first wedding anniversary and seemed to confirm that Thompson's success with *Brewster's Millions* had not been chance alone. Following a long Broadway run, it continued to thrive on the road. The New York department store Simpson Crawford tied in with a *Polly* gown and hat, and Taliaferro's portrait graced the city's fashionable women's magazines. Reviewers dismissed the drama but praised its uplifting influence. Thompson concurred: "Sunshine is the light that counts.... Why depict sordid things that exist in the dark?" Taliaferro, full of radiant youth, seemed bereft of shadows. "She is hardly bigger than the real children she plays with in one scene ... a fairylike youngster of about ninety pounds, suggesting all the experience of an actress who has lived twice her twenty years," commented the *Chicago Tribune*. The *Bohemian* was won over by the show's "eternal spirit of youth," the *Metropolitan* by its effect of making audiences feel "like children again in our pleasure and curiosity."[80]

With so much sunshine, though, shadows were bound to show up. Contained within the show's three-ring sermon on the benefits of circus performances was a special concern on the showman's part to correct the usual associations of female players with prostitutes. "To us," noted a Thompson press release, "circus women seem a race almost as alien as the Gypsy, and we are apt to dismiss them with that same familiar phrase, 'Women of the circus.'" Not so. *Polly* showed that amusements actually cultivate "sweet flowers of femininity rivaling sometimes in mental and physical fragrance their non-professional sisters." "In this production Frederic Thompson reaches out beyond the footlights and taps the conscience of the audience on its shrinking shoulders." Such preachiness suggests that Thompson had his wife in mind when he came to the defense of circus women; Taliaferro may not have been immune from this undesirable association even in her husband's mind. Whether the showman was reprimanding himself or his audience in these releases, the therapeutic stage romance between the patient-child Polly and the minister, with its reciprocal healing and asexuality, resembled the "Fredthompsons" on any number of points but the concluding one. Polly's respectability finally rests on her renunciation of self *and* shows. As she concedes toward the end, "Whither thou goest, I will go, for thy people shall be my people, and thy God, my God." Publicity releases for the show promised that Taliaferro's delivery of this line alone was enough to buoy "anyone who is pessimistic or gloomy, anyone who has lost faith, in fact anyone whose life is without sufficient sunshine." But the *Theatre* critic doubted that Polly got the better end of the deal, and Taliaferro herself finally proved less pliant and self-sacrificing than the woman of the circus.[81]

The tableau may have been wishful thinking on Thompson's part. With the show's success, Thompson again spoke of Taliaferro doing a "Polly," retiring to domestic life, but it was not long before he announced her return in another children's tale of unseen beauty triumphing over injustice—*Cinderella*. It never happened, probably because revenue considerations demanded Taliaferro's star presence in the *Polly* touring production (fig. 5.4). She played the role on the road for almost a year. *Polly* was her biggest hit in a long career on stage and screen, and her only success with Thompson. Her husband-manager developed additional and expensive roles for her, all syrupy romances with Taliaferro playing the delicate feminine creature at the center of larger male conflicts, but they flopped as badly as the Indian Durbar.[82]

These productions evinced Thompson's determination to construct, enhance, and merchandise his ingenue's virginal childishness. This enterprise merged with the showman's eye for novelty in 1909, when, convinced that her celebrity needed a boost, Thompson changed her name to "Nell." He announced the new identity for her debut in *Springtime*, written specially for her by Harry Leon Wilson and Booth Tarkington. In a promotional brochure, Thompson explained that Taliaferro

Fig. 5.4. This shot of the *Polly of the Circus* road company leaving for Chicago provides a rare view of the "Fredthompsons" together. Taliaferro stands above the crowd at the center of the train platform, her husband to her left. (*Billy Rose Theatre Collection, The New York Public Library for the Performing Arts, Astor, Lenox and Tilden Foundations.*)

was "foreign," too difficult for American tongues to pronounce. What is more, it "indicated the massive spread of a grand opera soprano rather than the slender delicacy of a young American girl," capturing none "of the daintiness and girlish charm of the little star." Of course, the label also alluded to the beloved literary heroine of Charles Dickens's *Old Curiosity Shop*. An actor changing names was not unusual, but to switch in the midst of a successful career seems a bewildering decision. Nor is there evidence that the couple agreed exactly on the strategy. It was one thing for a woman to change her married name, but quite another for a man to give his wife an entirely new name, and one that implied permanent infantilization. It was as if Taliaferro herself were composed of staff, as impermanent and subject to marketing needs as Luna's plaster palaces. The cover of the *Springtime* brochure suggested an underlying tension. Beneath her photograph, Taliaferro announced in script, "To my friends—Please in the future know me as Nell," then signed her original name in full. The degree of Thompson's cynical loyalty to Taliaferro's delicacy and charm and of his detached architectural regard for her as "nothing more nor less than scenery" was further disclosed in publicity releases detailing his efforts to register "Nell" as a trademark. When he ran into obstacles because she was not a product involved in interstate commerce, he transported the entire production of *Springtime* across the Hudson River to New Jersey and back.[83] That solved that problem, but it did nothing for the play or the marriage. *Springtime*, a revised and domesticated *Romeo and Juliet* that opened in October 1909, was notable for its expense, which was publicized (and likely exaggerated) as one hundred thousand dollars. In Thompson's hands, the play ended happily; the tragedy was at the box office. Critics loathed it and the performance of poor Nell, who shortly after the opening revived her old name.[84]

Even before Taliaferro's career began taking this unanticipated beating, the fairy tale behind the scenes was falling apart. In her later divorce suit, Taliaferro claimed that in August 1909, Thompson violently shook her "several times" and twisted her wrist, "which hurt me until I would cry out loud." This assault occurred shortly after the *Polly* tour had ended and the plans for "Nell" were announced, and several months before *Springtime*. Soon after this incident, Taliaferro left New York, explaining only that she and a friend from Chicago were taking "a trip to suit us." The gossip columnist for the *New York Dramatic Mirror* revealed that Thompson had "serious misgivings" about the trip, as well he might have. The vacation to Utah, California, and other Western scenes was later recounted by the friend in the *Ladies' World*, with no reference to the husband left behind. The author was another New Woman, the prolific magazine writer Clara E. Laughlin. What she did describe, and in a suggestively erotic vocabulary, were the two women's escape from the bonds of their lives and into a "female world of love" in the West. When Taliaferro came to her after the *Polly* tour, Laughlin later wrote in her autobiography, "the child was tired in body, mind, and soul." Their first stop was near Salt Lake City with the actor Ada Dwyer (Russell), who later became the "very intimate friend" of the poet Amy Lowell. In Dwyer's garden the women picked "big black California cherries" and ate to their "heart's content." On the California coast, in a Franciscan monastery, and in the hills above Santa Barbara, Laughlin and Taliaferro discovered a serenity and release from self that "we had been seeking all our lives." Among the few belongings Taliaferro had packed were volumes of mystical poetry and musings by "Fiona Macleod," the name of the feminine soul of the "flamboyant Celtophile"

William Sharp (1855–1905), one of the more eccentric literary inspira-
tions of the Celtic branch of late-nineteenth-century spiritualism.
Laughlin and Taliaferro basked in the western sunshine, played house
together, and filled themselves with Fiona's "most exquisite spirit." "We
spent a great deal of time hunting spots where the dark was deep and
velvety, and watching the stars go wheeling in the firmament—the
while we 'stretched' our souls, thinking about such things as stars suggest." Upon her return to New York in September, Taliaferro told a gossip columnist, the "Matinee Girl," "It was so good to lose ourselves."[85]

The illicit potential of Taliaferro's asylum among such "new" and
man-shunning women after the violent attack was not lost on Thompson. It would be problematic to label Laughlin a lesbian in the contemporary sense—that is, as a woman who exclusively desires females as
sexual partners. The term itself was only just coming into vogue among
sexologists and middle-class journalists, and intimate female friendships or "marriages" were not yet automatic evidence of sexual "perver-
sion." But her prose descriptions of luscious cherries and velvety
darkness suggest an eroticism in the friendship that must have troubled
the abandoned husband. Their relationship, at least as Laughlin described it, implied the "emotional intensity" and "sensual and physical
explicitness" characteristic of the "female world of love and ritual" that
Carroll Smith-Rosenberg has found among Northern women before the
Civil War. Such loving and often mothering relationships, which developed in the sex-segregated social atmosphere of the antebellum middle
class, were regarded as normal for the years prior to a woman's marriage. By the end of the nineteenth century, these same-sex friendships
were more often found among women who chose not to marry.[86] Laughlin, a determinedly itinerant and "scribbling" woman who stayed single,
toured with and mothered Taliaferro and referred to her in the diminu-
tive as a "child" or "Little Star." Her autobiography describes an instance of stage fright, during Philadelphia rehearsals for *Springtime*,
when Taliaferro, dressed in her "nightie," left the hotel room she shared
with Thompson and went to Laughlin's room. "May I come in your
bed?... Please! I'm *so* scared!" Laughlin "took her in and quieted her, and
soon she fell asleep." Both were awakened two hours later when
Thompson called in a panic, looking for his wife.[87]

What kind of sexual relationship Taliaferro and Thompson had is no
less a matter of speculation. Including Taliaferro's touring time, when

the couple often were together, they cohabited for four years. They never had children, but childlessness was not remarkable at a time when middle-class married couples in general were trying to limit family size and routinely practiced birth control. Over the previous century, fertility rates had declined by at least half for women of Taliaferro's race and class. Still, the on-and-off-again plans for retirement (implying childbearing) hint at confusion in the household, if not troubled intimacy. Middle-class women still expressed their femininity most concretely by bearing and rearing children, and men their masculinity by fathering offspring. Those particular gender interests, in their case, may have conflicted with material interests—namely, Thompson's investment in Taliaferro and his increasingly desperate revenue needs. But other considerations, which underwrote their respective identities as children, may also have argued against donning the uniforms of adulthood. Beyond keeping her off the stage, maternity presumably would have ruined Taliaferro's slender delicacy, and paternity eroded Thompson's pink-cheeked boyishness and nonchalant indifference to adult concerns. Given these conflicting dictates, we can only wonder how Peter Pan and his dainty ingenue managed their child identities in the conjugal playground. Offstage, did Taliaferro portray the sweet flower of femininity or a grown woman with carnal desires? Did Thompson assume the role of guileless, asexual boy or that of the raffish juvenile who shot the Chutes with a "girl" in either arm? From one perspective, it is reasonable to suspect that a man who sold pleasure to millions would insist on his share. But it seems more likely that Thompson pursued Taliaferro in the first place for the ways in which she assisted him in both evading and shouldering the responsibilities of being a man. Despite occasional protests, both relished thinking of themselves as prepubescent children; her wish to play Cinderella was matched by his determination to make her wish come true. When Taliaferro expressed a preference for the intimate company of Laughlin, she may well have reminded Thompson of what he sacrificed by dwelling in Never Land.[88]

In December 1909, in the midst of *Springtime*'s short season, the *New York Times* reported the couple's third anniversary gala, but domestic felicity had not returned permanently.[89] Taliaferro later charged in her divorce action that Thompson attacked her three more times in 1910. The first time, in January, occurred shortly "after retiring," to bed, when Thompson "got up and began abusing me and dragged me across the floor and threw me against the wall and pinched me and twisted my wrist." The "worst" incident was the following September, "and from that time on I never lived with him again."[90] She soon left for Chicago and settled "a few doors away from" Laughlin's house. The following February, Taliaferro sued for divorce, and the next month, she, Laughlin, and Laughlin's mother hopped a ship to Italy for a six-month vacation. Their only other companion was a doll that Taliaferro's landlady had given to the child-woman.[91]

Whether or not the women's friendship involved sexual intimacy, Thompson understood and portrayed it that way, if only as a way of deflecting the ugly light that the relationship cast on the scope of his boyishness. In his view, Laughlin had seduced his girl-wife and, in a sense, replaced him. His account of his and Taliaferro's alienation was poorly disguised in a pair of press releases in January 1911. For anyone familiar with the couple, the notices hardly concealed their threatening nature. Reporting from Reno, Thompson announced a forthcoming drama, written by himself, called *A Child of the Desert*. Denying that he was in Nevada to dissolve his marriage, the showman claimed he was gathering "true atmosphere and local color" for a new play. In it, a woman

> scarcely out of the rose-and-gold age of girlhood is off on the uncharted sea of matrimony with a jovial and practical young architect. From her earliest days her dreams and visions have been the paramount issue with her. She has steeped herself in weird literature and shunned life in all its forms. The modern world is to her a menace, a terror, a delusion, a very Valley of the Shadow of Death, and all reality is simply a prison to keep her from the wonderful lands she had read of in the masterpieces of Morris, Yeats, Fiona Macleod and the other mystics from the Mountains of the Moon.

The husband "laughingly agrees" to let her go west with "an older woman, an authoress," who has made her girlish nature restless with fantasies. "At last she feels she must forsake her husband and her home to wander over the world away from the monotony and in search of the mysteries that haunt her." In Nevada she discovers a world of sordid pleasures and falls prey to "an unscrupulous, adventurous genius who craftily plays upon her susceptibilities for reasons whose enormity she does not fathom, and enchants her with highly colored stories of life in that region of splendid days and dazzling nights, how he and his companion offer to lead her across the desert to her Paradise." The final scene in which she and her lover meet their deserved death would rival the yacht scene in *Brewster's Millions*. While gathering local color, Thompson was caught in a blistering storm in Death Valley. "I came to the surface clutching one of the biggest scenes ever seen in a theatre. Did I go through this for nothing? Well, hardly! Imagine a young woman at the mercy of such a storm! Let's get back to the camp at once. I want to work this out in detail." If Taliaferro had any lingering doubts about Thompson's rage, they surely were dispelled by the sandy demise of the wayward follower of Fiona Macleod. Thompson never intended to produce the show; he went to Reno to threaten and embarrass Taliaferro. Hinting at the influence of a third male party slandered her, although it is more likely that the diabolical seducer referred to Clara Laughlin, who had filled Taliaferro's head with dazzling stories and shown her "Paradise."[92]

For all her juvenile appeal, Taliaferro was not the dainty ingenue Thompson preferred her to portray, but an actor with remarkable powers of impersonation. He had tried to construct and manage her and his fairy-tale marriage on the same marketable foundation of play that he used with Luna Park, the Hippodrome, and *Little Nemo*. But Taliaferro proved less moldable even than staff and much too slippery to handle, just as his other enterprises were disappointing him or slithering out of his control. Thompson discovered he was unable to police the practical boundary separating the "girl wife" he married from the dainty ingenue he constructed for public consumption. Taliaferro, to his astonishment, actually lived in Never Land and probably reminded him that he did, too. At the same time, it must have bewildered and terrified her to be assaulted for playing the very part Thompson had created for her, a role that was different only in degree from that which he claimed for himself.

In other ways Thompson's rage is not hard to fathom. Taliaferro's principal attraction, her elfin unreality, was charming in the abstract, but it generated less revenue than he had anticipated and needed, especially when she threatened to take herself out of circulation. Her insurrections and his violent reactions to them reflected and were part of the more general degeneration of his imperial aspirations: losing the Hippodrome, the *Little Nemo* fiasco, the cancellation of *Cinderella*, Taliaferro's unanticipated road tour, the cycle of names, the *Springtime* money hole, and other flops such as *The Call of the Cricket*. Moreover, she was hardly a self-surrendering Polly, but a willful adversary. Unable to control or please her, Thompson, it seems, came to regard his dainty asset as a consuming liability who was devouring his wealth and energy. Between 1908 and 1911 Thompson's publicists still highlighted the "boyish smile" of the man who spent millions the way others parted with hundreds. But the pretense was getting too fantastic to support.[93] In addition to his notable stage failures, the divorce action belied his famous insouciance and disclosed a rage underlying the sunny disposition. It also publicized what Broadway insiders had known for some time: Thompson was dangerously unstable, a reckless gambler, an uncontrolled spender, and a heavy drinker who suffered long spells of intoxication. Taliaferro exposed his weaknesses, his inability to mold, manage, and market her, as well as the imbalance between his improvident outlays and his declining income. Thompson, and Taliaferro, too, must have felt keenly his diminishing vitality.

### Stage Sermons on Temperance and Women

For anyone paying close attention to or familiar with the erotically charged darkness of the cellar door of childhood, there was plenty of evidence that Thompson's infatuation with Taliaferro's asexual delicacy was genetically linked to a fascination with awe-inspiring women who, unlike Polly but too much like Mabel, could incapacitate the "Man with the Ideas." For all the concern for mothers, sisters, and Bible-quoting sweethearts, Thompson also produced the era's, if not the century's, most provocative consumer, the man-eating Vamp of *A Fool There Was* in 1909. Thompson liked to think that *A Fool* was serious drama, but it was no less fantastic than A Trip to the Moon; it just represented the dark side of the sphere. *A Fool* and Thompson's other successful drama, *The Spendthrift*, exposed the relentless undercurrent of unease and illicit desire that had bothered and inspired him since his earliest days as a builder of shows on world's fair midways. These anxieties, which had forced him to moderate or disguise the disorderly potential of even his most unrestrained depictions of spending and emancipation from responsibility, constituted much of what made him tremble deliciously at the dark opening of pleasure. For him, there was no apparent contradiction between selling trips to the Moon and denouncing the followers of lunar mystics. He could not discern the arbitrariness of the boundaries he drew between licit and illicit pleasures, manly play and insouciance and unmanly submission to desire, or vamps and virgins.

In March 1909, as Taliaferro was touring the nation in the *Polly* road company, Thompson published a manifesto in *Success* entitled "After the Salome Dance—What?" or, "How long will the American public tolerate low-minded theatrical performances?" The specific reference point, as the title indicates, was Oscar Hammerstein's revival of Richard Strauss's opera *Salome* in January 1909. Two years earlier the Metropolitan Opera Company had pulled the scandalous production after opening night.[94] The opera remained in exile even as the "Salome dance" became a standard parody and belly-dance routine in vaudeville. Then, in 1909, the dramatic soprano Mary Garden performed the infamous "Dance of the Seven Veils" and received John the Baptist's severed head before ten full houses at Hammerstein's Manhattan Opera House in New York, followed by a triumphant tour of Chicago and Philadelphia. Only Boston refused her.[95]

Thompson's essay on "cleanliness in amusements" enthusiastically joined in the censure of *Salome*, fixating on her "semi-naked" body while congratulating himself for running such filth out of Coney Island.[96] Yet his focus on the exposed female suppressed the affinity between Strauss's opera and his own melodrama *A Fool There Was*, which had opened that March. The opera, like other "Salomes" of the era, delivered a horrified condemnation of female desire and belonged to what Andreas Huyssen has called "the powerful masculinist and misogynist current within the trajectory of modernism," which "openly states its contempt for women and for the masses."[97] Although fully dressed and relocated to the sentimental domesticity of the late-Victorian American bourgeoisie, Thompson's *Fool*, no less than *Salome*, was a fevered thrill ride examining the forbidden extremes of consuming desire, which were represented as an essentially and seductively feminine threat to masculine order.

In the last twenty or so years *A Fool There Was* has received plenty of mostly hostile scholarly attention, but it has been the 1915 film, not the 1909 play, that has been dissected. Although overshadowed by its later film incarnation, the neglected stage show and the circumstances and context of its production deserve examination for what they suggest about "Peter Pans of stageland" such as Thompson and his playwright,

Porter Emerson Browne. *A Fool* was Browne's first play. Prior to his introduction on Broadway, he was a journalist and short-story writer for
magazines.[98] *A Fool*, which exploited the expanding cultural cash value
of "vampire women," would be his ticket.

His purported inspiration, Rudyard Kipling's poem "The Vampire,"
had been published in 1897 to accompany a painting of the same title by
Philip Burne-Jones, the son of the Pre-Raphaelite painter Edward
Burne-Jones and also a cousin of Kipling. The painting reflected the
artist's obsession with the "goddess siren symbol of the nineties," the
British actor Stella Campbell.[99] The publicity for Browne's play advertised this literary and artistic genealogy; the programs usually reprinted
the poem and the painting, which showed a lustful and scantily draped
"vampire" leaning triumphantly over her bloodless male lover.[100]
Browne's rendering of these sources was pretentiously highbrow. Instead of using personal names, he listed the characters as "The Husband," "The Wife," "The Child," "The Friend," and, of course, "The
Woman." Lest pedestrian American audiences be put off by this arti-
ness, Thompson published a thin brochure in which the author translated the symbolism into the vernacular. But critics (and probably
audiences, too) did not find the play's message opaque in the least.[101]
Browne's *Fool*, observed one, was a "heart-rending, soul-stirring and
sob-starting illustration of Kipling's shuddery poem ... a sort of a stage
sermon on temperance and women."[102]

What made it so shuddery was the mawkish detail with which
Browne dramatized the remarkably easy corruption and destruction of a
solid male citizen enslaved to unmediated female sexuality. In the first
act the audience learns that the loving father and faithful Husband,
John Schuyler, has been ordered on a short-term ambassadorial mission to England and must leave the suburban idyll he inhabits with Wife
and Child. Before Schuyler boards the transatlantic liner, which Thompson reproduced with fidelity on the stage, Browne inserted a heavy-
handed bit of foreshadowing: a scorned lover, "Young Parmalee,"
"haggard and dissipated, though bearing evidence of refinement," ap-
proaches a "tall, sinuous" woman, and thrusts a pistol in her face.[103]
"She looks at it unmoved a moment, then gazing into his wild eyes she
exclaims" the withering command that Theda Bara later edited and im-
mortalized in the silent film of the play: "Kiss me, my Fool!" Parmalee
refuses, turns the gun on himself, and fires. "The woman looks at the

stiffening body, laughs, and gathering up her skirts, moves on to her stateroom."

Moments after the bloody affair has been scrubbed from the deck, the Husband appears with the Wife. As the Woman passes along the deck, Schuyler "catches her eye, gives a sudden start and hesitates in his speech." Ignoring the crack in his composure, he asks the Friend about the commotion. After explaining, he asks Schuyler if he recalls Kipling's "The Vampire." Schuyler knowingly replies:

*A fool there was and he made his prayer*
       *(Even as you and I)*
*To a rag and a bone and a hank of hair.*
       *(We called her the woman who did not care),*
*But the fool he called her his lady fair*
       *(Even as you and I).*[104]

Laughing, he says such fools deserve their fate. By this time the Woman has seated herself on the spot where Parmalee died. "As the whistle blows and the ship moves out, Schuyler turns away from the rail and, catching sight of her, stands spellbound, gazing into her eyes."

By the end of the first act the outcome is obvious: the Husband's seduction, the heartless shaming of his family, the fruitless admonitions of his stalwart Friend, and the relentless leeching of Schuyler's vitality and morality (which in this case are synonymous) through the unrelenting sexual power of the Woman. At the end of act 3, Schuyler, raving with guilt, confronts his captor, who responds with a defiant "sneer." An astonishing exchange follows: Schuyler repeatedly slaps the Woman, who retaliates, with a mocking smile, "Kiss me, my fool!" He refuses, but his hands are shaking. She "hisses once more: 'Kiss me, my fool!' Gazing into her eyes his arm lowers unsteadily, and leaning over her as she sinks into a chair his lips slowly meet hers." The curtain lowered, usually to a standing ovation.

The end occurs a year after this incident. Having sucked the life from him, the Vampire has tired of her lover, as well she might, for by this point he is a brandy-soaked wretch. She stings him: "You are not as strong as you were, you know" (fig. 5.5). The remark steels him for a final, frenzied attempt to strangle his captor. But, as the *Toledo Blade* noted, "The mosses and fungi of lechery have gathered on the sickly

Fig. 5.5. "You are not as strong as you were," the Vampire sneers at the Husband near the end of Fred Thompson's production of *A Fool There Was*. (*Billy Rose Theatre Collection, The New York Public Library for the Performing Arts, Astor, Lenox and Tilden Foundations.*)

tree and his enfeebled frame and wrecked mind give way and death ends it all." "My fool!" the Woman exclaims, and "throwing a few crumpled rose leaves upon him laughs a heartless laugh." As if this were not enough, the curtain lowered momentarily before revealing a *tableau vivant* of the Burne-Jones painting, which underscored what made *A Fool* so unusual for its time: its unhappy ending allowed the Vampire to escape due punishment.[105]

Browne's essay on the play's symbolism explains that the dualistic warfare depicted in the conflict is "not merely the isolated struggles of several little human entities, but the worldwide battle of good against evil that wages—that has always waged—that will always wage—from East to West, from North to South—in all that place that lies between heaven and hell." But it was not a meaningless aesthetic coincidence that the worldwide battle was waged between the tormented "soul" of a man and a woman who symbolized, as Browne put it, "Sin, Vice, Evil, [and] the things that are bad."[106] In part, *A Fool There Was* and Strauss's opera both represented the "engulfing femininity" of mass culture, to use Andreas Huyssen's words, as a voraciously desiring woman. "The fear of the masses in this age of declining liberalism is always also a fear of woman, a fear of nature out of control, a fear of the unconscious, of sexuality, of the loss of identity and stable ego boundaries in the mass." Mass culture, according to this wisdom, beguiles its victims into unthinking, herdlike compliance in the same way that the Vampire captivated Schuyler with her irresistible gaze. "The lure of mass culture," writes Huyssen, "has traditionally been described as the threat of losing oneself in dreams and delusions and of merely consuming rather than producing."[107] Robert Hilliard, who played the Husband, said as much. "I don't think that vampire women are mercenary," he explained. "They are simply insatiable for love. They must possess a man completely while they have him. Then suddenly, and probably without understanding why themselves, they tire. They love this man no longer, but their natures demand love, and so they go to another—and it's the same story over again."[108] The story, presumably, was as old, or new, as that of Salome.

Such misogyny was an important corollary to the Victorian frame of mind, which attributed the great moving forces of public history to men and the private guardianship of the emotional resources of the home to women. "Officially," Nina Auerbach writes in her study of Victorian literature, *Woman and the Demon*, "the only woman worthy of worship was a monument of selflessness, with no existence beyond the loving influence she exuded as daughter, wife, and mother." Yet the Victorians' idealization of the domestic woman was matched by a fixation with shadowy, monstrous women in their art and literature—vampires, mermaids, goblins, Salomes, Judiths, and other "varieties of creation's mutants" such as the Woman in Browne's play. These fictional women in literature and art were anything but meek prisoners of the home. On the contrary, they were militant, demonic, powerful "outcasts from domesticity, self-creating rather than selflessly nurturing, regal but never maternal. Solitaries by nature and essence." Although usually depicted in premodern forms inspired by the nightmarish women of folklore and biblical apocrypha, her late-Victorian reference point was the New Woman, whom middle-class men feared as a supernatural threat to the solidity of patriarchal authority.[109]

Some late-twentieth-century readers, such as Bram Dykstra, have interpreted these "evil sisters" as evidence of a larger pattern of conservative male reaction in science, art, literature, and politics and as a functioning tool of political oppression. In this view, antimodernism also has rallied besieged white men against the encroachments of liberated "new" women, empowered socialist and labor groups, nonwhite colonial populations, dynamos and similar harbingers of technological change, and other economic challenges to bourgeois male authority. By captivating the stalwart male pillars of civilization with their unappeasable sexual appetite, these monstrous women officially warned of the dire social consequences of weakened white bourgeois male authority. Dykstra, in particular, has identified the "deadly racist and sexist evolutionary dreams of turn-of-the-century culture" and the "vicious eroticism" of such frightful females. These figures were not just symbols of disorder and chaos, but the core ideological instruments of repression and reaction, which sponsored and justified "a wide range of monstrously inhuman political practices" throughout the twentieth century.[110] Dykstra provides little actual evidence for the sweeping indictments or even the reactions of audiences to the silent movie. The social and cultural histories of the play (and of the movie, for that matter) are confined to what can be read from the images and words on the screen.

Still, much of the terror-stricken vocabulary and imagery that Thompson and his publicity men used to advertise the original Broadway *Fool* does suggest that Browne and his producer were more concerned about the fragile social and economic power of men like themselves than they were worried about actual consequences of extramarital sexual intercourse. Promotion for the play, for instance, included serious-minded, if shrill, disquisitions on the Vamp's larger significance. One such commentary was published under the name of Robert Hilliard, the actor whom Thompson made a star in the "Fool" role. Vampires, Hilliard explained, "slink through the world, bringing corruption to everything they touch." They are not necessarily beautiful ("many of them are homely"), but they "enchant when and wherever" they direct their eyes. This power "will cause a man ... to experience a sudden thrill when introduced to a certain woman, a thrill which takes him and shakes him as a terrier does a rat, never again leaving him alone until all the life and sense have been shaken from him, leaving him helpless on the sands of a realization of folly that has come too late."¹¹¹ His justification for repression, which presumably was aimed at promoting his own role in the play, focused obsessively on the invincible strength of his adversary and, by extension, the comparative weakness of her male victims. Although Browne's vampire exhibited none of the supernatural abilities of her kindred in Bram Stoker's 1897 novel, *Dracula*, the only way Hilliard could account for his character's capitulation was to attribute her influence to enchantment. After the long season on Broadway, the actor found himself as physically drained as his character had been sexually and morally depleted. "I had never played a part that so exhausted the vital forces."¹¹²

Hilliard's equation of vitality with power and physical and sexual exhaustion with impotence recalls the fears outlined in nineteenth-century sexual advice literature for men. These publications emerged at a time when Americans began to regard economic resources in terms of an apparent scarcity in a competitive marketplace and to treat social and sexual order as the outcome of individual will power and self-control rather than of the traditional community control of the individual. Advice writers such as the Congregationalist minister John Todd (1800–1873) and the pioneering gynecologist Augustus Kinsley Gardner (1821–76) were liberal economists at heart, who believed that a sound male mind and body were matters of steadily accumulating, instead of wasting, scarce resources. Both writers inveighed against male masturbation and nonprocreative sexual intercourse during marriage for squandering the vital and limited energies that men needed to make themselves effective in a market society. Sexual desire, in their minds, competed insidiously against the rational demands of economic life. Women could be especially draining, even in marriage. As wasters and spenders rather than producers or accumulators of wealth, they threatened to weaken and impoverish a man by consuming his sexual and economic wealth, which were interchangeable.¹¹³

The fear of women as consumers of men's energies demonstrates that the apprehension in Hilliard's diatribes and in the dramatic invective of Thompson and Browne belonged in part to nineteenth-century concerns about women, sexuality, and power. *A Fool There Was* pitted destructive femininity as a voracious consumer of sexual wealth against man, the producer of domestic order and stability and sexual equilibrium. A South Bend, Indiana, clergyman quoted by the management called the play "the most effective temperance sermon" depicting "the tragic ending of a life given to appetite" that he had ever encountered.[114] At the same time, however, *A Fool There Was*, with its voyeuristic, joyously terrifying scrutiny of sexual victimization, could not help publicizing the bad deeds that Browne purported to condemn. Even more than *Brewster's Millions*, *A Fool*'s fastidiously detailed exposé of sin, evil, and vice placed it in the tradition of "immoral reform." No doubt Browne meant for his dramas to awaken men to the menace at hand, but his and their responses to his stimulus could be mixed. For instance, Katherine Kaelred, the original Vampire, reported that on one occasion, a male spectator was "so worked-up" by her performance that he swore "he would have to submerge himself after the play in order to get calm again."[115] By "worked-up," Kaelred appeared to mean outraged, but her words also implied the need for a cold shower. This man's overwrought reaction suggests that the shuddery exposé concealed an erotic fascination that Thompson and his playwright were neither able nor wholeheartedly trying to subdue.

But perhaps *A Fool* was not just about men, ambivalent or otherwise. Recent feminist perspectives on the Vamp have readjusted the attention away from the men on stage and in the audience and given more consideration to the ambiguity of women's responses to the productions. Most of the scrutiny has been focused on the 1915 silent-film version of the play, which introduced the actor Theda Bara and briefly made her the preeminent dark goddess of the silver screen. This approach shows the influence of a wide range of scholarship that has undermined the notion that the messages of cultural texts are either unified or stable. Poststructuralist critics especially have argued that meanings are fluid and indeterminate because language itself is built out of arbitrary, shifting oppositions—masculine versus feminine, for instance. No position can be advanced without evoking and making visible ideas that the author wishes to render invisible. From another direction, some scholars have contended that, in consuming cultural products, audiences exercise an agency and discretion independent of the producer's intentions; the greater influences are their particular historical circumstances, which usually are described as a range or matrix of regional or national, class, gender, racial, and sexual identities. All of these critical positions have been taken in regard to the 1915 silent film. Andrea Weiss suggests in her study of lesbians in film that women no less than men may have been worked up by Bara's enticing representation of female power and the visible "pleasure of revenge" on men. The film historian Janet Staiger has argued that women may have identified sympathetically with the Vamp and been emboldened by her badness to contemplate "alternatives to the dutiful Victorian woman." The *Fool* narrative, which underscores Schuyler's vulnerability and the Vampire's invincibility, suggests that "a range of values about who was at fault and what were appropriate solutions was circulating in 1915."[116]

Critical accounts of audience's reactions from the time of the stage drama reinforce these less conclusive readings. Even though newspaper critics often censured the slapping incident (as one explained, "no real gentleman" would repeatedly strike "the face of a perfect lady, no matter how great the provocation"), the scene was a rousing crowd-pleaser.[117] "Robert Hilliard is always sure of several tumultuous recalls after he has caught his leading woman by the neck and soundly slapped her," reported the *Pittsburgh Leader*.[118] Some men in the audience may have found in this scene the regenerative thrill of defeat, which rallied them to the higher cause of all-out war against undomesticated New Women and all they represented.[119] But that reason would not necessarily explain the curious phenomenon noted by the Pittsburgh critic: "it is women who most loudly applaud the actor in this dramatic situation." Hilliard, no doubt, believed they were cheering him, although why women in particular would applaud his ineffectual last stand at gallantry is unclear. It may also have been the subversive message in the scene—the beating she gave him as much as his manly last gasp—that brought them to their feet. Women, and men for that matter, may have been cheering the Woman as a forceful, however hideously constructed, representation of female power. As Katherine Kaelred explained in another remarkably ambiguous reflection on her role, "I can imagine no better picture of the awfulness of wrong-doing than is presented in this play, and for that reason I think the character which I impersonate is going to do a lot of good."[120]

It is likely that, depending on the eyes of audiences, *A Fool* was all of the above—a rousing pornographic exposé of the decadent thrills of sexual excess, a passionate call to masculine "regeneration through violence," and a protofeminist vision of subversive revenge against men. But focusing exclusively on the silent film and viewing *A Fool* in relation only to other contemporary "bad women" movies, as the film studies tend to do, alienate it from the context of its original production and allow Bara's particular Vampire to set the terms of the debate. This approach obscures another curious aspect of the Vamp's arrival on the American scene: this shuddery stage sermon on temperance and women was sponsored by one of the era's more important proponents of intemperate consumption and of a life given to appetite.

Thompson's involvement becomes more curious when we consider his 1910 follow-up to *A Fool*, another hit melodrama by Browne called *The Spendthrift*. In this case, the battle of good against evil engaged husband against wife. Richard Ward is as industrious, responsible, and foresighted as his "butterfly wife" Frances is capricious and narcissistic. The play pits her insatiable material desires against his old-fashioned industry, self-restraint, and temperance in all matters save that of his wife, whom he cannot resist unwisely indulging. Concerned friends and family tell Richard he is a "fool!" for letting Frances squander his wealth on servants, automobiles, and frilly furnishings for the enormous house they cannot afford. Moreover, Frances is wholly neglectful of her predestined role as wife and mother. "A woman's sphere comprises something besides children," she responds when confronted with her barren household. Meanwhile her husband despairs over the empty returns on twenty years' labor—"a house that is no home, a woman that is no wife, and ruin." Fearing that she will lose all that she has spent so hard to attain, Frances foolishly borrows twenty thousand dollars from a shady character. To make matters worse, Richard wrongly suspects that she exchanged "treats" for the loan. The marriage between the bee and the butterfly breaks apart, only to be restored providentially in act 4. After disappearing from the marriage, Frances works as a governess, which teaches her the value of labor and her natural love of children; and Richard learns that Frances is no longer a spendthrift and never was a libertine. The melodrama of consumption ends happily with Frances a "woman transformed" and the Ward household's consuming desires brought in line with its needs and capacities.[121]

Once again Browne had attempted to portray a profound conflict, the meaning of which exceeded the specific ruin brought on by Frances Ward. *The Saturday Post* may have denounced the butterfly wife as "an obvious monster of feminine vanity, frivolity, and indeed mendacity," but what made *The Spendthrift* "a vital drama of to-day" was the way in which it linked the insatiable female spender, whose pathology was represented by her preference for home furnishings over children, to the

peril of "race suicide."[122] The historian Gail Bederman has shown that
the worry for the survival of the Anglo-Saxon race in the United States
was partly a response to the decline in the birthrate of native-born
whites. But the anxiety also reflected the widespread perception that
white men, as the Vampire put it so well, were not so strong as they
once were. In other words, the issue "was tied to a host of broader fears
about effeminacy, overcivilization, and racial decadence."[123] Thompson
shared these concerns. A painting commissioned to advertise *The
Spendthrift* was described this way: "On the snowy steps outside a closed
door stood a stork waiting in vain for a welcome from the house. Before
him he had deposited the burden which he had intended to present to
the occupants." The original title of *The Spendthrift* was *Waste*, but before it hit Broadway Thompson decided "waste" would not sell, perhaps
because it emphasized the victims rather than the villain—the spending
woman.[124]

### Now They Want Sheiks

Imagining himself as both the fun-loving toymaker of New York and
the beleaguered husband of his chameleon-like wife, Thompson was
well positioned to reflect on the ambiguous boundaries between prudent and wasteful spending that unsettled middle-class Americans in
the early part of the century. His personal fascinations, however, were
not eccentric. Time and again during this period, middle-class Americans expressed their unease with consumption by fixating on toys. Although the controversies usually identified child welfare as the
immediate concern, the exclamatory rhetoric exposed deeper anxieties.
When a craze for teddy bears erupted in the United States in 1906–7
and seemed to have made dolls a thing of the past, some voices warned
of the dire consequences to the nation's future mothers. The "toy beast
in the hands of little girls was destroying all instincts of motherhood,"
warned a Catholic priest in Michigan. He predicted that future generations would regard stuffed animals "as one of the most powerful factors
in the race suicide danger." Such worries about nurturing bestiality in
little girls expressed, in part, confusion and dismay about the child as
consumer, a new social and economic phenomenon. In competition
with the enticements of department store toy displays, middle-class parents often felt at a disadvantage in regulating their children's demands.

But the alarm about girls playing with bears instead of dollies also suggested the more pervasive and enduring concern about women in a culture of consumption: would they be unnatural, like Frances Ward, concerned only with pleasing or satisfying themselves, or would they rationally confine their shopping to the higher cause of family and household? These anxieties hardly troubled the toy industry. The teddy bear fad, which engrossed boys as well as girls, was a salient object lesson in the sales potential of novelty items and a major stimulant to domestic manufacturers, who relished the outcry. The trade journal *Playthings* reprinted accounts of the antibear crusade under the headline, "Hurrah for Teddy Bears! Getting Lots of Free Advertising."[125]

Dolls reclaimed much of their market share by the early 1910s, but the disquieting associations of toys with cultural decline persisted. By the early 1920s, the problem was not girls playing with stuffed animals but women carrying dolls, a fad that served to illustrate the aggressive marketing schemes of toy manufacturers no less than the disturbing ramifications when women preferred buying dolls to having babies. The implications for men of such consumer preferences were brought home in October 1922 in the case of Hazel McNally. The Hammond, Indiana, woman was arrested for murdering her twin infants, who—or which, as it turned out—were actually dolls; and not just any dolls, but Effanbee dolls, manufactured by Fleishaker and Bawm of New York. McNally's case landed her in newspapers across the country, but the real story turned out to be not the children, but the couple's troubled marriage. The husband was some thirty years older than Hazel, who had been his housekeeper. She was a divorcée and was sterile when she married McNally. The prosecution's parade of witnesses, including the bereaved father, swore that the children were children, but McNally insisted that it was her husband's "mania to pose before the world as a father" that led them to pass off "two skillfully constructed dolls" as their offspring. The court hearing underscored the generational shift in sexual and political expectations: a demanding older husband and a much younger, pleasure-seeking wife who rebelled once "her married life became slavery." The charges against McNally finally were dropped because of insufficient evidence, but an editorialist for the *Chicago Daily Tribune* described her real offense in a humorous indictment of "The New Ladies": "Once they were contented with good providers. Now they want sheiks. They have the vote. They pack guns. They have the men

Fig. 5.6. Once vindicated, the "Doll Mother" Hazel McNally purchased two new Effanbee Dolls, then posed for this photograph, which appeared in the November 1922 issue of the toy industry journal *Toys and Novelties.*

wholly on the run. Paternity is a gambling proposition."[126] McNally's behavior reinforced such conclusions. Vindicated, she announced that she would divorce her husband, then, perhaps, study law. For her first act of liberation, though, she bought two new Effanbee dolls. Her portrait, accompanied by the replacement twins, appeared the following month in the trade magazine *Toys and Novelties* as proof that dolls made in America were superbly lifelike: "When they are produced so close to life that they fool the father and the neighbors, it's going some" (fig. 5.6).[127] In the eyes of toymakers, at least, the woman who played with dolls and her husband's feelings was not frightful; she was free advertising. McNally managed to be both an unrepentant successor to the monstrous "spendthrift" and a discerning consumer, who knew a good doll when she saw one.

The women of *A Fool There Was*, *The Spendthrift*, and the toy departments of Hammond, Indiana, and other American cities all were "New Ladies" whose actions transcended the limitations of nineteenth-century ideals of the selfless, domesticated woman. No longer satisfied with mere providers, they wanted to multiply their enjoyment with sheiks. Instead of simply representing an exercise in male hegemony, these feminine monsters depicted consumption not as a passive activity, but as one that ascribed remarkable and, to some, frightening social and cultural power to women. They were what Jackson Lears calls the "mythic female consumer" who emerged in the Western imagination with the shift in the social role of women from producers in the household economy to consumers for the household in a market economy.[128] Whether as spenders or as sexual vampires, these mythical representations of women reflected the importance of a new social role and reality expanding in tandem with the growth of consumer capitalism in the United States. The urban culture at the turn of the century provided middle- and working-class women with an expanded range of public roles as shoppers and workers in the new commercial institutions, which encompassed retailing, amusements, the theater, restaurants, and many other services. In effect, women seized these new opportunities to be self-made. In spite of his best efforts, Browne's plays were less effective as sermons on production than as thrilling melodramas of consumption, which acknowledged the ascendant power of women in the urban marketplace even as they explored that culture's invitation to lose oneself in dreams and desires.[129] As Katherine Kaelred described the Vampire, she was "a vibrant creature, with an immense capacity for enjoyment. Whatever she enjoyed she enjoyed twenty times more than would an ordinary individual."[130]

But the fun that toymakers had publicizing the screeds against teddy bears and doll mothers suggests that such alarming indicators of cultural disorder also contained alternative possibilities for men, especially for those like Thompson, who were profiting from the new consumer industries. The Vamp was not just their most dreaded nightmare. She also was the deliciously terrifying distillation of "the spirit of modern consumerism" described by Colin Campbell, and, in that important sense, she was their fondest dream come true.[131] Instead of regarding *A Fool There Was* and *The Spendthrift* solely as reactionary responses to a more general sense of gender crisis for middle-class men like Thompson, we should be alert to how he and other men like him were fiends for just such consuming subjects.

We also need to consider how the showman used "bad women" to construct and naturalize new perspectives on manhood. At first glance, it appears paradoxical that one of the era's great spendthrifts produced dramas that portrayed the perils of consuming appetites. But if the evil sisters of *A Fool There Was* and *The Spendthrift* are regarded, not in isolation, but as the factious partners of their jovial brethren in *Brewster's Millions, A Yankee Circus on Mars,* and *Little Nemo,* Thompson's inconsistencies begin to make sense as a struggle, within himself and with his culture, to preserve the priority of male authority even as he reconfigured the boundaries of middle-class manhood. For one, the sisters' appetites alone underscored the unlimited potential of consumer markets. What seemed the awfulness of wrongdoing in one context also contained the potential for business expansion, especially for those who, like the Effanbee dollmakers, could spot an opportunity in a crisis. At the same time, frightening representations of uncontrolled feminine desire could be regarded as the rallying cry of bourgeois men, who were nostalgic for an old-fashioned model of prudential masculinity from a more patriarchal past, when, they imagined, men were producers instead of consumers and providers of services. But, it should be remembered, Monty Brewster appears healthy, rational, and winsome only from a late-twentieth-century perspective that expects men to play with their money. He, too, behaved in ways that violated dutiful Victorian gender ideals; from a late-nineteenth-century viewpoint, he was a hideous inversion of manly rectitude. In comparison to the Vampire, though, Monty (like Thompson) looked respectable, an agent of the occult order of the universe, powerful instead of puny. However much he resembled the licentious spendthrifts like Frances Ward, Monty was a daring cultural rebel with a cause: he made play pay. After all, even as the Vampire nightly lorded her superiority over the haggard form of the once upright John Schuyler, *Brewster's Millions* and *Little Nemo* were touring the United States spreading the good news that the only fools were men who did not dare to have fun.

### It's Proof I'm No Piker

By the spring of 1910 the stage tales of "bad women" must have helped Thompson make sense of his own private disorder, which was making him feel like, if not resemble, the wretched men in Browne's plays. His heedless spending, especially on his theatrical productions, had cost him dearly even if this problem was invisible outside the business world of the theater. His fortunes had been mixed at best for several years, both on Broadway and at Luna Park. Dundy's death was the first blow, followed by the financial panic of 1907–9. Taliaferro's decline reflected and fueled her husband's own consuming problems. All of these episodes contributed to his misfortune, but they did not cause it. Thompson's childish personality and genius for spectacle had allowed him to capitalize on private fantasies, but he was unable to build shows that subordinated all considerations to his labor, production, and profit needs. He dreamed of an octopuslike manufacturing and distribution system of vaudeville, summer and all-year amusement parks, hippodromes and circuses, but the boy at heart could not bring it off.

The self-delusion of his boyishness was staged for all to see in *Girlies*, his 1910 summer "roof garden" production. The Broadway rooftop theaters, which were designed to catch nocturnal winds and thereby to prolong theatrical entertainment into the summer months, tended to stage equally breezy musical comedies short on plot and long on chorus girls.[132] *Girlies* exaggerated the form with unusually extravagant costumes and sets and expensive stars, writers, and composers.[133] By opening night, Thompson already had spent himself into a hole, with thirty thousand dollars in preproduction expenses and obligations of another six thousand dollars in weekly operating costs. "Such fetching costumes and such display of lingerie and limb are calculated to make one gasp with awe," observed the *Dramatic Mirror*. But not to make a profit. Although the show usually played to capacity, *Variety* calculated that Thompson's cut from ticket sales brought him at most five thousand dollars a week. In other words, he was losing at least a thousand dollars a week on top of the thirty-thousand-dollar outlay. *Girlies* was a chorus of vampires sucking him dry.[134] Thompson had no choice but to sell the rights to *Girlies* and *The Spendthrift* to Klaw and Erlanger for one dollar; the expensive properties brought a paltry five thousand dollars.[135] The buyers did him (and themselves) a favor, but the transaction did not leave anyone smiling.

In August, Thompson still spoke as though his past only vaguely suggested his magnificent future, rattling off a list of startling new productions.[136] But by the following November, the *New York Review* reported "that conditions in the play world were not to his liking," and that Thompson, "as soon as he could do so advantageously, [planned] to close out his holdings."[137] *The New York Morning Telegraph* later countered, "Thompson Won't Desert Theatre," but his Broadway career was finished.[138] By this point the showman was as much as $140,000 in debt to Klaw and Erlanger. They shut him down on Broadway, for good, as it turned out.

Thompson was still rich in bravado. In September 1910 he announced a new venture: manufacturing aeroplanes. At the time the Wright brothers and others were trying to develop the aeroplane's potential as a military tool, but the toymaker of New York had other ideas.[139] He envisaged aeroplanes as personal consumer items, toys instead of practical tools, and announced three models, with the "Runabout" the least expensive at $1,750. Little ever came of the scheme.[140] Thompson's resurrection was dealt a final blow a year later on 11 December 1911. A fire at Luna Park destroyed several rides, but the mortal loss was his uninsured scenic studios, which were consumed along with properties for several new stage productions and for the *Polly of the Circus* and *Spendthrift* road companies. Thompson called it "a relatively small affair." "I suppose I shall be accused of having a press agent at the bottom of this fire."[141] In fact, the fire had consumed both his Broadway comeback and his "theatrical factory by the sea."[142]

Shortly after Christmas, Thompson collapsed while rehearsing George Barr McCutcheon's *Flyers*, which he was still hoping to use to stage his return. The newspapers called the seizure an attack of "acute neuritis." In February the *New York Review* reported that he still was very ill, and called his attack a stroke. The newspaper attributed the illness to Thompson's unusually sensitive and nervous personality and the physically exhausting demands of his work, although it is likely that his overindulgence in alcohol and his impending bankruptcy contributed most to his distress. The stroke marked the first of a series of mental and physical collapses that would plague Thompson during the last eight years of his life.[143]

The actual amusement empire fell in two stages, with Luna Park crumbling first. Around midnight on 2 April 1912, Thompson signed

Luna Park over to his creditors. Against the Luna Park Company's aggregate indebtedness of $2,684,000, he could offer minuscule assets.[144] The enfeebled signature effectively transferred ownership to the park's principal leaseholder, the Sea Beach Land Company, which joined with other leaseholders to form the Luna Amusement Company. The president of the new company announced plans to spend $300,000 on improvements and to hire Thompson as "managing architect."[145]

In June, two months after losing Luna, Thompson filed for personal bankruptcy in federal court in Brooklyn. The court papers provide a startling narrative of Thompson's excess. In addition to the Klaw and Erlanger debt, he owed his mother more than $30,000. He had never paid rent on the Fort George property and owed $150,000. The New York State Banking Department held two obligations against him, one for $100,000 and another for $109,000. Porter Emerson Browne was due back royalties, the Algonquin Hotel months of rent; dues were outstanding at the Players and Lambs Clubs, the Larchmont, Bensonhurst, and Manhasset Bay yacht clubs, and the Aero Club of America and its local chapter in New York. Thompson had accumulated personal debts of almost $665,000, and assets of $7,831. Valiantly playing Monty Brewster to the end, he told reporters, "It's proof I'm no piker, isn't it?"[146]

A cheapskate he was not. In fact, Thompson had been everything that he encouraged other men to be—the playful boy in Never Land, heedless of boundaries and limitations. For all his preaching to American audiences on the felicities and dangers of spending, and on the triumphs and destructions of spendthrifts, vampires, and fools, he also was speaking directly to and reassuring himself. His melodramas of consumption explored the delights and fears represented and aroused by the discovery of an economy of abundance and the commercial apparatus for manufacturing desire. Thompson offered his theatrical entertainments as cultural billboards for middle-class men like himself. His signs and signals guided them through the unfamiliar territory of the consumer marketplace, enticed them with visions of plenty, and alleviated their reluctance to indulge by alerting them to the hazards of excess.

Although the sources for his dramas were diverse, they seem in many respects to have issued from his confusion at the way his own personality mirrored the commercial culture around him, the marketplaces of play that he had built on the protean ambiguity of his purported childlike personality and insatiable longings. "The Woman" was the key instrument in this enterprise. She had immediate personal importance to Thompson, taking the fall for the precipitous deterioration of his marital and business fortunes and serving as a scapegoat onto whom he could displace the very desires that were consuming him. But Thompson's personal problems were also cultural problems. By taking on the risks and dangers of a life given to appetite, the Woman also helped Thompson face and make uneasy sense of the more bewildering and disturbing implications of the new commercial culture that he was helping create. Long before the crash of the amusement empire in 1912, he had spent himself nearly to death, consumed by the irresistible lure of fun, novelty, sensation, thrills, and, no doubt, alcohol. At the end of a decade of exciting the craving for thrills and exploiting the "billion-dollar smile," all the time trying to control and steer desires into profitable and acceptable channels, Thompson personally had little to show for his brilliance except the proof he was no penny-pincher. Luna Park would not last beyond midcentury and the Hippodrome was flattened in 1939. Yet the symbols of middle-class Americans' divided attitudes toward consumption have endured in the figures of the jovial Monty Brewster and his evil sister, the femme fatale of *A Fool There Was.*

SIX

# We're Playing Games

The Toylands of Peter Pan Culture, 1912–30

O N 14 October 1911, as many as a hundred thousand people gathered in San Francisco's Golden Gate Park to watch the president of the United States, William Howard Taft, stab a silver shovel into the ground, symbolically beginning construction of the Panama-Pacific International Exposition of 1915. Once Taft had deposited the "sacred soil" in a redwood and crystal casket and a hundred doves were released, the "Lilly of the North," the renowned American soprano of Wagnerian opera, Madame Lillian Nordica, led the "vast assemblage" in the "Star-Spangled Banner." In the solemnly terse words of the exposition's official historian, Frank Morton Todd, "It was a great day's work."[1]

Virtually two years to the day later, on 13 October 1913, Fred Thompson summoned a crowd of children to a construction site on the exposition grounds to consecrate the beginning of Toyland Grown Up, a fourteen-acre amusement park of animated fairy tales and nursery rhymes and hundred-foot-tall toys that he planned for the Joy Zone, the fair's boulevard of commercial amusement. Under Thompson's direction, each child planted a toy in the ground specially prepared for the ceremony. He comforted the unsure children with assurances that these playthings were magical seeds, which over the next year and a half

Fig. 6.1. In 1913, Fred Thompson helped San Francisco children plant dolls, gingerbread men, and cake—the "seeds" of his Toyland Grown Up at the 1915 Panama-Pacific International Exposition. (*San Francisco History Center, San Francisco Public Library.*)

would grow to an immense size (fig. 6.1). Then fertilizer—gingerbread men, candy, nuts, cakes, chicken and cranberry sauce, plum pudding, and ice cream—was scattered on the toys, which the children, using little rakes and shovels, helped cover with dirt. Finally the field was liberally watered with California "champagne." Unfortunately the only music at the ceremony was the din of the children's noisemakers. The "Beautiful Kitty Gordon," a comic-opera star then appearing locally in Victor Herbert's *Enchantress*, suffered a "nervous collapse" upon arriving at the site, which prevented her from presiding as Toyland's "princess." No matter, according to Todd. "The delectable foolishness went on for hours and brought a mist to the eyes of many a grown-up who realized that only in some such fairyland as this could he ever be a child again."[2]

On that day, Fred Thompson was in robust promotional form, manifesting no signs of his recent troubles back east. Squatting down with the children to lay the groundwork for his fanciful enterprise, he played the role of Peter Pan as zestfully as ever. Yet Thompson was not just having some fun attracting attention in his usual manner. The correspondence in the timing and structure of his ceremony with that of the grand event two years earlier suggests that he knew what he was doing with this bit of foolishness. Although there is no evidence that anyone other than he got the joke, Thompson must have grinned inwardly at the way his "great day's" play poked fun at the earlier, laborious demonstration of the main exposition's breathless civic religion and high-mindedness.

The Panama-Pacific usually has been described as the last of the great and confident Victorian expositions. Such fairs were supposed to be "colossal" universities that instructed "the people by means of the best object lessons the Western Hemisphere can produce."[3] The 1915 fair, with its neoclassical warehouses of industry and culture, was not unusual in this regard. The city's leading financiers, politicians, and industrialists designed, inaugurated, and staged their exposition to commemorate the opening of the Panama Canal and San Francisco's revival from the 1906 earthquake. The official representation of the fair, which appeared in posters and on guidebook covers, featured a muscled, nude male splitting the continents for the canal, the "thirteenth labor of Hercules," with the exposition city shimmering dimly in the background beneath his buttocks (fig. 6.2). Here was Man's conscious and progressive triumph over nature, a fitting symbol for the nation that had joined the two oceans and for the city that had rebuilt itself from destruction.[4] Boosters promoted the event as a selfless celebration of the enterprising genius and the global benevolence of Western, and especially American, industry, art, and science, and contended that the fair would preserve and enshrine timeless categories of civilized taste and cultural leadership. The "final and lasting effect," the critic Eugen Neuhaus predicted, will be "the great enduring lesson of beauty which the Exposition so unforgettably teaches."[5]

With this high-flown rhetoric and imagery in the air, Thompson's show seemed impishly parodic: the winsome Kitty Gordon rather than the formidable Nordica; Victor Herbert instead of Richard Wagner; children with toy spades in place of the president with a silver shovel. If the Panama-Pacific, like the canal itself, resulted from Herculean labor, then his Toyland for grown-up kids would arise from the play of children. Yet Thompson's theatrical joke amounted to more than cheek. In comparison to the presidential fantasy of high civic purpose, the Toy-

Fig. 6.2. The official image of the San Francisco exposition was Perham Nahl's poster, "The Thirteenth Labor of Hercules." (*Larson Collection, Special Collections, California State University, Fresno.*)

land ceremony enacted an antic, infantilist fantasy of material indulgence and wish fulfillment, which mocked the Panama-Pacific's cult of masculine progress and enterprise and its conflation of Western civilization and industrial capitalism with the mythic body of Hercules. The point of the caricature, it seems, was to expose not the differences between the rival enterprises of play and work so much as their essential sameness. "We're all just tots grown," he explained the next year in the toy-industry publication *Playthings*. "We're playing games, and the toys may be the theater, the mart of trade, the stock ticker, the factory or the laboratory, but they're toys just the same."[6]

### Titania's Playground

That work was play, and that modern adults were, in reality, unhappy children, were hardly new ideas for Thompson, but Toyland was the clearest expression of the dreams that inspired and troubled his personal investment in Peter Pan culture. Thompson designed it to be nothing less than the exposition's preeminent feature; visions of Buffalo and A Trip to the Moon must have danced in his head. His newest "playground for the human race" took the form of a well-appointed playroom of an indulged middle-class child, with giant-sized toy figures strategically littered about its grounds as though an enormous four-year-old had abruptly abandoned them for other notions of fun.[7] By the summer of 1915, when the venture wobbled on the edge of bankruptcy and even its most ardent supporter had decided that it was a delusion, the entire project, in retrospect, seemed doomed from the start. But in 1913 and for nearly two years afterward, the fair's hierarchy had greeted and backed Thompson's proposal with genuine excitement.

Thompson may have been amused by the hospitality. After all, however profitable, his projects at earlier world's fairs had scuttled on the periphery of official culture, like, as he once put it, a "side show to be more or less ashamed of."[8] The exposition's eagerness for Toyland indicated, in part, the respectability commercial amusements had achieved by the mid-1910s. But the enthusiasm also hinted at the growing appeal of eternal childhood and other aspects of the commercial culture of Peter Pan in the United States. In fact, within weeks of opening day, some writers happily declared that the exposition was not the "noble educational institution" described in official guidebooks, but a "great playplace."[9] Katherine Dunlap Cather, writing in the children's magazine *St. Nicholas*, insisted the exposition should really be called "Titania's Playground," alluding to *A Midsummer Night's Dream*. "Can't you shut your eyes and see the Fairy Queen and all her fays flitting along" its broad avenues?[10] Granted, Dunlap was writing for a leading middle-class children's publication, but others who targeted an exclusively adult audience shared her vision of the exposition. "Educational bosh!" a writer for the *San Francisco Bulletin* exclaimed. "Education only as it lures, as it is had in the spirit of the child at play, not in a sense of strenuous stern duty."[11]

These complementary visions of the Panama-Pacific as a dream landscape of magically animated toys and as a playground for the cast of *A Midsummer Night's Dream* suggest that the image of hardworking Hercules was not sufficient to contain all the meanings either of the fair or, by extension, of civilization. Observers had long noted the enchanting quality of exposition cities with their spectacular lighting, animate machinery, and impermanent plaster palaces that seemed, like a dream, to disappear as quickly as they came into being.[12] What was extraordinary about the Panama-Pacific was how its designers, for all their talk of "strenuous stern duty," encouraged an outlook that earlier fairs in the United States had labored to exile to the borderlands of seriousness. They deliberately created an ephemeral fairyland of magic, play, and wonder that competed with more-conventional representations of a mature capitalist civilization.

The San Francisco fair was not eccentric in this regard. On the contrary, it signaled the new depth to which Peter Pan culture had penetrated into the consciousness of middle-class Americans. There was no place else on earth like Luna Park when Thompson and Skip Dundy opened it in 1903. But by the time Toyland Grown Up came into being between 1912 and 1915, Thompson's venture was only the most grandiose of the many "toylands" that were in business in American cities. The transformations in attitudes and expectations that were indicated by the surprising ordinariness of Toyland Grown Up were particularly visible in the new American toy business, one of the fastest growing domestic industries after 1910. In many respects, the men—or, rather, "toy men," as they were called—who led the revolution in the manufacturing and retailing of playthings had grown up with Fred Thompson. They, too, dealt in calculated regression or "the stuff that dreams are made of," as the industry's leading publication, *Playthings*, often described the outlook appropriate for profitable "dealing with childhood." Like Thompson, too, they had no easy time charting a new frontier for manly endeavor within the stigmatized world of consumption, especially the business of play and children's toys. They needed constant encouragement to treat their work as play—advice that often was underscored by threatening reminders that they could ill afford to do otherwise. As *Playthings* insisted in 1927, whether "from choice or circumstance," toy men were the chosen representatives "of Peter Pan the Playfellow."[13]

## None Can Enter Who Is Not Willing to Play

The summers of 1914 and 1915 were an inauspicious time in which to stage an international exposition that either paid homage to the harmony and vitality of Western civilization or celebrated the carefree joy and innocent pleasures of the universal child spirit of play. In August 1914, Britain declared war on Germany, and the Panama Canal connected the Atlantic with the Pacific under the protection of the United States. In February 1915 the Panama-Pacific exposition opened in San Francisco, and the following May a German U-boat sank the *Lusitania*, turning American public opinion on the European war sharply against the Germans.

Within this configuration of international events, the Panama-Pacific's boosters, many of them leading industrialists or financiers, raced to complete their "microcosm" of civilization. The exposition city spread along the northern shoreline of San Francisco Bay.[14] More than half the 635-acre site was set aside for what the critic Neuhaus called "the seriously designed main body" of the fair.[15] The Joy Zone was allotted a stubby, seventy-acre finger appended to the eastern edge of the site, across the Avenue of Progress.[16] The exposition's architecture, generally Beaux Arts neoclassicism, reflected the Progressive drive for harmony and organicism that was typical of earlier fairs. Leading American architects were assembled as a commission in 1912, and, although a chief was named, the emphasis was on the cooperative striving for the ideal. "Architect, sculptor and painter are in perfect accord," explained the architect Henry Bacon, who had designed the Lincoln Memorial in Washington, D.C. To ensure harmony, the development of the major aesthetic aspects of the fair—lighting, public art, architecture, landscaping, and color—was closely coordinated and supervised. Instead of assigning architects to discrete structures, the exposition appointed them to the courtyards formed where the exterior walls of different exhibition palaces converged or intersected. The aim was to eliminate the egoism of the individual architects, who might undermine the unity of the exposition city by designing competing buildings. According to the official historian, Todd, the "enjoyment and intellectual stimulus of the people" achieved precedence over the socially disruptive individual interests of the designers. "All chance of discord had been eliminated, and a harmony created that had never been seen on any such scale before."[17]

To preserve and protect the exposition's image of revelatory beauty and high seriousness, the planners screened the Joy Zone behind the vast Machinery Hall and on the wrong side of the Avenue of Progress. The Joy Zone consisted of a broad concourse more than half a mile long, and for the most part offered the usual collection of curiosities, illusions, rides, primitive or exotic villages, and naughty appeals to male sexual appetites.[18] But in some ways the Joy Zone was different. The concessions director, Frank Burt, had promised to stock the street with "geniuses with great ideas," such as Fred Thompson. Although all plans had to be approved by the fair's Division of Works, Burt disclaimed any intention of imposing order on the appearance of the competing businesses. However, Burt did require concessionaires to construct "fantastic" façades for their attractions, which would "express without any reading sign if possible, what was offered inside."[19] The directive resulted in an avenue of mammoth sculptural oddities—a gigantic Uncle Sam beckoning customers to a souvenir shop, the stereotyped clownish black faces at the "Old Plantation," the giant toy soldiers flanking Toyland's main entrance—which had more in common with the exaggerated and brightly colored action of the Sunday supplement comics than with the main exposition's iconography. Whereas guidebooks encouraged visitors to linger contemplatively in the exposition's courtyards, the Joy Zone was built for immediate and easy consumption. Its "total synthesis of advertising and architecture" did not require reflection or cultivation; any child could read its signs. The buildings also lent a degree of grotesque absurdity or premeditated surrealism to the Joy Zone, which distinguished it from earlier exposition midways.[20] The Joy Zone's cultural reversion was further expressed in its practice of lining structures with unfrosted bulbs, which cast the entertainments in the "glare of the bizarre."[21] For all these reasons, as Todd put it, the Joy Zone "was not and could not be a part" of the harmonious exposition. It "was a picture in and by itself, a thing extraneous."[22]

Yet Todd and others exaggerated the Joy Zone's seclusion and difference. They overlooked the ways in which the deployment of magic and fairy tales joined, rather than divided, the opposing faces of the exposition. Hercules still spoke for much of the fair, which collectively represented, as one guidebook explained, "the Spirit and Romance of Man's Development, Energy, Adventure, Aspirations and Achievements."[23] But another voice, less rational and masculinist, also laid claim, with considerable success, to defining the fair's meanings. The spiritualist writer Cora Lenore Williams, for one, belittled the "arts and crafts of human industry" as the "fumbling and groping of earth's creatures." Williams detected instead "a new heaven and a new earth" revealed in the "fourth-dimensional aspect" of the fair. The truth of the exposition, in other words, was glimpsed through intuitive and, by implication, less grown-up eyes.[24] A writer for the *San Francisco Examiner* identified the Never-Landish atmosphere of the fair in a more Thompsonian vocabulary: this exposition "just won't stand for seriousness. It laughs and wants the world to laugh with it."[25]

Although Fred Thompson made clear from the start his intention of making light of the exposition city's solemnity, it appears that all those in authority in San Francisco took his foolishness seriously. Thompson had disclosed his interest in the San Francisco exposition the week after Christmas 1912 at a reception he threw at the New Amsterdam Theatre in New York. The showman had virtually disappeared from Broadway in the year or more since the ruinous fire at Luna Park. This occasion served to announce that he was "hard at work" on projects for both Luna Park and the theater, but he also planted rumors of something big for the 1915 world's fair.[26] No new theatrical projects panned out, but after ending his formal affiliation with Luna Park in July, he left for San Francisco to sell his ideas for Toyland. Once there he proposed to build what the theatrical daily, the *New York Morning Telegraph*, described as a "miniature city" that was "large, spacious, novel and comprehensive." The fair's Division of Concessions and Admissions endorsed the Toyland proposition and awarded him the concession. Thompson returned to New York "confident," according to the newspaper, that Toyland would "be his biggest and best contribution to the world's amusements."[27]

From these grandiose beginnings in magic and ballyhoo, however, Toyland's history split onto parallel but inseparable tracks: one involving the actual amusement, the other the figment of Thompson's overblown imagination. Frank Burt, the Joy Zone's director, had opened the Panama-Pacific door for Thompson. Burt was a veteran show businessman and had managed or owned an interest in a number of well-known urban parks—Chicago's Sans Souci and Denver's Lakeside, or White City—before his appointment in San Francisco. Burt came recommended to the exposition by, among others, A. L. Erlanger. Yet there is no evidence that he knew of Thompson's recent bankruptcy or reputation as a drunk and spendthrift. He told the fair management that Thompson was "the Peer of all Exposition Builders." Burt's support is less surprising than Thompson's ability to convince anyone he could un-

Fig. 6.3. A smiling Fred Thompson appeared relaxed and confident in this shot at the Toyland construction site, probably in mid-1914. His Noah's Ark office building is in the background. (*Collection of Donna Ewald Huggins.*)

dertake a venture projected to cost $750,000 (the advertised price was $1,000,000). A later investigation of the Toyland fiasco claimed Thompson had gone to San Francisco in 1913 with the backing of "Bet-a-Million" Gates. If he actually made this claim, it was a daring humbug; Gates had been dead for two years.[28] Whether or not he dropped that particular name, Thompson must have seduced the management with his New York reputation, the originality of his designs, and a "big money front," a skill he acquired in his early show days (fig. 6.3). But there was nothing goodnatured about this charade; any pretense of financial soundness would have constituted a conscious fraud on his part. In 1913 Thompson still was in personal bankruptcy and his puny assets remained in the hands of a trustee. When the venture collapsed in May 1914 because Thompson was virtually broke, the fair ceded the concession to the Toyland Amusement Company, a team of investors headed by E. W. A. Waterhouse, a local automobile parts manufacturer.[29] They retained the showman as designer and manager and scaled back the original proposal. But anyone familiar with *Little Nemo* or *Springtime* could have warned them that Thompsonian amusements were, by definition, immune to economy. The actual Toyland became the grandest embarrassment of the Joy Zone, and brought more than tears to the eyes of its investors, who lost at least $70,000 and probably far more.[30] "Toyland G. U.," one fair official later observed, "was a miserable failure."[31]

Exactly what amusements were built at Toyland is hard to determine; records of its operation are scanty at best, probably because of its continuous state of financial crisis. What evidence there is, however, indicates that only a fraction of the amusements that Thompson promised in 1913 made it off the drawing board. Yet even if the actual show was a poor excuse for a playground for the human race, the Toyland that Thompson sold the fair management, as Burt and others realized early on, was fantastic to contemplate, and one did not have to believe in fairies to agree with Thompson when he promoted his venture as "a real novelty and departure from the conventional."[32]

When a local newspaper described Toyland as a "Barrie-like fantasy,"[33] it put a name to the narratives and images the showman generated to sell the enterprise. The original design even included a "City of Peter Pan" with streets named for J. M. Barrie and the actor Maude Adams.[34] But even without these literal signposts, Toyland was steeped in the exploitable antimodern longings of Peter Pantheism. As the *New York World* explained in an early description, "none can enter here who is not willing to play, for the G.U. [Grown Up] tin soldiers will guard the entrance against all those nasty modern people who keep on killing the fairies by not believing in them."[35] The newspaper's warning linked Toyland to the moment in *Peter Pan* when the fairy Tinker Bell has drunk poison meant for the eternal boy. Desperate to save her life, Peter appeals to the audience, explaining that she will recover only if they show their belief in fairies by applauding. Audiences invariably responded and Tinker Bell never died.[36] Thompson attempted a similar appeal with Toyland, clouding the nastiness of commercial exchange at the point of admission while (he hoped) profiting nonetheless from his audience's willingness to pay to be children.

As Thompson told the story, the idea for Toyland Grown Up had occurred to him several years earlier at a holiday gathering. As the company congregated around the Christmas tree, he selected a "particularly interesting" toy from the abundant array spread over the tree and asked, "Can you imagine this one 200 feet high?" "The idea seemed odd and original to my friends, but the novelty of it made such a strong appeal to them that I decided to bring into being an entirely new and original form of amusement. That was the beginning of Toyland Grown Up."[37] Although this account may well have been apocryphal, the narrative surrounded Toyland with an aura of sentiment, magic, wonder, and the material splendor of the middle-class celebration of Christmas. The story specifically recalls "The Nutcracker and the Mouse King," the mid-nineteenth-century tale by E. T. A. Hoffmann. This story was the basis of Tchaikovsky's ballet "The Nutcracker Suite," first produced in the 1890s and, for much of the twentieth century, a staple of middle-class entertainment for children during the holiday season. The dramas of Thompson's Toyland history, Hoffmann's story, and Tchaikovsky's ballet all commence at a Christmas party amid a luxurious profusion of children's playthings and culminate in a dream world of magically enlarged and animated toys. In the sixth tableau of the ballet, in particular, the girl protagonist Clara dream-watches as the "Christmas tree grows and reaches enormous proportions" and the dolls and other toys stir to life.[38]

Whether or not Thompson consciously copied the tale, the parallels indicate how he cast himself in the role of a smiling, well-meaning sorcerer, like Hoffmann's genial toymaker Drosselmeyer. Thompson was no less a participant in this fantasy than were his prospective patrons. Promotions claimed that "His Majesty Santa Claus" ruled the "Principality of Toyland." Even as the cost of the enterprise was publicized as one million dollars, the managerial touch and profit motives of showmen or capitalists were masked. The *San Francisco Examiner* observed that Thompson "has bubbling inside him a wholesome, effervescent play impulse which has met entirely too much suppression under the exigencies of modern industrial life. He wants to unloose the fountain."[39] A writer for the *San Francisco Bulletin* described the showman as "a man with an elf-like manner and a wise gnome-like smile."[40] The *San Francisco Chronicle*, in yet another reference to *A Midsummer Night's Dream*, called him "the modern 'Puck'" who "has impishly outdone himself in his assaults upon human dignity."[41] Thompson identified himself in his San Francisco letterhead as the "Plenipotentiary and Envoy Extraordinary" of Toyland, and listed his address as "His

Majesty's Council Chamber, Court of Youth." The professional credentials following his name were not the "A.I.A." of the American Institute
of Architects, but six stylized toy blocks, "A B C X Y Z."[42] Running the
whole business from his office, a roomy Noah's Ark that he built on the
Toyland site, Thompson made light of Hercules in everything he did.
He "knows how to make grown-ups play," the *Examiner* reported late in
1913. "While he works happily in the spirit of play, he has studied deeply
the science of prodding sluggish imaginations."[43] For Thompson, it
seems, living in Never Land was not a matter of banishing commercial
considerations, nor did it involve actually being a powerless child. The
showman claimed unique, studied qualifications that enabled him to
enact power in new and profitable ways. He knew how to make people
pay to play.

So it was not exactly in a spirit of innocence that Thompson designed
Toyland to look as though a child had built it. Although it offered some
of the usual Coney Island attractions, these were ancillary to its conceptual novelty. Luna's palaces had always implied a reference to the external claims that a harried man escaped at Coney Island. At least from a
distance, they looked substantial, even though they were not. With Toyland, Thompson sought to stifle these references, to give freer rein to
the unsecured, endlessly desiring self that he valued so highly. His illustrations show an off-balance and asymmetrical city. A precariously balanced stack of spools composes a tower; buildings appear to have been
improvised by a child using whatever materials were on hand.[44] Thompson wanted the patrons of Toyland to feel as if they were entering the
playroom of a gargantuan child or an outsized toy store teeming with
mechanical life. "The beautiful fancies of Grimm, Andersen and Lewis
Carroll, fantastically supplemented by Thompson's million-dream
power imagination, will take form in a wilderness of Brobdingnagian
toys," promised the *Examiner*. "Toyland will be a fantasy of color, a playful, happy warping and twisting of the set relationships of life."[45]

Thompson's illustrations indicate that he designed Toyland with
men like himself in mind and that he wanted to shake their solidity of
identity and needs. Immense toy soldiers guard the entry, while a band
plays beneath the dome of a gigantic mushroom (fig. 6.4). Grown men
try to traverse Cobweb Lake, a lacework of thick ropes over a lagoon. A
mammoth toy duck ferries passengers down a canal.[46] In the rear, Old
Mother Hubbard's cupboard, five stories high, serves as the Toyland

Fig. 6.4. Even supplemented by brass bands, Toyland's playroom architecture and features could not drum up enough business to put the venture in the black. (*Billy Rose Theatre Collection, The New York Public Library for the Performing Arts, Astor, Lenox and Tilden Foundations.*)

Grand Hotel. Inside, "one great big shelf" is the main ballroom, where couples dance on an enormous plate to the tunes of an orchestra seated in a champagne glass.[47] There were to be many other features, but the implication in all was the mocking of maturity, responsibility, and any external claim that constrained a man's sense of self. Santa Claus was to be Toyland's patron, Noah's Ark the management's headquarters, and the one church an upside-down structure dangling from the chain of a derrick, with a sign announcing "Church Picnic To-Day."[48] A ninety-foot doll, carrying a pennant declaring "Votes for Women" (which figure was actually built), marks the entrance to "Crazy Town," which one journalist described as "a veritable topsy-turvy land." Inside "you duck your head to pass under a crazy clothesline bearing men's garments and come face to face with the legend, 'Votes for Men.'"[49]

If such features indicated that politics and religion had become laughing matters for men, so, too, had work. In the sketches, automa-

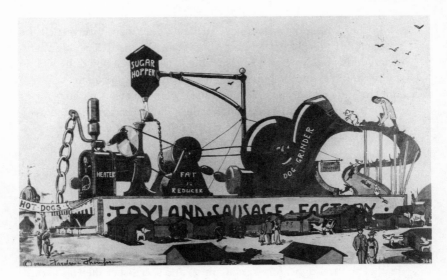

Fig. 6.5. Thompson's design for a hot-dog stand at Toyland Grown Up poked fun at sentimental pet owners and earnest advocates of "pure food" regulations. (*San Francisco History Center, San Francisco Public Library.*)

tons, not people, do the work of Toyland, plying cranks and levers to energize the park's machinery of fun, freeing men and women from the drudgery, discipline, and even the sight of human labor. The Toyland roller coaster is a treacherous tangle of scaffolding at a construction site; mechanical men race wheelbarrows loaded with passengers along the reticulated network of planks.[50] At the hot-dog stand, customers select an actual canine for lunch; a mechanical Chinese figure leads the raw materials into a "dog grinder" and other exaggerated processors that transform it into a chain of wienies (fig. 6.5).[51] It is hard to imagine that Thompson believed middle-class patrons would buy either of these features, especially the facetiousness of his Sausage Factory, which exploited the racial stereotype of dog-eating Asians even as it satirized Progressive exposés of the meatpacking industry such as *The Jungle* by Upton Sinclair (1906). At a time when growing numbers of bourgeois Americans had come to cherish animals for their apparently humanlike qualities, the humor of this gruesome slaughterhouse might have been lost on many people.[52]

In these and other examples, Toyland's inefficiency travestied the efficiency of industrial manufacturing. Thompson may have been criticizing industrial work as dehumanizing to laborers, although he was no more willing to question the necessity of industrial capitalism than were the fair's major patrons.[53] Furthermore, he anticipated that his patrons would be from the middle class, if not the affluent professional and managerial class; people, in other words, who had little if any direct experience with industrial machinery or labor, except, perhaps, to manage or profit from it. How such people would have regarded his park is a matter of speculation, but it is apparent that Thompson expected their views to be like his. The citizens of Toyland were freed from having either to work or to worry about the plight of workers. By inverting work, religious, and civic settings as playgrounds and picnics and turning inexhaustible mechanical laborers into toys, he sought to put a smiling face on the concerns that vexed white-collar men like himself, who lived in a topsy-turvy land of political rights for women, union and socialist challenges to capitalist authority, and corporate managerial structures that distanced them from both property ownership and the point and act of production. The idea that work should be like play was appealing from the perspective of the brokers and buyers of consumer goods and services, who had an emotional and financial stake in the dream life of consumer capitalism. It also may have comforted a broader middle-class audience that worried about both the welfare and the potential insurgence of the men and women whose labor made their pleasure possible.[54] Yet Toyland also distorted an aspect of industrial life in which actual working women and men found little to thrill them. From their vantage, the claim that factories and stock markets were "toys just the same" suppressed the crucial inequalities between and within these social settings.

The nature of the delight and hope that Thompson wished to sell was apparent in his illustration of *The Wishing Well* (fig. 6.6). This house of mirrors was

The Place Where
Fat People Can Get Thin
Thin People Can Get Fat
Small People Can Get Tall
Tall People Can Get Small
Or Anything They Wish[.][55]

Fig. 6.6. In the Wishing Well, as in the park as a whole, patrons who believed in the "Barrie-like fantasy" of Toyland could wish for anything and be anything they wished. (*Larson Collection, Special Collections, California State University, Fresno.*)

The amusement suggests a new twist on Thompson's long-standing conviction that vanity—"the overpowering ambition of those grown-up children called the human race to be seen 'doing things'"—is an essential element of human nature that begs to be exploited by the shrewd impresario.[56] Although it appears the Wishing Well never was built, its conception offers an alternative to the usual associations of vanity and self-indulgence with decadence and effeminacy.[57] In his sketch, most of the wishful patrons are male and their payoff is not personal corruption, but a happy warping of self in the Valentine "Land of Hearts," which lies at the bottom of the well.[58] In the Principality of Play that Thompson imagined, the choices and preferences ordinarily associated with disorder, such as vanity, would be courted, not corrected. Like other agents of the new consumer economy, Thompson encouraged all Americans to buy his fun, but his message was aimed at those middle-class men whom he had once described as the tragic victims of set circumstances. Toyland invited them to disregard religion, work, civic identity, and the welfare of others, and to subject themselves, their longings and dissatis-factions, to the alchemical wonders of the marketplace where they could be "Anything They Wish."

Wishes alone could not bring Toyland into existence, however. The fictional foundation of the enterprise was revealed early in 1914. The concessions management as well as the exposition's highest authorities increasingly had become concerned about the solvency of Thompson's company. A year before the exposition's scheduled opening, the pres-sure was mounting on Thompson to demonstrate that he could put to-gether the financing for the project. He had little to show for his efforts. An imprecise financial statement he submitted in mid-February 1914 revealed that the million-dollar playground was little more than a fan-tasy. For an amusement that would cost around $700,000, Thompson had only $2,500 in cash and no investors in sight. What was equally dis-tressing was that the showman was drinking heavily, the exposition's managers learned. Three months later the situation had not improved. Burt argued that Toyland "should be financed, if possible." It had been promoted for almost a year as the gem of the Joy Zone, and officials knew that its failure would leave an unacceptable dark spot on the boulevard. It was obvious by this point, however, that Thompson was washed up emotionally and financially.[59] Shortly afterward, the fair managers forced him to sign an abandonment of his concession to the exposition.[60]

The total cost of Toyland continued to be heralded as $1,000,000, although the new owners planned to spend just $150,000 on their ver-sion.[61] But from the moment they took control, Toyland consumed every dollar that could be squeezed out of them. By the end of August 1914, when the war in Europe was escalating, Waterhouse had sold only $5,000 in stock to friends. When he threatened to back out, the exposition arranged a way to keep Toyland solvent. Over the course of building the project, the fair lent the company almost $140,000; Waterhouse himself threw away almost $100,000 of his own money on the amusement.[62]

In the meantime Thompson had forged ahead with construction. The building costs, increased by the wet San Francisco fall and winter, mounted. On the opening day of the fair, visitors wandered through the unfinished Toyland, much of it covered with canvas. The company rushed to complete the job, which sent labor costs staggeringly high. By the time it actually opened, six long weeks without revenue into the fair, the total cost had risen to $278,000. Less than a week later Waterhouse and his partners were ready to shut it down. Toyland, in the words of the official historian, Todd, had fallen "flatter than Babylon." A week later Thompson hocked his prized collection of lucky miniature elephants and fled to New York. He told the newspapers there that he would devote his energies to "picturizing" the Bible as a moving picture; a few months later, he suffered a nervous breakdown and narrowly avoided dying of a kidney ailment. Soon after Thompson's departure from San Francisco, Toyland's untiring advocate, Frank Burt, declared the project a "myth, the dream of a distorted brain. No possible salvation."[63] Yet another concessions official was left marveling at what might have been. As he wrote five months later, "Whether, under the best of conditions, the fantastic dreams of this wonderful genius could have been realized would only be wildest conjecture. Had he [Thompson] been successful and able to give only one full dress rehearsal according to his plans, those who were fortunate enough to witness the scenes would have had something to tell their grandchildren that would rival all fairy tales put together."[64]

### Mellow Enough to Eat

Thompson's claims to capital had been mythic from the start, but his dream, as Burt apparently believed, was not so far-fetched. Toyland was neither extraneous nor foreign to the main body of the exposition. Both of the opposed aspects of the exposition—its serious main body as well as its antic amusement appendix—were part of Titania's Playground. The chief architects who unconsciously integrated the two parts of the exposition city were the American artist Jules Guérin, who was appointed to supervise and impose a system of color on the exposition as a whole, and Walter D'Arcy Ryan, the designer of its spectacular lighting scheme. Both men firmly believed they were advancing the established cultural hierarchies and polarities championed by earlier fairs. For instance, Ryan insisted that the illumination of the exposition "was highly educational in character."[65] What was remarkable was how they sought to replace ugliness with beauty—by reenchanting the disenchanted, by incorporating magic and childlike wonder into their celebrations of Western civilization. Their aesthetics suggested the same discomfort and unease that Thompson had with Herculean civilization. Like Thompson, both were popularly regarded as "magicians," wielding the instruments of color, light, and electricity. In doing so, they advocated—and much more effectively than Toyland Grown Up—the cultural consciousness informed and shaped by the commercial culture of Peter Pan.

Before San Francisco, Jules Guérin's work was probably as visible in America as that of any artist of his day, even if his name was not widely known. He had painted the topographical murals that decorated Pennsylvania Station in New York and the allegorical murals in the new Lincoln Memorial. In addition to his contributions to such upscale publications as *Harper's* and *Scribner's*, Guérin had illustrated Robert Hichens's deep-purple-prose accounts of travels in the Middle East, *Egypt and Its Monuments* (1908) and *The Near East: Dalmatia, Greece, and Constantinople* (1913). He was best known among artists as a master architectural delineator. He had produced the illustrations in *The Plan of Chicago* (1909), the landmark City Beautiful design by the architects Edward H. Bennett and Daniel Burnham. Guérin's work often was compared favorably to that of Maxfield Parrish, his friend and also an illustrator of books by Hichens. The appointment of Guérin in San Francisco was engineered by his friend and colleague Edward Bennett, the fair's chief planner.[66] The artist's involvement marked an important shift in the representation of "culture" at and by world's fairs. Most obviously, color had been a minor key at previous American fairs, which rarely deviated from the white staff composition of Chicago's White City. At San Francisco, though, Guérin was charged with designing a spectrum of colors that muralists and architects would apply in their respective contributions. His decree that "there shall be no white" distinguished the 1915 fair from its predecessors, but it also marked how he, in league with the architects, made the color of the palaces a centrally important aspect of their symbolic language of progress. The primary exterior base was a softly tinted, buff-colored staff composition resembling Roman travertine limestone. On top of this base, Guérin applied "rich and soft" variations of Mediterranean greens, reds, oranges, pinks, and blues to the architectural and sculptural features. "I resolved," he said, "that even the roofs should be harmoniously colored: so that when those who throng the avenues on the land side of the exhibition look down upon them they will see a great party-colored area of red tiles, golden domes, and copper-green minarets." The entire exposition was color-coordinated; even security guards wore khaki uniforms to match the buildings.[67]

In part, Guérin's color scheme affirmed the artistic aspirations and reformist values of the exposition's management and the artist himself. The official historian, Todd, attributed their interest in color to the rediscovery of the ancients' use of tints in decorating classical sculpture and architecture. The president of the exposition rashly predicted that the fair would influence cities across America to establish "color commissions" to regulate domestic paint jobs, "in order that there may be a harmony of tone instead of the present discord."[68] But in addition to the Progressive concern for harmony and organization in aesthetics and politics, Guérin's designs demonstrated the enormous advances in color and dye techniques that had shaped the textile industries and fashion design in Europe and the United States since the late nineteenth century. The Panama-Pacific, in other words, reflected and encouraged the growing business of and consumer appetite for color.[69]

Guérin's integration with consumer culture is disclosed in another way. His exposition paint job corresponded to his own gauzy, almost abstract compositions of light and color that, according to one critic, had showed "not only the architecture but the very atmosphere" of Robert Hichens's travels in the Near East.[70] Guérin's association with Hichens is especially revealing of his ties to the contemporary consumer economy. The British writer's best-known work was *The Garden of Allah*, a sensationalist novel about an unmarried Englishwoman who escapes "the pettiness of civilized life" by escaping into the forbidden night of the Arabian desert, where she discovers the "barbarian" in herself. Although Hichens eventually punishes his heroine for her daring adventures, American audiences found the novel's sensual Orientalism more appealing than its moral. The novel was adapted to the stage, first in 1907 and then again in 1912, when its New York revival sparked an Arabian craze. The "Garden of Allah" was recreated in hotel lobbies, restaurants, and department store fashion shows; in 1912 the New York Wanamaker store hired members of the Broadway cast to lend authenticity to its Hichens-inspired fashion show. Hichens's vogue was one aspect of a larger Orientalist frenzy in the United States. The principal cause was the rapid and national expansion of American consumer industries, which incorporated Orientalism's primitive and sensual appeal into their sales apparatus.[71]

Guérin applied his "'Oriental' palette of stucco tones"[72] to the San Francisco palaces and courts as though he were painting a vast Hichens landscape that exuded the warm colors and luxurious comfort of the East. "Imagine," he urged a writer in 1913, "a gigantic Persian rug of soft melting tones, with brilliant splashes here and there, spread down for a mile or more, and you may get some idea of what the Panama-Pacific Exposition will look like when viewed from the distance."[73] The image, another writer predicted, "will be Oriental, a brightened Constantinople with Latin architectural strength and character."[74] Here, stated clearly, were the competing themes of the fair: the allure of the childlike Orient's luxury, ease, and desire, and the imperturbable strength of Hercules. Guérin's fantasy of a cityscape turned Oriental carpet and the vision of a new and improved Constantinople aglow in colors that were "mellow enough to eat," as Todd put it, positioned the exposition as the cultural ally of the institutions of consumption that engaged Orientalist sensuality and indulgence to sell goods.[75]

Walter D'Arcy Ryan wielded a similar wand. In 1915 he was the chief illuminating engineer at General Electric's Nela Laboratory and the leading designer of public and spectacular lighting in the United States. By that time he already had demonstrated his ability to work on a canvas even more extensive than that of Guérin. His most famous projects used light to illuminate peculiarly American icons—Niagara Falls, the Panama Canal, the Singer tower in New York—as well as such grandiose civic pageants as the 1909 Hudson-Fulton celebration in New York. Ryan's work provided not just objective lighting, but a luminous narrative of progressive and spiritual enlightenment. He practiced lighting as a combination of physical science, behaviorist psychology, expressive art, and secular religion.[76] His selection as "Chief of Illumination" indicated the degree to which the provision of spectacular artificial light was conceded by 1915 to encompass subjectivity as well as the objective phenomena of science. Ryan was assigned the task not only of lighting the fair, but also of creating the spectacular effects, designing the lighting standards and fixtures, and selecting the appropriate glass for the exposition's buildings and lighting fixtures. The Chief of Illumination was part engineer, architect, scenic decorator, artist, dramatist, and spiritualist.[77] He claimed to have built up "a new science out of chaos," which brought together the conflicting fields of art and science and, by implication, religion.[78] The poet and critic Edwin Markham could not contain himself after seeing Ryan's work in San Francisco, which he nominated as "the greatest revelation of beauty that was ever seen on the earth."[79]

Ryan staged the fair's revelatory beauties according to an evolutionary scale, moving from the primitive glare at the periphery to the civilized glow at the center. He regarded outlining buildings as a contemptible form of illumination and confined it to the stigmatized Joy Zone. On the Avenue of Progress dividing the Joy Zone from higher expressions of civilization, an "intermediate step or carnival effect" was installed to suggest the liminal transition from the "blaze" of the Joy Zone to the "soft illumination of the palaces." The transition gave "the visitor an opportunity to contrast the light of the past with the illumination of the future." Leaving the Joy Zone, one "looked from the semi-shadow upon beautiful vistas and the Guérin colors, which fascinating in the daytime, were even more entrancing by night." The result was theatrical, using lighting to create mood and setting rather than merely to shed light on objects. The fair's centerpiece, the Tower of Jewels, "standing mysteriously against the starry blue-black of the night," was the illuminated future. Here was a vision of "the science of lighting and the art of illumination." It "surpassed," Ryan said, "the dreams of Aladdin."[80]

The reference to the boy with three wishes in the *Arabian Nights* linked Ryan's lighting theatrics to Guérin's good-as-new Constantinople, revealing their common use of industrial technologies and organizational techniques to create an Orientalized landscape that restored enchantment to a disenchanted world and made wishes come true. According to Todd, Ryan's floods created an unearthly "fairyland at night," an atmosphere of "ghostly light and shadow." The Court of Abundance was a "grotto of wizardry," the Court of the Universe a scene from the Oriental "fancies of Maxfield Parrish." Buildings appeared to be alive— to glow on their own—as Ryan had hidden or obscured the lighting sources. Todd recalled that Ryan's illuminating "witchcraft" transformed plaster sculptures into "living flames in air" that "glowed with life and power." Ryan's "Scintillator"—forty-eight powerful searchlights that played in the sky above the exposition—was operated by squads of Marines commanded by "four corporals who received their orders by telephone from a first sergeant and megaphoned them to the men." The nineteenth century's symbol of social and industrial progress, a locomotive, was effectively rendered a toy, locked into position and run at sixty miles an hour to generate great clouds of steam, on which the Scintillator screened shafts of light. Todd, like others, marveled at the system and "punctuality" that organized and managed the enchantment of the exposition. "Such magic," he explained, "was wrought through modern organization and appliances," noting especially the contributions of the General Electric research laboratories.[81]

Time and time again Ryan reminded fellow engineers and the ordinary public that his "dreams of Aladdin" were "the result of a concentrated study in the best uses and applications of artificial light."[82] Like Thompson, he had studied how to prod imaginations and to make grown-ups believe in fairies. But in the many published discussions of the lighting, magic and Titania's playful fays got the better part of the attention. "The god of mirth descends upon the Exposition at night," observed a writer for the *San Francisco Examiner*, who did not mention Ryan's "uniform system" and planning. By day the exposition "feeds the brain" and "talks business to the man of affairs, science to the erudite and just plain astonishment and wonder to the average man and woman." But at night, it "shuts the book of learning" and "jests and plays with old and young alike." At that time the exposition becomes a "magic city," and no scholar can maintain his "somber" outlook, no "paterfamilias" his seriousness. "It somehow dispels the cares of life; it quenches ambition temporarily and calls for enjoyment.... The brains of those men whose life ordinarily is a round of prosaic dry as dust facts and business—those brains, too, are thrilled and softened."[83]

Many regretted that, in November, the lights of the "magic city" were extinguished, but Ryan returned the next year to make Wonderland a permanent aspect of the city's commonplace life. In October 1916, the local Downtown Association unveiled the "Path of Gold," an urban lighting system that Ryan had designed for Market Street, the city's major commercial and transportation artery. Although a downtown merchant described the "installation" as "a first-class, modern, efficient, distinctive system" that would uphold San Francisco's "reputation as 'a city that does things,'" such dry-as-dust assessments were silenced by descriptions of Market Street's dreamlike splendor. The 155 lighting standards cast a shadowless white glow on the façades of the business and civic structures, transforming the city's center into a "lane of lure." On the night the lights came on for good, large crowds "poured forth from their homes in an expectant throng, lining the roped curbs in a mass." Newspaper accounts proclaimed the enchantment of the city's most important business street: they spoke of the "Wonders of Fairy Street," "'Magic of Aladdin's Lamp' Lights City's Main Thoroughfare," "Traced by Fairy Wand." The celebratory parade featured fourteen illuminated floats, which told the "story of lighting, from the days of the cave-men and their pine knots down to the present day of high-power filament bulbs." The last float was the "climax of the pageant," showing "the powerful light of To-day. Upon a high throne sat the 'Great God—Mazda,' devotees before him doing homage." The designer of the urban lighting scheme, the furnisher of facts for the pageant of "the evolution of man and the advance of light," and the toast of the town that night was Walter D'Arcy Ryan. According to the *San Francisco Examiner*, "thousands of Peter Pans" cheered his "wizardry" and "accepted it, regardless of the fact that the quality of the light was not golden at all."[84]

Like most of those published about the event, the *Examiner* account was unabashed boosterism, but the references underlying its enthusiasm are worth examining. They linked the "lane of lure" to the two major consumer texts of the era, Barrie's *Boy Who Would Not Grow Up* and L. Frank Baum's story about the Land of Oz, where everything was green only because people believed it was so. The integration of San Francisco's well-lit business district into the universe of Oz and Never Land suggest the growing literacy in—and legitimacy of—the fundamental fantasies of Peter Pan culture. Market Street, the polychromatic and sparkling Panama-Pacific exposition, the dreamscape of Toyland Grown Up—all appeared as if they had been "wished into being with fairy wand."[85] Or, as Fred Thompson might have said, all of these fantastic projects were kid's stuff, all toys just the same. The demand for a quotient of child's play on top of the usual managerial concerns for modern and efficient installations still raised serious misgivings about men who claimed or wished to be boys. But evidence for the rewards of never growing up was mounting, well beyond the examples of San Francisco's various Toylands.

### A New Love for Toys

Such rewards eluded Fred Thompson. Little was heard from him after his return to New York. "Picturizing" the Bible may have seemed a way of restoring order to his life and assets to his balance sheet, but there is no evidence that anything ever came of the project. For the next four years it was Thompson's poor health, rather than his successes, that made headlines, and small ones at that. Then in mid-April 1919, when he actually had only two months to live, he entertained a writer from the *New York Sun* in his Manhattan apartment. The newspaper reported that, despite his near disappearance since 1915, the showman was "clear of eye again and his mind as young and keen as ever"—vague references to Thompson's immediate history of physical illness, mental breakdown, and chronic drunkenness. The return of his health seemed also to have revived his promotional energies and fervor to entertain.[86]

Thompson let the paper in on a scoop: he was about to launch an ambitious plan to make America the preeminent toymaking and toy-buying country in the world. The walls of his apartment were covered with recently completed illustrations of a Principality of Toyland for the center of New York City. The purpose this time around, though, was not profit, but a public-spirited incorporation of the child spirit that would restore play to a disenchanted world. "In these days of American efficiency," he explained, "toys are stamped out as a cold commercial proposition on a par with the dollar watch." Toys lacked drama, action, and life, and the "abhorrent" result was a nation of children "too sophisticated" to regard them as anything more than objects.

The New York Toyland would counteract this deplorable condition, taking children back to Never Land and teaching them to see the material world with new eyes. Instead of having joyless laborers tending machines that issued a stream of things, Thompson's wonderland would be a manufacturing amusement park, decorated in resplendent colors and operated by crippled war veterans, blind people, midgets, and giants, all dressed in fanciful costumes. The fruits of their labor would be copyrighted under Toyland's trademark and distributed, for a royalty, for mass production by manufacturers around the country. Cynical juveniles would watch how "Santa and his workers made the toys before one's very eyes, among lathes and wheels that are not grimy and greasy like the factory wheels of earth, but which whang and bang and whizz in myriads of colors." At the conclusion, the youngsters would board a "golden elevator" and return to the commonplace world. But they would leave rehabilitated, their "belief in Santa" restored along with "a new love for toys."

The Principality of Toyland, which rehearsed a lot of ideas that had gone nowhere in San Francisco, also suggested how little Thompson's decline had changed him. However clear his eye, he was seriously ill and virtually penniless; yet he still believed in toys and play and his own unending childhood. For all practical purposes, though, the scheme was another hallucination, a therapeutic fantasy that reflected the ailing showman's unconscious identification with the physical and social invalidism of wounded soldiers, the blind, and midgets, not to mention the play-starved children who were the ostensible reasons for the project. The Principality of Toyland was a massive convalescent ward for a nation that seemed too modern to embrace an aging and dying Peter Pan.

Thompson may have lost his grip on reality, but he was far from losing his mind. The skeptical reporter for the *New York Sun* deserves some credit for recognizing how "gripping the hearts and minds of the children" necessarily increased "by millions the toylovers in the young world." More believers in Santa Claus ultimately entailed an expanding demand for playthings. Integrating industry into dreamland may have seemed a cure for what ailed Americans, but it also outlined a therapeutic strategy that was well suited to market exploitation. Yet, whereas Thompson had been ahead of most Americans in marketing play and eternal youth at the Buffalo world's fair in 1901 and on Coney Island two years later, his ideas by 1919 were, if anything, a sideshow to the nationwide efflorescence of the commercial culture of Peter Pan. He may not have realized it, but he was describing, rather than prescribing, changes. Contemporary designers of the urban retail economy already were hard at work making a case for the profit potential of eternal childhood, absorbing and expanding the strategies embedded in Thompson's earliest successes into an integrated institutional network for the design, production, distribution, and consumption of fantasy, childhood, and play. These tactics were visible throughout the urban economy, from the gaudy pageantry of department store retailing to the choruses of women riding "Kiddie Kars" in the 1916 Ziegfeld Midnight Frolic.[87]

If any sector of the consumer economy did not need Thompson's guidance in integrating the industrial with less material ideas, it was the

American toy industry. By 1919, the United States already was rapidly becoming the world's leading producer and consumer of toys. The industry's history shows both the widening appeal of boy-manhood and workplace hedonism and the dilemmas posed by these historical developments. It also exposes in detail how Thompsonian and other playthings marketed in a Peter Pan culture operated as prototypes for the merchandising techniques of twentieth-century consumer capitalism. The culture of eternal boyhood operated well beyond the boundaries of leisure-time occupations; it also encompassed and abetted new middle-class expectations of work and of business success.

Thompson's ventures, from the Tennessee centennial through his last desperate fantasy, laid out the need for toys and how to sell that need. Perhaps as important, his exploits also suggested how to stand tall as a man who made or sold play for a living. Before 1915, domestic toy-makers believed they were struggling on two fronts: first, against the more experienced and established German manufacturers who controlled domestic markets, and second, against Americans themselves, who tended to disregard both toys and the men who owned the businesses that made or sold them. Hence the importance of Fred Thompson's record of achievement. The major trade publications, *Playthings* in New York and *Toys and Novelties* in Chicago, frequently carried news of his ventures. (Both published regular dispatches on Toyland Grown Up at the San Francisco fair.) In these accounts the showman appeared as one of their own, although on a grand scale. His Luna Park and Hippodrome theater were universally loved, and seemed already to have broken into a vast and to this point unexploited market for play. Even as toy men envied his success, they also felt the slights of which Thompson complained throughout his career, especially the sense of being a minor tributary to the main currents of American life. Thompson's achievements—the wealth and notoriety no less than the joy his work gave him—lent legitimacy to the play industry and to the men who built and identified themselves with it. The showman was an object lesson in the manly potential of eternal boyhood, which was just the lesson that toy men sorely felt they needed.

Although the growth of the American toy industry constituted a story of steady and impressive commercial success, the white-collar men who actually worked in or supervised the businesses still felt they had to prove themselves as men. As they conventionally told the story, in the

early phase of the business, before 1905 to 1910, the domestic toy industry and toys in general constituted an incidental, even despised part
of American life. In the days of German-made toys, *Playthings* explained
in 1919, toys "boasted of no mercantile prestige.... The public bought
them because children had to have playthings of one kind or other." Descriptions of these early days emphasized the petty stature, the physical
weakness and dependency of the business, and echoed Fred Thompson's defensive denunciations of the "distinguished" men who scorned
his amusements. Compared with other commercial ventures, the toy
industry seemed either "young" (which toy men regarded as a slight to
their pride) or "trivial." Manufacturers and leading urban department
stores viewed toymaking and selling "as a side show" limited to the
Christmas season.[88] Many of the century's earliest domestic producers
began making toys as a seasonal sideline, often as a production consideration to use up scrap materials or to keep a factory busy during times
when the principal line of business was not in production.[89] In addition,
the men who were put in charge of the scorned retail department were
ill fit to resist their marginalization. They tended to be marked by a condition of dependence and powerlessness: "the boss's little brother," or
the "unfortunate" man "whose good nature prevented refusal," or,
finally, the "uninformed buyer from another department" who knew
nothing about toys and simply bought and sold what he was told. In all
respects, the body of the early toy business and of the toy man himself
resembled that of toyless children as the industry defined them in the
salubrious postwar years: "Poor, pale little devils, flat chested, spindle
legged and hollow cheeked with sunken and lack lustre eyes."[90]

Toy men sought to build themselves up—to make themselves
plenipotentiaries of play—in a number of ways. Some tried to hire men
instead of women for the department, but given the low status of toymaking and selling, they had difficulty keeping male clerks in their departments. Between 1890 and 1940, store managers and the public in
general believed that women were more suited than men to sales positions as a whole, and not just in toys. Women could be paid less than
men, and it was widely assumed in the business that women possessed
qualities peculiar to their sex—a capacity for sympathy and concern
with others' needs, skills of manipulation, a keen appreciation of domestic duties and responsibilities, a desire to please—that were adapt-
able to the service ethos of modern merchandising and could profitably

be exploited.[91] Service itself was problematic for men in a culture with roots in republicanism, which was wary of the motives of servile men.[92] Yet toy selling seemed to carry a stigma even greater than that of other sales jobs because of its association with child's play. Although there appeared to be no consensus among managers on the necessity of having male clerks, many believed sex was relevant to toy merchandising. As a Kansas City toy man explained, "Women clerks should be placed in charge of dolls, dolls' accessories, etc., and the sterner sex in charge of trains, lanterns and electrical toys."[93] However, even if they believed "every toy department should have at least one man on the permanent selling force," they were unable to keep the "sterner sex" in the department. Men would clerk anywhere—suits, furniture, even millinery—before toys. The male clerk, an exasperated buyer complained, "seems to feel that such departments offer a man 'man's' work." This buyer was advised to try to bribe "a good man, or a likely boy" with a higher salary.[94]

### Creators, Not Imitators

A more effective strategy among retailers for asserting the seriousness of the toy man paralleled Fred Thompson's neverending effort to build an expanded, year-round market for toys and play. Retailers would no longer accept the straitjacketing custom and habit that limited toy buying to the Christmas season. In pursuing this goal, toy men believed that they had a number of advantages in their favor. First, they regarded children as "the easiest of all customers to influence." It was just a matter of putting "a little thought on the subject to take advantage of this fact to the benefit of [the retailer's] own pocketbook." There also was the issue of what toy men made and sold and to whom. In addition to being insatiable and capricious, children were also numerous and destructive. Toy men thrilled at the thought of "twenty-five million children in the United States 'of a toy age.'" "Imagine that huge army of toy-shop invaders—and, mark you, they are also toy destroyers—ready, at the beginning of each year, to consume your manufactures." The problem, then, was not in getting children to buy. As one noted with delight, give kids "a nickel, a dime or a quarter, stand them before a display of toys, and see how long it takes the coin to change hands." Rather, the problem lay in changing how the retailing establishment and the consuming public regarded toys. Playthings had to be "taken out of the Christmas tree class and put into every day life."[95]

For toy men, "making" a market was an expression of masculine aggression and independence, as opposed to the passive and weakly dependent position of the "boss's little brother."[96] It meant actually acquiring or conquering territory in the store, a kind of property ownership, expanding the temporary Christmas toy section to the permanent toy floor for every day life. As *Playthings* editorialized, the industry was held in submission by "a certain attitude of the human mind." It was not "creating a field for itself." During the war years, when German supplies dried up, toy demand grew so rapidly that even smaller stores established permanent toy displays, following the example set by some of the largest stores a decade before. Yet toy men preferred to see themselves not as the beneficiaries of fortunate circumstances, but as aggressive, self-made men who controlled their destinies. "It is by this method of creating a market rather than following blindly along established lines," explained *Playthings*, "that the great strides have been made by American toy manufacturers." No longer content to let children decide what they wanted, toy men were, as an ad for the Erector line of construction toys claimed, going "Over the Top in 1918," conquering new markets, acquiring new territory in the store, and telling children what they desired. In early 1920 a toy man requested "just another year or two"; by then, "the toy industry will have imbedded itself in the world of commerce so deeply, substantially and permanently that nothing under the sun will ever move it or distract it from its rightful position." Other toy men already felt the changes. As one had proclaimed a year earlier, "we are finding all our latent talents coming to the surface. We are giving expression to the best in us and thus becoming creators, not imitators. We are relying more on our own resources."[97] Like Fred Thompson, they were learning to make play pay.

Yet in conquering their territory and capturing the "twenty-five million children," toy men had to answer to a paradoxical imperative. The only way to penetrate markets and to secure the territory of Toyland was to combine executive ability and boyish dreams, to become themselves the child-man inhabitants of Fairyland, the playful, good-hearted friends of their little customers. As one toy writer insisted, "each toy department and each toy store must consider itself as a commercial business, with a sentimental work to perform."[98] This prescription would have made no sense in the nineteenth century, when "sentimental" was a synonym for "unmanly."[99] To mix business with such emotions was not just to confuse the separate moral spheres and natures of men and women, but to invite disaster.[100] But in the commercial culture of Peter Pan, to repeat the novelist Samuel Merwin's assessment of Fred Thompson, such a combination was one of the rarest and one of the finest things in the world. Marketplaces of play required a new kind of man, one more in tune with the emerging suburban ideal of "masculine domesticity." In the early twentieth century, magazines and other sources of expert advice were urging middle-class fathers to claim a greater presence in their children's lives. Rather than acting like stern Olympian patriarchs, they should pal around with the kids and act like caring older companions, especially to their sons.[101] Merchants commercialized this ethos, adjusting themselves both to the new child-centeredness of the suburban ideal and to the demands of the marketplace. As the buyer for New York's Fourteenth Street Store asserted in 1909, the "girls and men" of the toy department "must enter into the spirit of hearty childhood themselves; they must be children to their friends, calling them by name, if possible.... If a little girl gets her little toe stepped upon, she is kissed and comforted. If a small boy bumps into a swing that refuses to get out of his way, his wounds are rubbed and he is coaxed into a new game." Another suggested that the best way to get the "customer's viewpoint of playthings" was to have his clerks "dress in the well loved costumes of Mother Goose and the Fairy Tales."[102] Costuming salesclerks as Bo-Peep and Jack Horner was a fine combination of sentiment and salesmanship, although by 1927 it was not so rare as during Thompson's early years in New York.[103]

The commercialization of the "spirit of hearty childhood" was an accurate indicator of the way in which toy selling was at the center of significant changes in American retailing. Christmas toy sales had been an increasingly important aspect of urban retailing since the early 1890s, and special decorative features, particularly in window displays, had frequently accented the Christmas seasons.[104] Beginning in 1912 (around the time Fred Thompson leaked his idea for Toyland at the New Amsterdam reception), leading American department stores substantially increased the use and elaborateness of holiday decorations and entertainment features. "It is not sufficient to get the customers into the stores," *Playthings* observed that year; "they must be entertained there, and this is the real secret of merchandising at this season." That year, for example, the Wanamaker store in New York abandoned the "distinctly businesslike atmosphere" that had marked its toy department in the past and installed a "Fairyland," decorating the sales floor with "impressive green dragons" and "plaster heads of comic figures." With each succeeding Christmas season at Wanamaker's, *Playthings* reported in 1915, "there has been shown a disposition to stage Toyland in a manner really theatrical in its appeal and truly electrical in its impression. The idea was to delight and dazzle beyond description." Prior to 1915, *Playthings* noted, the New York Gimbels toy department had been weighted down with "a sort of majestic dignity that ... had some of the purely educative atmosphere of the museum." No longer; that year, Gimbels installed a "Santa Claus Land" and some of its decorations and features resembled "a three-ring circus gone mad." Such toy displays were achieving the status of "real show spots of the town for juvenile New Yorkers" and adults.[105] In big and small cities alike, retailers were following the guidelines of Titania's playground: selling had to be done in the spirit of the child at play, not in the sense of strenuous, stern duty.[106]

Dazzling adult and child customers with decorative features was part of a larger scheme to banish—or, rather, disguise—the commercialism and pressured sales tactics that permeated the "adult" areas of the store. "If possible," advised one toy man, "get away from the fixed and stiff business-like appearance of the adults' end of the store because nothing so grates on the soul of the child as a matter-of-fact stiffness." W. G. Hegeman, the influential toy buyer for Macy's, instructed fellow buyers in 1913 to appeal to the "happy, care-free nature of the child" and to expel from their departments "the ordinary more or less sordid merchandising appeal" that was used to sell apparel, furniture, and appliances.[107] "Let the spirit of play" rule the toy department, urged Kitty Walker, the buyer for the Grand Leader store in St. Louis. "Without it the child feels restrained and stricken with awe." In 1919, Bloomingdale's in New York advertised its "Happyland" as "just the sort of [place] that every child will love—not one of those cold, *stand-off, hands-off* shows with 'Don't Touch' signs bobbing up everywhere, but an Affair of toys and joys." Yet in addressing "every child," toy men knew that the people who read ads and bought toys usually were adults. The elaboration of the "fairyland spirit of toys" actually was aimed at grown-ups.

"By all means," implored a writer in *Playthings*, "let us realize that the dear public is just begging for merchants to forget the strictly commercial, particularly in respect to toys, and to give them the glimpse of Fairyland that toys by their very nature promise all of us." Ads told women and men to go to Toyland to "forget about your troubles—forget that you are grownups—go back to your childhood days."[108]

In part, this sales strategy reflected the dominant retail service ideal that the great urban merchants, Marshall Field and John Wanamaker, pioneered in the late nineteenth century. To banish the transparently commercial was not unusual advice; most merchants sought to "disarm the customer by replicating the [anticommercial] ambience of a bourgeois home."[109] Yet the "toy department spirit," as it was often described and proposed, aimed even more completely to transform merchandising, disarming its adult and child customers by creating an antipatriarchal atmosphere of parentless freedom, intergenerational equality, and wish fulfillment. Managers of toy departments were urging a version of "masculine domesticity" on each other. To make sales, they had to become a new kind of men, by suppressing the male passions of selfishness and determination to acquire wealth and by assuming what was traditionally a woman's role as selfless nurturer and companion of children. The "toy man's proposition," as one writer defined it, was "to put sharp commercial considerations aside." A veteran of the doll firm Fleishaker & Baum urged the buyer to "put all of himself and all of his love for the littles[t] ones into his work and while he may not get as big a money return for his labor as some other departments may, the reward in the happiness brought to the children will pay better than gold." Another cautioned that "the makers and sellers of play[th]ings must know children and must have a high regard for children"; obvious advice perhaps, but also necessary because middle-class men had, for most of the nineteenth century, spent little time with their children, male or female.[110] In fact, few of the preconditions for success as a toy man conformed to nineteenth-century prescriptions of manly respectability. What kind of Victorian man could fulfill the twelve qualifications for successful toy selling enumerated by a *Toys and Novelties* writer in 1918, the foremost of which was, *"Can be a child once again yourself"?*[111]

As all of these quotations suggest, the illusion of free play and spontaneous desire, of "childhood days" in "Happyland," was more important than actually letting adults or children do as they wanted or get what they wished. Appearances notwithstanding, liberty in the toy department was largely structured by and subordinate to the merchandising needs of the store. The idea of making the child feel as if she or he were the proprietor of the store was founded on the faith that loyalty won during childhood ensured "a good customer in after life." The meanings and symbols of the toy department were designed not to free children or adults but, as a veteran clerk explained in 1929, "to create the desire for ownership whenever the children come into the store. Place the toy doll or game in their hands, place him astride the velocipede. In every case make the kid believe he or she owns that toy." Yet as toy men talked to each other and encouraged these schemes and practices, they insisted that it was both good business and actually the case that the toy department was, as it should be, not "cold or so lonely," but an "oasis" of innocence in the pecuniary "world commercial."[112] Toyland offered an icily instrumental market solution to the antimodernist yearning for a refuge of warmth and community in the heartless, impersonal, pervasively commercial modern world.[113]

In truth, hiding the pecuniary reality of the toy department only meant masking the exercise of power. For toy men to become children again did not amount to infantilization. On the contrary, by cultivating the boy inside, a toy man did not surrender power so much as devise new ways of enacting it by disguising its influence. W. A. Finnerty, the toy man at New York's Wanamaker store, was a case in point. "Friendliness," according to Finnerty, must be "the prevailing spirit" of the department, but they were to be decidedly lopsided friendships. Like most toy men, he maintained that the "pressure of high-powered salesmanship" did not work in the toy department, which should have an atmosphere of freedom and ease. According to the Finnerty plan, when a mother brings her children to Wanamaker's, a salesclerk does not pounce on them but waits for an opportunity to play with the children, to become their friend. "No one urges [the mother] to buy, but as she strolls through the department with her children, friendly eyes keep track of them." If interest is shown, the clerk is "ready to serve, but otherwise, she plays the part of a friend of the child." Here selling was not only "playing" but also playacting. Retail toy men like Finnerty practiced the art of "handling people," of winning them as friends in order to influence them as customers by playing with them. The issue at stake in these prescriptions was power, how to have it and how to use it invisibly, inoffensively, but effectively in an era of salesmanship and administration.[114]

By the end of the 1920s these apparently contradictory imperatives— to be the sturdy man and the winsome boy, the playful friend and the playacting salesman, the conquering proprietor and the yielding servant, the dealer in fancy and the generator of profits—were uneasily contained in the model of manhood embodied by toy men with big ideas, such as Bob Davis, who was described as the "Richest Man" in Cincinnati in a 1926 Christmas ad for Hanke's Department Store. As a toy buyer, Davis had "the next happiest job to being Santa Claus himself." But he was not handed the job on a plate; no, "he made this job!" His success was attributed to a number of factors: a youthful eye that could see "into several million [children's] hearts so understandingly"; a determination to drive hard bargains, dealing directly with overseas producers, making "huge contracts with toy factories," to bring the savings home to "nearly all the children of Greater Cincinnati"; and, finally, skillfully "directing the many duties of more than one hundred able assistants." And yet, for all this hard work, "there isn't a younger person in Hanke's than 'Bob' Davis. If you could see him today,... you would never believe that he has been a full grown man for more than forty years." The ad concludes, "See Toyland tomorrow—lose your worldly worries in a fairyland of children's joys."[115] Bob Davis had more fun and was a better man *and* manager for staying a boy at heart, which constituted a new kind of manhood that was enacted in and made necessary by a culture of consumption.

### Play is the Business of the Child

Bob Davis (or at least the advertised version of him) may have figured out how to combine managerial science and industrial ideas with less-material childish sentiment, but the very way in which the boast was voiced suggests that the ad copy was not describing reality so much as pleading a case for it. Toy men felt that the battle for the status of their wares and of themselves was far from over. Even with a decade of mounting sales behind them, the editor of *Playthings* scolded the annual gathering of the industry in 1927: "We [toy men] must, ourselves, remember and we must make the world understand that toys of today are tools of youth ... [and] no longer mere gewgaws to distract the juvenile mind."[116] Such an argument, with its juxtaposition of constructive tools and fancy gewgaws, was partly a reminder never to be satisfied with existing sales; but it also indicated that toy men did not separate market expansion from their continuing struggle to show that they, like the wares they dealt in, were not a shameful sideshow. During and after the war years, efforts within the industry to build sales by defining the meaning and importance of toys often engaged the suspicion that toys corrupted children. The debate revolved around the concerns that had bothered Thompson and continued to worry the sales force of Peter Pan culture: were toys "mere playthings" that effeminized or weakened the child, or "constructive tools for learning" that prepared the manly bearing of the child?

Selling toys, then, almost inevitably meant selling middle-class Americans—and toy men themselves were included in this category—on the authentic virility of toys and the men who dealt in them. For example, in 1910 a writer in *Playthings* explained why girls' and boys' toys were fundamentally different: "The first lives in a land of unreality, the latter in one of stern roughness and practicality." There was little unusual for the time in categorizing tender idealism as feminine, and muscular, factual realism as masculine. The new basis of "passionate" manhood that emerged in the late nineteenth century focused on the male body and what a man aggressively did with it as opposed to his character and how uprightly he bore it. The difference in toys outlined here, though, also recalls Fred Thompson's too-energetic assurance that he was not an actor in shows, but "an inventor and constructor" of them. As with the showman, the mere act of drawing the distinction betrays the toymakers' uneasiness. Defining a hierarchy that favored the manly child who combined knowing with doing or preferred toys that "fill the youthful brain with burning facts about the great world in which it is to live" may have been more effective at explaining away the trouble than at alleviating the discomfort of being a toy man.[117]

In 1919 Marshall Field's toy-buying handbook expressed the central metaphor for the masculinization of play as "the business of a child," a version in miniature of the peculiarly adult male behavior of middle-class work. By 1920 the *New York Journal* was demanding "more toys ... [for] the boy half working, half playing, intensely interested and willing, to develop his mind along the line of his future work."[118] This instrumentalist ethos became an essential component of the sales pitch for the many new "educational toys" and the vast array of American-made playthings that duplicated the material life of adults in miniature, all of which rolled out of American factories in record numbers after 1910. Toy men quoted and often worked closely with the new experts on children, who confirmed that "toys are the means by which children live in miniature the daily life of their elders."[119] Notwithstanding the use of gender-neutral references, the universal model of the playing child implicit in this view of play almost invariably was the little masculine doer, the toy man himself in miniature. A 1920 editorial in *Playthings* identified the "purchasing power" of playing boys as the backbone of the new American industry. The universal Little Johnny at play was "a thinking, reasoning personality with the ideas of manhood and of business surging in his brain. He wants to do things, he wants to create things." For Little Johnny no less than for the toy man, play was serious business. Marshall Field's "Inspiration" advertisement for its toy department, which identified commodity play as the foundation of man-made civilization, was celebrated in the trade in the early 1920s: "As kings dream of dynasties, warriors of conquest, and explorers of continents—so children dream through the inspiration of toys." "In this Universe of Playdom are the milestones marking the road to maturity. Here are toys constructive and instructive—for occupation, recreation, and education. Here is Science at its source; Art in its adolescence; Power at its portal!" In America, children had no time for mere amusement. As the editor of *Playthings* asserted in 1924, American toys "are made for useful play rather than for playful use."[120]

After 1914 and continuing into the 1920s, however, some American toy men used the words that only a few years earlier had distinguished boys' from girls' toys to establish a new hierarchy that was more attuned to the circumstances of the war and postwar era. They sought to masculinize play as an activity that, with the right *American-made* commodities, led to the acquisition of the sturdy body of manhood. Beginning in the war years, toymakers initiated a national campaign advertising American toys as an essential element of "The Trinity that Builds Patriotism / The Home—The School—The Playhour," the last of which was designated the "greatest" of the three, "the toy hour."[121] During but especially after the war, toy men also endeavored to establish the masculine character and manly effects of all domestically produced toys—not just those made for boys—as the distinguishing mark of their peculiarly American quality. Toy men invented their toys' masculinity and defended their newly won market monopoly by setting their commodities against the marked femininity and effeminizing effects of the German-made variety. This chauvinistic take on play and toys was a fine combination of sentiment and business, a profitable mix of gender hierarchies, "100 percent Americanism," and the particular market interests of the toy industry. According to the new convention, American-made toys were sturdier, "last longer," educational, "health-building," scientific, "well built," "substantial," made for a definite purpose, realistic, original, priced for value, and tailored to children's "needs," not whims or desires.[122] In comparison, German-made toys were the gendered "other": "hanky-panky, flimsy," "frail," "made only for amusement," cheap, imitative, "baubles to last for a day."[123]

Dolls seemed especially to embody the differences, a condition that in all probability reflected the desperation of American dollmakers to break the German monopoly. Prior to the war, German dolls dominated domestic sales and were envied for their high quality;[124] in the new era, their advantages became liabilities, and they were savaged for living in a feminized land of unreality. "The German doll is a doll," Benjamin Goldenberg, of the pioneering American dollmaker E. I. Horsman Co., explained in 1923. "It is dressed like a doll. If it has a soul, it is the soul of a doll." American dolls, on the other hand, were like "real babies and real children."[125] An American doll, a toy man explained, "is not only stronger and made to last, but it is also made to represent a natural face and attire of an American child, instead of the empty fairy-looking face of the German doll without expression, and only overdone in unnatural beauty."[126] As one writer explained in 1919, in an article that owed as much to *A Fool There Was* as it did to tariff debates, prewar American doll men were held in a kind of sexual captivity to a foreign-made "siren" doll. He called her "Big Bertha, the Vampire Doll," and she stood for any large and inexpensive imported doll—"The Biggest in the City for a Dollar." American manufacturers could not match her low cost. Retailers and consumers could not resist her size and price. The triumph of the American toy industry in trade competition with German producers promised the restoration of gender, sexual, and domestic order by assuring the American dominance of the toy market.[127]

As effective as it seemed to be in shoring up the sturdiness of the

American toy industry, there were problems with the instrumentalist ethos. If play was the manly business of the child, what constituted the difference between a child and an adult, or more precisely, between a boy and a man? Toys obviously destabilized the time-honored moral boundary between manhood and boyhood, an effect that appealed to an increasing number of middle-class men who were unsure of their manhood in a corporate consumer society and who envied the energy and fun-loving zest of boys. Also, as committed as retailers were to toys as educational tools, they sold them in settings that were far less instrumentalist and masculinist in their depiction of play. As almost everyone in the business understood, selling toys required using sentiment, theatricality, and fantasy—putting on shows. Many sought to banish practical concerns from the toy department and to make it a place of "sheer joy" where "the ghosts of dead fireflies go."[128] What, then, was Toyland: the place of "burning facts" or fanciful fireflies? It seems that Toyland, like toy men, was not so much either as both, a syncretic combination of these contrasting and gendered qualities. When the maker of the popular construction toy Structo introduced in 1917 the advertising slogan, "Makes Men of Boys—Makes Boys of Men," it effectively summarized both the ambiguous returns of Peter Pan culture.[129]

### Be a Man and a Magician

Within the new American industry of play and childhood, two figures, A. C. Gilbert and Tony Sarg, stand out for the ways in which they embodied the boundless identity and mediated the paradoxical imperatives of Peter Pan manhood. These toy men had their most impressive business achievements after 1915, but their singular successes were only partly attributable to their particular ingenuities and talents. They also tapped into the sudden proliferation of new market outlets and consumer demand for commodities of childhood, which Thompson's years of building toylands had foretold. Ambitious entrepreneurs, they publicized their work as play and their identities as boys who had never grown up, even as they labored, like Thompson, to demonstrate that their manhood was not compromised, but enhanced, by their investment in not growing up.

Perhaps no one voiced his concerns for the sturdiness of the toy industry and the boy at play more insistently than A. C. Gilbert. His Erector construction toy, a box of metal girders and axles that he introduced in 1913, aimed to stimulate "the constructive side of a boy's nature" and "the ambition to become somebody, to be something big."[130] Erector's immediate popularity positioned Gilbert to become a leading figure in the American toy industry during its extraordinary growth period from 1915 to 1925. In 1915 Gilbert was instrumental in founding the Toy Manufacturers of the U.S.A. The trade association united domestic manufacturers independently of wholesale houses, which had dominated the American market through their control of imported playthings. Elected the first president of the organization, Gilbert led it through the critical years during and after the Great War when American toymakers exploited the advantages brought by the embargo of German-made goods. But Gilbert also was instrumental in the association's campaign to define the meaning and vital importance, not of playthings in general, but of American-made toys in particular. His aim, as he put it, was to build an Erector-like industry that "exert[s] the sort of influences that go to form right ideals and solid American character."[131]

Gilbert's biography, however, suggests the difficulties toy men faced in finding a solid footing in a consumer industry that mixed hard facts and fireflies. Born in 1884, Gilbert was reared in modest prosperity in Salem, Oregon, where his father was a businessman and insurance broker. In many ways, Gilbert had the red-blooded energy for unusual success in American business. He was an ambitious, competitive youth, athletically gifted, "wiry and strong," fleet of foot; he displayed little interest in or patience for the modest pursuits of his father. What excited him was watching someone performing "an exciting feat" entailing daredevil agility or cunning, which he immediately set out to imitate or to surpass. "I wanted to do it myself," he explained in his autobiography, *The Man Who Lives in Paradise*. Gilbert's compulsion to do it himself was fulfilled on the athletic field, where he became a champion pole vaulter at Pacific University, at Yale, and finally at the 1908 Olympics.[132] Yet the "biggest and most exciting" stunt he witnessed during his youth occurred on the stage, not the athletic field. It was performed by Hermann the Great, a magician who went to Salem when Gilbert was about twelve. The boy already had learned some tricks from a magic set he won selling subscriptions to *Youth's Companion*, but when he witnessed the master at work, he "was as baffled as those who thought he possessed supernatural powers." When Hermann unwittingly called the boy out of the audience to assist him, Gilbert played a few of the tricks he had up his own sleeve, which won him an invitation backstage. That visit "set me firmly on a magic hobby-horse that would in time carry me to heights I never dreamed of."[133] Gilbert's fascination and skill with illusion, play, and public performance were the credentials that gained him entrance to the commercial culture of Peter Pan in the 1910s and 1920s.

The boyish tricks became more than a hobby or sideshow when Gilbert went east to study medicine at Yale. At first he entertained friends and professors, but soon he was performing in clubs from New York to Boston. He added more hocus-pocus to his act, worked up new tricks, and "branched out," as he put it, "into mind-reading and spiritualistic acts." When he graduated in 1909, he abandoned thoughts of medicine. The previous year he and a partner had formed the Mysto Manufacturing Company to produce boxes of magic tricks for would-be boy performers like himself. Their success encouraged them to expand to a full line of magic supplies for professionals and to open a retail outlet in Times Square. All the while Gilbert continued to perform, in clubs and in show windows where he demonstrated his wares. "What made me feel good was getting asked back over and over again to the same places," he recalled. "That meant people liked the show I put on." He later constructed the sales pitches for his toys around the concept of the performing self, what he called the "natural born booster—the man or woman who has a good thing to say for those with whom he works, and for whom he has worked, and for society in general."[134] For Gilbert, performance was the essential tool for achieving the twin goals of popularity and sales.

Much as Fred Thompson insisted he was not a shady trickster, Gilbert dodged the darker implications of his showmanship by claiming to be a new kind of magician. He may have been a fiend for tricking people, but he avoided fiendish trappings. On stage, he said, he did not play the typical vaudeville Mephisto "with black pointed beard" and "dashing black cape." Instead he portrayed a clean-shaven, virile sorcerer for the modern age, an athletic champion practicing a wholesome version of the black arts. Gilbert the sorcerer resembled the boy bursting with optimism and energy who appeared on the cover of Mysto's magic catalogue of 1911: polished, yet solid and reliable, a trustworthy, Boy Scout practitioner of what a contemporary magician called "a sort of pleasant fraud ... upon a good-natured public." Whereas competitors used images of demons to promote their wares, Gilbert advertised a progressive form of magic. He wanted "to place magic on a footing where it has never been before.... to build up a reputation ... for honesty and reliability." His "new idea" combined reliable, honest masculinity, like his sturdy athletic body, with good-natured trickery. According to his ads, the Mysto trademark "stands for character." "Magic," stated the catalogue, "is legitimate merchandise if manufactured by honest and reliable firms." This offer may have been his neatest trick: Gilbert claimed to reconcile deceit with character, magic and illusion with sincerity and reliability, performance with being. "Be a man and a magician," the catalogue exhorted boy customers. "Learn to entertain," encouraged a Mysto ad.[135]

Gilbert's determination to combine magic, performance, and character took an important turn in late 1911, when he began thinking "how fascinated boys might be in building things out of girders," the idea behind the Erector set. The magic business was "fun," he explained, but "not enough to satisfy me."[136] Perhaps, but he also may have worried that a man who dealt in deception for a living would never amount to much. Erector, which was one of the important success stories in the new American toy industry, presented no such problems. Through aggressive selling and advertising, Gilbert turned Erector into one of the biggest-selling and most widely recognized brand names on the domestic market. By 1920 sales were approaching two million dollars and Gilbert had expanded the original line with other new toys for constructive work-play.[137]

Yet tricks remained Gilbert's stock in trade. Selling his goods meant selling himself. The ads for Erector and his later autobiography merged his athletic virility, energy, love of magic, eternal boyishness, and desire to win public affection through performance in a coherent narrative for achieving boy-manhood by way of constructive play with his particular commodity. Much like the friendly-eyed toy retailers, Gilbert played the part of buddy to his young customers. In the hearty salutation that appeared in Erector ads—"Hello, Boys! Make Lots of Toys!"—he addressed his potential customers as what he himself claimed to be, a fellow boy, a pal. He wrote ads to read "as if they were personal messages from me to the boys. It was not just good selling, as it turned out, but I meant it.... I was convinced that boys became interested and excited when a *person*, not a corporation, spoke to them." He invited boys to write back to him, and the "best letters" were published in *Toy Tips*, an advertising publication disguised as a newspaper and circulated freely "to any boy who wrote in for it." The company boasted a distribution of seventy-five thousand in 1921. As *Printers' Ink Monthly* put it, the boy "is made to feel that he is writing direct to A. C. Gilbert, and the letter he gets in reply is signed by A. C. Gilbert." The letters were, like the ads, a pleasant fraud. As *Playthings* reported in 1920, "about 1,500 letters a day come into the Gilbert office, and all are answered, most of them necessarily, by form letters."[138]

Gilbert's finest performance of sincerity occurred in 1918 during a much-publicized debate over whether, as a wartime necessity, Christmas gift giving should be temporarily suspended. Such was the recommendation of the Council of National Defense, which included a number of cabinet-level officials. Even though retailers predicted the council's action would have little effect on Christmas spending, the toy trade association weighed in as if the nation's heart were at stake. To "rob American *children* of their joy on Christmas," Gilbert's company protested in an ad, "to cheat children of childhood play—that must not be." Gilbert, as the toy association's president, led a mission to Washington to defend the interests of American children. He won a retraction and a bonanza of publicity. Gilbert insisted that American toys were neither luxuries nor gimcracks. "The greatest influences in the life of a boy are his toys.... A boy wants fun, not education." Then he opened cases of sample toys, and the decorum of the meeting broke apart. Cabinet members, one newspaper reported, began to play with the toys as though they "were boys again." A council member explained: "Toys appeal to the heart of every one of us, no matter how old we are." Gilbert was widely praised for saving the holiday and for boosting the prestige of domestic toys. The toymaker regarded the event as "one of the happiest and most successful undertakings" of his career, and attributed his achievement to a simple, if redundant, approach: "I was earnest, I was honest, and I was sincere."[139] Few lobbyists have ever claimed otherwise. But for Gilbert, his stratagems did not constitute undue influence because they were deployed in the spirit of play. After all, he had made serious men break down and have some fun—and saved Christmas in the bargain. This formula worked for him. As he explained in 1923, "To many men business is a burden: something to be taken solemnly and groaned over. Not to me! I am having the time of my life."[140]

### A Man Who Plays with Dolls, and Admits It

For all the fun Gilbert was having, though, the very smugness of his claims betrayed the undercurrent of doubt that bothered the business-men of Peter Pan culture. These worries were even more apparent in the case of Tony Sarg, who, as a number of writers noted, made and played with dolls for a living and was not ashamed to admit it. Begin-ning in 1917, Sarg's puppet plays of fairy and folk tales prompted a surge of popular interest in marionette theater in America. By the early 1920s he had expanded beyond the elitist art theaters of the time into an industry for merchandising childhood and fairy tales for adults as well as children in public festivals, department stores, restaurants, night clubs, hotels, and product advertising. Sarg became an emblem as well as an entrepreneur of play, although that he was so remained the most remarkable and puzzling aspect of his identity.

Sarg was born in Guatemala in 1880 and lived on his family's plan-tation there until his German father sent him to a German military academy. Against his father's wishes, he moved upon graduation to London, where he became a commercial artist.[141] Another of his child-hood passions was collecting toys, including puppets. In England he was captivated by marionettes and began an intense self-directed study of the art. He claimed to have watched more than fifty performances of *Salome* by the English puppeteer Thomas Holden. Sarg asked Holden to show him how he made the seductress dance so fluidly, but Holden re-fused to divulge the secrets of his craft to the enthusiastic upstart. "Nev-ertheless," Sarg later explained, "I have a mechanical eye, and by watching carefully I managed to guess a number of Holden's secrets." He discovered that, unlike the stiff, wooden bodies of ordinary puppets, Holden's marionettes had flexible, hollow torsos, which "made it possi-ble for the figures to walk in a lifelike manner." To supplement this covert insight, he devised a way to increase the number of strings on his puppets, which magnified the ways in which they could be manipulated without hindering their operation. Sarg's marionettes could even smile.[142]

In 1914, Sarg and his American wife left wartime London for New

York, where he established puppeteering as a commercial art.[143] His break came unexpectedly in 1916, when the impresario Winthrop Ames hired him to replace a European marionette troupe whose New York performance had been canceled by the war. Ames was a leader in the "little theater" movement, an effort to establish "an intellectually aristocratic drama" in small, noncommercial "art" theaters in the United States. Ames also was an early supporter of marionette performances at his Little Theater in New York. Modernist artists of the time found the childlike appeal of the puppet and the travesty of the human condition represented by its absurdly tethered and exaggerated actions a potent source for attacking the arid empiricism and spiritless rationality of modern life. In 1927 the American critic Mary Cass Canfield explained the attraction in the ethical vocabulary of Peter Pan culture. Toys, she said, "are manna in the wilderness" for those who crave "escape from fact" and "ever-flowing actuality" and who possess "a passion for the impossible." "No better toys," she added, "have ever been invented than marionettes, because they belong to that half of art which is a flight from everyday existence."[144] Fred Thompson could not have phrased it any better. In many respects, the new vogue of aristocratic puppet theater continued nineteenth-century Romanticism's celebration of folk primitivism. But Canfield's contention that acting dolls delivered the observer from a desiccated existence by reawakening a lost childhood also reprised the advertised claims for adult play in amusements such as Luna Park and the Hippodrome, in the toy displays of department stores, and in the polychromatic fantasies of Guérin and Ryan. In the culture of Peter Pan, boundaries joined, instead of separated, the noncommercial art of highbrow culture and the billion-dollar smile.[145]

After his first professional performance in 1917 in New York, Sarg achieved a level of praise and attention unprecedented for puppet players in the United States. On opening night four hundred children packed the theater; on the second night, four hundred adults occupied the seats. Sarg's plays teemed with puppet spectacle: jugglers, snake charmers, materializing ghosts, a bucking donkey whose rider nimbly hopped on and off. The writer Anne Stoddard praised his "humor, skill, ingenuity, trained sense of color and composition, and instinctive understanding of the child heart," which gave his acting dolls "the stature of living persons."[146] His plays were swarmed with fairies and magical figures whose identities and forms changed cleverly and fluidly on the puppet stage. "Our Doctor Magicus," according to Sarg, "could make thin people fat, and fat people thin; short people, tall, and tall people, short, before the eyes of the audience!" The description repeats, almost word for word, the promise of Fred Thompson's Wishing Well. Like Thompson, Sarg made wishes come true. "I like plays," he professed in a telling allusion to *Peter Pan*, "which make people believe in fairies."[147]

Sarg's doll plays responded to an adult desire to consume child culture that antedated his arrival in New York and, in any event, was too powerful to be confined to the "intellectually aristocratic" space of institutions such as the Little Theater. Always alert to the main chance, Sarg emerged during the 1920s as a singularly visible figure in translating toys, fairy tales, and play into the market world of consumption. The demand for his talents reflected the emerging status of the child as consumer, but it also demonstrated the powerful and broad appeal of playthings and play to adult consumers. As *Toys and Novelties* had exclaimed to the trade in 1922, "grown-ups have taken to dolls! Dolls are fads!"[148]

Like Fred Thompson's playthings, the Sarg puppets were toys that reflected the preferences of middle-class urban men. For one, the marionettes resembled their master. "Their bodily gyrations equal easily the acrobatic antics of any human athletes," the critic Clayton Hamilton observed. The transformations and stunts of which his dolls were capable also reflected his passion for machines and problems of mechanics. As one writer put it, Sarg was "first of all, a mechanician." His animated dolls appeared at the same time that American toymakers were designing and mass producing "lifelike" dolls. In both cases, the application of "realism" defeminized doll making. At the same time, however, he wanted his mechanical wonders to make people believe in fairies. Marionettes, he contended, "can literally carry out many of the fairy stories of our childhood," and make the audience believe in them in spite of their impossibility. According to a Boston critic, Sarg's dolls make the spectator forget "what his brain well knows, that the dolls are controlled by threads.... They do not, even to the most childish fancy, become human beings; they remain dolls—but dolls actuated by their own energy, their own sentiments and passions, their own pumping hearts of blood."[149]

Although the *San Francisco Examiner*'s Redfern Mason found Sarg's marionettes an antidote to the "soul-killing materialism" of the twentieth century, Sarg was a commercial artist from the start.[150] He quickly became deeply invested in modern mass retailing, especially at Christmas and at Macy's department store in New York. In 1923 he designed an elaborate, mechanically automated puppet show for the store's block-long wall of show windows. The following year Macy's introduced its annual Thanksgiving Day parade; that event followed by the premiere of a new Sarg window show became a yearly attraction. In 1927 Sarg introduced what would become the signature feature of the parade, giant balloon figures—that is, "upside-down" supermarionettes.[151] The puppeteer designed toy sections for other department stores, painted murals in hotels, and constructed automated marionette shows for restaurants. In 1926 he turned a dreaded ordeal into play with a chain of children's barber shops for department stores. Little customers entered a circus tent, purchased haircuts at a ticket booth, and then were clipped while sitting on carousel animals and watching a mechanical puppet show.[152] Sarg developed his own line of illustrated children's books, animated films, wallpaper, silks, and other textiles. His designs sold breakfast cereal and cigarettes.[153] In 1933, he staged his grandest spectacles to date at the Century of Progress Exposition in Chicago: *Alice in Wonderland* at the children's midway pavilion; *Venus on the Half Shell* for mature patrons of the "Streets of Paris" show; and a cabaret of dancing groceries at the A&P corporate pavilion. Under Sarg's tutelage, New York, Chicago, and other cities got their Toyland principalities.[154]

In 1926, *American* published a flattering profile of Sarg, which marveled at his energy and enterprise. Here was a hard-working, tirelessly productive businessman, who supervised workers, accumulated capital, and converted virtually every idea that came to mind into a money-making scheme. And yet, the article's headline exclaimed, "Tony Sarg Has Never Done a Stroke of Work in His Life!" For Sarg, work was not work, which he associated with drudgery and debilitating seriousness. It was and should be play. As a rival eulogized him after his death in 1940, Sarg had been "a good business man, a hard worker, and one who also knew how to play."[155]

Only twenty years earlier, the three-hundred-strong Martian chorus in *A Yankee Circus* had explained to the audiences of the New York Hippodrome why their planet was so different (and superior) to Earth. On Mars, they proclaimed in unison, "We work and we sing a song / We call it play!" By the end of the 1920s, the advantages of Mars, while still suspect, no longer seemed so alien to Yankee Land as they had when

Thompson opened his grand theater. Competing conceptions of manliness had hardly disappeared, and they continued to disturb the peace of mind of men who played for a living. After all, the predictable news angle on Tony Sarg was his unforced admission that he played with dolls for a living. The emphasis on their personal vigor and stamina, the sturdy body of their industries, the mechanical proficiency of their toys, the constructive, educational value of their commodities, and the heaps of money they made in the process betrayed toy men's persistent defensiveness about their boy-man way of making a living. These posturings were conventional and backward looking in many respects, and suggested how little had changed since the days when Thompson was consigned to the margins of the Buffalo world's fair. At the same time, however, these men also were forward looking in identifying the consumer marketplace as the new workplace and stage for achieving and performing their manhood. By the end of the 1920s, what had once been inconceivable—that a man should simultaneously be a child and an adult, that he could offer security and certainty and also be a master of illusion, that the world might be turned upside down and still turn a handsome profit—was being promoted as a recognized route to achievement in a consumer age. Tony Sarg, for one, did not groan over his burdens or deny himself anything; work, for him, was a merry-go-round of unrestrained indulgence. "My pleasure, my thrills," he said, "all come from the things I am doing. To me the great secret is being able to do the thing you most like to do in life."[156] Such enthusiasm could have described a spree of shooting the Chutes at Luna Park. The movers and shakers of the new consumer economy were not forsaking work or divorcing their sense of entitlement and self-realization from achievements at the factory, laboratory, or mart of trade, but for Sarg and other men like him, embracing consumption and having fun were becoming preconditions of manly fulfillment. If a "great day's work" still was not just the same as fooling with toys, Sarg, A. C. Gilbert, Bob Davis, and men like them were playing nonetheless—and, they insisted, having the time of their lives doing it.

# SEVEN

# A Kindergarten Preacher in Toys

FRED Thompson died early on 6 June 1919 at St. Vincent's Hospital, New York, following an operation for a range of physical disorders involving gallstones, appendicitis, and hernia. His surgery the previous Monday had been his seventeenth trip to the operating table in the four years since the debacle in San Francisco, but he had persevered to the end. "His cheerfulness under the burden of suffering and constant anticipation of more operations was the marvel of his physicians," reported the *New York Sun*, "and they thought for a time that his gameness alone would pull him through." In the days after his last operation, though, a late-spring heat wave settled over the city and brought on a deterioration in his condition that Thompson's merry disposition could not reverse. He lost consciousness and never regained it. He would have been forty-six years old the following Halloween.[1]

Thompson was buried next to his mother on the periphery of Woodlawn Cemetery, the scenic resting place in the Bronx for many of the city's most powerful financiers, industrialists, speculators, retailers, and stage personalities. He had an ordinary plot located a short but meaningful distance from the gaudy tombs of gilded grandees such as "Bet-a-Million" Gates, who had clamored only fourteen years earlier to be among the first to invest in his amusements. The showman had not mounted a major project in four years; his estate, after paying for his funeral, was valued at seven hundred dollars.[2] So hard up was Thompson at the time of his death that a headstone was not placed on his grave until 1922, by which time his friends and former associates had collected enough money to commission a modest monument. The memorial, unveiled on the third anniversary of his death, reflects on Thompson's ephemeral grandeur. Miniature versions of the Hippodrome's columns carved in stone frame the showman's profile in bronze bas-relief, surmounting the following information:

Sacred to the Memory
of
Frederic Thompson
Creator Of Joy For Millions,
The Hippodrome
Luna Park, Toyland.

A Poet, A Painter, Philosopher,
An Architect, A Kindergarten
Preacher In Toys— .

1873–1919[3]

The stone recorded his most important public works: Luna Park, which helped establish the twentieth-century paradigm of outdoor amusement parks for the masses; the Hippodrome, the gargantuan inefficiency of which nevertheless incorporated a prescient vision of a middle-class demand for luxurious fantasies at prices they would pay; and Toyland Grown Up, the dream of giant playthings on the edge of San Francisco Bay.

But it is the second half of the epitaph that warrants examining. The last words on Thompson, as one might expect, screen out the hustler side of the showman in a way that, ironically, tries to hustle his record. For instance, the word choice leaves us with the familiar and misguiding image of Thompson as an artisanal builder of shows, not a crafty actor in them. The phrase "A Kindergarten Preacher In Toys" is odd, too. One thinks of kindergarten teachers, not preachers; likewise, kindergarten teachers at that time were (and usually still are) women, and preachers in most cases men. Thompson, as his eulogists must have realized, played with these boundaries, all in the service of having a good time and making good money, too. He was very much a preacher for the twentieth century, but his sermons were indulgently affirming and reassuring rather than sternly reproving. Like his kindred spirits in the toy industry, he made friendliness and play the prevailing themes of his enterprises. The eye he kept on his customers did not deny the ultimate ends of his instruments and designs; it was just part of the smiling face of his business. As he had explained in 1915, "Life should be fifty per cent work and fifty per cent play.... A showman has as much responsibility as a hundred preachers; his business is to provide fifty per cent of life."[4] Thompson's claim to have supplanted preachers is striking, especially given the long historical link between showmanship and the work of Satan, but it captures how he and his many amusement projects both encouraged and reflected the ways in which middle-class Americans had warmed up to secular play and fun. The reigning philosophy of the kindergartens of pleasure he constructed for modern Americans concisely expressed the ethos of the Peter Pan culture that he had helped build and the consuming boy-manhood that he had brilliantly represented for more than a decade.

All of Fred Thompson's physical contributions to mass amusements in the United States in his brief but impressive tenure as New York's toy-maker and everyday Peter Pan have been erased from the American landscape. Luna, which proved to be the most durable of his monuments to the child spirit, was finally brought down by three fires in the 1940s and was not rebuilt (fig. 7.1). And yet his anxieties about adulthood, and his strategies for soothing them, have survived to the present day, though adjusted to the suburbanization and "automobility" of middle-class America. Rather than jumping ahead to the opening of Disneyland in 1955, the best place to observe what happened to Thompson's ideas after 1920 is Playland, which opened in Rye Beach, New York, in 1928. From one perspective, Playland shows the transition from Luna to the post–World War II amusement economy of year-round, middle-class suburban theme parks such as the Six Flags, Great America, and Disney chains, surrounded by asphalt parking lots and linked to major express-ways. Although a seasonal park, Playland has stayed in business since its first day. Its name as well as its unified architecture pay tribute to Thompson's conception of amusement, but with important differences

Figure 7.1. Luna Park had been in decline for decades when a series of catastrophic fires in the early 1940s closed the amusement for good. The remnants from the last fire in 1944 are shown here. (*Brooklyn Collection, Brooklyn Public Library.*)

that have often characterized such enterprises in the ensuing years. Unlike the plaster, irregular, and ever-changing Luna, Playland's elegant Art Deco buildings were constructed with fireproof concrete blocks at a high fixed capital cost; as a result, the exteriors of many of the original structures remain today pretty much as they were in 1928.[5] Playland also has catered to suburban—not urban—families who were transported in privately owned automobiles to its setting in an affluent seaside suburb, rather than on the undeveloped fringe of a crowded city. Finally, at its inception and for much of its tenure, Playland was owned and operated by the Westchester County Park Commission, which tore down two shabby Luna-era parks and constructed the new attraction as a byway from the county's growing system of publicly funded parkways. These roads connected the area's rapidly growing population of commuters to New York City, encouraged the decline of the rural environs of cities as semi-isolated enclaves of the rich, and heralded the rise of the new suburban affluence of the corporate middle class.[6]

Public support of Playland in this model suburban neighborhood amounted to more than eliminating eyesores and nuisances on its beaches. It also indicated that by the late 1920s Peter Pan culture enjoyed enough respectability that the government was willing to subsidize its vision of the good life.[7] By this time, "summer amusement," as Thompson had once called it, was settling into a schedule of durable expectations, which were less antic alternatives to everyday life than subsets of the new leisure economy. Like its plaster predecessors, the original Playland offered itself as an adult's refuge from care. The slogan of its "Kiddyland," which was only for children, was Thompsonese modified by the vocabulary of car culture: "Park 'em and forget 'em."[8] But such hostility toward the little ones, as Thompson's later ventures had shown, was fading even as the valuation of children as consumers was rising. In 1925 the National Association of Amusement Parks had underscored the new market orientation when it designated 4 August as "National Kiddie Day," when special devices for children would be showcased.[9] Playland forecast its movement in the direction of suburban families with children on opening day. More than two thousand free tickets were distributed to area schoolteachers, and the park's director inaugurated the venture by handing the "golden key to happiness" to a three-year-old Rye boy, who represented the county's "youth."[10] (Thompson had once performed a similar publicity stunt, except that the recipient of the jewel-studded key to Luna was a grown-up boy, the theater monopolist A. L. Erlanger.)[11] Playland was advertised as "America's Premier Playground," and, like Luna, it incorporated folklore and fairy tales. Such features were tools, as one account put it, "to promote an atmosphere of relaxation and play."[12] No one needed to worry about eccentric falling statues at Rye Beach, just as there was little of Thompson's sense that adults are "thrill-hungry" children. The genealogy of the Rye Beach resort was less Luna Park than the private playground of the new suburban backyard, with all of its specialized commodities to amuse and occupy the kids, from sandboxes to seesaws.[13]

The tension between play and respectability was still an issue in 1928, although Playland seems mainly to have raised concerns that it would be a noisy intrusion of modernity into Arcadia. When grumpy residents expressed concern about noise and riff-raff, the park's director reassured them: "Our loud speakers never play jazz. They always play good music."[14] Playland has loosened up over the years; what originally struck its wealthy neighbors as an unwelcome harbinger of modernity now impresses visitors as charming, quaint, even antimodern. (It was designated a protected "National Historic Landmark" in 1987.)[15] What matters from a historical perspective, though, is that public officials in 1928 thought it reasonable to expect ventures such as Playland to attract residents to the area, to generate a consistent stream of fees and tax revenue, and to do so without violating that particular community's canons of propriety.[16] Playland's future was staked on the permanence, predictability, and respectability of the market for adult and family play.[17] Middle-class Americans continued to struggle in the twentieth century to reconcile their desire and perceived need for recreation, vacations, and pleasure with their psychological commitment to work and production and their persistent fears about the dangers of idle hands.[18] In the early 1950s, for instance, Walt Disney had to hustle to get financing for the "large dose of pure fun" that he had in mind for suburban Los Angeles because bankers and his own brother, the financial director of the Disney studios, would have nothing to do with his folly.[19] Disneyland remains a monument to the bankers' shortsightedness. Suspicions of amusement remain today, but when fun has won out in the bourgeois calculation of the costs and benefits of play, suburban pleasure spots such as Playland and Disneyland have been only a short drive away for the whole family.

### Playboys and Boys at Play

With its dignified historical pedigree and location in the dreamland of suburban Westchester County, Playland still seems fantastic today, but even in 1928 it already was crucially modifying Peter Pan culture's insurrection against the grim mandates of productive labor, repressed desires, and rational leisure that constrained the bourgeois paterfamilias. For although a man was free to cavort as a kid would at Playland, he may not have felt free to do anything else. Such healthy play threatened to become yet another chore, one more obligation for the harassed suburban father. An amusement park, in other words, could support as well as oppose the "breadwinner ethic" of the twentieth-century middle-class father. In 1951, the sociologist Martha Wolfenstein underscored the uncertain returns of Peter Pan culture in an essay on the "fun morality" that had arisen in American culture since 1940. Not only had play and fun lost their evil associations; more important, they had gained "a new obligatory aspect."[20] Although "fun morality" was not so new as she suggested, Wolfenstein had exposed the oppressive potential that underlay Never Land even in Thompson's day. Steering the family to the Rye playground, the lord of the suburban household may have been not free but required to go there; sitting behind the wheel of the car may have felt little different from being strapped to it.

The critic and historian Barbara Ehrenreich has argued that, by the 1950s, middle-class men were actually feeling this way, slaves or martyrs to the breadwinner ethic. Throughout the twentieth century, as she has put it, American men have been told "to grow up, marry and support their wives. To do anything else was less than grown-up, and the man who willfully deviated was judged to be somehow 'less than a man.'" This ethic ruled more or less unchallenged until the fifties and 1953 in particular, when Hugh Hefner began publishing the glossy men's magazine *Playboy* as a rebellious alternative. With its nude centerfolds and self-help guides on scoring with young women and appointing a playboy "pad," the magazine flouted the constraints that unmanned the middle-class suburban male—from presiding over backyard barbecues to pleasing the other half to, perhaps, hauling the family to Playland. *Playboy* was not opposed to either women or play, just the versions that came with the penalties of marriage and family. Nor did it object to capitalism. Implicit in its pages was the ponderous assumption that frolic must not get out of hand; swank digs required money and the liberty to spend it. *Playboy*'s radicalism, rather, was in divorcing manliness from marriage and allying it with heterosexual sex. "You could call [the magazine] 'immature,'" writes Ehrenreich, "but it already called itself that, because maturity was about mortgages and life insurance and *Playboy* was about fun."[21]

The cultural mutiny of the "boy at play" and his hedonistic rebellion against the masculine "convention of hard-won maturity" actually began long before Hefner either exploited such insubordination in the postwar period or located the "cellar door of childhood" on an actual female body. The roots of *Playboy*, like those of Playland's "fun morality," were in the culture of Peter Pan and the commercial immaturity that Fred Thompson and his fellow playmates brought to the consumer marketplace in the early twentieth century. These early Peter Pans implicitly challenged the breadwinner ethic by incorporating their dread of everyday responsibilities and their passion for the impossible into the new economy's array of possibilities. What they resisted was the alienation of middle-class men from the joy of living and the world of delight that was consumer culture's principal enticement. After all, these men built that world; they were fools not to enjoy it. The moneymaking antics of such Peter Pans suggest that the middle-class male flight from responsibility in the 1950s and afterward was a continuation and expansion of an earlier longing of American men to evade the implications of modernity by doing the opposite of what they were supposed to do.[22]

Fred Thompson may not have been the first "playboy" in the Hefner sense. The sly voice in which he described the archetype of Luna Park thrills no less than his shrill tirades against Salome and Coney Island prostitutes disclosed his worst nightmares about sexual appetites. But *Playboy* has never had much truck with such women either. After all, its escapist fantasies, while not asexual, needed the help of "bunnies," who were (and still are) *playmates*. The contrast implicit here was not just between Hefner's ideal of the fetching girl next door and the predatory wife or Vamp, both of whom had a withering effect on a man's sexual and financial wealth. The bunny also was an alternative to older ideals of manly friendship, which bound men to each other with claims of loyalty and reciprocity that counterbalanced self-interest.[23] A playmate came with no such strings attached. In the privacy of the reader's imagination, she was there to play with or not, wholly in the present moment, with no claim on the future, all of which composed a daydream of power in which the playboy-man got to call the shots. *Playboy*, as Ehrenreich has shown, was all about escaping from breadwinning to an all-male Never Land—either between its pages, where presumably only men would prowl, or inside its clubs, to which only men had keys. Hanging out in such homosocial quarters, as in Thompson's time, roused second thoughts, which was why centerfolds of the "American Girl" were literally at the center of *Playboy*; they legitimized "what was truly subversive about" the magazine, "that a playboy didn't have to be a husband to be a man."[24] The similarities can be overdrawn, but both Thompson the boy at play and Hefner the playboy conceived of their enterprises as rebellious claims for freedom, joy, and pleasure for men like themselves. For both, too, playthings and playmates were the essential tools of manly insurrection against the chains of respectability.

### The Peter Pan Syndrome

Hefner's juvenile enterprises suggest that the consuming ethos of Peter Pan culture and the form of masculinity it endorses remain as tempting, hopeful, and troublesome today as they were in the era when men had to fly to the Moon or Mars to escape the severities of Yankee Land. One reason for the durability of the attraction lies in Peter Pan's guarantee not just of eternal youth and adventure, but of youthful power, a promise that still expresses and responds to the undercurrent of discontent felt by middle-class men as they weigh their options in a global corporate workplace and consumer marketplace. Today, as in Thompson's time, voices still deplore the pernicious effects of a culture that values having fun too highly and distracts adults—usually men—from graver matters. Such critics lament what they identify as the marked decline of character in the postwar era, the male flight from responsibility, the confusion of boys and men in the wake of the feminist and gay revolutions, and the "commitment to non-commitment."[25]

Such diagnoses of America's late-century ills have had broad appeal, although they frequently have been expressed in promises of reinvigorating the individual middle-class male rather than in terms of revitalizing the community. Perhaps the most popular rendition of the chief terminology and logic of these complaints was Dan Kiley's *Peter Pan Syndrome: Men Who Have Never Grown Up*. This thoroughly secular self-help therapy sold two hundred thousand copies in hardback and was translated into twenty-two languages upon its publication in 1983. A principal selling point was its insight that middle-class American men only appear to be on top of the world. In reality, they are weak, frightened little boys, as averse to real maturity as Peter Pan, a "soft, effeminate boy who wouldn't grow up." Kiley took the conventional short-term view that "PPS" (as he called it) was not somatic in nature but social and cultural, a postwar pathology peculiar to the permissive 1950s consumer culture of ease and abundance. Parents who substituted money for time and attention and encouraged immediate over delayed gratification had reared a generation of young men who "take their food, shelter, and safety for granted and concentrate their efforts on finding new ways to purchase pleasure." Men—and it is obvious that he meant white men—were spoiled by families "too affluent for their own good"; they no longer had to grow up. Part of the proof consisted of the unafflicted populations: past generations of men, who could take nothing for granted, and nonwhite men of the ghetto, whose poverty immunizes them. Women, on the other hand, whether rich or poor, possess a different sort of advantage. They can "actualize both the masculine and feminine sides of their personality" and are thus immune to the sex-role confusion that besets achievement-oriented and successful males. Men must suppress their feminine sides, which makes them insensitive narcissists blind to the needs of their mates and children. In Kiley's estimation, then, all of white men's advantages actually are liabilities.[26]

This message appears to have appealed to men as well as to women, although Kiley laid a lot of the blame on the latter group. The psychological imbalance within men had empowered women with a "pseudostrength," which they used to keep men from growing up. He especially scolded women who "Wendy" men by playing protective mother to their juvenility. Kiley encouraged women to surrender their control and to help the PPS victim become the man he really needs to be, "a caring, fragile human being like the rest of us." Instead of doting, Wendyish mothers, men needed Tinker Bells—women who would appreciate and preserve their boyish gusto for spontaneous fun but have no patience with the tantrums. What a man needed, in other words, was a better playmate, and one who remained a sidekick to the main character.[27]

His invocation of Tinker Bell shows, too, that Kiley was not counseling austerity or telling men to leave Never Land altogether. Inordinate self-denial or excessive seriousness would only make matters worse. Instead, he offered a developmental compromise—a definition of healthy manhood that encouraged men to retain boys' happy-go-lucky and devil-may-care spontaneity and love of pleasure even as they became more responsible and concerned for others than for themselves. Such a man would not only act more grown up; he also would be "full of energy," still able "to be young and silly" if he wanted. In Kiley's revised Peter Pan manhood, maturation entailed no net loss of play, youth, or energy. On the contrary, a successfully rehabilitated Peter Pan would grow up and still believe in fairies, like "Larry," the out-of-control lawyer whose case study concluded Kiley's book. Larry's tyrannically remote and sexually brutal father and overbearingly affectionate mother had turned him into a textbook "Peter Pan." As an adolescent, he was a self-loathing chronic masturbator, ashamed of himself and his private pleasure. As an adult, he became a misogynistic, womanizing hedonist. His marriage, home, and professional life a wreck, Larry subjected himself to two kinds of therapy, one at the hands of a "shrink" (Kiley) who helped him "make sense" of the fears that ruled him, and the other with "Connie," a lover whose "maturity, strength, and sanity drew Larry closer to her each time they talked." Larry gradually learned to "actualize" both sides of his personality, "that it's okay to be hard on the outside and soft on the inside." The result was like a trip to the playground. During their first congress, Larry and Connie "made love for two days." Larry had never been so "totally comfortable just being naked and talking." Moreover, he was "full of energy" (in addition to marathon sex, he started jogging again). He had not felt this good since he was a boy. He had thought that waking up to "reality" would weaken him; instead, it made him stronger. "This time he *wanted* to be young and silly." Realizing that there is nothing wrong with being afraid freed him from his perpetual childhood, but with a twist. "Now I'm free," he told Kiley. "I can be young forever." At its core *The Peter Pan Syndrome* rescued its boymen by helping them overcome their fear of pleasure, although it did so by insisting that women let men be "young and silly" without making them feel weak or unmanly doing so.[28] Women had to help men redeem Fred Thompson's promise: that they could grow up *without growing old*.

In the 1980s Kiley's therapy was a best-seller in the United States, Japan, and Brazil, but it has since fallen out of circulation. For one thing, it was politically problematic, blaming women for men's troubles while simultaneously putting women in charge of rehabilitating their juvenile charges.[29] Moreover, *The Peter Pan Syndrome* was written for the deficit, "zero-sum" mentality of the early and mid-1980s. The best it could offer was a careful compromise between responsibility and eternal youth, which with luck and a Tinker Bell playmate would provide abundant quantities of each. A larger and sunnier library of "inner child" therapies has since taken its place. Leading the list has been the work of John Bradshaw, whose *Homecoming: Reclaiming and Championing Your Inner Child*, first published in 1990, in many ways launched the decade. To the usual complaints about the immature Peter Pan personality (a term Bradshaw does not use), *Homecoming's* author makes several crucial adjustments, which enabled his self-help system to flourish in the surplus material economy of the 1990s. The "inner child" was more than a catchy phrase; it also allowed him to include women in the afflicted population, which democratized the pain, at least in gender terms. Brad-

shaw also shifted the source of the problem from affluence to deprivation, which redirected the focus from the spoiled man to the neglected
and impoverished "inner child" (not, it should be noted, to the actual
poor). Perhaps most important, whereas Kiley envisioned the bourgeois
male self torn by conflicting commands to control itself and to let go,
Bradshaw established a strategic, interactive partnership of playmates—
indulgent outer adult and wishful inner child.[30]

For Bradshaw, the phrase "inner child" almost physically embodies
the well of childhood resentments and injuries that women and men
harbor inside them as they grow up. On the outside they may look like
everyone else, but dwelling within is a child who wants "to cry out in
rage and indignation." This needy, frightened, and demanding juvenile
rules the adult, paralyzing his development with its fits and demands.
The physical body has grown tall, but the emotional self has become a
"child adult." Bradshaw urges the suffering adult not to punish the
inner child for its misbehavior or to turn a blind eye to its tantrums. Instead, he advises him to rescue himself by "fathering" (or "mothering,"
as the case may be) the wounded inner child back to health. This attention, which must be continuous, finally gives the "lonely boy" (or girl)
inside what he needs; and what he needs, according to Bradshaw, is
what he desires, whether it is gentle discipline, tender affection, or material indulgence. In the healing that occurs, the wounded child yields to
the "wonder child" it was meant to be, which unleashes a torrent of "creative and transformative energy" inside the adult.[31]

The author of Homecoming might say that The Peter Pan Syndrome,
with its grumpy ambivalence toward wealth and permissiveness,
reflected the cultural or psychological hold of "original sin," an idea that
Bradshaw regards as "a major source for many repressive and cruel
child-rearing practices" that fill the child with shame and self-hatred.
The problem lies in the suggestion that there is something wrong with
children, whether actual or "inner." He avers that there is "no clinical
evidence to support any kind of innate depravity in children." More to
the point, Kiley's therapy was deficit oriented; even its visions of abundance betray fears of scarcity. Homecoming, on the other hand, seemed
tailor-made for the new economic era of the 1990s. Fears of scarcity, explains Bradshaw, are childish fears. He counsels his readers to promise
wondrous abundance and to deliver on those promises instead of scarring the inner child by forcing unwarranted and undesired limits on

him. Even when his own inner boy has to wait for what he wants, Bradshaw says "no" in a way that leaves the boy feeling okay, if not better about himself. After all, Bradshaw explains, "I'm proving to him that we can have *more* pleasure if we delay gratification."[32]

While there is a certain levelheadedness to some of his advice, often Bradshaw's therapy, at least as he describes his own experiences, is little more than another name or a justification for guiltlessly indulging in or buying playthings and pleasures. He has revised the anthem of *Little Nemo*: what fools people are to deny their inner children. His inner child, for instance, likes flying first class, playing golf, and riding in limousines, which his outer adult benevolently permits. Granting permission in this manner is important. Certainly such gestures feel good to the child, but they also display the power of the outer adult. Here the dubiousness of conspicuous consumption is transformed into beneficial therapy. In fact, most of the items on Bradshaw's list of "ten things" or advantages of "potency" that a man has over his inner boy involve the privileges of the purse: owning a car, having a bank account with money in it, the ability to "buy myself interesting toys," or "all the ice cream and candy I want," or to "do whatever I want to do." The inner child needs to hear about these strengths; he "will be very impressed!" and trust will build between him and his "father." In Bradshaw's therapy, the orphaned Lost Boys of *Peter Pan* are found, but they are not exiled from paradise. Rather, they get to stay there because being "parented" no longer has to be the austere alternative to Never Land that it once had seemed.[33]

As different as they appear, the "decline of values" critics of Peter Pantheism, adjustment therapists such as Kiley, and "inner child" advocates such as Bradshaw are not fundamentally at odds with one another. Instead, they often are compatible, complementary, mutually reinforcing participants in the century-long, dynamic discourse about the prospects for men in a capitalist economy that requires unbounded production and consumption, self-denial and self-indulgence, cold rationality and warm fairy tales. Regardless of whether they include women in the calculus or of where they fall in the spectrum of value preferences between the poles of manly production and effeminate consumption, all have been engaged in searching for a way to achieve authentic masculinity and powerful selfhood in the shifting and shifty cultural terrain of consumer capitalism. Rather than resolving the issue, they have tended to quibble over the specific qualities or over the ideal ratio of boyishness to maturity and of denial to indulgence. The disagreements have only reinforced the idea that the consumption of goods and the pursuit of wealth, underwritten and guided by some formula of "boymanhood" that enables men to get comfortable with their childishness, remains the enduring hope of American life.

### The Arrested Development of Hollywood

For the last twenty-five years Hollywood has served as the nation's unofficial petri dish for studying the dilemmas of Never Land. In many ways, this story is an old one. Since the days of Douglas Fairbanks and Mary Pickford, movie stars and their films have exploited the dream of unlimited play and eternal youth—and laid themselves open to dissection in movies such as *Sunset Blvd.* (1950).[34] Yet, since the mid-1970s, Hollywood has seen a particular efflorescence of movies, moviemakers, and stars who exhibit and explore the implications of Peter Pan manhood. None have been more influential or more closely watched (and often admired) in this regard than Robin Williams, Tom Hanks, and Steven Spielberg. Not only are they three of the wealthiest, most powerful, and most recognizable figures in the American entertainment business today;[35] they also have built careers and entertainment empires by either playing or being identified as boys who have resisted, failed, or—especially in the case of Spielberg—lately succeeded at growing up.

Williams, for instance, launched his stardom as the gibberish-speaking overgrown boy alien Mork, an exile from the humorless planet of Ork, in the late-1970s television comedy *Mork and Mindy*. Since then, his movies usually have been built on the supposed conflict between the exuberant, creative energy of boyishness (which he usually and hyperactively represents) and the life-choking tyranny of excessive seriousness and maturity (which he sometimes portrays as an enfeebled adult who learns—and shows us—how to play): *Good Morning Vietnam* (1987), *Dead Poets Society* (1989), *Hook* (1991), *Mrs. Doubtfire* (1993), and *Jack* (1996), to name some of the most obvious examples. Although Tom Hanks ordinarily portrays his characters at a lower voltage than Williams, many of his most popular and celebrated movies—*Splash* (1984), *Big* (1988), *Forrest Gump* (1994), *Apollo 13* (1995), *Toy Story* (1995), *The Green Mile* (1999)—have fostered the myth that arrested development or everlasting childhood, while scorned by those too serious to comprehend its potential, can revitalize us all. The paragon of this genre, though, has been Spielberg. Since *Jaws* in the summer of 1975, virtually everyone has regarded him as the preeminent Peter Pan of American popular culture. Yet even as he has almost continuously delighted moviegoers, critics often have questioned whether Spielberg could produce anything more substantial than pleasing trifles such as *Raiders of the Lost Ark* (1981). Once he appeared to get serious in the 1990s, news of the greatness of such films as *Schindler's List* (1993) and *Saving Private Ryan* (1998) was uttered in the same breath with proclamations that he had finally grown up.[36]

Spielberg's newfound maturity is one clue that the apparent wall of seriousness dividing featherweight late-1980s fantasies such as *Big* from more-adult films of the late 1990s such as *Saving Private Ryan* actually obscures what these two movies in particular have in common. Rather than being in fundamental conflict, they are engaged in a kind of sibling rivalry over the uncertain returns of Peter Pantheism. *Big*, which starred Tom Hanks as a twelve-year-old boy inside a man's body, was one of the highest-grossing and most profitable films of 1988.[37] It was written in part by Anne Spielberg, which encouraged rumors that Hanks's character was modeled after her famous brother Steven. Reviewers did not regard this pedigree as a problem, and almost universally endorsed the movie's proof of the "hidden child in each of us." *Big*, observed one writer, "begs the question why adults get so serious when there is fun to be had in almost any situation." Hanks got most of the credit for establishing this self-evident logic. "Boyishness," one reviewer observed, "comes naturally to him—that's part of his appeal in any role. He has small, fleshy lips, arched eyebrows, and rounded eyes—he looks like a young and graceful clown."[38]

In *Big*, Hanks plays Josh Baskin, a middle-class boy whose drama is provoked by the wrenching, perhaps even "scarring," experience of deprivation endemic to suburbia: he is denied admission to an amusement park ride because he is too small, and his affections for an older girl are unrequited. He wishes he were "big," and, miraculously, the wish is granted. He awakens the next morning the literal embodiment of Bradshaw's therapeutic metaphor: a boy in a man's body. Exiled from his home, where even his mother does not recognize him anymore, he flees to Manhattan in search of the magic key to restore his body to its rightful size. It is *The Wonderful Wizard of Oz*, but without witches. Josh's boyish innocence and zest for life charm all but those most crippled by the artificial concerns of adulthood. He coincidentally finds work at a multinational toy corporation and moves up in a flash from the rags of data processing to the riches of a vice president's office. Josh's new "work" does not actually involve making any goods, generating any unwanted sweat, or owning any capital. His work really is "play." As he explains, "I play with all this stuff and then I go in and I tell them what I think." "And they pay you for that?" exclaims his twelve-year-old best friend. "Suckers!" What Josh does is come up with ideas for commodities that make people—stockholders as well as toy buyers—happy. The secret to his success (on the job as well as off, as the budding romance with his attractive fellow executive Susan shows) is that, in growing up, Josh has not grown old. He is the metaphorical antonym of MacMillan Toys, where marketing ideas have gone stale and employees have turned cynical under the excessively rational and grown-up corporate managers. Josh's sincere boyishness and sheer love of play and toys restore vigor and excitement to the company; sales are soaring, employees are loving their work, and Paul, the hotshot M.B.A. who once was the darling of the company, now finds himself bested by Josh at every turn, in the boss's no less than in Susan's eyes. "What is so special about Baskin?" Paul demands. "He's a grown-up," Susan answers. What this irony lacks in subtlety it makes up for in earnestness.

*Big*, of course, exploits an ancient theme ("a little child shall lead them," prophesied Isaiah) that Hollywood has played with for decades: *Mr. Smith Goes to Washington* (1939), *It's a Wonderful Life* (1946), *Miracle on Thirty-fourth Street* (1947), and, in a less reassuring vein, *Being There* (1979).[39] Its marketplace setting is at least as old as Horatio Alger's post–Civil War romances. Books such as *Ragged Dick* (1868) showcased winsome boys who catch the eye of the well-placed adult with their ingenuous charm and plucky dispositions; then they race past more advantageously positioned rivals, exposing them for their leaden conventionality and sophisticated cunning in the process. But most of *Big's* direction is derived from the logic of Kiley's revised Peter Pantheism and Bradshaw's wonder childishness. A healthy, mature man (and, by extension, a profitable business) retains some of the playful boy within him. *Big's* success story directly equates aging with corruption, weakness, and bad business sense; youth, on the other hand, means innocence, energy, and marketing genius. Josh is not the only vehicle for this message. The old-fashioned CEO of the firm is a no-nonsense businessman who is still a kid inside. When his corporate sycophants throw "favorability ratings" and marketing reports at him, he tells them to save the "bullshit": "If a kid likes a toy, it sells. That's all." Josh wins his big promotion not by kissing up to the boss, but by playing with him. They perform a duo of "Heart and Soul" and "Chopsticks" on the outsized piano keyboard at the 1980s corporate symbol of the high-end play spirit, the F.A.O. Schwarz store on Fifth Avenue in New York.

In the second half of the movie, Josh undergoes two transformations. The first results from an evening of sexual intimacy with his colleague Susan, which sends him rocketing overnight into manhood. When Josh arrives at the office the next morning, as one critic put it, he "walks about like a rooster after his first successful day in the henhouse."[40] But the grin on his face cannot conceal that he has lost something in the bargain. His ideas for toys no longer have the zip they once did. Now he is working late hours, neglecting his best buddy for dates with Susan (with whom he is now occasionally disagreeable), drinking coffee, and wearing suits. He misses the child he once was and his mother, two longings that bring on the final transformation. Forsaking Susan, he wishes himself small again, in effect returning to a presexual Never Land that Fred Thompson could have comprehended—just boys, no girls, except, of course, his mother. He finds the charm that delivers him back to genuine childhood on the quaint boardwalk at—where else?—Playland.

Some critics at the time accused *Big* of cynically cozying up to "acquisition-guilty yuppies" and playing to the late-1980s spirit of corporate excess.[41] Perhaps, but the assessment seems shortsighted. *Big* was participating in a century-long investigation of the relation of toys to manhood. Josh Baskin is as much the kid brother to the Peter Pan fantasies of Fred Thompson and Tony Sarg as he is to those of John Bradshaw's inner child flying in the first-class compartment. Much like the Luna Park version of boys' play, *Big* also retains the enduring suspicion that women will swipe the best thing that men have going for themselves—the fun-loving boy inside. *Big*'s story was neither peculiar to postwar America nor limited to the antifeminist reaction of the Reagan-Bush years. Nor did it exhaust the theme. Wonderful boys in grown-up bodies have continued to make appearances in films associated with

Hanks: the "wise fool" Forrest Gump, a role that won Hanks his second Academy Award; and the African-American death-row inmate in *The Green Mile*, John Coffey, who possesses a magical healing gift that rejuvenates the cynical guard Paul Edgecomb, who is played by Hanks. (Among other beneficial outcomes of Coffey's ministrations, Edgecomb can again have sexual intercourse with his attractive wife.) Whether Hanks is using or being healed by it, his roles keep demonstrating the redemptive power of neverending childhood to men suffering from what Fred Thompson once diagnosed as tuberculosis of the heart.

The persistence of these juvenile features made the actor's appearance in 1998 at the head of Steven Spielberg's cast of infantrymen storming the beaches of Normandy in *Saving Private Ryan* all the more revealing of that film's entanglement in the paradoxes of eternal boyhood. For the past twenty-five years Spielberg and his movies have been participants in this larger drama. For the period from 1975 to 1994, the moviemaker seemed to represent both sides of the Peter Pan syndrome—the happy-go-lucky charm and the confounding immaturity—in films such as *Jaws*, *Close Encounters of the Third Kind*, *E.T. the Extra-Terrestrial*, and the Indiana Jones series. Biographical assessments of the director tended, in Kiley fashion, to lay responsibility for his apparent developmental deficit on the shoulders of his neglectful and divorced suburban parents. Like the Peter Pans diagnosed by the doctor, Spielberg grew up impoverished amid his family's comparative affluence—fearful, soft, weak, unable to be a man.[42] Then, in the late 1980s and early 1990s, Spielberg went through a period of middle-class male adversity—turning forty, fatherhood, marriage, divorce, and remarriage—which forced him to reassess the direction of his life. In 1997 his father described the new man to *Time*: "He's a mature guy now, and the biggest reason is his family."[43] The new Spielberg was reflected in the much-acclaimed seriousness of *Schindler's List* (1994), his celebrated treatment of the Holocaust. Whether Spielberg has forsaken childish things is beside the point. What matters here is the narrative, which relies on a familiar trope in American critical literature on the performing arts—one that defines the aesthetic progress from puerile melodrama to hard-headed realism in terms of "growing up."[44] As critics have told the story, *Schindler's List* was the director's coming of age. "Spielberg's bar mitzvah movie," *Jewish Frontier* said of the Holocaust film. The "boy of *Jaws*," pronounced *Time*, "has become the man of *Schindler's List*."[45] Gender is an essential element of these assessments, defining Spielberg's metamorphosis, not from childhood to adulthood, but from boyhood to manhood.

The notion that aesthetic progress recapitulates a man's life cycle necessitates a period of adolescence in which Spielberg could prepare for his bar mitzvah. In his case, he had to come to terms with Peter Pan. This process began on a literal note in 1990–91, when he and fellow boy-man Robin Williams collaborated on *Hook*, the most recent big-budget version of Barrie's drama. The movie, which wonders what Peter Pan would be like if he grew up, was vastly over budget, ridiculed by reviewers, and indifferently received by moviegoers. As a number of writers observed at the time, *Hook* owed as much to John Bradshaw as it did to James Barrie. The *New Yorker* called the "whole sorry spectacle ... an illustrated lecture on finding the inner child."[46] (Bradshaw, who concluded *Homecoming* with a reflection on Spielberg's *E.T.*, actually was consulted on the *Hook* script, and his daughter was cast in the production.)[47] Even with its reliance on the therapeutic paraphernalia of inner-childhood, *Hook* owed much of its punch to the century-long suspicion that modern life has made fools of middle-class white men.

Spielberg's *Hook* insists that *Peter Pan* (no matter how many women have played the part) is a man's story. Squeezing the famously wooly body of Robin Williams into Pan's tights underlines the point. Williams plays the mature Peter Pan Banning, a corporate raider who prefers crushing the business competition to hugging his family.[48] The child is buried so deeply within him that he has become the enemy—a pirate—which is to say he displays all the symptoms of excessive seriousness: he is out of shape, wears three-piece suits (Hollywood's universal symbol of prematurely enfeebled male maturity), and misses his son's Little League baseball game. Desperate, his wife Moira skips recounting his obligations as a parent and appeals instead to his self-interest: "Your children love you. They want to play with you. How long do you think that lasts?" Workaholism is depriving him of the greatest fun of life—fatherhood. In the end, in Spielberg's words, Banning comes around and "evolves into this wonderful man-child."[49] His return to Never Land constitutes not infantilization, but a new kind of empowerment, as he relearns to soar, slays the pirates, and restores his standing in the eyes of his Little Leaguer son. Returning to the "real" world, he is rejuvenated—more, rather than less, Peter-Panish. He nimbly scrambles up a drainpipe to rejoin his family and gives Moira an ardent kiss. His son and wife are now beaming, knowing that, from now on, they both will be getting some quality playtime with Father.

At the time of the film, a press aide for Spielberg explained that *Hook* "isn't really about pirates. It's about Steven's views of modern parenthood."[50] *Hook* actually has little to say about parenthood. Its chief concern is fatherhood, which Spielberg defines and justifies by calculating the hedonistic returns on the patriarch's investment of time and energy. He shows that maturity does not have to connote the marriage penalty of the self-denying, duty-bound, joyless breadwinner. Banning learns that the joys of money are sorry substitutes for the real fun of playing with his children. Men do not lose in the bargain of fatherhood; they are enriched and enlivened. The movie thus thrives on the suspicion that King Morpheus articulated eighty years earlier in Fred Thompson's *Little Nemo*: that the dependents—women and children—are having all the fun. Although some writers have described *Hook* as "harsh" and "self-critical," such words seem ill suited to the regeneration at work here.[51] Rather than losing himself in his children (as women, regrettably, tend to do) or in his work (as he used to do), Banning finds himself in and among his children—an alternative and pleasurable form of fulfillment that dodges the pinch of self-sacrifice. The implication is that, from here on out, he will not just be on time for baseball games; he will find work that is fun and leaves him feeling more rather than less like a man.[52]

Although impressive, climbing a drainpipe hardly solves the persistent dilemmas of Peter Pan manhood, which is what makes *Saving Private Ryan* less a departure from Never Land than a continuing adventure in it. The main claim for the brilliance of *Private Ryan* is the "reportorial candor" with which Spielberg reproduced the American forces' D-Day invasion of France. The movie, from this perspective, manfully shows war exactly as it was experienced by fighting men instead of softening it with narrative or pictorial sentiment that panders to audiences' childish wishes for gung-ho heroism. "Spielberg makes you look at the consequences of war," explains the historian Stephen Ambrose. "He makes you look at these young kids, the terror, the confusion, the chaos, the noise, the heartbreak of these young lives being stamped out."[53] What *Saving Private Ryan* seems to affirm, then, is not just the greatness of the invading Allied soldiers, but especially the maturity of Spielberg. By demonstrating how D-Day made men out of the boys who participated in the invasion, *Private Ryan* likewise proves just how much Hanks and Spielberg themselves had grown in the decade since they appeared, literally and figuratively, in *Big*. Boys could not tell the truth about war, part of which is that fun is not to be had in all situations. Like *Big* and *Hook*, *Saving Private Ryan* was (and is) as much about the Peter Pan syndrome as it was about World War II.

Since its release, *Saving Private Ryan* has become inseparable from the popular filial pietism and "postheroic" anxieties associated with *The Greatest Generation*, the title of a collection of reminiscences and reprimands that the television news personality Tom Brokaw collected from veterans of World War II and published to best-selling acclaim in late 1998.[54] Although Brokaw claims that his interest in compiling the book was to pay tribute to the greatness of the war generation, he also gives considerable attention to their complaints that today's women and men seem, in comparison to their fathers and mothers, frivolous, childish, and excessively concerned about material possessions. In Brokaw's words, the "greatest generation" believes that the younger set has "too many toys, too much play time, too little concentration on what really counts."[55] Such gripes position *The Greatest Generation* and other war productions such as *Saving Private Ryan* in relation to the claims and charms of Peter Pan culture and the persistent worry that contemporary men do not measure up to earlier generations of men—a worry that was as prevalent in the 1910s and 1940s as it is today. It seems unlikely that Spielberg would have put his cast of millionaire actors, including the perennial boy-man Tom Hanks, through five days of real-life basic training under a former Marine to make them grow up—or, in his words, to "put them in a frame of mind where they understood that we weren't playing around, that we were making a serious picture about war"—if he were not worried that, in reality, he and they were only playing around.[56]

*Saving Private Ryan* and *The Greatest Generation* underscore the continuing necessity of exploring, celebrating, and condemning the ambiguous effects of consumer culture on men—how its toys and playtime distractions from what really counts seem to make men feel more and less powerful at the same time. In this sense, little has changed since the early twentieth century, when the inventor of Luna Park insisted that work had to be fun and built playgrounds where men had to do only what they wanted to do. There is a good deal of Fred Thompson in the image of the revitalized and revised patriarch Spielberg, overseeing his part of the multinational entertainment conglomerate DreamWorks, his priorities set straight by the lessons of D-Day and the demands of presiding over a continuously expanding brood of youngsters. His second wife explained the practical details of the new man her husband had become: he still works hard, but "if one of the kids asks him to build a castle, he's immediately down on the floor, building that castle. The kid runs away, Steven crawls back on the couch and gets back to [his] business."[57] Spielberg, it seems, has achieved the promise of Peter Pan culture in the fashion of Josh Baskin. Yet, as in the time of Fred Thompson, this developmental achievement is a balancing act, which necessitates combining power with play into an authentic masculine compound of storming the beaches at Normandy, building dream castles, and managing DreamWorks. If Spielberg has eluded the diminished expectations and the disenchantments that have soured contemporary life for other middle-class suburban men, it is because he has grown up without growing old, which, in his case, means that he remains no less a capitalist than an amusement inventor and perennial small boy.

Such attitudes seem genetically inscribed in today's information economy and the hip, playful, toy-building entrepreneurs who claim to be engineering it, such as Steve Perlman. One of the forces behind WebTV, Perlman was once described by his associates as a thirty-eight-year-old "brilliant guy who doesn't want to grow up." Perlman's outlook on work is vintage Fred Thompson. "The only things I will do," he says, "is stuff that I am interested in doing." When he quit his position at Apple Computer (a firm with a mythic history deeply enmeshed in Peter Pantheism) because it had become too stodgy for him, he delivered his farewell in a "white paper" on keeping innovation alive, subtitled "Growing Up without Growing Old." Before he fled the Microsoft corporation in 1999 to start his own company, Perlman was making his fellow executives there feel a little uneasy. "He wants power without responsibility," someone at the company said, "and at Microsoft that just doesn't fly."[58]

Whether Peter Pan will fly at Microsoft is not the issue. His airworthiness and utility seem, if anything, more assured and important today than when he and Fred Thompson joined hands now nearly a century ago. One reason is the very elasticity of the idea of Never Land. It suggests a way of escaping from the world and making the most of its opportunities; it both sanctions and censures risk and recklessness. Another reason is the monopoly that men claim on the prerogatives of eternal childhood. A Maude Adams, Mary Martin, or Cathy Rigby may play the role to great acclaim, but in American culture a woman cannot so easily be Peter Pan. The director of *Big*, Penny Marshall, understood as much. She briefly toyed with the idea of casting a "girl" in the lead role. Then she remembered Josh's sexual initiation, which commences when he "sees Susan's breast for the first time and reaches out reverentially to touch it." Marshall decided girls need not apply. "It doesn't work the other way," she explained. "I mean, it's a little more acceptable that a thirteen-year-old boy has an experience with a woman. The other way, it's impossible.... Plus, what's she gonna touch? No. There's just no way."[59] The image of an eternal girl crowing like a rooster after a night in the henhouse is too topsy-turvy, too horrible to contemplate. "It's Polanskiville," Marshall said, alluding to the film director Roman Polanski, who was accused in 1977 of raping a thirteen-year-old girl.[60] Eternal boyishness continues to bother American men, but it does not necessarily conjure up such alarming associations. On the contrary, even when he appears at his worst—feckless, narcissistic, confoundingly immature—a boy-man sustains the possibility that his discovery of new doorways to pleasure and privilege will advance the cause of self and civilization. Even if the dilemmas of Never Land cannot be resolved, the eternal boy remains useful in justifying the bounty and in explaining away the deficits that contemporary middle-class men experience in their everyday lives. If men will follow the boy's example, he will teach them to fly like him. After all, for most of the twentieth century, American culture provided stages on which Peter Pan was free to soar and pulleys and guy wires to make sure he could get off the ground, even if the strings were there for all to see.

*Chapter 1: Uncle Sam's a Boy at Play*

1.  "What Fools We Mortals Be," from the Broadway musical *Little Nemo*, produced by Klaw and Erlanger, New Amsterdam Theatre, New York, 20 October 1908. The song is reprinted in *Klaw and Erlanger Present "Little Nemo"* (New York: Cohan and Harris, 1908), 23–27, book by Harry Smith, music by Victor Herbert; based on Winsor McCay's Sunday supplement cartoon, *Little Nemo in Slumberland*, published in the *New York Herald*.

2.  On the comic strip, see Winsor McCay, *The Complete Little Nemo in Slumberland*, vols. 1–4, edited by Richard Marschall (Seattle: Fantagraphics Books, 1990); John Canemaker, *Winsor McCay: His Life and Art* (New York: Abbeville Press, 1987); and Jackson Lears, *Fables of Abundance: A Cultural History of Advertising in America* (New York: Basic Books, 1994), 330–31. On comic strips in general, see Ian Gordon, *Comic Strips and Consumer Culture, 1890–1945* (Washington, D.C.: Smithsonian Institution Press, 1998).

3.  "Messrs. Klaw and Erlanger Will Stage Little Nemo," Paris edition of the *New York Herald*, 10 September 1907, and "Victor Herbert and H. B. Smith Fit Nemo for Stage," *New York Herald*, 27 May 1908, both in Erlanger Collection Scrapbooks, Billy Rose Theatre Collection, New York Public Library at Lincoln Center, Astor, Lenox, and Tilden Foundations (hereinafter cited as TCNYPL).

4.  On the cost of the production, see "Plays and Players: The Cost of Musical Comedy," *American Magazine* 70 (May 1910): 105–13.

5.  Clipping from *Spotlight*, 27 October 1906, Frederic Thompson clipping file, TCNYPL.

6.  The Broadway agency of Cohan and Harris owned the last quarter of the production. For an account of the legal and financial arrangements of the produc-

tion of *Little Nemo*, see the *Little Nemo* contract file, series 3, no. 57, in the collection of the Shubert Archive, New York, New York. See also the synopsis of the financial arrangements for the production in the Klaw and Erlanger Plays—Corporation Series, Shubert Archive.

7. John Murray, "Building a Great Spectacle," *Green Book Album* 1 (March 1909): 638–39; "Nemo Travels in Style," *New York Morning Telegraph*, 20 September 1908, and Sam McKee, "All the Family Will See 'Nemo,'" *New York Morning Telegraph*, 27 September 1908, in Erlanger Collection Scrapbooks, TCNYPL; final scene, "Little Nemo in Slumberland: An extravaganza in Three Acts," Harry B. Smith Collection, *Little Nemo* file, script, n.d., Theatre Collection, Museum of the City of New York; "In Happy Slumberland," in *Klaw and Erlanger Present "Little Nemo,"* 132–34; "Little Nemo Will Be Matinee Idol," *New York Morning Telegraph*, 29 September 1908, in Locke Collection, vol. 192, "Master Gabriel" clippings, TCNYPL; "Remember the Old Continentals," in *Klaw and Erlanger Present "Little Nemo,"* 118–22.

8. "Luna Park Is Opened; 60,000 People There," *Brooklyn Daily Eagle*, 17 May 1903, 6.

9. Edwin E. Slosson, "The Amusement Business," *Independent* 57, 21 July 1904, 134; "Otto Herschman Is Buying for Kahn Bros.," *Playthings* 11 (October 1913): 104. On Luna Parks around the world, the World Wide Web is a useful source, although the websites change constantly. For examples of Luna Parks on other continents, see the following: for Melbourne, Australia (1912), the website http://www.lunapark.com.au, which reports that seven Luna Parks were opened in Australia on the Coney Island example, but only those in Melbourne and Sydney still exist; for Sydney, http://www.lunaparksydney.com; for the one in Buenos Aires, Argentina (1912), http://www.lunapark.com.ar. For a photograph of Luna in Berlin, see V. R. Berghahn, "Germany's America," *American Heritage* 46 (May-June 1995): 62–69; for Luna Park in the former Soviet Union, see the film *Luna Park* (1991), directed and written by Pavel Lungin, IMA Films, 105 minutes, New Yorker Video, 1994, videocassette.

10. Robert Grau, *The Business Man in the Amusement World: A Volume of Progress in the Field of the Theatre* (New York: Broadway, 1910), 328.

11. Promotional brochure, *Luna Park: The Heart of Coney Island* (1903), 8, in the collection of the Brooklyn Historical Society.

12. Clipping, "Toy-Maker for Grown-Ups," *New York Journal*, 5 May 1916, in Thompson and Dundy clipping file, TCNYPL.

13. Thompson's second wife, Selene Thompson, quoted in a letter from Marguerite Merington to the *New York Sun*, 24 May 1929, reprinted in the *Nashville Banner* as "Fine Tribute Paid Nashville Woman," in scrapbook 1, Avery Collection, Manuscript Division, Tennessee State Library and Archives, Nashville; "Frederic Thompson's Tribute to Toys," *Playthings* 7 (July 1909): 115. On gift giving, see Stephen Nissenbaum, *The Battle for Christmas: A Cultural History of America's Most Cherished Holiday* (New York: Vintage, 1997), 132–75.

14. David Nasaw, *Going Out: The Rise and Fall of Public Amusements* (New York: Basic Books, 1993), 3, chaps. 1–4; Kathy Peiss, *Cheap Amusements: Working Women and Leisure in Turn-of-the-Century New York* (Philadelphia: Temple University Press, 1986); Jack Poggi, *Theater in America: The Impact of Economic Forces* (Ithaca, N.Y.: Cornell University Press, 1968), 3–27; Lewis Erenberg, *Step-*

*pin' Out: New York Nightlife and the Transformation of American Culture,
1890–1930* (Westport, Conn.: Greenwood Press, 1981); Alfred L. Bernheim, *The
Business of the Theatre: An Economic History of the American Theatre, 1750–1932*
(New York: Benjamin Blom, 1932).

15. Glenmore Davis, "Our Billion-Dollar Smile," *Success* 11 (December 1908): 766.

16. Frederic Thompson, "Amusing People," *Metropolitan* 32 (August 1910): 601.

17. Review of *Peter Pan*, *Theatre* 5 (December 1905): 27. What is *Peter Pan* "all
about?" one critic asked rhetorically. "Can you describe how you would feel if
you saw yourself again in your mother's arms?" See the clipping "Maude
Adams's Peter Pan Takes One Back to Childhood Days," *Los Angeles Examiner*, 9
July 1907, in Locke Scrapbook, vol. 5, TCNYPL.

18. J. M. Barrie, *Peter Pan, or The Boy Who Would Not Grow Up*, act 5, scene 2, in *The
Plays of J. M. Barrie in One Volume* (New York: Charles Scribner's Sons, 1948),
91. Although "Never Land" sounds strange to contemporary ears, I have used it
throughout this book because it is the wording in the published version of Barrie's play.

19. For an alternative vision of the American future, see Nick Salvatore, *Eugene
Debs: Citizen and Socialist* (Urbana: University of Illinois Press, 1982); John Up-
dike, speech to the National Arts Club, 1984, quoted in James B. Twitchell, *Ad-
cult U.S.A.: The Triumph of Advertising in American Culture* (New York:
Columbia University Press, 1996), vii.

20. Pauline Jacobson, "Forty Winks at the Exposition," *San Francisco Bulletin*, 13
February 1915, 13; William Leach, *Land of Desire: Merchants, Power, and the Rise
of a New American Culture* (New York: Pantheon, 1993), 90; Jean-Christophe
Agnew, "Coming Up for Air: Consumer Culture in Historical Perspective," *Intellectual History Newsletter* 12 (1990): 15. On the gender implications of con-
sumption, see the useful essays in Victoria de Grazia, ed., *The Sex of Things:
Gender and Consumption in Historical Perspective* (Berkeley and Los Angeles:
University of California Press, 1996). The introductory comments by de Grazia
(1–10, 11–24, 151–61, 275–86) are especially insightful. On men and consumer
culture, see Michael S. Kimmel, "Consuming Manhood: The Feminization of
American Culture and the Recreation of the Male Body, 1832–1920," in *The
Male Body: Features, Destinies, Exposures*, edited by Laurence Goldstein (Ann
Arbor: University of Michigan Press, 1994), 12–41; Michael S. Kimmel, *Man-
hood in America: A Cultural History* (New York: Free Press, 1996), 101–12; Peter
G. Filene, *Him/Her/Self: Sex Roles in Modern America* (1974; reprint, Baltimore:
Johns Hopkins University Press, 1986), 69–93, esp. 71–80; E. Anthony Rotundo, *American Manhood: Transformations in Masculinity from the Revolution to
the Modern Era* (New York: Basic Books, 1993), 167–246; John D'Emilio and Estelle B. Freedman, *Intimate Matters: A History of Sexuality in America*, 2d ed.
(Chicago: University of Chicago Press, 1997), 222–35; Gail Bederman, *Manliness and Civilization: A Cultural History of Gender and Race in the United States,
1880–1917* (Chicago: University of Chicago Press, 1995), 10–20; Gail Bederman, "'The Women Have Had Charge of the Church Work Long Enough': The
Men and Religion Forward Movement of 1911–1912 and the Masculinization of
Middle-Class Protestantism," *American Quarterly* 41 (1989): 432–65; Margaret
Marsh, "Suburban Men and Masculine Domesticity, 1870–1915," in *Meanings
for Manhood: Constructions of Masculinity in Victorian America*, edited by Mark

C. Carnes and Clyde Griffen (Chicago: University of Chicago Press, 1990), 111–27; and Elliott J. Gorn, *The Manly Art: Bare-knuckle Prize Fighting in America* (Ithaca, N.Y.: Cornell University Press, 1986), 206–47.

21. In her introduction to *The Sex of Things*, Victoria de Grazia contends that scholars need to examine "the immense transformative powers of capitalist-driven consumption as it constantly refashions notions of authentic, essential woman- and mankind" (1–10, quotation on 8). On gender and the writing of history, see Joan W. Scott, *Gender and the Politics of History* (New York: Columbia University Press, 1988), esp. 1–50; see also John Higham, "The Reorientation of American Culture in the 1890s," in *Writing American History*, edited by John Higham (Bloomington: Indiana University Press, 1970), 79; and Lears, *Fables of Abundance*, 42–43. Higham's influential essay, which I quote here, has been a starting point for talking about the fin de siècle "crisis of manhood." Recent treatments are Rotundo, *American Manhood*, 247–55; Michael S. Kimmel, "The Contemporary 'Crisis' of Masculinity in Historical Perspective," in *The Making of Masculinities*, edited by Harry Brod (Boston: Allen and Unwin, 1987), 121–54; Kimmel, *Manhood in America*, 81–188; and Bederman, *Manliness and Civilization*. I find Bederman's nuanced and dialectical approach the most helpful.

22. Lears, *Fables of Abundance*, 273; John F. Kasson, *Amusing the Million: Coney Island at the Turn of the Century* (New York: Hill and Wang, 1978), 105–9; Leach, *Land of Desire*.

23. Nasaw, *Going Out*.

24. See the excellent discussion in Mary Louise Roberts, "Gender, Consumption, and Commodity Culture," *American Historical Review* 103 (June 1998): 817–44; see also Lawrence Levine, "The Folklore of Industrial Society: Popular Culture and Its Audiences," in *The Unpredictable Past: Explorations in American Cultural History* (New York: Oxford University Press, 1993), 291–99, quotations on 295–296. Lizabeth Cohen has similarly argued that alternative mentalities did not simply wither under the onslaught of consumer capitalism's revolutionary promises and enticements. Her work emphasizes the influence of unanticipated historical events, such as the widespread social devastation of the Great Depression, intersecting with the preferences and priorities of consumers (working-class immigrants, for example), whose patronage of chain or grocery stores and whose purchase of phonographs were not necessarily de facto rejections of their ethnicity or ethnic ways. When Italian Chicagoans listened, alone or in groups, to recordings of Sicilian songs or comedians, they reinforced their "collective experience as immigrants." See Lizabeth Cohen, *Making a New Deal: Industrial Workers in Chicago, 1919–1939* (Cambridge: Cambridge University Press, 1990), 99–158; quotation on 105. William Leach's examination of L. Frank Baum is an especially skillful execution of this mode of investigation of consumer culture's architects; see his essays "The Clown from Syracuse: The Life and Times of L. Frank Baum" and "A Trickster's Tale: L. Frank Baum's *The Wonderful Wizard of Oz*," in L. Frank Baum, *The Wonderful Wizard of Oz*, edited by William Leach (1900; reprint, Belmont, Calif.: Wadsworth, 1991), 1–34, 157–88. The final quotation is from Stewart Culin, *The Road to Beauty*, typescript, Culin Archival Collection, Brooklyn Museum of Art Archives (Research and Writings: Road to Beauty [5.2.006], chaps. 1–4, 1925), 49–50. For a discussion of Culin as Peter Pan, see Woody Register, "Everyday Peter Pans: Work,

Manhood, and Consumption in Urban America, 1900–1930," *Men and Masculinities* 2 (October 1999): 197–227.

25. Peter Ackroyd, "Biography: The Short Form," *New York Times Book Review*, 10 January 1999, 4.

26. Thompson, "Amusing People," 604. The biographers whose work I admire and have sought to emulate include Neil Harris, *Humbug: The Art of P. T. Barnum* (Chicago: University of Chicago Press, 1981); Kathryn Kish Sklar, *Catharine Beecher: A Study in American Domesticity* (New Haven: Yale University Press, 1973) and *Florence Kelley and the Nation's Work: The Rise of Women's Political Culture, 1830–1900* (New Haven: Yale University Press, 1995); and John L. Thomas, *Alternative America: Henry George, Edward Bellamy, Henry Demarest Lloyd, and the Adversary Tradition* (Cambridge, Mass.: Harvard University Press, 1983). My indebtedness to William Leach's biographical scholarship, especially his edition of *The Wonderful Wizard of Oz* and his major study of American consumer culture, *Land of Desire*, is obvious.

27. Thompson, quoted in Frances A. Groff, "Exposition Moths," *Sunset* 35 (July 1915): 135.

*Chapter 2: The Moon For a Plaything*

1. Frances A. Groff, "Exposition Moths," *Sunset* 35 (July 1915): 133, 138.

2. William Leach, *Land of Desire: Merchants, Power, and the Rise of a New American Culture* (New York: Pantheon, 1993), 5–12, quotations on 7.

3. On the revaluation of leisure in the hands of liberal ministers, Progressive reformers, and inspirational writers such as Ralph Waldo Trine, see Daniel Rodgers, *The Work Ethic in Industrial America, 1850–1920* (Chicago: University of Chicago Press, 1979), 94–124. Quotation from "Toy-Maker for Grown-Ups," *New York Journal*, 5 May 1916, in Thompson and Dundy clipping file, TCNYPL.

4. Groff, "Exposition Moths," 134.

5. Quoted in Paul Krause, *The Battle for Homestead, 1880–1892: Politics, Culture, and Steel* (Pittsburgh: University of Pittsburgh Press, 1992), 102. On Debs, see Nick Salvatore, *Eugene Debs: Citizen and Socialist* (Urbana: University of Illinois Press, 1982), 18. On the economic depression of the 1870s, see Philip S. Foner, *The Great Labor Uprising of 1877* (New York: Monad Press, 1977).

6. *New York Tribune*, quoted in Salvatore, *Eugene Debs*, 31; John L. Thomas, *Alternative America: Henry George, Edward Bellamy, Henry Demarest Lloyd and the Adversary Tradition* (Cambridge, Mass.: Harvard University Press, 1983), 77–82, quotations on 79.

7. Linda Wagner-Martin, *Telling Women's Lives: The New Biography* (New Brunswick, N.J.: Rutgers University Press, 1994), 1–10.

8. On Casey Thompson's birth and immigration, see the obituary for his brother, George W. Thompson, "Designed Many Fine Buildings," *Nashville Banner*, 22 February 1910, 7. According to the obituary, the Thompson family emigrated from Chatham, England, in 1850. The scanty information available suggests that Casey Thompson was a skilled ironmaster who may have supervised a steel-rolling mill. The 1878 city directory for Portsmouth, Ohio, where the Thompsons moved when Fred was one year old, lists a Frederick Thompson who "works rolling mill." See *Portsmouth Directory* (Portsmouth, Ohio: Wiggins and McKillop's, 1878), 135. In a published interview, Thompson says his father "es-

tablished" the Burgess Steel Works in Portsmouth. See "Frederic Thompson, the Proof of Youth," *New York Sunday Telegraph,* 2 April 1905, 7. In this interview Thompson almost certainly exaggerated Casey's role. The Burgess mill had existed for some years in 1873, when its poor financial condition forced its major creditor to take over operations. Casey Thompson probably began working at Burgess under the new management. On the Burgess Steel and Iron Works, see Frank H. Rowe, *History of the Iron and Steel Industry in Scioto County, Ohio* (Columbus: Ohio State Archaeological and Historical Society, 1938), 38–41.

9. Robert B. Westbrook makes a comparable point in *John Dewey and American Democracy* (Ithaca, N.Y.: Cornell University Press, 1991), 1–2.

10. "Frederic Thompson, the Proof of Youth." See also "Frederic Williams Thompson," in *The National Cyclopaedia of American Biography* (New York: James T. White, 1926), 19: 105–6. On stained-glass work, see Groff, "Exposition Moths," 134; see also Worthington Pump and Machinery Corporation, *One hundred Years, 1840–1940, Worthington* (Harrison, N.J.: Worthington Pump and Machinery, 1940), 7–19.

11. Rodgers, *Work Ethic,* 95, 102, 123, *Chautauquan* quotation on 102. My work is deeply indebted to Rodgers's study, although it should be noted that his chapters on changing attitudes regarding leisure and play—"'Mechanicalized' Men" and "Play, Repose, and Plenty," 65–124—focus principally on religious and secular reform voices.

12. Krause, *Battle for Homestead,* 350–51, 10; David Montgomery, *Workers' Control in America: Studies in the History of Work, Technology, and Labor Struggles* (Cambridge: Cambridge University Press, 1979), 4, 13. I also have been influenced by Joshua B. Freeman, "Andrew and Me," *Nation* 255 (16 November 1992), 572–80.

13. On Holley, see Krause, *Battle for Homestead,* 67–77, quotation on 70.

14. Groff, "Exposition Moths," 134; Raymond Williams, *The Country and the City* (New York: Oxford University Press, 1973), 60–67; Lewis Mumford, *Technics and Civilization* (New York: Harcourt Brace, 1934), 25, 45–55, quotation on 53; Frederic Thompson, "Amusing People," *Metropolitan* 32 (August 1910): 601.

15. On "mechanicalized" men, see Rodgers, *Work Ethic,* 65–93; Mumford, *Technics and Civilization,* 51. Thompson's nostalgia for the pleasures of the shop floor of his childhood was rendered most fully—and pleasingly—in his 1908 Broadway production *Via Wireless,* the opening scene of which involved a fully operating, realistically detailed blast furnace of a steel mill. See the description in Glenmore Davis, "Building a Play," *Success* 12 (February 1909), in Locke Scrapbook, series 2, vol. 113, TCNYPL, 128. The play itself is discussed in chap. 4.

16. Carroll Smith-Rosenberg, "Davy Crockett as Trickster: Pornography, Liminality, and Symbolic Inversion in Victorian America," in Smith-Rosenberg, *Disorderly Conduct: Visions of Gender in Victorian America* (New York: Oxford University Press, 1985), 108. For accounts of sons who rebelled against the "market revolution," see Paul M. Johnson and Sean Wilentz, *The Kingdom of Matthias: A Story of Sex and Salvation in Nineteenth-Century America* (New York: Oxford University Press, 1994), and Richard L. Bushman, *Joseph Smith and the Beginnings of Mormonism* (Urbana: University of Illinois Press, 1984).

17. On "boy culture," see E. Anthony Rotundo, *American Manhood: Transformations in Masculinity from the Revolution to the Modern Era* (New York: Basic Books, 1993), 31–55; quotations on 55, 71.

18. Rotundo, *American Manhood*, 55; see also Gail Bederman, *Manliness and Civilization: A Cultural History of Gender and Race in the United States, 1880–1917* (Chicago: University of Chicago Press, 1995), 16–20.

19. Michael Paul Rogin, *Ronald Reagan, the Movie; and Other Episodes in Political Demonology* (Berkeley and Los Angeles: University of California Press, 1987), 135; Rotundo, *American Manhood*, 71; Parkman, quoted in Rogin, *Ronald Reagan*, 137; Robin D. G. Kelley, *Race Rebels: Culture, Politics, and the Black Working Class* (New York: Free Press, 1996), 29–30.

20. Rotundo, *American Manhood*, 55, 61, 71, 191.

21. On these transformations in general, see Peter G. Filene, *Him/Her/Self: Sex Roles in Modern America* (1974; reprint, Baltimore: Johns Hopkins University Press, 1986), 69–93, 71-80; Alan Trachtenberg, *The Incorporation of America: Culture and Society in the Gilded Age* (New York: Hill and Wang, 1982); Robert Wiebe, *The Search for Order, 1877–1920* (New York: Hill and Wang, 1967), esp. 111-95; Krause, *Battle for Homestead*, esp. 47–152; Salvatore, *Eugene Debs*; Carroll Smith-Rosenberg, "The New Woman as Androgyne: Social Disorder and Gender Crisis, 1870–1936," in Smith-Rosenberg, *Disorderly Conduct*, 245–96; William R. Leach, "Transformations in a Culture of Consumption: Women and Department Stores, 1890–1925," *Journal of American History* 71 (September 1984): 319–42; Susan Porter Benson, *Counter Cultures: Saleswomen, Managers, and Customers in American Department Stores, 1890–1940* (Urbana: University of Illinois Press, 1986), 75–226; Rotundo, *American Manhood*, 167–246; John D'Emilio and Estelle B. Freedman, *Intimate Matters: A History of Sexuality in America*, 2d ed. (Chicago: University of Chicago Press, 1997), 222–35; Bederman, *Manliness and Civilization*, 10–20; Gail Bederman, "'The Women Have Had Charge of the Church Work Long Enough': The Men and Religion Forward Movement of 1911–1912 and the Masculinization of Middle-Class Protestantism," *American Quarterly* 41 (1989): 432–65; Elliott J. Gorn, *The Manly Art: Bare-knuckle Prize Fighting in America* (Ithaca, N.Y.: Cornell University Press, 1986), 192.

22. Rotundo, *American Manhood*, 167–283; Michael S. Kimmel, *Manhood in America: A Cultural History* (New York: Free Press, 1996), 13–116; Bederman, *Manliness and Civilization*, 10–15; Warren Susman, "Culture Heroes: Ford, Barton, Ruth," in Susman, *Culture As History: The Transformation of American Society in the Twentieth Century* (New York: Pantheon, 1984), 141–49.

23. Margaret Marsh, "Suburban Men and Masculine Domesticity, 1870–1915," in *Meanings for Manhood: Constructions of Masculinity in Victorian America*, edited by Mark C. Carnes and Clyde Griffen (Chicago: University of Chicago Press, 1990), 111–27; on the Boy Scouts, which emerged after 1910, see David Mcleod, *Building Character in the American Boy: The Boy Scouts, Y.M.C.A., and Their Forerunners, 1870–1920* (Madison: University of Wisconsin Press, 1983); Bederman, *Manliness and Civilization*, 77–120, 170–215; Lois Banner, *American Beauty* (New York: Knopf, 1983), 244–48; Rotundo, *American Manhood*, 258–59; Theodore Roosevelt, *The Rough Riders* (New York: Charles Scribner's Sons, 1899), 1–38; Owen Wister, *The Virginian* (1902; reprint, New York: Penguin, 1988), 51.

24. Bederman, *Manliness and Civilization*, 15–16; Elizabeth Lunbeck, *The Psychiatric Persuasion: Knowledge, Gender, and Power in Modern America* (Princeton, N.J.: Princeton University Press, 1994), 229–30.

25. "Frederic Thompson, the Proof of Youth"; "Designed Many Fine Buildings"; "Frederic Williams Thompson," *National Cyclopaedia*, 19:105–6. For a list of the work of George W. Thompson, see William W. Howell, "Hugh Cathcart Thompson: Native Tennessee Architect," School of Architecture, University of Tennessee, 1975, 108–18, in the Tennessee State Library and Archives. For examples of George Thompson's designs and of Frederic Thompson's delineations, see *Selections from Executed Work and Sketches by Thompson and Zwicker, Architects—Nashville* (Louisville, Ky.: Southern Publishing and Advertising, 1896).

26. See the listings for Thompson in *Nashville City Directory* (Nashville, Tenn.: Marshall and Bruce, Publishers 1891–99). There was no listing for Thompson in either 1890 or 1900. On "gala days," overspending, and "young fellows," see "Frederic Thompson, the Proof of Youth"; see also "Frederic Williams Thompson," *National Cyclopaedia*, 19:105–6; Groff, "Exposition Moths," 134.

27. So far as I know, Thompson never gave himself the impressive pedigree that recent chroniclers of Coney Island have assigned him. See, for example, Ric Burns's widely admired documentary "Coney Island," broadcast on the PBS television series *The American Experience* (directed by Ric Burns, produced by Ric Burns and Buddy Squires, written by Richard Snow; WETA-TV, 4 February 1991). An Internet site that repeats the error is the Amazing Fredini's at http://fargo.itp.tsoa.nyu.edu/~fredini/qtvr/. On nineteenth-century architects, see William H. Jordy, *Progressive and Academic Ideals at the Turn of the Twentieth Century*, vol. 4 of the series American Buildings and Their Architects (New York: Oxford University Press, 1972), 79–80; on training at the École des Beaux Arts, see William H. Wilson, *The City Beautiful Movement* (Baltimore: Johns Hopkins University Press, 1989), 59; and Louis H. Sullivan, *The Autobiography of an Idea* (1924; reprint, New York: Dover, 1956), 213.

28. Gregory F. Gilmartin, "Joseph Urban," in *Inventing Times Square: Commerce and Culture at the Crossroads of the World*, edited by William R. Taylor (Baltimore: Johns Hopkins University Press, 1996), 271–83.

29. The best account of the Chicago fair is James Gilbert, *Perfect Cities: Chicago's Utopias of 1893* (Chicago: University of Chicago Press, 1991). Gilbert estimates that of the twenty-seven million paid admissions, half or more were repeat visits (121). Also, on turn-of-the-century American world's fairs and the Chicago fair in particular, see Robert Rydell, *All the World's a Fair: Visions of Empire at American International Expositions, 1876–1916* (Chicago: University of Chicago Press, 1984); Robert W. Rydell and Nancy Gwinn, eds., *Fair Representations: World's Fairs and the Modern World* (Amsterdam: VU University Press, 1994); and David E. Nye, *Electrifying America: Social Meanings of a New Technology, 1880–1940* (Cambridge, Mass.: MIT Press, 1990), 29–47.

30. Trachtenberg, *Incorporation of America*, 208–34, quotation on 211; Warren Susman, "The City in American Culture," in *Culture As History*, 237–51; on "civic spirit," see Wilson, *City Beautiful*, 60; on the moral function of architecture, see Gilbert, *Perfect Cities*, 19.

31. Groff, "Exposition Moths," 133–48; "Frederic Thompson, the Proof of Youth."

32. Gilbert, *Perfect Cities*, 1–44; quotation from Gordon S. Wood, "The Wandering Jewish Prophet in New York," *New York Review of Books* 41, no. 17, 20 October 1994, 56. Of the vast literature on the Second Great Awakening, see Nathan O.

Hatch, *The Democratization of American Christianity* (New Haven: Yale University Press, 1989); Mary P. Ryan, *Cradle of the Middle Class: The Family in Oneida County, New York, 1790–1865* (Cambridge: Cambridge University Press, 1981); Paul M. Johnson, *Shopkeepers' Millennium: Society and Revivals in Rochester, New York, 1815–1837* (New York: Hill and Wang, 1978); and Johnson and Wilentz, *Kingdom of Matthias*.

33. Gilbert, *Perfect Cities*, 38–44, 148–49, quotations on 42, 149.

34. The quotation on rising gradually appears in Ann Fabian, *Card Sharps, Dream Books, and Bucket Shops: Gambling in Nineteenth-Century America* (Ithaca, N.Y.: Cornell University Press, 1990), 122. James Gilbert notes that Pullman's generation, while excelling in self-confidence and success, "lacked the language and categories to explain its accomplishments. A fondness for values of an earlier, parsimonious agricultural world did little to articulate the consumer culture, with its extravagances of promise and profits that these men had concocted" (*Perfect Cities*, 42).

35. Gilbert, *Perfect Cities*, 108–30; Rydell, *All the World's a Fair*, 55–68; John F. Kasson, *Amusing the Million: Coney Island at the Turn of the Century* (New York: Hill and Wang, 1978), 23.

36. Sol Bloom, *The Autobiography of Sol Bloom* (New York: G. P. Putnam's Sons, 1948), 9–110, quotations on 107.

37. Gilbert, *Perfect Cities*, 44; John Calvin Brown, "Mission of the Amusement Park," *Show World* 2 (21 March 1908) 3. Much as it had been in his San Francisco theater days, when among other roles he had been a claquer (someone hired to applaud the performance), Bloom's sole concern was packing the house, not presenting authentic exhibitions of the cultural life of "all nations." After seeing the Parisian Algerian village, he later recalled, he doubted "very much whether anything resembling it was ever seen in Algeria, but I was not at the time concerned with trifles. The Algerians themselves were genuine beyond question, and what was really important was that they presented a varied entertainment that increased in excitement in proportion to my familiarity with it.... I was sure I could make a fortune with them in the United States" (*Autobiography*, 107).

38. "Frederic Thompson, the Proof of Youth," and "Frederic Williams Thompson," *National Cyclopaedia*, 19:105-6.

39. Rodgers, *Work Ethic*, 65-93.

40. Howard P. Chudacoff, *The Age of the Bachelor: Creating an American Subculture* (Princeton, N.J.: Princeton University Press, 1999), 45–54, 75–105. For Thompson's residential addresses, see *Nashville City Directory* (1889–1899). On the Edgefield neighborhood, see Don H. Doyle, *Nashville in the New South* (Knoxville: University of Tennessee Press, 1985), 88. See also Martin A. Berger, "Negotiating Victorian Manhood: Thomas Eakins and the Rowing Works," *Masculinities* 2, no. 3 (fall 1994): 6.

41. I am grateful to Peter Laipson for his thoughtful comments: the *Forum* quotation appears in his essay, "Manhood and Bachelor Respectability in the Late-Nineteenth-Century City" (in my possession). See chap. 4 for a discussion of Thompson's first marriage.

42. Neil Harris, "Collective Possession: J. Pierpont Morgan and the American Imagination," in Harris, *Cultural Excursions: Marketing Appetites and Cultural Tastes in Modern America* (Chicago: University of Chicago Press, 1990), 250–75;

T. J. Jackson Lears, *No Place of Grace: Antimodernism and the Transformation of American Culture, 1880–1920* (New York: Pantheon, 1981), 106; William Dean Howells, "Pernicious Fiction," in *The American Intellectual Tradition*, edited by David A. Hollinger and Charles Capper (New York: Oxford University Press, 1993), 2:25–28, quotation on 27; W. Churchill Williams, "Red Blood in Fiction," *World's Work* 6, no. 1 (May 1903): 694–700.

43. Berger, "Negotiating Victorian Manhood," 6; Sullivan, *Autobiography of an Idea*, 322; "rough game" quoted in Rotundo, *American Manhood*, 224; Louis H. Sullivan, *Kindergarten Chats and Other Writings* (1918; reprint, New York: Dover, 1979), 29.

44. Henry B. Fuller, *With the Procession* (1895; reprint, Chicago: University of Chicago Press, 1965), quotations on 200, 115, 15, 7, 226, 16, 117–18, 71–72, 118, 226, 3, 274. On the literature of businessmen as artists, see Harris, "Collective Possession," 255–56.

45. Fuller, *With the Procession*, 16, 17, 226.

46. "Frederic Thompson, the Proof of Youth," and "Frederic Williams Thompson," *National Cyclopaedia*, 19:105–6.

47. "Frederic Thompson, the Proof of Youth," and "'Fred' Thompson Tells of the Trials and Joys of a Showman's Life and Says That to Be Successful, Be Cheerful," *New York Herald*, 1 January 1905, sec. 3, 9. On Thompson and Zwicker's work at the centennial, see Minutes of the Executive Committee, 21 and 29 November 1895, Records of the Tennessee Centennial and International Exposition, 1897, Manuscript Division, Tennessee State Library and Archives. Fred Thompson's delineations appear in *Selections from Executed Work*. See Chester H. Liebs, *Main Street to Miracle Mile: American Roadside Architecture* (Baltimore: Johns Hopkins University Press, 1995), 39-73, quotations on 39, 49. Also see the discussion of "The Long Island Duckling" in Robert Venturi, Denise Scott Brown, and Steven Izenour, *Learning from Las Vegas: The Forgotten Symbolism of Architectural Form*, rev. ed. (Cambridge, Mass.: MIT Press, 1989), 87–93.

48. Thompson's account of the Blue Grotto appears in "'Fred' Thompson Tells of the Trials and Joys." Also see Herman Justi, ed., *Official History of the Tennessee Centennial Exposition* (Nashville, Tenn.: Brandon, 1898), 205–6. For further discussion of Vanity Fair and Bunyan's *Pilgrim's Progress*, see chap. 3. On Monte Cristo, see A. Nicholas Vardac, *Stage to Screen: Theatrical Method from Garrick to Griffith* (Cambridge, Mass.: Harvard University Press, 1949), 59–62, and Bruce A. McConachie, "Pacifying American Theatrical Audiences, 1820–1900," in *For Fun and Profit: The Transformation of Leisure into Consumption*, edited by Richard Butsch (Philadelphia: Temple University Press, 1990), 65.

49. "Frederic Thompson, the Proof of Youth." On "activism," see Lears, *No Place of Grace*, 106–7, 98–139. Quotation describing grotto from Justi, *Official History*, 206.

50. Justi, *Official History*, 207.

51. This description is taken partly from the patent specifications: United States Patent Office, letters patent no. 612,993, granted 25 October 1898; application filed 30 October 1897 by Frederic Williams Thompson and Frank G. Rogers of Nashville, Tennessee. See also Justi, *Official History*, 207–8.

52. Kasson, *Amusing the Million*, 26–27; Reid Badger, *The Great American Fair: The World's Columbian Exposition and American Culture* (Chicago: Nelson Hall,

1979), 108; David F. Burg, *Chicago's White City of 1893* (Lexington: University of Kentucky Press, 1976), 223–24; Benjamin C. Truman, *History of the World's Fair, Being a Complete and Authentic Description of the Columbian Exposition from Its Inception* (1893; reprint, New York: Arno, 1976), 583–86.

53. The Giant Seesaw also followed him wherever he went, to later world's fairs in Omaha and Buffalo and, eventually, to Steeplechase Park on Coney Island, where it remained as Thompson moved on to build Luna Park.

54. Thompson's account of the Trans-Mississippi and International Exposition appears in "'Fred' Thompson Tells of the Trials and Joys" and "Frederic Thompson, the Proof of Youth."

55. Thompson quotations are from "'Fred' Thompson Tells of the Trials and Joys" and "Frederic Thompson, the Proof of Youth." "Glimpses of the Midway," *Omaha World-Herald*, 25 August 1898, 2. According to the *Omaha World-Herald*, "'Darkness and Dawn' closed the exposition season after earning the greatest reputation of any show that ever went on a Midway. Opened on the 18th of August, and has since shown to 110,000 people, more for the time than any other of the forty-three Midway attractions." See "Heaven and Hell," *Omaha World-Herald*, 30 October 1898, 8. Thompson claimed that he and Dunnavant each reaped a profit of forty thousand dollars. However, Darkness and Dawn was another of Thompson's fictions in an additional way. The amusement itself, which was a spoof of Dante, had appeared at earlier world's fairs—as the *Café de la mort* in Paris and as Night and Morning in Nashville (and probably at other American fairs, too). Thompson's invention, in other words, was not the amusement, but the publicity. On the Nashville version, see Bobby Lawrence, *Tennessee Centennial, 1897* (Charleston, S.C.: Arcadia, 1998), 79.

56. See "'Fred' Thompson Tells of the Trials and Joys" and "Frederic Thompson, the Proof of Youth."

57. Fabian, *Card Sharps*, 1–107. Middle-class Americans, as Fabian has shown, had a psychological and material stake in demonstrating that their work, which made the abstraction of money without actually producing things, was fundamentally different from the nonwork of men who gambled, such as card sharps and reckless speculators.

58. Jonas Barish, *The Antitheatrical Prejudice* (Berkeley and Los Angeles: University of California Press, 1981), 114, 117.

59. For the Puritans, according to Barish, theater enacted "a perpetual carnival, or parody of the good society, in which hectic merriment will replace ordered work, a *regnum diaboli* dominated by the anarchy of the sexual instincts" (*Antitheatrical Prejudice*, 82-83); Richard Wightman Fox, "The Discipline of Amusement," in Taylor, *Inventing Times Square*, 83–98; Henry Ward Beecher, *Lectures to Young Men on Various Important Subjects* (New York: Saxton and Miles, 1846), 215–51; Karen Halttunen, *Confidence Men and Painted Women: A Study of Middle-Class Culture in America, 1830–1870* (New Haven: Yale University Press, 1982), 1–55. On the theatrical versions of *Ten Nights in a Barroom* and *Uncle Tom's Cabin*, see Jeffrey D. Mason, *Melodrama and the Myth of America* (Bloomington: Indiana University Press, 1993), 61–126.

60. Fox, "Discipline," 90, 96; William Leach, "The Clown from Syracuse: The Life and Times of L. Frank Baum," in L. Frank Baum, *The Wonderful Wizard of Oz*, edited by William Leach (1900; reprint, Belmont, Calif.: Wadsworth, 1991), 8.

61. For salacious details of fiendish designs, few texts could match *The Quaker City; or, The Monks of Monk Hall,* George Lippard's popular 1845 novel about a sinister, quasi-Masonic lodge in Philadelphia; edited by David S. Reynolds (Amherst: University of Massachusetts Press, 1995). See also Halttunen, *Confidence Men,* 1–32 and Jackson Lears, *Fables of Abundance: A Cultural History of Advertising in America* (New York: Basic Books, 1994), 60. David S. Reynolds discusses this literature at length in *Beneath the American Renaissance: The Subversive Imagination in the Age of Emerson and Melville* (Cambridge, Mass.: Harvard University Press, 1988). See also the references to the "fiendish barbarity" of slaveholders in Frederick Douglass, *Narrative of the Life of Frederick Douglass, an American Slave* (1845; reprint, Boston: Bedford Books, 1993), 45, 65.

62. "Jumping" quotation appears in an advertisement for a Christmas puppet display at the R. H. Macy department store, New York, *New York Times,* 24 November 1923, 5. On "tricksters" in nineteenth- and early-twentieth-century America, see Neil Harris, *Humbug: The Art of P. T. Barnum* (Chicago: University of Chicago Press, 1981); Halttunen, *Confidence Men,* esp. 198–210; Fabian, *Card Sharps*; William Leach, "A Trickster's Tale: L. Frank Baum's *The Wonderful Wizard of Oz,*" in Baum, *Wonderful Wizard of Oz,* 174–75; and Lears, *Fables of Abundance,* esp. 17–133.

63. William James, *The Varieties of Religious Experience,* edited by Martin E. Marty (1902; reprint, New York: Penguin, 1982), 106. Also see the discussion of James and L. Frank Baum in Leach, "Clown from Syracuse," 5–8, and "Trickster's Tale," 167–80; Leach, *Land of Desire,* 195; Theodore Dreiser, "A Vanished Seaside Resort," in *The Color of a Great City* (1923; reprint, Syracuse, N.Y.: Syracuse University Press, 1996), 127.

64. Dreiser's *The Financier* and *The Titan* formed the first installments of what the writer called his "trilogy of desire."

65. Adams, quoted in Gordon S. Wood, ed., *The Rising Glory of America, 1760–1820* rev. ed. (Boston: Northeastern University Press, 1990), 137–38; Joyce Appleby, *Capitalism and a New Social Order* (New York: New York University Press, 1984), 42, 93; Sean Wilentz, "Artisan Republican Festivals and the Rise of Class Conflict in New York City," in *Working-Class America: Essays in Labor, Community, and American Society,* edited by Michael H. Frisch and Daniel J. Walkowitz (Urbana: University of Illinois Press, 1983), 50; the Reverend George W. Bethune, "Leisure—Its Uses and Abuses," *Merchants' Magazine and Commercial Review* (November 1839): 399; also see Rotundo, *American Manhood,* 222–83.

66. Robert C. Allen, *Horrible Prettiness: Burlesque and American Culture* (Chapel Hill: University of North Carolina Press, 1991), 49; Frederic Thompson, "The Making of Coney Island," *Bohemian* 12 (June 1907): 784–85.

67. Steven M. Gelber, "Do-It-Yourself: Constructing, Repairing, and Maintaining Domestic Masculinity," *American Quarterly* 49, no. 1 (March 1997): 74; see also Gelber, *Hobbies: Leisure and the Culture of Work in America* (New York: Columbia University Press, 1999), 155–294.

68. Attendance at Omaha in 1898 was an astonishing 2.7 million, a small fraction, perhaps, of the 27 million who attended the Columbian exposition, but an enormous number for a small Midwestern city such as Omaha. More importantly, the fair paid a 92.5 percent dividend to its stockholders. See Rydell, *All the World's a Fair,* 124. On Thompson's education at the League, see "Frederic

Thompson, the Proof of Youth." According to his enrollment cards at the Art Students League (in my possession), Thompson studied antique, sketching, illustration, and perspective in the winter and spring of 1899 and again in the fall of 1900. The enrollment cards are incomplete and suggest that he may have been enrolled for more than these two periods. I am grateful to Lawrence Campbell of the Art Students League for providing this information. "Frederic Thompson, the Proof of Youth." Bloom, *Autobiography*, 98.

69. On the Pan-American as a "colossal university," see the article "Some Information Regarding the Pan-American Exposition," in the promotional releases collected as Pan-American Exposition Literature, New York Public Library; Rydell, *All the World's a Fair*, 126–53 (the "unity" quotation appears on 127); Eugene Richard White, "Aspects of the Pan-American Exposition," *Atlantic Monthly* 88 (July 1901): 89.

70. Richard H. Barry, *Snap Shots on the Midway of the Pan-American Exposition* (Buffalo: Robert Allen Reid, 1901), 6–8. For a discussion of the racist ideology of the fair, see Rydell, *All the World's a Fair*, 127–53. On attendance, see White, "Some Aspects," 91.

71. Thompson's claims are in "Frederic Thompson, the Proof of Youth." For a list of the buildings Thompson designed, see Barry, *Snap Shots*, 145; on "the kid," see T. J. Sullivan, "Creator of Enormous Amusement Enterprises," *Human Life* 2, no. 2 (November 1905): 8. According to Sullivan, the Buffalo showmen described Thompson "as the man who furnished about all of them with ideas for their shows, as well as with plans for their Midway buildings."

72. "Press Release," August 1900, in the collection of Pan-American Exposition Literature, New York Public Library.

73. This inscription and others can be seen in *Views of the Pan-American Exposition*, n.d., Pan-American Exposition Literature, New York Public Library, 139, 141. In some four hundred images the photographer felt were worthy of preserving, the midway was almost entirely ignored.

74. Barry, *Snap Shots*, 7. Also see Mary Bronson Hartt, "The Play-side of the Fair," *World's Work* 2, no. 4 (August 1901): 1097–1101.

75. Thompson, "Making of Coney Island," 787–88.

76. Barry, *Snap Shots*, 40. Other discussions of A Trip to the Moon include Kasson, *Amusing the Million*, 61; Michele H. Bogart, "Barking Architecture: The Sculpture of Coney Island," *Smithsonian Studies in American Art* 2 (winter 1988): 7; and Judith A. Adams, *The American Amusement Park Industry: A History of Technology and Thrills* (Boston: Twayne, 1991), 45–46. The building dimensions for Thompson's attractions are listed on a site map contained in Pan-American Exposition Literature, n.d., New York Public Library. (By contrast, the Pan-American edition of Darkness and Dawn occupied 20,000 square feet, and Old Plantation 12,700 square feet.) The fullest description of the Trip's mechanical operation and dramatic effects appears in the patent specifications, which Thompson filed in November 1902: United States Patent Office, "Scenic Apparatus," patent no. 725,509, granted 14 April 1903; application filed 15 November 1902, by Frederick William [*sic*] Thompson, of New York, N.Y.

77. Julian Hawthorne, "Some Novelties at Buffalo Fair," *Cosmopolitan* 31 (September 1901): 490; Barry, *Snap Shots*, 40; see also the description in the promotional brochure, *Pan-American Exposition* (Buffalo, 1901), 29, collected in

Pan-American Exposition Literature, n.d., New York Public Library; H. G. Wells, *Seven Famous Novels* (Garden City, N.Y.: Garden City, 1934), viii.

78. Barry, *Snap Shots*, 37, 40, 42; Hawthorne, "Some Novelties," 490–91.

79. Groff, "Exposition Moths," 135; Robert Grant, "Notes on the Pan-American Exposition," *Cosmopolitan* 31 (September 1901): 460, 462; Barry, *Snap Shots*, 40. Construction costs were alleged to have been $52,000, but in one season in Buffalo and three on Coney Island, according to one account, Thompson and his partner "cleaned up over $250,000 with it." See "Frederic Thompson, the Proof of Youth." A contemporary account in *Billboard* magazine called the moon trip "a great success, and could make a great deal more money if it had the capacity. The mistake was made in constructing a building with so small a capacity for visitors." See Dr. de Garmo Gray, "On the Midway," *Billboard* 13, 21 September 1901, 10. In later years, extravagant claims would be made about the illusion. The initial novelty of the amusement both in Buffalo and on Coney Island may have generated $250,000 in profits, although it is unlikely. Millions were said to have taken the trip. However, according to an affidavit of Thompson's auditor given in 1912, A Trip to the Moon averaged revenues of $20,000 annually, which, at ten cents apiece, meant two hundred thousand riders. By that time the novelty had worn off, and Thompson had even eliminated it from his park at one point, only to bring it back later in the updated form of A Trip to Mars by Aeroplane. See affidavit of Roman Debes, August 1912, *In the Matter of Frederic Thompson, Bankrupt*, United States District Court for the Eastern District of New York, Brooklyn, New York; these records are stored at the National Archives and Records Administration, Bayonne, New Jersey. A good account of Thompson's amusement is Frank H. Winter and Randy Liebermann, "A Trip to the Moon," *Air & Space* (October-November 1994): 62–67. They argue that "Thompson's originality lay in his creation of the first electrical and mechanical space extravaganza, the forerunner of all amusement park space rides." On "E.T.," see the Universal Studios Orlando theme park website: http://www.universalstudios. com/unicity2/inpark/rides/et.html.

80. Nye, *Electrifying America*, 41–46; White, "Aspects," 85; David E. Nye, *Narratives and Spaces: Technology and the Construction of American Culture* (New York: Columbia University Press, 1997), 113–24; promotional brochure collected in Pan-American Exposition Literature, n.d., New York Public Library.

81. Leach, "Trickster's Tale," esp. 157–59.

82. Robert Musil, *Young Törless*, translated by Eithne Wilkins and Ernst Kaiser (1908; reprint, New York: Pantheon, 1955), 8.

83. Lears, *No Place of Grace*, esp. 218–41.

84. Edward Said, *Orientalism* (New York: Random House, 1978).

85. Addams, quoted in Micaela de Leonardo, *Exotics at Home: Anthropologies, Others, American Modernity* (Chicago: University of Chicago Press, 1998), 3. Also see Peter Duus, ed., *The Japanese Discovery of American: A Brief History with Documents* (New York: Bedford Books, 1997).

86. Leach, "Trickster's Tale," 158; Winter and Lieberman, "A Trip to the Moon," 62–63, 65–66.

87. Flammarion, quoted in William Sheehan, *The Planet Mars: A History of Observation and Discovery* (Tempe: University of Arizona Press, 1998), online address: http://www.uapress.arizona.edu/online.bks/mars/chap06.htm. H. G. Wells,

"The First Men in the Moon," *Cosmopolitan* 30 (November, December 1900; January, February, March, April 1901): 65–80, 195–206, 310–23, 415–29, 521–34, 643–56; Albert A. Hopkins, *Magic Stage Illusions and Scientific Diversions* (New York: Munn and Co., 1901), 348–51. The Moon of Thompson's illusion, like that of Wells's story, was populated by Selenites and Moon Calves.

88. Sonu Shamdasani, "Encountering Hélène: Théodore Flournoy and the Genesis of Subliminal Psychology," in Théodore Flournoy, *From India to the Planet Mars: A Case of Multiple Personality with Imaginary Languages*, edited by Sonu Shamdasani (Princeton, N.J.: Princeton University Press, 1994), xi–xv, quotation on xiii.

89. Ann Braude, *Radical Spirits: Spiritualism and Women's Rights in Nineteenth-Century America* (Boston: Beacon Press, 1989); Leach, "Clown from Syracuse," 5–8; James, *Varieties*, 88, 117; Bruce F. Campbell, *Ancient Wisdom Revived: A History of the Theosophical Movement* (Berkeley and Los Angeles: University of California Press, 1980). Vivekenanda is quoted in Leach, *Land of Desire*, 229.

90. Braude, *Radical Spirits*, 82–83; Shamdasani, "Encountering Hélène," xi.

91. Leach, *Land of Desire*, 191–260, *Pollyanna* quotation on 245; Leach, "Trickster's Tale," 184; Donald Meyer, *The Positive Thinkers: Popular Religious Psychology from Mary Baker Eddy to Norman Vincent Peale and Ronald Reagan* (1965; reprint, Wesleyan, Conn.: Wesleyan University Press, 1988), 81.

92. Daniel B. Vermilye, "Translator's Preface," in Théodore Flournoy, *From India to the Planet Mars: A Study of a Case of Somnambulism with Glossolalia* (1900; reprint, New Hyde Park, N.Y.: University Books, 1963), xxiii. All of the textual references are to the 1994 reprint edition of Flournoy: fig. 11, 102; fig. 105; 38, 23–25, 171; Shamdasani, "Encountering Hélène," xxv, xxxii.

93. Shamdasani, "Encountering Hélène," xi–xvii; Barry, *Snap Shots*, 40.

94. Frederic Thompson, "Amusement Architecture," *Architectural Review* 16 (July 1909): 89; "Intelligent Advertising That Reaches the Masses Means Exposition's Success," *Buffalo Courier*, 4 August 1901, 1.

95. Advertisement for "Millionaire Midway Day," *Buffalo Courier*, 28 July 1901, 16; "106,315 Pass Gates; Dedication Day Record Broken," *Buffalo Courier*, 4 August 1901, 1. In later accounts, Thompson claimed, probably not without reason, that more than 146,000 attended Midway Day.

96. "Conglomeration of the Midway's World Wonders," *Buffalo Courier*, 4 August 1901, 1.

97. "Intelligent Advertising"; "Boom Fair Like a Circus," *Buffalo Courier*, 5 August 1901, 7.

98. Rydell, *All the World's a Fair*, 152–58.

99. "The Buffalo Fiasco," *Billboard* 13, no. 45, 9 November 1901, 8; "Boom Fair."

100. Fred Thompson, "Fooling the Public," *Delineator* 69 (February 1907): 265–66.

101. Thompson, "Fooling the Public," 266; Gilbert, *Perfect Cities*, 206.

### Chapter 3: Life is Only a Merry-Go-Round

1. "Coney Island Opened Up," *New York Sun*, 14 May 1905, 7.

2. Frederic Thompson, "Amusing People," *Metropolitan* 32 (August 1910): 601.

3. Michael R. Booth, *Victorian Spectacular Theatre, 1850–1910* (Boston: Routledge and Kegan Paul, 1981), esp. 1–30, 60–92. Kathy Peiss, in *Cheap Amusements: Working Women and Leisure in Turn-of-the-Century New York* (Philadelphia:

Temple University Press, 1986), 136, argues that Luna was the culmination of nineteenth-century amusement forms instead of the beginning of a twentieth-century aesthetic.

4. Alexis de Tocqueville, *Democracy in America*, edited by J. P. Mayer, translated by George Lawrence (New York: Harper Perennial, 1969), 460.

5. "Frederic Thompson's Tribute to Toys," *Playthings* 7 (July 1909): 115.

6. For an account of the formation of the Thompson and Dundy partnership, see clipping, "The Hippodrome Builders Tell How It Happened," *Chicago Inter-Ocean*, 18 February 1906, in Frederic Thompson clipping file, TCNYPL. On Dundy's speculative activities and gambling reputation, see Oliver Pilat and Jo Ranson, *Sodom by the Sea: An Affectionate History of Coney Island* (Garden City, N.Y.: Doubleday, Doran, 1941), 141–54, and clippings "Dundy May Be a Millionaire," *New York Dramatic Mirror*, 29 July 1905, and "Dundy, Theatrical Manager, Is Dead," *New York World*, 6 February 1907, both in Thompson clipping file; see also "Great Showman Died When Dundy Succumbed," *Brooklyn Daily Eagle*, 6 February 1907, 7.

7. Peiss, *Cheap Amusements*, 124–25, 134–36; Frederic Thompson, "The Making of Coney Island," *Bohemian* 12 (June 1907): 786–87; Edo McCullough, *Good Old Coney Island: A Sentimental Journey into the Past* (1957; reprint, New York: Fordham University Press, 2000), 302–4.

8. Pilat and Ranson, *Sodom by the Sea*, 6–7; Catharine Brody, "A New York Childhood," *American Mercury* 14 (May 1928): 57–66. Peiss reports that steamships charged fifteen to twenty-five cents for a round-trip in 1901, and trolleys a nickel or dime for the trip to Coney. See Peiss, *Cheap Amusements*, 115–38.

9. Elmer Blaney Harris, "The Day of Rest at Coney Island," *Everybody's* 19 (July 1908): 26–27; Robert Wilson Neal, "New York's City of Play," *World To-Day* 11 (August 1906): 822; Brody, "New York Childhood," 64.

10. Theodore Dreiser, "A Vanished Seaside Resort," in *The Color of a Great City* (1923; reprint, Syracuse, N.Y.: Syracuse University Press, 1996), 121; Richard Lingeman, *Theodore Dreiser: At the Gates of the City, 1871–1907* (New York: G. P. Putnam's Sons, 1986), 135–41.

11. David Nasaw, *Going Out: The Rise and Fall of Public Amusements* (New York: Basic Books, 1993), 80–95: Peiss, *Cheap Amusements*, 122–25.

12. *New York Times*, 24 October 1909, part 5, 7.

13. Peiss, *Cheap Amusements*, 122–25.

14. Harris, "Day of Rest," 26, 33.

15. "Would Buy Up Coney Island," *Brooklyn Daily Eagle*, 5 December 1902, 2.

16. John F. Kasson, *Amusing the Million: Coney Island at the Turn of the Century* (New York: Hill and Wang, 1978), 57–61; Pilat and Ranson, *Sodom by the Sea*, 130–41; Peiss, *Cheap Amusements*, 127–29; Robert E. Snow and David E. Wright, "Coney Island: A Case Study in Popular Culture and Technical Change," *Journal of Popular Culture* 9 (spring 1976): 966–67.

17. Thompson, "Making of Coney Island," 782.

18. Peiss, *Cheap Amusements*, 122–38.

19. Thompson, "Making of Coney Island," 787.

20. Pilat and Ranson, *Sodom by the Sea*, 144–46.

21. "Splendid Midway Chief Feature of the New Coney Island," *Brooklyn Daily Eagle*, 23 November 1902, section 3, 3.

22. See "Splendid Midway." Of the attractions Thompson offered during his first Luna season, at least the following, or a close variation thereof, had been in Buffalo: A Trip to the Moon; Infant Incubators; Venice in New York; Eskimo, Philippine, and Hawaiian villages; circus performances and wild-animal shows; Japanese Gardens; and Old Germany.

23. "Luna Park Is Opened; 60,000 People There," *Brooklyn Daily Eagle,* 17 May 1903, 6; "Luna Park First Night," *New York Times,* 17 May 1903, 2; *Luna Park: The Electric City by the Sea,* promotional brochure published by Luna Park, 1903, Brooklyn Historical Society; "Big Crush at Coney; Crowd Record Eclipsed," *Brooklyn Daily Eagle,* 6 July 1903, 5.

24. "Luna Park Is Opened"; "Big Crush at Coney." Robert E. Snow and David E. Wright report that Luna had four million visitors in the summer of 1904 even with the competition of Dreamland; they do not, however, cite their source for this figure. See Snow and Wright, "Coney Island," 968.

25. There are many sources for this claim. See, for instance, Thompson, "Making of Coney Island," 788–89, and Pilat and Ranson, *Sodom by the Sea,* 148.

26. Editorial, "Coney Island," *New York Times,* 17 May 1909, 8.

27. Thompson, "Amusing People," 608. For an account of Luna's operations, see the affidavit of Roman Debes, August 1912, *In the Matter of Frederic Thompson, Bankrupt,* United States District Court for the Eastern District of New York, Brooklyn, New York, at the National Archives and Records Administration, Bayonne, New Jersey.

28. Edo McCullough, in his unfootnoted 1957 history, *Good Old Coney Island,* credited Gates with putting "up a large share" of the money (304). A 1907 newspaper article identifies Gates and a Chicagoan, John B. Drake, as "big early backers of Luna Park." See Malcolm MacDonald, "Gossip of Plays and Players," *Cleveland Plain-Dealer,* 9 October 1907, in Thompson clipping file, TCNYPL. According to Lucy P. Gillmann, "Coney Island," *New York History* 36, no. 3 (July 1955): 277, the "estimated $700,000 to cover the cost of construction, came from the Coney racing crowd and Wall Street."

29. Thompson, "Making of Coney Island," 787.

30. On the transformation of the American theater, see Richard Butsch, "Bowery B'hoys and Matinee Ladies: The Re-gendering of Nineteenth-Century American Theater Audiences," *American Quarterly* 46, no. 3 (September 1994): 374–405; Robert W. Snyder, *The Voice of the City: Vaudeville and Popular Culture in New York* (New York: Oxford University Press, 1989); Robert C. Allen, *Horrible Prettiness: Burlesque and American Culture* (Chapel Hill: University of North Carolina Press, 1991); Bruce A. McConachie, "Pacifying Theatrical Audiences, 1820–1900," in *For Fun and Profit: The Transformation of Leisure in Consumption,* edited by Richard Butsch (Philadelphia: Temple University Press, 1990), 47–70; Lawrence W. Levine, *Highbrow/Lowbrow: The Emergence of Cultural Hierarchy in America* (Cambridge, Mass.: Harvard University Press, 1988), esp. 171–242.

31. The best social history of this class is Olivier Zunz, *Making America Corporate, 1870–1920* (Chicago: University of Chicago Press, 1990); see also Nasaw, *Going Out,* 4–5, 43–6.

32. Neil Harris, "Urban Tourism and the Commercial City," in *Inventing Times Square: Commerce and Culture at the Crossroads of the World,* edited by William R. Taylor (Baltimore: Johns Hopkins University Press, 1996), 66–82. A measure

of Coney's attraction to tourists can be had at any meeting of trade card and postcard collectors. The ones I have attended in Rhode Island have displayed hundreds of Coney Island cards that usually had been mailed to New England friends and family reporting a "fine time."

33. Harris, "Day of Rest," 24–34 quotations on 24, 28, 34.

34. Peiss, *Cheap Amusements*, 115–38.

35. *The Crowd*, directed by King Vidor, screenplay by King Vidor and John V. A. Weaver 1928, Metro Goldwyn Mayer, MGM/UA Home Video, 1989, videocassette.

36. Reginald Wright Kauffman, "Why Is Coney? A Study of a Wonderful Playground and the Men That Made It," *Hampton's* 23 (August 1909): 219.

37. Luna Park advertisement from *Brooklyn Daily Eagle*, 27 May 1911, Coney Island section, 1.

38. I am grateful to Peter Laipson for sharing the manuscript of his essay, "Manhood and Bachelor Respectability in the Late-Nineteenth-Century City" (in my possession).

39. Frederic Thompson, "Amusing the Million," *Everybody's* 19 (September 1908): 386, 378.

40. On Dreamland, see Pilat and Ranson, *Sodom by the Sea*, 160–73.

41. "Mammoth Amusement Park," *Theatre* 4 (October 1904): v.

42. David E. Nye, *Electrifying America: Social Meanings of a New Technology, 1880–1940* (Cambridge, Mass.: MIT Press, 1990), 122–32; Nasaw, *Going Out*, 80; Roy Rosenzweig, *Eight Hours for What We Will: Workers and Leisure in an Industrial City, 1870–1920* (Cambridge: Cambridge University Press, 1983), 171–90.

43. John Calvin Brown, "Mission of the Amusement Park," *Show World* 2, 21 March 1908, 3.

44. "Directory of Amusement Resorts," *Midway* 1 (September 1905): 36–38. In April 1901, the theatrical weekly *Billboard* listed the names and locations of 120 parks throughout the United States, but the list included all manner of "parks, pleasure resorts and summer gardens." See "Parks," *Billboard* 13, 27 April 1901, 21. These lists are not definitive (*Billboard* published a longer list later in 1901) but they accurately indicate the growth of outdoor amusement parks after the Luna opening.

45. "Summer Parks," *Variety* 1, 13 January 1906, 12.

46. J. L. Hoff, "Luna Park, Heart of Coney Island, a Gem," *Show World* 2, 9 May 1908, 13.

47. For an impressive copy of Luna's form and ethos, see "White City Is Opened," *Chicago Record-Herald*, 27 May 1905; available at the website "Jazz Age Chicago!—White City Amusement Park," http://www.suba.com/~scottn/explore/sites/parks/w_city03.htm.

48. Thompson, "Amusing People," 601; for parks in other cities, see Nasaw, *Going Out*, chap. 7, esp. 89–91.

49. For a discussion of the cannibalism of commercial art, see Gregory F. Gilmartin, "Joseph Urban," in Taylor, *Inventing Times Square*, 272–73.

50. Edward C. Boyce, *Modern Amusement Parks* (New York: 302 Broadway, 1905), n.p. Boyce's relationship to the White City park in Chicago is described in "White City Is Opened."

51. Edward W. Byrn, "The Progress of Invention during the Past Fifty Years," *Scientific American* 75, 25 July 1896, quoted in Thomas P. Hughes, *American Genesis:*

*A Century of Invention and Technological Enthusiasm, 1870–1970* (New York: Viking, 1989), 14.

52. On A Trip to the Moon, see United States Patent Office, "Scenic Apparatus," patent no. 725,509, granted 14 April 1903; application filed 15 November 1902, by Frederick William [*sic*] Thompson, of New York, N.Y. For 20,000 Leagues, see United States Patent Office, patent no. 739,236, granted 15 September 1903; application filed 4 March 1902, by Frederick [*sic*] Williams Thompson, of New York, N.Y.

53. On patents, see the lists of "amusement devices" for the years 1900–1911 in the *Annual Report of the Commissioner of Patents* (Washington, D.C.: Government Printing Office, 1900–11).

54. John S. Lopez, "Summer Playthings in the Making," *Green Book Album* 3 (June 1910): 1183.

55. Thompson, "Amusing People," 604.

56. Kauffman, "Why Is Coney?" 224.

57. "Fortunes in Novelties for Amusement Parks," *Show World* 2, 11 January 1908, 34.

58. Edwin E. Slosson, "The Amusement Business," *Independent* 57, 21 July 1904, 138. How far showmen would go in showcasing danger or cruelty was indicated by the execution of Topsy, one of Luna Park's elephants, who was poisoned and finally electrocuted as a gruesome spectacle. See Judith A. Adams, *The American Amusement Park Industry: A History of Technology and Thrills* (Boston: Twayne, 1991), 49–50; "Coney Island," broadcast on the PBS television series *The American Experience*, directed by Ric Burns, produced by Ric Burns and Buddy Squires, written by Richard Snow, WETA-TV, 4 February 1991.

59. Lopez, "Summer Playthings in the Making," 1186.

60. Henry James, *The American* (1877; reprint, Boston: Houghton Mifflin, 1962).

61. William Leach, *Land of Desire: Merchants, Power, and the Rise of a New American Culture* (New York: Pantheon, 1993), 4–5.

62. See Andrew Jackson, "State of the Union Address, Dec. 6, 1830," in *The Cherokee Removal: A Brief History with Documents*, edited by Theda Perdue and Michael D. Green (Boston: Bedford Books, 1995), 119–20.

63. Leach, *Land of Desire*, 4–5; on the emergence of the fashion industry and merchandising, see 91–111; Simon Nelson Patten, *Product and Climax* (New York: B. W. Huebsch, 1909), 29–30, 62. The quotation on "traditional restraints" appears in Leach, *Land of Desire*, 239.

64. Patten, *Product and Climax*, 28.

65. Colin Campbell, *The Romantic Ethic and the Spirit of Modern Consumerism* (Oxford: Blackwell, 1987), 39–40.

66. Campbell, *Romantic Ethic*, 77–95; quotation on 86.

67. Campbell, *Romantic Ethic*, 89. The fundamental drive to buy goods, according to Campbell, "is the desire to experience in reality the pleasurable dramas which [consumers] have already enjoyed in imagination, and each 'new' product is seen as offering a possibility of realizing this ambition." But because neither things nor people can live up to their imagined effect, longing becomes a "permanent mode" of existence, *the* modern condition (89–90).

68. Campbell, *Romantic Ethic*, 47. As Jean-Christophe Agnew has summarized this argument, "Consumer letdown and the longing that disappointment nourished

were indeed consequences of manipulation, but of a manipulation ... in which consumers pulled their own strings." Agnew, "Coming Up for Air: Consumer Culture in Historical Perspective," *Intellectual History Newsletter* 12 (1990): 8.

69. The most complete statement of Thompson's psychology of summer amusement appears in Thompson, "Amusing People," 601–10.

70. Frederick A. [sic] Thompson, "The Summer Show," *Independent* 62, 6 June 1907, 1461.

71. John Locke, *Some Thoughts Concerning Education*, edited by John W. Yolton and Jean S. Yolton (New York: Oxford University Press, 1989), and Jean-Jacques Rousseau, *Emile; or, On Education*, edited and translated by Allan Bloom (New York: Basic Books, 1979). See the recent discussion in Gary Cross, *Kids' Stuff: Toys and the Changing World of American Childhood* (Cambridge, Mass.: Harvard University Press, 1997), 18–20.

72. Friedrich Schiller, *On the Aesthetic Education of Man*, translated by Reginald Snell (New York: Frederick Ungar, 1983), 79–80.

73. Richard Hofstadter, *Anti-Intellectualism in American Life* (New York: Vintage, 1963), 359–90. Hofstadter notes the importance of the work of Romantic theorists such as Rousseau, Johann Heinrich Pestalozzi, and Friedrich Froebel to the students of education and childhood at the turn of the century, in particular John Dewey. Michael Steven Shapiro discusses the importance of Froebel to the kindergarten movement during the same period in *Child's Garden: The Kindergarten Movement from Froebel to Dewey* (University Park: Pennsylvania State University Press, 1983).

74. Joseph F. Kett, *Rites of Passage: Adolescence in America, 1790 to the Present* (New York: Basic Books, 1977), 111–43; Mary P. Ryan, *Cradle of the Middle Class: The Family in Oneida County, New York, 1790–1865* (Cambridge: Cambridge University Press, 1981); Nancy F. Cott, *The Bonds of Womanhood: "Woman's Sphere" in New England, 1780–1835* (New Haven: Yale University Press, 1977), 19–100.

75. Gail Bederman, *Manliness and Civilization: A Cultural History of Gender and Race in the United States, 1880–1917* (Chicago: University of Chicago Press, 1995), 77–120, quotations on 95, 99.

76. William A. Gleason, *The Leisure Ethic: Work and Play in American Literature, 1840–1940* (Stanford, Calif.: Stanford University Press, 1999), 1–16, 100–14; Dominick Cavallo, *Muscles and Morals: Organized Playgrounds and Urban Reform* (Philadelphia: University of Pennsylvania Press, 1981), 49–72, 73–87, 150; Jane Addams, *The Spirit of Youth and the City Streets* (1909; reprint, Urbana: University of Illinois Press, 1972), 6, 7, 13.

77. Cross, *Kids' Stuff*, 121–45, quotation on 137.

78. William Leach, "Child World in the Promised Land," in *The Mythmaking Frame of Mind: Social Imagination and American Culture*, edited by James Gilbert et al. (Belmont, Calif.: Wadsworth, 1993), 209–38.

79. "Toyland on State Street," *Toys and Novelties* 12 (April 1915): 31; Leach, "Child World," 211–2; Bill Brown, "American Childhood and Stephen Crane's Toys," *American Literary History* 7 (fall 1995): 443–44.

80. Miriam Formanek-Brunell, *Made to Play House: Dolls and the Commercialization of American Girlhood, 1830–1930* (New Haven: Yale University Press, 1993), 15–16; "Pioneers in the Toy Trade: John T. Doll," *Playthings* 5 (May 1907): 32; Leach, "Child World," 210–11.

81. "The Great American Toy Industry," *Toys and Novelties* 15 (February 1918): 123; Leach, "Child World," 212-13; James T. Patterson, *America in the Twentieth Century: A History*, 3d ed. (Ft. Worth: Harcourt Brace Jovanovich, 1989), 119-22; "Made-in-America," *Toys and Novelties* 14 (February 1917): 69. In 1914 the United States imported $7.7 million in German toys; in the five months prior to declaring war in 1917, $19,045. See "Allies Compete for World's Toy Market," *Toys and Novelties* 15 (March 1918): 99; Franklin Butler, "United States Supreme Toy Market," *Toys and Novelties* 15 (February 1918): 169; "Toy Manufacturers Association of the U.S.A. File Brief with Ways and Means Committee," *Toys and Novelties* 18 (June 1921): 72. The TMAUSA represented only a fraction of the industry. The value of domestic toys compared to imports also suggests the rapidly mounting dominance of American makers. In 1914 the United States imported $9 million and produced $13.7 million; in 1917 imports dropped to $3 million while domestic production soared to $26 million, which represented 90 percent of the domestic market. See Butler, "United States Supreme Toy Market," 169.

82. "Toyland on State Street," 31; "Chicago Christmas Season Smashes All Records," *Playthings* 18 (January 1920): 260-62; Harry Edwin Booth, "Buyers Preparing for Record Business in 1920," *Toys and Novelties* 17 (January 1920): 235; "How 'Go to It Gibson' Made Good," *Playthings* 18 (January 1920): 270–1; "American Appetite for Toys Insatiable," *Toys and Novelties* 20 (December 1923): 162; Leach, "Child World," 213; "New and Old Merchandising Problems in the Toy Industry," *Toys and Novelties* 24 (December 1927): 177; "Keep and Use This Book," *Playthings* 23 (January 1925): 361.

83. Kauffman, "Why Is Coney?" 221.

84. Addams, *Spirit of Youth*, 127.

85. Thompson, "Amusing People," 605.

86. "Toys Bring Children's Trade; Why the Youngsters Are the Best Spenders," *Toys and Novelties* 9 (June 1913): 70.

87. Jackson Lears, *Fables of Abundance: A Cultural History of Advertising in America* (New York: Basic Books, 1994), 75.

88. Thompson, "Amusing People," 604–5.

89. Robert Wilson Neal, "New York's City of Play," 819–20.

90. Quoted in Cavallo, *Muscles and Morals*, 51; see also Bederman, *Manliness and Civilization*, 96.

91. Fred Thompson, "Fooling the Public," *Delineator* 69 (February 1907): 264.

92. Quotations in Peiss, *Cheap Amusements*, 137. On the decline of genteel hegemony, see Kasson, *Amusing the Million*, esp. 3–28.

93. Morton White, *Social Thought in America: The Revolt against Formalism* (New York: Viking, 1949).

94. Susan Strasser, *Satisfaction Guaranteed: The Making of the American Mass Market* (New York: Pantheon, 1989), 27, 159, 161.

95. Leach, *Land of Desire*, 385–86.

96. Thompson, "Amusement Architecture," *Architectural Review* 16 (July 1909): 85–88. I have been influenced in this discussion by Jonas Barish, *The Antitheatrical Prejudice* (Berkeley and Los Angeles: University of California Press, 1981). As Barish writes, "All the emblems for permanence and dependability come from an inanimate world of minerals or a world of conceptual abstractions, a world

essentially unfeeling and inhuman, and hence exempt from change. Our own slang preserves echoes of this situation, with justice as 'a square deal,' or honesty as 'on the level,' or (pejoratively) that which is inflexible, rigid, and sharply bounded by conventions, as 'square.'" (104).

97. Thompson, "Amusement Architecture," 88.

98. Thompson, "Amusing People," 609.

99. "The Annual Awakening of the Only Coney Island," *New York Times*, 6 May 1906, part 4, 8.

100. On Parrish, see Leach, *Land of Desire*, 52–55; on McCay, see the foreword by Maurice Sendak in John Canemaker, *Winsor McCay, His Life and Art* (New York: Abbeville Press, 1987), 9. Also see the 12 August 1906 episode of *Little Nemo*, which is reprinted as the frontispiece of Canemaker's book; in this cartoon, which the author calls "the single most beautiful comic strip page ever," Little Nemo is dressed as Peter Pan.

101. On this phenomenon in general, see Edward Said, *Orientalism* (New York: Vintage, 1979); the list of characteristics appears on 40. See also Linda Nochlin, *The Politics of Vision: Essays on Nineteenth-Century Art and Society* (New York: Harper and Row, 1989), 33–57, quotation on 44.

102. On merchandising, see Leach, *Land of Desire*, 104–11. For a further discussion of Orientalism in merchandising, see chap. 6.

103. "Coney as a National Midway," *Brooklyn Daily Eagle*, 15 September 1902, 4. The message of this editorial suggests strongly that the unnamed businessmen credited with leading this transformation were headed by Thompson and Dundy.

104. James A. Schmiechen, "The Victorians, the Historians, and the Idea of Modernism," *American Historical Review* 93 (April 1988): 288–316.

105. "Annual Awakening of the Only Coney Island."

106. Lopez, "Summer Playthings in the Making," 1189.

107. "The 1906 Coney Island:—Crowded, Brilliant, Gay!" *Brooklyn Edison* 4 (August 1906): 149.

108. Harris, "Day of Rest," 33–34.

109. Descriptions of these attractions are taken principally from Harris, "Day of Rest," 33–34; "The Mechanical Joys of Coney Island," *Scientific American* 99, 15 August 1908, front page and 108–10; "The Mechanical Side of Coney Island—Where the Imaginative Inventor Holds Sway," *Scientific American* 103, 6 August 1910, 104–5, 112; and Lopez, "Summer Playthings in the Making," 1185. For excellent photographs of the Human Toboggan Slide, Witching Waves, and other rides discussed here, see "Mechanical Joys of Coney Island," 108–9 and front page. For a technical description of the slides, see Thompson's patents: United States Patent Office, Frederick [sic] Williams Thompson, "Amusement Apparatus," patent no. 830,853, application filed 10 June 1904, granted 11 September 1906; and patent no. 861,919, application filed 17 April 1907, granted 30 July 1907.

110. Thompson, "Amusing People," 605.

111. See *To Luna: 1913 Pictorial Program and Souvenir Book* (Brooklyn, N.Y.: Luna Amusement Company, 1913), n.p., at the Brooklyn Historical Society.

112. Paul Barber, in *Vampires, Burial, and Death: Folklore and Reality* (New Haven: Yale University Press, 1988), 98–99, 133–46, observes that nineteenth-century scholars attributed the phenomenon of vampires to the accidental or "premature" burial of living persons. According to Barber, the signs of premature bur-

ial—scratch marks in coffins, bodies crawling out of the earth, the hideous facial expressions of exhumed corpses, and the like—are actually the normal
signs of natural bodily decomposition. Two publications examining the danger
and contemporaneous with Luna Park are Franz Hartmann, *Buried Alive: An
Examination into the Occult Causes of Apparent Death, Trance, and Catalepsy*
(Boston: Occult Publishing, 1895), and William Tebb, *Premature Burial and How
It May Be Prevented: With Special Reference to Trance, Catalepsy, and Other Forms
of Suspended Animation* (London: S. Sonnenschein, 1905).

113. Edgar Allan Poe, "The Premature Burial," in *Collected Works of Edgar Allan Poe*,
edited by Thomas O. Mabbott (Cambridge, Mass.: Harvard University Press,
1978), 954–55, 956. Other Poe stories in which his fascination with premature
burial occurs are "Berenicë," "Loss of Breath," and "The Fall of the House of
Usher."

114. The description of Night and Morning appears in an untitled clipping, 18 May
1907, in the Thompson clipping file, TCNYPL.

115. David S. Reynolds, *Beneath the American Renaissance: The Subversive Imagination
in the Age of Emerson and Melville* (Cambridge, Mass.: Harvard University Press,
1988), 169–210, quotation on 169.

116. In general, see Timothy J. Gilfoyle, *City of Eros: New York City, Prostitution, and
the Commercialization of Sex, 1790–1920* (New York: W. W. Norton, 1992).

117. Poe, "How to Write a Blackwood Article," also known as "The Psyche Zenobia,"
in *Collected Works*, 340.

118. Reynolds, *Beneath the American Renaissance*, 225-48, quotations on 226.

119. See Poe, "The Premature Burial," in *Collected Works*, 955, including the explana-
tory note, 969.

120. Thompson, "Amusing People," 607; Poe, quoted in Reynolds, *Beneath the
American Renaissance*, 227.

121. Thompson, "Amusing People," 607.

122. Kauffman, "Why Is Coney?" 220-21.

123. Adams, *American Amusement Park Industry*, 46–52; Kasson, *Amusing the Million*; Nasaw, *Going Out*.

124. "Annual Awakening of the Only Coney Island."

125. Gillmann, "Coney Island," 282.

126. "A Look at Luna Park," *New York Herald*, 6 May 1906, part 3, 14.

127. "Annual Awakening of the Only Coney Island."

128. John F. Kasson highlights the use of the word "manufacture" in Thompson's
most frequently cited article, "Amusing the Million," published in 1908. (See
Kasson, *Amusing the Million*, 82.) Thompson adds that all "great mass meetings" from church picnics to political rallies rely on advance men to create the
"impression that there will be things doing, to get emotional excitement into
the very air.... You see, it's all the same." See Thompson, "Amusing the Million," 379. The quotations indicate not only the usual interpretation of the ma-
nipulative and unfree quality of his amusements, but also the increasingly
prevalent sense that the material world was largely shaped and given meaning
through artifice. See, for instance, the related artifice of publicity discussed in
James L. Ford, "The Men Who Manufacture Fame," *Success* 11 (May 1908):
293–94.

129. Glenmore Davis, "Our Billion-Dollar Smile," *Success* 11 (December 1908): 814.

130. "A Look at Luna Park."

131. Lears, *Fables of Abundance*, 97.

132. Lears, *Fables of Abundance*, 33.

133. Thompson, "Amusing People," 601.

134. Thompson, "Amusement Architecture," 89. For an account, photograph, and diagram of the "eccentric statue," see "Mechanical Side of Coney Island," 103–4, 112.

135. From Barbara G. Walker, *The Woman's Encyclopedia of Myths and Secrets* (New York: Harper San Francisco, 1983). Also see the section on "leuk-" in the appendix "Indo-European Roots," in *The American Heritage Dictionary of the English Language*, edited by William Morris (Boston: Houghton Mifflin, 1976), 1526–27.

136. Victoria de Grazia, "Changing Consumption Regimes," in *The Sex of Things; Gender and Consumption in Historical Perspective*, edited by Victoria de Grazia (Berkeley and Los Angeles: University of California Press, 1996), 14–15.

137. Comments condemning the Sans Souci "Tea Assembly" in Gordon S. Wood, *The Rising Glory of America, 1760–1820* (1971; reprint Boston: Northeastern University Press, 1990), 137–9. In 1905, the new magazine *Midway* listed five Sans Souci parks in the United States. See "Directory of Amusement Resorts," *Midway* (September 1905): 36–38.

138. Thompson, "Amusing People," 610.

139. Thompson, "Amusement Architecture," 87.

140. Thompson, "Amusing People," 602.

141. See the further discussion of Thompson's appetites in chap. 5. My discussion here benefited enormously from conversations with Peter Laipson and Bruce Dorsey, and the suggestions of Karen Halttunen.

142. On treating and the rise of heterosocial leisure, see Peiss, *Cheap Amusements*, and Beth L. Bailey, *From Front Porch to Back Seat: Courtship in Twentieth-Century America* (Baltimore: Johns Hopkins University Press, 1988).

143. Harris, "Day of Rest," 32.

144. Thompson, "Amusing People," 601.

145. George Chauncey, *Gay New York: Gender, Urban Culture, and the Making of the Gay Male World, 1890–1940* (New York: Basic Books, 1994), 111–26.

146. Chauncey, *Gay New York*, 117.

147. Christina Simmons, "Modern Sexuality and the Myth of Victorian Repression," in *Passion and Power: Sexuality in History*, edited by Kathy Peiss and Christina Simmons, (Philadelphia: Temple University Press, 1989), 163–64.

148. See also Kevin J. Mumford, "'Lost Manhood' Found: Male Sexual Impotence and Victorian Culture in the United States," *Journal of the History of Sexuality* 3 (1992): 33–57; see also Jonathan Ned Katz, *The Invention of Heterosexuality* (New York: Penguin Books, 1995).

149. Harris, "Day of Rest," 28.

150 E. Anthony Rotundo, *American Manhood: Transformations in Masculinity from the Revolution to the Modern Era* (New York: Basic Books, 1993), 48–53, quotations on 48, 50.

151. For an account that emphasizes antebellum white Americans' repulsion at and erotic attraction to nonwhite, savage childhood, see Eric Lott, *Love and Theft: Blackface Minstrelsy and the American Working Class* (New York: Oxford University Press, 1993).

152. The best discussion of nineteenth-century boyhood is Rotundo, *American Manhood*, esp. 31–108.
153. Rotundo, *American Manhood*, 55.
154. Anthony Rotundo uses similar phrasing in describing fathers in his discussion of "boy culture," *American Manhood*, 48–49.
155. Compare the regressive fare of Luna Park with Anthony Rotundo's description of respectable Victorian manhood: "A man—unlike a boy—needed a sense of responsible commitment. He could not throw over his family, disregard his business partners, or quit his job on a whim. A man had to have a sense of duty based on enduring loyalty, not on the strongest impulse of the moment" (*American Manhood*, 55).
156. See the description of the Tickler in Harris, "Day of Rest," 34.
157. Kasson, *Amusing the Million*, 82.
158. Jackson Lears, in *Fables of Abundance*, 273, restates John F. Kasson's conclusion in *Amusing the Million*.
159. By the 1970s, as Barbara Ehrenreich has shown, new markets for pornography would be built around an expanded version of regressive escape, the fantasy of retreating to "babyhood," which *Swank* (a publication Ehrenreich describes as "a magazine devoted to full-color crotch shots") hailed as "the ultimate escape" from the pressures "to perform, to succeed, to 'score' with women." See Ehrenreich, *The Hearts of Men: American Dreams and the Flight from Commitment* (Garden City, N.Y.: Anchor Books, 1983), 126.
160. Channing Pollock, "'Coney'—1909," *Green Book Album* 2 (September 1909): 544.
161. I have been influenced in the following discussion by Wolfgang Schivelbusch, *Disenchanted Night: The Industrialization of Light in the Nineteenth Century*, translated by Angela Davies (Berkeley and Los Angeles: University of California Press, 1988).
162. See the following promotional brochures issued by the park: *Luna Park: The Electric City by the Sea* (1903) and *Luna Park: The Heart of Coney Island* (1903), 9, both in the collection of the Brooklyn Historical Society.
163. "The Old Coney Island and the New and the Part Edison Service Has Played in the Transformation," *Brooklyn Edison* 1 (August 1903): 121.
164. Schivelbusch, *Disenchanted Night*, 82.
165. "The Old Coney Island," 121–22. The Brooklyn Edison Company quickly recognized the propaganda value of Luna Park and initiated an annual Coney Island edition of its house magazine beginning in August 1903. The magazine closely followed the amusement developments on the island, especially after the company signed a contract with the island's next amusement venture, Dreamland, in the fall of 1903; it claimed Dreamland was "the largest contract for permanent service ever made by any central station in the world." See "Dreamland," *Brooklyn Edison* 2 (November 1903): 2.
166. "Old Coney Island," 116–17, quotation on 116.
167. Thompson, "Making of Coney Island," 782.
168. Matthew Luckiesh, *Artificial Light: Its Influence upon Civilization* (New York: Century, 1920), 111–62, 208–24.
169. Schivelbusch, *Disenchanted Night*, 137.
170. See, for instance, James G. Huneker, "Coney Island," in *New Cosmopolis: A Book of Images* (New York: Scribner, 1915) 166.

171. "Frederick Thompson Tells How Electricity Has Revolutionized Mechanics behind the Scenes, Exemplified in New York's Hippodrome," *New York Herald*, 12 February 1905, section 3, 10.
172. Nye, *Electrifying America*, x, 1–136.
173. David E. Nye, *Narratives and Spaces: Technology and the Construction of American Culture* (New York: Columbia University Press, 1997), 113–24, quotations on 113, 124.
174. On Stieringer, see David T. Day, "Light: The Civilizer," *American Illustrated Magazine* 61 (April 1906): 661–64, quotation on 661. Stieringer died 18 July 1903, of consumption, at the age of fifty-eight. See his obituary in *Engineering Record* 48, 25 July 1903, 108. The mantle of his genius passed to Walter D'Arcy Ryan, the illumination wizard at General Electric; see the discussion in chap. 6.
175. Luther Stieringer, "Electrical Installation and Decorative Work in Connection with Exposition Buildings," *Engineering Record* 44, 12 October 1901, 350; Day, "Light: The Civilizer," 661, 662; Schivelbusch, *Disenchanted Night*, 178.
176. Luckiesh, *Artificial Light*, 300.
177. Maxim Gorky, "Boredom," *Independent* 63 (August 1907): 309.
178. Huneker, "Coney Island," 165.
179. Gorky, "Boredom," 311.
180. Huneker, "Coney Island," 163–64.
181. Kauffman, "Why Is Coney?" 220.
182. Thompson, "Amusement Architecture," 89. A similar statement occurs in Thompson, "Amusing the Million," 385.
183. "How Mardi Gras Came to Be," *Brooklyn Daily Eagle*, 19 September 1906, 7; Pilat and Ranson, *Sodom by the Sea*, 120–21. On attendance, see, for example, the various reports in the *New York Times*, including "Mardi Gras Festival Attracts 300,000," 23 September 1905, 9; and "Throng of 700,000 at Coney," 20 September 1908, part 2, 9.
184. Lears, *Fables of Abundance*, 2.
185. See, for instance, Alfred D. Chandler, Jr., *The Visible Hand: The Managerial Revolution in American Business* (Cambridge, Mass.: Harvard University Press, 1977), and E. P. Thompson, "Time, Work-Discipline, and Industrial Capitalism," *Past and Present* 38 (December 1967): 56–97.
186. "The Spectacle," *Brooklyn Daily Eagle*, 19 September 1906, 7; "How Mardi Gras Came to Be," 7; "1906 Coney Island," 148–49.
187. "The Spectacle"; on "work-obsessed visions," see Lears, *Fables of Abundance*, 127; see also his discussion of the "Land of Cockaigne," 22–26.
188. Thompson, "Amusing People," 601.
189. Other grandiose plans that were floated as news or rumors but never came to fruition included the following: producing, as opposed to just booking, vaudeville acts ("Thompson Enters Vaudeville War," *New York Times*, 15 March 1907, 9); purchasing a Broadway theater ("Theatre for Frederic ... [fragment]," *New York Morning Telegraph*, 18 February 1908, Thompson and Dundy clipping file, TCNYPL); a Thompson and Dundy circus ("New Circus in the Field," *New York Sun*, 12 January 1905, and "Novelty in Tent Shows," *New York Press*, 12 January 1905, in Burnside Scrapbook, TCNYPL); a Luna Park for Rochester, New York, and for North Bergen, New Jersey ("Luna Park Not Yet for Rochester," *Rochester Post Express*, 16 January 1905, and "Schuetzen Park To Be Transformed," *Hobo-*

*ken Observer,* 28 March 1905, both in Burnside Scrapbook, TCNYPL); and a "permanent world's fair" on top of the new Pennsylvania Railway station ("Thompson Merely Thinking," *New York Morning Telegraph*[?], 21 February 1908, in Thompson and Dundy clipping file, TCNYPL).

190. "Busy Days at Hippodrome, Will Open with New Year," *New York Evening Telegram,* 26 September 1904, in Burnside Scrapbook, TCNYPL.

191. John Bunyan, *The Pilgrim's Progress* (1678; reprint, New York: New American Library, 1981), 85.

192. In "Allegory as Sacred Sport: Manipulation of the Reader in Spenser and Bunyan," in *Bunyan in Our Time,* edited by Robert G. Collmer (Kent, Ohio: Kent State University Press, 1989), 93–112, James F. Forrest emphasizes Bunyan's masterly skills as a storyteller.

193. David E. Smith, *John Bunyan in America* (Bloomington: Indiana University Press, 1966), 89.

194. Alcott, quoted in Madelon Bedell, *The Alcotts: The Biography of a Family* (New York: Clarkson N. Potter, 1980), 11.

195. See various essays in *Ante-bellum Reform,* edited by David Brion Davis (New York: Harper and Row, 1967), esp. William G. McLoughlin, "Charles Grandison Finney," David Brion Davis, "The Emergence of Immediatism in British and American Antislavery Thought," and John L. Thomas, "Romantic Reform in America, 1815–1865," 97–107, 139–52, 153–76.

196. Nathaniel Hawthorne, *The Celestial Railroad and Other Stories* (New York: Signet Classic, 1963), 185–202; Smith, *John Bunyan in America,* 94–97.

197. Louisa May Alcott, *Little Women, or Meg, Jo, Beth, and Amy* (1868; reprint, Boston: Little, Brown, 1924), 10–11.

198. Quoted in Canemaker, *Winsor McCay,* 79; examples of the cartoon appear on 79–80.

199. Other borrowings include the "green spectacles," which were necessary to behold the brilliance of the Emerald City, and the mark placed on Dorothy's forehead by the Witch of the North. Ruby slippers were an alteration for the 1939 movie version. On the correspondence between the two works, see William Leach, "A Trickster's Tale: L. Frank Baum's *The Wonderful Wizard of Oz,*" in L. Frank Baum, *The Wonderful Wizard of Oz* (1900; reprint, Belmont, Calif.: Wadsworth, 1991), 160–61. On silver shoes, see Baum, *Wonderful Wizard of Oz,* 44, and Bunyan, *Pilgrim's Progress,* 93–94; on spectacles, see Baum, 87, and Bunyan, 142 ("the reflections of the sun upon the city ... was so extremely glorious, that they could not, as yet, with open face behold it but through an instrument made for that purpose"); on the forehead mark, compare Baum, 46, and Bunyan, 42; on Emerald City, see Baum, 89–92, and Bunyan, 141–42.

200. Leach, "Trickster's Tale," 160–61.

201. The two most influential interpreters of this message are highly deductive, relying on little evidence of Baum's actual life or aims: Henry M. Littlefield, "The Wizard of Oz: Parable on Populism," in *Things in the Driver's Seat: Readings in Popular Culture,* edited by Harry R. Huebel (Chicago: Rand-McNally, 1972) 35–48, and Fred Erisman, "L. Frank Baum and the Progressive Dilemma," *American Quarterly* 20 (autumn 1968): 616–23. Leach's reading is an important corrective to these methodologically and empirically weak interpretations.

202. See the prefatory note "To the Reader" in L. Frank Baum, *A New Wonderland:*

*Being the First Account Ever Printed of the Beautiful Valley, and the Wonderful Adventures of Its Inhabitants* (New York: R. H. Russell, 1900), n.p.

203. William Leach, "Strategists of Display and the Production of Desire," in *Accumulation and Display of Goods in America, 1880–1920*, edited by Simon J. Bronner (New York: W. W. Norton, 1989), 106–10, quotation on 108; Leonard S. Marcus, *The American Store Window* (New York: Whitney Library of Design, 1978), 12–13.

204. Leach, "Strategists," 108; Baum, *Wonderful Wizard of Oz*, 36.

205. "Summer Parks," *Variety* 5, 12 January 1907, 11; "Summer Parks," *Variety* 7, 7 September 1907, 9; "Balloon Park for New York," *New York Times*, 3 November 1907, part 2, 1; schedule of unsecured debts, *In the Matter of Fred Thompson, Bankrupt*, United States District Court for the Eastern District of New York, Brooklyn, New York; "Another Monoplane Enters Chicago Race," *New York Times*, 24 September 1910, 3.

206. See chap. 5 for a more detailed account of Thompson's bankruptcy.

207. Joyce Appleby, *Capitalism and a New Social Order* (New York: New York University Press, 1984), 1–23; Agnew, "Coming Up for Air," 15.

208. The motto can be seen in the photograph of the Bunny Hug, which appears in *To Luna*. Lyrics are taken from "Life is a Merry-Go-Round," words by John L. Golden, music by Benjamin Hapgood Burt, from Fred Thompson's "musical satire" *Girlies*, copyright 1910 by Jerome H. Remick and Co., New York and Detroit. *Girlies* was produced by Thompson at the New Amsterdam Theatre Roof Garden, 13 June 1910, for eighty-eight performances. For all the women in this "leg show," the song was performed by men: the veteran "dialect" comedian Joseph Cawthorn and "a complement of male voices." See untitled review of *Girlies*, *New York Dramatic Mirror*, 25 June 1910, in Locke Scrapbook, series 2, vol. 41, TCNYPL.

### Chapter 4: New York's Gigantic Toy

1. "General Advertising by Means of Electric Signs," *Brooklyn Edison* 3 (January 1905): 36–38. The first public display of a "talking sign," otherwise known as the Mason Monogram, was at Thompson's alma mater, the colossal people's university at Buffalo, in 1901. See J. A. Goldberg, "The Development of Motion Effects in Electrical Signs," *Illuminating Engineer* 2 (February 1908): 852; "The 'Talking' Electric Sign," *Brooklyn Edison* 1 (June 1903): 82–83.

2. Clipping, "'Big Store' Idea to Give Masses Entertainment," *New York Morning Telegraph*, 26 September 1904, Burnside Scrapbook, TCNYPL.

3. Untitled clipping, Hippodrome Scrapbook no. 9872, TCNYPL, ca. 13 April 1905.

4. Robert Grau, *The Business Man in the Amusement World: A Volume of Progress in the Field of the Theatre* (New York: Broadway, 1910), 328.

5. Neil Harris, *Humbug: The Art of P. T. Barnum* (Chicago: University of Chicago Press, 1981), 243–46, 260.

6. The information that follows is taken from the biography of MacKaye written by his son, Percy MacKaye, *Epoch: The Life of Steele MacKaye, Genius of the Theatre*, 2 vols. (New York: Boni and Liveright, 1927). For a discussion of the pageantry movement, see Trudy Baltz, "Pageantry and Mural Painting: Community Rituals in Allegorical Form," *Winterthur Portfolio* 15 (autumn 1980): 211–28.

7. Jean-Christophe Agnew, "Times Square: Secularization and Sacralization," in *Inventing Times Square: Commerce and Culture at the Crossroads of the World*, ed-

ited by William R. Taylor (Baltimore: Johns Hopkins University Press, 1996), 5–6, MacKaye quotation on 5.

8.  MacKaye, *Epoch*, 311.

9.  Agnew, "Times Square," 6.

10. A. H. Saxon, *Enter Foot and Horse: A History of Hippodrama in England and France* (New Haven: Yale University Press, 1968).

11. Michael R. Booth, *Victorian Spectacular Theatre, 1850–1910* (Boston: Routledge and Kegan Paul, 1981), 60–92.

12. MacKaye, *Epoch*, 348; see clipping, "Frederic Thompson, The Proof of Youth," *New York Sunday Telegraph*, 2 April 1905, 7, in Burnside Scrapbook, TCNYPL; "Zoo, Circus, Spectacle, All in One," *New York Times*, 3 July 1904, 21.

13. William Leach, *Land of Desire: Merchants, Power, and the Rise of a New American Culture* (New York: Pantheon, 1993), 15.

14. The best account of these historical developments is Leach, *Land of Desire*, 15–150.

15. H. Gordon Selfridge, *The Romance of Commerce* (London: John Lane, 1918), 365.

16. Theodore Dreiser, *Sister Carrie* (1900; reprint, Boston: Houghton Mifflin, 1959), 22.

17. Leach, *Land of Desire*, 112–50, Wanamaker quotation on 112; Susan Porter Benson, *Counter Cultures: Saleswomen, Managers, and Customers in American Department Stores, 1890–1940* (Urbana: University of Illinois Press, 1986), esp. 12–30, "democracy" quotation on 20; and Alfred D. Chandler, Jr., *The Visible Hand: The Managerial Revolution in American Business* (Cambridge, Mass.: Harvard University Press, 1977), 225–29. The Field creed served as the title of a history of the firm: Lloyd Wendt and Herman Kogan, *Give the Lady What She Wants: The Story of Marshall Field and Company* (Chicago: Rand McNally, 1952). On displays in department stores, see William Leach, "Strategists of Display and the Production of Desire," in *Consuming Visions: Accumulation and Display of Goods in America, 1880–1920*, edited by Simon J. Bronner (New York: W. W. Norton, 1989), 99–132.

18. The "gentrifying" process is discussed in chap. 3.

19. "'Fred' Thompson Tells of the Trials and Joys of a Showman's Life and Says That to Be Successful, Be Cheerful," *New York Herald*, 1 January 1905, section 3, 9; on prices, see advertisement in the *New York Times*, 9 April 1905, pictorial supplement, n.p.

20. On refined vaudeville and the reform of its entertainments, see Robert Snyder, *The Voice of the City: Vaudeville and Popular Culture in New York* (New York: Oxford University Press, 1989), 21–41, and David Nasaw, *Going Out: The Rise and Fall of Public Amusements* (New York: Basic Books, 1993), 27–33.

21. Lary May, *Screening Out the Past: The Birth of Mass Culture and the Motion Picture Industry* (Chicago: University of Chicago Press, 1983), 147–66.

22. "'Big Store' Idea to Give Masses Entertainment"; "'Fred' Thompson Tells of the Trials and Joys"; Harold Ackerman, "The New York Hippodrome," *Broadway* (April 1905), in Hippodrome Scrapbook no. 6453, TCNYPL. The theater "had to be kept filled to make real money," said R. H. Burnside, who directed the Hippodrome's productions for twelve of the years between 1908 and 1923. "To raise seat prices was to drive away a large part of the audience." See R. H. Burnside, "Secrets of the Hippodrome," typescript, 15 March 1932, 20, TCNYPL.

23. See the following clippings in Burnside Scrapbook, TCNYPL: "'Big Store' Idea to Give Masses Entertainment"; untitled clipping from the *Chattanooga Times*, 29 January 1905; "Record Breaking Hippodrome Sale," *New York Herald*, 11 April 1905; untitled clipping from the *New York Inquirer*, 4 March 1905; Ackerman, "New York Hippodrome"; unidentified clipping, 12 November 1904. See also clipping, "The Elephants, the Lions, and Maeterlinck," *Life*, 2 November 1905, Hippodrome Scrapbook no. 9872, TCNYPL. *Broadway* quotation in Ackerman, "New York Hippodrome." On Progressives, see William R. Taylor, "Walter Lippmann in *Vanity Fair*," in Taylor, *In Pursuit of Gotham: Culture and Commerce in New York* (New York: Oxford University Press, 1992), 109–18.

24. Vincent Sheean, *Oscar Hammerstein I: The Life and Exploits of an Impresario* (New York: Simon and Schuster, 1956), 118–19; see also the following two untitled clippings, Burnside Scrapbook, TCNYPL: *New Haven Register*, 4 December 1904, and clipping, "The Usher," n.d.; Milton Epstein, "The New York Hippodrome—From Luna Park to Sixth Avenue," master's thesis, New York University, 1982, 18–20; clipping, "New York Theatre Seats, $1," 12 December [?] 1904, in Burnside Scrapbook, TCNYPL.

25. On the circus war, see the following clippings in the Burnside Scrapbook, TCNYPL: "Circus War Is Soon to Begin," *New York Herald*, 23 January 1905; "Hippodrome and the Circus," *New York Morning Telegraph*, 25 February 1905; "Barnum and Bailey Enjoin Their Clown," *New York American*, 7 April 1905; "Will There Be a Circus War?" *New York Dramatic News*, 28 January 1905; "Herbert Barnum Seeley Now Ticket Seller in New York Hippodrome," *Bridgeport Standard*, 28 March 1905.

26. The information in this paragraph is taken from Lloyd Wendt and Herman Kogan, *Bet a Million! The Story of John W. Gates* (Indianapolis: Bobbs-Merrill, 1948); this book's account of Gates's association with the Hippodrome contains numerous errors.

27. "Opening of the Hippodrome and New Plays of the Week," *New York Herald*, 9 April 1905, section 3, 9. See the following clippings in the Burnside Scrapbook, TCNYPL: "Saunterings," *Town Topic*, 9 March 1905; "Gates President of Hippodrome Co.," *New York Commercial*, 30 September 1904; "Long Time Loan for New Hippodrome Co.," *New York Wall Street Summary*, 17 September 1904. See also Norman Clarke, *The Mighty Hippodrome* (South Brunswick, N.J.: A. S. Barnes, 1968), 21–22, and "Black Faction Wins in U. S. Realty Fight," *New York Times*, 16 January 1904, 16. The *Annual Report of the Superintendent of Banks, Relative to Savings Banks, Trust Companies, Safe Deposit Companies, and Miscellaneous Corporations for the Year 1904* (Albany: Brandow Printing, 1905), 526, lists the directors of the New York Security and Trust Company, several of whom also were on the board of U. S. Realty when the Hippodrome deal was sealed, including James Stillman, who was identified as a principal backer of the Hippodrome.

28. In addition to the technical magazines examined below, see, for example, the detailed descriptions in "Wonders of the Hippodrome," *New York Sun*, 9 April 1905, 10, and "Frederick Thompson Explains How Electricity Has Revolutionized Mechanics behind the Scenes, Exemplified in New York's New Hippodrome," *New York Herald*, 12 February 1905, section 3, 10. On the fascination with quantification, see William R. Taylor, "The Evolution of Public Space in New York City: The Commercial Showcase of America," in Bronner, *Consuming*

*Visions*, 294–96. On the values of organized bigness and efficiency to contemporary political and social changes, see Robert H. Wiebe, *The Search for Order, 1877–1920* (New York: Hill and Wang, 1980), esp. 111–223.

29. Clarke, *Mighty Hippodrome*, 14–16.

30. "The New York Hippodrome," *Scientific American* 92, 25 March 1905, 242; "The Erection of the New York Hippodrome Roof Trusses," *Engineering Record* 51, 18 March 1905, 334–35.

31. "Wonders of the Hippodrome"; "Steel Work in the New York Hippodrome," *Engineering Record* 51, 25 March 1905, 352–53; "The New York Hippodrome," *Architects' and Builders'* 6 (August 1905) 490–98.

32. *New York Clipper*, quoted in Clarke, *Mighty Hippodrome*, 26.

33. James A. Schmiechen, "The Victorians, the Historians, and the Idea of Modernism," *American Historical Review* 93 (April 1988): 288–316.

34. "Theatrical Incidents and News Notes," *New York Tribune*, 16 April 1905, 9; "New York Hippodrome Opens in a Blaze of Glory," *Billboard* 17, 22 April 1905, 20; "Frederick Thompson Explains How Electricity"; Burnside, "Secrets of the Hippodrome," 19. The best statement of Thompson's ideas about architecture appears in Frederic Thompson, "Amusement Architecture," *Architectural Review* 16 (July 1909): 85–89.

35. Samuel Merwin, "Thompson and His Hippodrome," *Success* 9 (July 1906): 467.

36. On Romeo, see Epstein, "New York Hippodrome," 25–26. On Temple, see untitled clippings in the Edward P. Temple clipping file, TCNYPL; on Klein, see "The New Hippodrome Ballet under Rehearsal," *New York Sun*, 29 January 1905, part 2, 3, and Charles Darnton, "The Man Who Staged the Biggest Show on Earth," *New York Evening World*, 15 April 1905, 9. On Carrigan and Thomas, see Merwin, "Thompson and His Hippodrome," 467. On Hagen, see Grau, *Business Man in the Amusement World*: 168–69; "Not Much Balm for Hagan [sic]," *New York Morning Telegraph*, 16 December 1904, Burnside Scrapbook, TCNYPL; and Claude Hagen, letters to Lee Shubert, 7 and 16 October 1908, and 15 August 1908, General Correspondence, 1908–10, Shubert Archive, New York. Klein's previous composition was *Mr. Pickwick*, produced in January 1903. See Burns Mantle and Garrison P. Sherwood, eds., *The Best Plays of 1899–1909 and the Year Book of the Drama in America* (New York: Dodd, Mead, 1944), 427. On Melville, see "Death of Frank J. Melville," *New York Morning Telegraph*, 5 December 1908, 2.

37. "American Woman Charms Famous European Costumer," *New York Times*, 18 December 1904, part 3, 7.

38. Colgate Baker, "Arthur Voegtlin, The Genius of the Hippodrome," *New York Review*, 13 July 1912, in Voegtlin clipping file, TCNYPL; clipping, "Big Things Conceived for New Hippodrome," *New York Commercial*, 6 March 1905, in Burnside Scrapbook, TCNYPL; "How Arthur Voegtlin Dreams His Big Spectacles," *New York Times*, 8 September 1912, part 5, 12; Dana Gatlin, "Arthur Voegtlin," *American Magazine* 76 (August 1913): 38–39; Arthur Voegtlin, "Paint's Part in Successful Play," *Pittsburgh Leader*, 25 November 1910, in Locke Collection file no. 2439, TCNYPL; Djuna Barnes, "Interviewing Arthur Voegtlin Is Something Like Having a Nightmare," in Barnes, *Interviews* (Washington, D.C.: Sun and Moon Press, 1985), 76–84; Arthur Voegtlin, *The Great Train Robbery: A Realistic Drama Spectacle in Three Scenes* (n.p.: ca. 1905), Harris Collection of American

Poetry and Plays, John Hay Library, Brown University. On "Venice in New York," see "Duss's 'Venice' on View," *New York Times*, 1 June 1903, 7.

39. On Voegtlin's post-Hippodrome career, see "The National Merchandise Fair," *Dry Goods Economist* 77, 7 July 1923, 15–21; "Merchandise Fair Opens in Three Buildings," *New York Times*, 2 July 1923, 14; and "Arthur Voegtlin, Stage Producer, 90," *New York Times*, 20 January 1948, 23. On brokers of culture, see William Leach, "Brokers and the New Corporate, Industrial Order," in Taylor, *Inventing Times Square*, 99–117.

40. Lewis A. Erenberg, *Steppin' Out: New York Nightlife and the Transformation of American Culture, 1890–1930* (Chicago: University of Chicago Press, 1981), 40–56.

41. Editorial, *Architectural Review* 16 (July 1909): 93; "Studies of Notable Installations: Scenic Effects in Interior Illumination," *Illuminating Engineer* 3 (December 1908) 555–58, quotation on 557; "Studies of Notable Installations: Spectacular Effects in Interior Lighting," *Illuminating Engineer* 3 (August 1908): 326–29, quotation on 326.

42. Darnton, "The Man Who Staged the Biggest Show on Earth."

43. "Frederick Thompson Explains."

44. La Rue Vredenburgh, paper read at the convention of the National Electric Light Association, Denver, Colorado, 6–11 June 1905, reprinted as "Sign and Decorative Lighting," *Electrical Age* 34 (June 1905): 425.

45. Taylor, "Evolution of Public Space in New York City," 290.

46. "A Truly Successful Advertising Scheme," *Thompson's Mile-a-Minute Specials*, 27 November 1908, Thompson and Dundy clipping file, TCNYPL.

47. Valentine Cook, Jr., "The Great White Way," *Illuminating Engineer* 1 (May 1906): 146; "Electricity at the New York Hippodrome," *Electrical World* 47, 5 May 1906, 916.

48. "Electricity at the New York Hippodrome," 916; E. L. Elliott, "The Illumination of the New York Hippodrome," *Illuminating Engineer* 1 (April 1906): 75; clipping, untitled article by Alan Dale, ca. 13 April 1905, in Hippodrome Scrapbook no. 9872, TCNYPL. Michele H. Bogart makes a similar point about Luna's lighting and architecture in "Barking Architecture: The Sculpture of Coney Island," *Smithsonian Studies in American Art* 2 (winter 1988): 3–17.

49. Elliott, "Illumination of the New York Hippodrome," *Illuminating Engineer*, 75, 77.

50. "Electricity at the New York Hippodrome," 913–14; Elliott, "Illumination of the New York Hippodrome," 74; "Frederick Thompson Explains."

51. John F. Kasson, *Civilizing the Machine: Technology and Republican Values in America, 1776–1900* (New York: Penguin, 1977), 139–80.

52. "Mechanical Plant of the New York Hippodrome," *Engineering Record* 52, 26 August 1905, 229–30.

53. Chandler, *Visible Hand*, 259–66, quotation on 262.

54. Leach, "Strategists of Display," 101.

55. Selfridge, *Romance of Commerce*, 363.

56. Comments on the design of the Hippodrome are taken from the plans of the Hippodrome published in *American Architect and Building News* 87 (13 and 20 May 1905), international ed. (n.p).

57. Merwin, "Thompson and His Hippodrome," 467.

58. "New Hippodrome Ballet under Rehearsal."

59. Zoe Anderson Norris, "One Woman's Impressions of the 'Hippo's' Opening," *New York Times*, 16 April 1905, part 4, 6; clipping, "The New Hippodrome Opens," *New York Sun*, 13 April 1905, in Thompson clipping file, TCNYPL; Clarke, *Mighty Hippodrome*, 28, 31.

60. McCardell, "Hats Off to the Hippodrome!"; Norris, "One Woman's Impressions of the 'Hippo's' Opening"; "New Hippodrome Opens."

61. On Erlanger, see chap. 5; on Keith et al., see Snyder, *Voice of the City*, 26–41.

62. "Behind the Scenes at the Hippodrome," *New York Sun*, 30 April 1905, section 2, 3; Colgate Baker, "Through the Hippodrome Wonderland," *New York Review*, 15 October 1910, in R. H. Burnside clipping file, TCNYPL. The Hippodrome was comparable to the wonders of modern transportation, such as Pennsylvania Station in New York. See Lorraine B. Diehl, *The Late, Great Pennsylvania Station* (New York: American Heritage, 1985), and Taylor, "Evolution of Public Space in New York City," 287–309.

63. Charles Darnton, "A Peep at the Hippodrome," *New York Evening World*, 8 April 1905, 9.

64. John Golden and Viola Brothers Shore, *Stage-Struck John Golden* (New York: Samuel French, 1930), 135–38.

65. For the scenario of the play, see the review in *New York Dramatic Mirror*, in *Via Wireless* clipping file, TCNYPL; quotation from review dated 20 January 1909 in the same file.

66. Review in *Washington Star*, 25 October 1908, in Thompson and Dundy clipping file, TCNYPL.

67. Clipping, Glenmore Davis, "Building a Play," *Success* (February 1909), in Locke Scrapbook, series 2, vol. 113, TCNYPL.

68. Selfridge, *Romance of Commerce*, 362–63. Selfridge's "Organisation Chart of a Twentieth Century Department Store," which folds out of his book, is thirty-seven inches wide.

69. George W. Perkins, "The Modern Corporation," in *The Currency Problem and the Present Financial Situation: A Series of Addresses Delivered at Columbia University, 1907–1908* (New York: Columbia University Press, 1908), 156.

70. Davis, "Building a Play"; review, *Cincinnati Inquirer*, n.d., and untitled clipping, *Des Moines Register*, 28 June 1908, Thompson and Dundy clipping file, TCNYPL; "Little Nemo to Be a Great Spectacle," *Show World* 3, 12 September 1908, 13.

71. See the following clippings in the Thompson and Dundy clipping file, TCNYPL: "The President Sees Via Wireless 'Play,'" *New York Morning Telegraph*, 19 October 1908; "Frederic Thompson's Coup," *New York Morning Telegraph*, 29 January 1909. See also "The Call Boys Chat," *Philadelphia Inquirer*, 31 January 1909, section 1, 10.

72. Davis, "Building a Play"; Frederick Winslow Taylor, *The Principles of Scientific Management* (1911; reprint, New York: W. W. Norton, 1967), quotations on 6, 49; for Taylor's celebrity, see Sudhir Kakar, *Frederick Taylor: A Study in Personality and Innovation* (Cambridge, Mass.: MIT Press, 1970), 174–78, and his period at Midvale, 41–50; Thomas Hughes, *American Genesis: A Century of Invention and Technological Enthusiasm, 1870–1970* (New York: Viking, 1989), 184–203; Harry Braverman, *Labor and Monopoly Capital: The Degradation of Work in the Twentieth Century* (New York: Monthly Review Press, 1974), 91–97, 111–12.

73. Edward Bellamy, *Looking Backward, 2000–1887* (1888; reprint, New York: New American Library, 1960), 93, 125; Henry Ford and Samuel Crowther, *My Life and Work* (Garden City, N.Y.: Doubleday, Page, 1922), 72–73; Warren I. Susman, "Culture Heroes: Ford, Barton, Ruth," in *Culture as History: The Transformation of American Society in the Twentieth Century* (New York: Pantheon, 1984), 131–41.

74. Leach, "Strategists of Display," 132.

75. "New York Hippodrome Opens in a Blaze of Glory," 20; advertisement in *New York Times*, 9 April 1905.

76. "Opening of Hippodrome," 10; untitled clipping fragment, 13 April 1905, Locke Scrapbook no. 9872; "Greatest of Hippodromes Is Opened with Splendor," *New York Herald*, 13 April 1905, 1. According to Mantle and Sherwood, *Best Plays of 1899–1909*, 489, *A Yankee Circus on Mars* was performed 120 times at the New York Hippodrome, including daily matinees; it was arranged by Frederic Thompson, with book by George V. Hobart, lyrics by Harry Williams, music by Manuel Klein and Jean Schwartz, produced by Thompson and Dundy, 12 April 1905; *Andersonville: A Story of Wilson's Raiders*, was arranged by Frederic Thompson, with book by Carroll Fleming and music by Manuel Klein.

77. See "Opening of Hippodrome," and various untitled clippings in Hippodrome Scrapbook no. 9872, TCNYPL, all ca. 13 April 1905; see also "New York's Mammoth Pleasure Palace" and "Theatrical Incidents and News Notes."

78. Darnton, "Peep at the Hippodrome." On the limitations of the plot, see Epstein, "New York Hippodrome," 91–92.

79. The account that follows is taken from several sources, including a typescript of *The Yankee Circus in Mars* [*sic*], Script Collection, Shubert Archive, New York; Norris, "One Woman's Impressions of the 'Hippo's' Opening"; Clarke, *Mighty Hippodrome*, 26–37; and "New Hippodrome Opens."

80. *Yankee Circus*, scene 1, 6–23, quotation on 6.

81. "New Hippodrome Opens"; Clarke, *Mighty Hippodrome*, 31; *Yankee Circus*, scene 2, 2–4; Norris, "One Woman's Impressions of the 'Hippo's' Opening."

82. *Yankee Circus*, "Aurora Borealis," scene 2, n.p.

83. "New Hippodrome Opens."

84. Clarke, *Mighty Hippodrome*, 34–36, 41. *Andersonville* was later replaced by *The Romance of the Hindoo Princess*, which featured the Hippodrome's elephants sliding down a stage mountain into the lake.

85. "Lady Volumnia's Song" or "Tainted Gold," act 1, scene 1, 15–19, typescript of *A Society Circus*, Script Collection, Shubert Archive, New York; program, *A Society Circus*, Locke Collecton Scrapbook 12, 523, TCNYPL.

86. "A 'Society Circus' Is Vastest of Spectacles," *New York Times*, 14 December 1905, 7; "Electricity at the New York Hippodrome," 915–16.

87. Fred Stone, *Rolling Stone* (New York: McGraw-Hill, 1945), 131–43.

88. Both *The Wizard of Oz* and *Babes in Toyland* originated in Chicago, not New York, and were produced by the team of Fred R. Hamlin and Julian Mitchell. *The Wizard of Oz*, with book and lyrics by L. Frank Baum and music by Paul Tietjens and A. Baldwin Sloane, opened in Chicago in 1902 and toured the eastern and southern United States before it played 293 performances at the Majestic Theatre, New York, beginning 21 January 1903; it returned a year later for 48 additional performances. *Babes in Toyland*, with libretto by Glen MacDonough and music by Victor Herbert, after a hit opening in Chicago in the summer of 1903,

played 192 performances at the Majestic Theatre, New York, beginning 13 October 1903. J. M. Barrie's *Peter Pan* opened on 6 November 1905, at the Empire Theatre in New York, for 223 performances, Charles Frohman, producer; it reopened a year later for another 40 performances. *A Society Circus* was performed 596 times at the New York Hippodrome, beginning 13 December 1905; book by Sydney Rosenfeld, lyrics by Rosenfeld and Manuel Klein, music by Klein and Gustav Luders, produced by Thompson and Dundy. See Mantle and Sherwood, *Best Plays of 1899–1909*, 427, 440, 500, 503.

89. Many accounts claim that Barrie wrote *Peter Pan* with Maude Adams in mind. John D. Williams quoted Barrie in 1909, "When *Peter* took flight from my fancy he found haven in the spirit of Maude Adams," and reported that Barrie always referred to the character as "Peter Adams." See "The Barrie That Frohman Knows," *Green Book Album* 1, no. 5 (May 1909): 1013–15. According to a 1937 *Theatre* article quoted in Phyllis Robbins, *Maude Adams: An Intimate Portrait* (New York: G.P. Putnam's Sons, 1956), 106, Adams played the role of Peter "more than 1,500 times. Others have played him well, but he will always be identified here with Miss Adams."

90. Louise Boynton, "Maude Adams in 'Peter Pan,'" *Century* 51 (December 1906), 320; Otheman Stevens, "Maude Adams without Rival in Public Regard," *Los Angeles Examiner*, 7 July 1907, clipping in Locke Scrapbook, vol. 5, TCNYPL.

91. Ada Patterson, *Maude Adams: A Biography* (1907; reprint, New York: Benjamin Blom, 1971), 79. Offstage Maude Adams also was a mystery, although of a different kind and one worthy of a critical study. She was born Maude Kiskadden in 1872, the child of a stage-actor Mormon mother and a "gentile" father. She was a child actress, but as an adult was best known for playing boys: Peter, the young Napoleon in *L'Aiglon, Chantecler*. She was famous as a recluse who abhorred publicity. "Asceticism is the keynote of her life," wrote Patterson, whose biography nonetheless publicized her severe privacy, including a description of the ten-by-twelve nun's cell that she constructed in her New York home and that was modeled after the one in which she stayed during a retreat to a French convent, although without the Christian symbols. "No noise from the street ever reaches this retreat.... Here Maude Adams finds the silence and the peace she loves." Patterson also notes that Herbert Spencer was Adams's favorite author, which adds a dimension to her asceticism (79, 83–87). See other accounts in the Locke Scrapbook, vols. 5 and 6, on Adams, TCNYPL.

92. On Rigby, see the revival's official website: http://www.peter-pan.com/. Williams starred in *Hook*, directed by Steven Spielberg, produced by Gary Adelson and Craig Baumgarten, TriStar Pictures, Columbia Pictures, Amblin Entertainment (1991), videocassette.

93. Boynton, "Maude Adams," 320; "Bids Farewell to 'Peter Pan,'" *New York Morning Telegraph*, 5 January 1908, in Locke Scrapbook, vol. 6, TCNYPL.

94. Review, *Theatre* 5 (December 1905): 288–89. *Hook* is examined in chap. 7.

95. Boynton, "Maude Adams," 320.

96. "Childhood Young and Old: What Some Grown-Ups Learned at a Performance of 'Peter Pan,'" *New York Times*, 17 December 1905, part 4, 4.

97. Otheman Stevens, "Maude Adams's Peter Pan Takes One Back to Childhood Days," *Los Angeles Examiner*, 9 July 1907, in Locke Scrapbook, vol. 5, TCNYPL.

98. Alan Dale, "'Peter Pan' a Riddle and There's No Answer," *New York American*, 7

November 1905, in Locke Scrapbook, vol. 5; Fannie Fair, review of *Peter Pan,* *New York Evening Telegraph,* 20 November 1905, Locke Scrapbook, vol. 6, TCNYPL.

99. Review, *Theatre,* 288–89.

100. William Leach, "Transformations in a Culture of Consumption: Women and Department Stores, 1890–1925," *Journal of American History* 71 (September 1984): 319–21; Selfridge, *Romance of Commerce,* 15-16.

101. "His devotion to her was almost childlike," reported the *Morning Telegraph,* "and it was to her that he outlined first the plans for his numerous big achievements." See "Frederic Thompson's Mother Dies," *New York Morning Telegraph,* 11 September 1917[?], in Thompson and Dundy clipping file, TCNYPL.

102. Clipping from *Spot Light,* 27 October 1906, in Thompson clipping file, TCNYPL; "Ballet Girls Put on Horseback and Elephants Put into Autos," *New York Sun,* 8 January 1905, part 2, 10; Darnton, "Peep at the Hippodrome," 9; "The Hippodrome's Birthday," *New York Sun,* 14 April 1906, 5; McCardell, "Hats Off to the Hippodrome!"; Merwin, "Thompson and His Hippodrome," 528. Merwin followed Thompson closely one summer and used the showman as the model for a character in the novel he and Henry K. Webster wrote, *Comrade John* (New York: Macmillan, 1907). See "Thompson as a Book Hero," *New York Morning Telegraph,* 8 November 1907, in Thompson and Dundy clipping file, TCNYPL.

103. "Ballet Girls Put on Horseback."

104. Merwin, "Thompson and His Hippodrome," 528.

105. May, *Screening Out the Past,* 96–146.

106. See the following clippings in Thompson clipping file, TCNYPL: "Seen and Heard by Lady Gay," *New York Morning Telegraph,* 25 November 1906; "Fred Thompson's New Home," source unknown, 10 September 1905.

107. For a description of the yacht, see J. L. Hoff, "Luna Park, Heart of Coney Island, a Gem," *Show World* 2, 9 May 1908, 13. See also the following clippings in Thompson and Dundy clipping file, TCNYPL: "Thompson and Barr Collaborate," *New York Morning Telegraph,* 25 June 1908; "Thompson Yacht Likes the Going," *New York Morning Telegraph,* 6 June 1907; "Elephant Laughs When Yacht ...," *New York Morning Telegraph,* 8 July 1908; "Thompson and the Sea," *Frederic Thompson's Mile-a-Minute Specials,* 4 September 1908.

108. "Frederic Thompson, the Proof of Youth"; "Little Nemo on the Stage Soon," *New York Herald,* n.d., Locke Scrapbook, vol. 448, 95.

109. See the following clippings in the Thompson and Dundy clipping file, TCNYPL: "Theatre Special Off for Chicago," *New York Morning Telegraph,* 28 August 1908; "Fred Thompson's Show Makes a Quick Flit," *New York Morning Telegraph,* 12 April 1909; "Runs His Shows 'Via Wireless,'" *New York Morning Telegraph,* 30 November 1908; "Made Chicago in 16-Hour Record to See His Wife," source unknown, 29 September[?] 1908. See also "Wireless on Fast Train," *New York Times,* 28 February 1909, 3; and Jean Eldredge, "Protecting the Stars," *Green Book* 1 (April 1909): 792.

110. These lines from the original New York production of *Peter Pan* are quoted in "The Story of Peter Pan," *Metropolitan* (February 1906), in Locke Scrapbook, vol. 5. The published edition of the drama in *The Plays of J. M. Barrie in One Volume* (New York: Charles Scribner's Sons, 1948), contains a variation on these lines in act 5, scene 2: "I'm youth, I'm joy ..." (84). An original typescript of the

play is missing from the Library for the Performing Arts of the New York Public Library.

111. "Behind Scenes at Hippodrome with 450 Actors," *New York Herald*, 13 April 1905, 4; "Fred Thompson, the Wizard," *Cleveland Leader*, n.d., in Thompson and Dundy clipping file, TCNYPL; Merwin, "Thompson and His Hippodrome," 468; "The Hippodrome's Birthday," *New York Sun*, 14 April 1906, in Thompson clipping file, TCNYPL; untitled clipping from *New York Globe*, in Thompson and Dundy clipping file, TCNYPL; "Sunday Benefits Realize $17,000," source unknown, 30 May 1906; "Well What's This?...," *New York World*, 17 May 1908, Locke Scrapbook, vol. 448, TCNYPL.

112. On the legend of Santa Claus, see Stephen Nissenbaum, *The Battle for Christmas: A Cultural History of America's Most Cherished Holiday* (New York: Vintage, 1996), esp. 169–75.

113. "'Fred' Thompson Tells of the Trials and Joys."

114. "Frederic Thompson of Luna Park," *Spot Light* (July 1908), in Thompson and Dundy clipping file, TCNYPL.

115. "Luna Park Not Yet for Rochester," *Rochester Post Express*, 16 January 1905, and "Schuetzen Park to Be Transformed," *Hoboken Observer*, 18 March 1905, both in Burnside Scrapbook, TCNYPL; "Frederic Thompson Interested in Long Beach," *New York Dramatic News*, 19 June 1909, and "Thompson Merely Thinking," source unknown, 21 February 1908, both clippings in Thompson and Dundy clipping file, TCNYPL; Malcolm MacDonald, "Gossip of Plays and Players," *Cleveland Plain Dealer*, 9 October 1907, in Thompson clipping file, TCNYPL; "Busy Days at Hippodrome, Will Open with New Year," *New York Evening Telegram*, 26 September 1904, and "Work on the Great Hippodrome," newspaper unknown, n.d., both in Burnside Scrapbook; see also "Thompson and Dundy in Westchester," *Variety* 1, 13 January 1906, 2.

116. "Colonial Music Hall, New York City," *Billboard* 17, 21 January 1905, 5; "'Fred' Thompson Tells of the Trials and Joys"; "Thompson Enters Vaudeville War," *New York Times*, 15 March 1907, 9.

117. "'Fred' Thompson Tells of the Trials and Joys."

118. Untitled clipping, *Engineering News*, 15 September 1904, and "Hippodrome for Chicago," *Billboard*, 11 March 1905, Burnside Scrapbook, TCNYPL; "Hippodrome for London Next," *New York Morning Telegraph*, 14 February 1906, Thompson clipping file, TCNYPL; "Thompson-Marinelli," *Variety* 1, 27 January 1906, 2; "Notes from London," *Variety* 2, 24 March 1906, 13.

119. On circus plans, see "New Hippodrome Scheme," *New York Times*, 12 January 1905[?], and "New Circus in the Field," *New York Sun*, 12 January 1905, Burnside Scrapbook, TCNYPL; "Thompson & Dundy's Tent Shows," *Variety* 3, 1 September 1906, 2.

120. Merwin, "Thompson and His Hippodrome," 528.

121. "Hip's Big Bear Act Cancelled," *Variety* 3, 4 August 1906, 2.

122. "Hippodrome Celebrates," *New York Times*, 13 April 1906, 7.

123. "Thompson and Dundy at Odds," *Variety* 1, 20 January 1906, 2.

124. "'Hipp' to Resume Old Scale," *Variety* 1, 10 February 1906, 2.

125. "Thompson and Dundy versus Gates," *Variety* 1, 3 February 1906, 2.

126. "Dundy Stood by Thompson," *Variety* 1, 3 March 1906, 2. *Variety* also noted that the theater management ran an expensive advertising campaign—reportedly

spending thirty-six thousand dollars—during the spring 1906 showing of Barnum and Bailey's circus in New York.

127. "Thompson and Dundy Leave the Hippodrome," *Variety* 3, 16 June 1906, 4; "Thompson & Dundy Quit the Hippodrome," *New York Times*, 9 June 1906, 9. The Shuberts were not publicly named the new managers of the Hippodrome until July; see "Hippodrome Leased to the Shuberts," *New York Times*, 8 July 1906, 1.

128. "Frederic Thompson, The Proof of Youth."

129. There is little evidence of Thompson's alcoholism except in nonscholarly accounts of Coney Island and the Hippodrome. The only actual reference to his drunkenness that I have found is in the records of the Panama-Pacific International Exposition of 1915; this evidence is discussed in chap. 6. The accounts of his alcohol addiction given in these works—Oliver Pilat and Jo Ranson, *Sodom by the Sea: An Affectionate History of Coney Island* (Garden City, N.Y.: Doubleday, Doran, 1941), 141, 154–57, 164; Clarke, *Mighty Hippodrome*, 21, 40–41; Edo McCullough, *Good Old Coney Island: A Sentimental Journey into the Past* (1957; reprint, New York: Fordham University Press, 2000), 316–17; John F. Kasson, *Amusing the Million: Coney Island at the Turn of the Century* (New York: Hill and Wang, 1978), 111—are backed up by the evidence of violence against his wife and his collapses, the frequency of which increased after the breakup of his first marriage (see the discussion in the following chapter). McCullough, in particular, writes that both Dundy and Thompson were "sick men," and that Thompson drank himself to death (316–17).

130. On Burnside's and Dillingham's tenures at the Hippodrome, see Clarke, *Mighty Hippodrome*.

### Chapter 5: Millionaires and Monsters

1. George Barr McCutcheon, *Brewster's Millions* (New York: Grosset and Dunlap, 1902).

2. The *New York Morning Telegraph* reported on 31 May 1906, near the time of Thompson and Dundy's departure from the Hippodrome, that the partnership intended to produce the book as a play. Untitled article in Thompson clipping file, TCNYPL.

3. Frederic Thompson, "Amusing People," *Metropolitan* 32 (August 1910): 605.

4. Alfred L. Bernheim, *The Business of the Theatre: An Economic History of the American Theatre, 1750–1932* (New York: Benjamin Blom, 1932), 43–57, quotation on 50; *Chicago Tribune* quotation on 49. For additional information on the Theatre Syndicate monopoly, see Peter A. Davis, "The Syndicate/Shubert War," in *Inventing Times Square: Commerce and Culture at the Crossroads of the World, 1880–1939*, edited by William R. Taylor (Baltimore: Johns Hopkins University Press, 1996), 147–57.

5. Lawrence W. Levine, *Highbrow/Lowbrow: The Emergence of Cultural Hierarchy in America* (Cambridge, Mass.: Harvard University Press, 1988), 13–81.

6. David Grimsted, *Melodrama Unveiled: American Theater and Culture, 1800–1850* (Chicago: University of Chicago Press, 1968), 204–48, quotation on 222.

7. Peter Brooks, *The Melodramatic Imagination: Balzac, Henry James, Melodrama, and the Mode of Excess* (New Haven: Yale University Press, 1976), ix, 4.

8. James L. Smith, *Melodrama* (London: Methuen, 1973), 66; James, quoted in

Thomas Postlewait, "From Melodrama to Realism: The Suspect History of American Drama," in *Melodrama: The Cultural Emergence of a Genre*, edited by Michael Hays and Anastasia Nikolopoulou (New York: St. Martin's, 1996), 56.

9. For a recent historian's reflection that Coney Island attractions were "thrilling drama without imaginative effort," see John F. Kasson, *Amusing the Million: Coney Island at the Turn of the Century* (New York: Hill and Wang, 1978), 81–82.

10. Porter Emerson Browne, "The Mellowdrammer," *Everybody's* 21 (September 1909): 347.

11. Browne, "Mellowdrammer," 347, 348.

12. Browne, "Mellowdrammer," 347, 354.

13. Quoted in Grimsted, *Melodrama Unveiled*, 41–42; on melodrama "as a theatrical form of polarized excesses," see Postlewait, "From Melodrama to Realism," 53–56, quotation on 54.

14. Quoted in Brooks, *Melodramatic Imagination*, 4.

15. Grimsted, *Melodrama Unveiled*, 229–31, quotation on 230.

16. Postlewait, "From Melodrama to Realism," 39–56, quotations on 45, 43.

17. Brooks, *Melodramatic Imagination*, 4.

18. A. Nicholas Vardac, *Stage to Screen: Theatrical Method from Garrick to Griffith* (Cambridge, Mass.: Harvard University Press, 1949), 20–67, 108–35; Brenda Murphy, *American Realism and American Drama, 1880–1940* (New York: Cambridge University Press, 1987).

19. The best biographical source on McCutcheon is A. L. Lazarus and Victor H. Jones, *Beyond Graustark: George Barr McCutcheon, Playwright Discovered* (Port Washington, N.Y.: Kennikat Press, 1981). Editorial, "Romance out of Indiana," *New York Times*, 24 October 1928, 28. For a list of his publications, see "Geo. B. M'Cutcheon Dies at a Luncheon," *New York Times*, 24 October 1928, part 1, 22.

20. Lazarus and Jones, *Beyond Graustark*, 74; "Geo. Barr McCutcheon," *New York Times*, 21 July 1912, part 6, 418.

21. For a definition of farce, see William Harmon and C. Hugh Holman, *A Handbook to Literature*, 8th ed. (Upper Saddle River, N.J.: Prentice Hall, 2000), 209. Thompson did not bother with such fine distinctions, as he explained: "Whether 'Brewster's Millions' is light comedy and farce, or melodrama, we leave it to our audience to decide." What mattered, he claimed, was that it amused audiences. See New Amsterdam Theatre program for the week of 28 January 1907, *Brewster's Millions* program file, TCNYPL.

22. For a description of this scene, as well as critical commentary on its unconvincing operation, see Vardac, *Stage to Screen*, 85–87. A review of the New York opening called the foundering yacht scene "eminently successful as an effect" although hardly a necessary part of the play. See untitled and undated review, *Brewster's Millions* clipping file, TCNYPL.

23. McCutcheon, *Brewster's Millions*, 282, 55. Here and below, unless otherwise noted, I am relying for plot details and quotations on McCutcheon's 1902 novel rather than the stage play, which, in terms of the aspects I am discussing here, did not differ in any significant regard. There are, however, important details in the novel that are missing in the play, although they are not relevant to the present analysis. With some desperation and remarkable serendipity, Thompson let his stage manager, Winchell Smith, take a shot at adapting the novel to the effects Thompson had already built. Although now forgotten, Smith earned the

title "the Play Doctor" in a career launched by *Brewster's Millions* and spanning more than twenty years, during which he wrote only one original play, but "doctored" many hit productions, including several of Thompson's shows. Although himself a notorious spendthrift, Smith died in 1933 leaving a multi-million-dollar fortune that the *New York Times* speculated was "perhaps the largest, ever amassed by an American playwright." See "Winchell Smith, Playwright, Dies," *New York Times,* 11 June 1933, 30, and articles in Winchell Smith clipping file, TCNYPL. For the actual script, see Winchell Smith and Bryan Ongley, *Brewster's Millions: A Comedy in Four Acts* (1907; reprint, Samuel French, 1925).

24. McCutcheon, *Brewster's Millions,* 312; the "Fairies" reference to *Peter Pan* was added for the stage production; see Smith and Ongley, *Brewster's Millions,* 17.

25. "Fine Bills at Chicago Theaters," *Show World* 1, 24 June 1907, 7.

26. New Amsterdam Theatre program for week of 28 January 1907, *Brewster's Millions* program file, TCNYPL.

27. *Brewster's Millions* played for 163 performances in New York in 1906 and 1907 and spawned touring companies in the United States, England, and Europe. See "Noted Here and There," *Chicago Evening Post,* 22 June 1907, 9. Its run was unusually long for the first decade of the twentieth century; a few dozen performances were more common, while the extraordinary popularity of *The Merry Widow,* which ran for 416 performances, rarely was matched. For instance, compare the theatrical offerings in Burns Mantle and Garrison P. Sherwood, eds., *The Best Plays of 1899–1909 and the Year Book of the Drama in America* (New York: Dodd, Mead, 1944), 346–584; the figures for *Brewster's Millions* and *The Merry Widow* appear on 530 and 548.

28. The claim for the popularity of *Brewster's Millions* is in the promotional brochure "Frederick Thompson Presents Edward Abeles in Brewster's Millions," no date, in *Brewster's Millions* (Cinema 1935) clipping file, TCNYPL. After being out of print for a number of years, the book was republished in 1999 by Indiana University Press. The best resource for the technical details of the various film versions of *Brewster's Millions* is the Internet Movie Database (www.imdb.com). The Billy Rose Theatre Collection, New York Public Library, also has a file on each of the film versions and the one radio version. A representative ending is that of *Miss Brewster's Millions:* "The close of the film finds Polly broken-hearted, once more an extra, making the rounds. But Tom has learned to love the girl, and surprises her by saying that all is not lost. There's still a little left from the wreck. Smile. Kiss. Closeup." See Paramount press sheet, "Bebe Daniels in 'Miss Brewster's Millions,'" 31 July 1926, TCNYPL. The "hard labor" quotation is in Smith and Ongley, *Brewster's Millions,* 66.

29. David S. Reynolds, *Beneath the American Renaissance: The Subversive Imagination in the Age of Emerson and Melville* (Cambridge, Mass.: Harvard University Press, 1988), 59–84, 211–24.

30. "Frederick Thompson Presents Edward Abeles in Brewster's Millions."

31. *Brewster's Millions* pamphlet, hand-dated 2 April 1907, in *Brewster's Millions* clipping file, TCNYPL.

32. "Frederick Thompson Presents Edward Abeles in Brewster's Millions."

33. Rennold Wolf, "Rattling Good, 'Brewster' Play," *New York Morning Telegraph,* n.d., *Brewster's Millions* clipping file, TCNYPL.

34. Jackson Lears, *Fables of Abundance: A Cultural History of Advertising in America*

(New York: Basic Books, 1994); Daniel Horowitz, *The Morality of Spending: Attitudes toward the Consumer Society in America, 1875–1940* (Baltimore: Johns Hopkins University Press, 1985); Joyce Appleby, *Capitalism and a New Social Order* (New York: New York University Press, 1984); Victoria de Grazia, "Changing Consumption Regimes," in *The Sex of Things: Gender and Consumption in Historical Perspective*, edited by Victoria de Grazia (Berkeley and Los Angeles: University of California Press, 1996), 1–21.

35. McCutcheon, *Brewster's Millions*, 137, 323–24.
36. Ann Fabian, *Card Sharps, Dream Books, and Bucket Shops: Gambling in Nineteenth-Century America* (Ithaca, N.Y.: Cornell University Press, 1990), 111–28, quotations on 2, 112; Karen Halttunen, *Confidence Men and Painted Women: A Study of Middle-class Culture in America, 1830–1870* (New Haven: Yale University Press, 1982), 16–22.
37. Fabian, *Card Sharps*, 153-202, quotation on 9.
38. See, for instance, E. Anthony Rotundo, *American Manhood: Transformations in Masculinity from the Revolution to the Modern Era* (New York: Basic Books, 1993), 248-51.
39. McCutcheon, *Brewster's Millions*, 2, 10, 8, 33, 46–47, 286.
40. Lears, *Fables of Abundance*, 75.
41. McCutcheon, *Brewster's Millions*, 315–25.
42. On retailing as public service, see William Leach, *Land of Desire: Merchants, Power, and the Rise of a New American Culture* (New York: Pantheon, 1993), 146–48.
43. McCutcheon, *Brewster's Millions*, 54, 272.
44. Letter to Mrs. Frederic Thompson from Margaret Mayo, dated 8 March 1929, in Margaret Mayo papers, Cage Collection, TCNYPL.
45. Kasson, *Amusing the Million*, 111; Oliver Pilat and Jo Ranson, *Sodom by the Sea: An Affectionate History of Coney Island* (Garden City, N.Y.: Doubleday, Doran, 1941), 154–57; Edo McCullough, *Good Old Coney Island: A Sentimental Journey into the Past* (1957; reprint, New York: Fordham University Press, 2000), 316–17.
46. An obituary for Dundy reported that he had already handed over his financial end of the partnership to an associate in order to free his time to pursue his own speculative investments in western gold mines and other risky projects. See "Great Showman Died When Dundy Succumbed," *Brooklyn Daily Eagle*, 6 February 1907, 7. That article notes that John Kilborn, brother of a vice president of the National City Bank, had "attended to practically all of the financial affairs of the concern for the last year," and was promoted to treasurer with Dundy's death.
47. Glenmore Davis, "Our Billion-Dollar Smile," *Success* 11 (December 1908): 815.
48. Maurice Sendak, "Foreword," in John Canemaker, *Winsor McCay: His Life and Art* (New York: Abbeville Press, 1987), 9; Lears, *Fables of Abundance*, 330.
49. "Messrs. Klaw and Erlanger Will Stage Little Nemo," Paris edition of the *New York Herald*, 10 September 1907, in Erlanger Collection Scrapbooks, TCNYPL. In the summer of 1906, *Variety* reported that the first new managers of the Hippodrome planned "a stupendous spectacular presentation" of *Little Nemo*, with the master of high-end melodrama, David Belasco, as stage manager. See Coulton Waugh, *The Comics* (New York: Macmillan, 1947), 19; "Hippodrome's New

Production," *Variety* 3, 11 August 1906, 2; "Belasco Will Stage Hippodrome Productions," *Variety* 3, 14 July 1906, 2; Canemaker, *Winsor McCay*, 119–26.

50. Ian Gordon, *Comic Strips and Consumer Culture, 1890–1945* (Washington, D.C.: Smithsonian Institution Press, 1998), 6, 37–42, quotations on 6, 41. Gordon figures that in 1908, eighty-three newspapers in fifty locations carried comic strips. On the history of "brand name" commodities, see Susan Strasser, *Satisfaction Guaranteed: The Making of the American Mass Market* (New York: Pantheon, 1989).

51. On the merchandising of "Buster Brown," see Gordon, *Comic Strips*, 46–58.

52. "Messrs. Klaw and Erlanger Will Stage Little Nemo."

53. "Plays and Players: The Cost of Musical Comedy," *American Magazine* 70 (May 1910): 113.

54. "Victor Herbert and H. B. Smith Fit Nemo for Stage," *New York Herald*, 27 May 1908, in Erlanger Collection Scrapbooks, TCNYPL; John Murray, "Building a Great Spectacle," *Green Book Album* 1 (March 1909): 638–39; "Nemo Travels in Style," *New York Morning Telegraph*, 20 September 1908, Erlanger Collection Scrapbooks, TCNYPL; "Little Nemo to Be a Great Spectacle," *Show World* 3, 12 September 1908, 13.

55. Edward N. Waters, *Victor Herbert: A Life in Music* (New York: Macmillan, 1955), 1–49, 69–71, 73–81, 116, 128, 140–49, 232–33, 240–51, 257–64, 300–302, 372–76, 412–15, 504–8; see also the clipping "Sunday Benefits Realize $17,000," newspaper unknown, 30 May 1906, in Thompson clipping file, TCNYPL.

56. "Little Nemo to Be Produced on the Stage," *Chicago Record*, 5 July 1908, in Locke Scrapbook, series 2, vol. 19.

57. "Messrs. Klaw and Erlanger Will Stage Little Nemo."

58. Untitled clipping in Locke Scrapbook, series 2, vol. 192, 99–100, TCNYPL; advertisement for Brown Shoe Co. in *Dry Goods Economist* 62, 12 September 1908, 5.

59. Neil Harris, *Humbug: The Art of P. T. Barnum* (Chicago: University of Chicago Press, 1973), 49–50.

60. "A Chronicle of the Passing Show," *Philadelphia Telegraph*, 12 December 1906, in Locke Scrapbook, series 2, vol. 192, TCNYPL.

61. Compare the photo of Gabriel as Little Nemo in Locke Scrapbook, series 2, vol. 191, with that of McCay's son in Canemaker, *Winsor McCay*, 127.

62. Untitled clipping in Locke Scrapbook, series 2, vol. 192, 99–100, TCNYPL.

63. Untitled clipping in Locke Scrapbook, series 2, vol. 192, 58, TCNYPL.

64. "The Happy Land of Once upon a Time," from the Broadway musical *Little Nemo*, produced by Klaw and Erlanger with Frederic Thompson, New Amsterdam Theatre, New York, 20 October 1908. The song is reprinted in *Klaw and Erlanger Present "Little Nemo"* (New York: Cohan and Harris, 1908), 18–22. Book and lyrics by Harry Smith; music by Victor Herbert. Based on Winsor McCay's Sunday supplement cartoon, *Little Nemo in Slumberland*, published in the *New York Herald*.

65. Sam McKee, "All the Family Will See 'Nemo,'" *New York Morning Telegraph*, 27 September 1908, in Erlanger Collection Scrapbook, TCNYPL.

66. Undated review in *Theatre*, Erlanger Collection Scrapbook, TCNYPL.

67. "Fred Thompson Elopes with Miss Taliaferro," *New York Globe*, 1 December

1906; untitled clipping, 8 December 1906, both in Locke Scrapbook, vol. 448, TCNYPL.

68. "Personality Her Secret of Success," *Toledo Times*, 3 January 1908, in Locke Scrapbook, vol. 448, TCNYPL; "Frederic Thompson Wins," *Show World* 2, 30 May 1908, 16.

69. See the following clippings in Locke Scrapbook, vol. 448: Rennold Wolf, "Mabel Taliaferro," *Smith's* (June 1908); "Mabel Taliaferro in 'Cinderella' New Amsterdam's Holiday Event," *New York Morning Telegraph*, 2 May 1908. See also "Miss Mabel Taliaferro," *Collier's Weekly* (January 1911), and illustration for "Listening to the Fairies," *Detroit News Tribune*, 23 January 1910, both in Locke Scrapbook, series 2, vol. 297. The record of productions that starred Taliaferro and that actually made it to the stage is unclear. For instance, although she was announced to appear in *Cinderella*, there is no record that it ever was produced. Other roles included *Ingomar*, *Listening to the Fairies*, *The Land of Heart's Desire*, and *King Rene's Daughter*.

70. Mabel Taliaferro, "My Yesterdays," *Bohemian* 14 (April 1908): 484.

71. Clipping of "Stage Romance of Cincinnatian Ends in a Suit," *Cincinnati Times-Star*, [3?] December 1911, in Thompson and Dundy clipping file, TCNYPL; and clippings of the following articles in Locke Scrapbook, vol. 448, TCNYPL: "Fred Thompson Elopes with Miss Taliaferro"; "Mabel Taliaferro—Child Actress Grown Up," *Theatre* 4, 1 August 1904, 197–98, 200; untitled clipping, 16 March 1901; untitled clipping, 3 May 1902; Marian the Maid, "'Lovey Mary' above Caramels," 4 September 1904; untitled, *New York Dramatic Mirror*, 24 September 1904; review of Boston performance of W. B. Yeats, *The Land of Heart's Desire*, 10 May 1901. Mabel Taliaferro's weight is taken from "Discovering the Yellowstone with Mabel Taliaferro," *Green Book Album* 3 (March 1910): 573.

72. Eileen Wiley Todd, *The "New Woman" Revised: Painting and Gender Politics on Fourteenth Street* (Berkeley and Los Angeles: University of California Press, 1993), 19–24; Elizabeth Lunbeck, *The Psychiatric Persuasion: Knowledge, Gender, and Power in Modern America* (Princeton, N.J.: Princeton University Press, 1994), 185–228.

73. Anna A. Rogers, "Why American Marriages Fail," *Atlantic Monthly* 100 (September 1907): 289–98, quotations on 290, 292, 297, 292.

74. Carroll Smith-Rosenberg, "The New Woman as Androgyne: Social Disorder and Gender Crisis, 1870–1936," in *Disorderly Conduct: Visions of Gender in Victorian America* (New York: Oxford University Press, 1985), 247.

75. "Stage Romance of Cincinnatian Ends in a Suit"; "Mabel Taliaferro—Child Actress Grown Up," 197–98, 200.

76. Smith-Rosenberg, "New Woman as Androgyne," 253.

77. "Fred Thompson Elopes with Miss Taliaferro"; "Little Mabel's Summer," *Chicago Inter-Ocean*, 16 June 1907, clipping in Locke Scrapbook, vol. 448, TCNYPL.

78. Typescript of press release no. 17 in the *Polly of the Circus* clipping file, TCNYPL.

79. For the plot of the play, see Margaret Mayo, *Polly of the Circus*, prepared by Nathaniel Edward Reeid (New York: Longmans, Green, 1933).

80. Margaret Mayo, *Polly of the Circus*, produced by Frederic Thompson at the Liberty Theatre, 23 December 1907. Sets by Thompson and staged by Winchell Smith; 160 performances. See Mantle and Sherwood, *Best Plays of 1899–1909*,

553. See also "Quaint Model for Girls," *New York Telegram*[?], 8 April 1908, Locke Scrapbook, vol. 448, TCNYPL; Thompson quotation from typescript of press release no. 15, "What Frederic Thompson Says of the Drama of Today," in clipping file of *Polly of the Circus*, TCNYPL; *Chicago Tribune* quoted in "Dainty Star Given Warm Greeting Here," *Show World* 3, 5 September 1908, 7; reviews in Taliaferro Scrapbook, vol. 448, TCNYPL, from the *Bohemian* (May 1908) and the *Metropolitan* (March 1908).

81. See the following typescripts of press releases in the *Polly of the Circus* clipping file, TCNYPL: "Polly of the Circus," no number; nos. 23, 10, and 14; review in *Theatre* (February 1908) in Locke Scrapbook, vol. 448, TCNYPL; also see the articles in Locke Scrapbook, vol. 448, quoting Thompson and Taliaferro protesting the ignominy heaped on theatrical couples. Thompson seemed particularly sensitive to the ill repute in which theatrical people were held.

82. "The Youngest Dramatic Star," *Dramatic News and Dramatic Times*, 2 May 1908, in Locke Scrapbook, vol. 448, TCNYPL; "Play for Miss Taliaferro," *New York Times*, 2 May 1908, 9; untitled clipping from *New York Dramatic News*, 9 May 1908, in Locke Scrapbook, vol. 448; "Little Nemo to Be a Great Spectacle," 13; "Stage Romance of Cincinnatian Ends in a Suit." Among the other productions were Booth Tarkington and Harry Leon Wilson's *Springtime* in October 1909, Samuel Peple's even greater though less-expensive failure, *The Call of the Cricket* in April 1910, and Forrest Halsey's *My Man* in August 1910.

83. "Thompson's Mysterious 'Nell,'" *New York Morning Telegraph*, 9 June 1909, in Thompson and Dundy clipping file, TCNYPL; *Springtime* promotional brochure in *Springtime* clipping file, TCNYPL; "Thompson Gets His Trademark," *New York Morning Telegraph*, 11 September 1909, in Thompson and Dundy clipping file, TCNYPL.

84. "Mr. Thompson Believes in Tears," *Chicago Tribune*, 17 August 1909, in Thompson and Dundy clipping file, TCNYPL. For restoration of Taliaferro's original stage name, compare the programs for 19 October and 1 November in *Springtime* program file, TCNYPL. For a typical review, see "'Springtime' Drips with Lachrymose Gaspings," *New York Press*, 20 October 1909. The Theatre Syndicate's ally, the *New York Morning Telegraph*, was nearly, if not completely, alone in finding the play delightful; for *New York Morning Telegraph* and other reviews, see *Springtime* clipping file, TCNYPL.

85. See "Bill for Divorce," 2 December 1911, and "Affidavit of Mabel Taliaferro Thompson," 13 December 1911, quotations on 3, in *Thompson v. Thompson*, file no. S-290973, Archives, Office of the Circuit Court Clerk of Cook County, Chicago, Illinois; "The Matinee Girl," *New York Dramatic Mirror* 62, 11 September 1909, 4; Clara E. Laughlin, "A Vacation with a Star," *Ladies' World* (March 1910), in Locke Scrapbook, series 2, vol. 297, TCNYPL; Clara E. Laughlin, *Traveling through Life: Being the Autobiography of Clara E. Laughlin* (Boston: Houghton Mifflin, 1934). On Ada Dwyer Russell, see Richard Benvenuto, *Amy Lowell* (Boston: Twayne, 1985), 9–10. On "Fiona Macleod" and William Sharp, see the discussion of her/his relationship to William Butler Yeats in R. F. Foster, *W. B. Yeats: A Life*, Vol. 1, *The Apprentice Mage, 1865–1914* (Oxford: Oxford University Press, 1997), 80–81, 180–81, quotation on 80. According to Foster, "Sharp's writings (from 1893 in secret disguise as 'Fiona Macleod') would eventually help to broadcast Celticism to the world" (80).

86. John D'Emilio and Estelle B. Freedman, *Intimate Matters: A History of Sexuality in America* (Chicago: University of Chicago Press, 1997), 189–94; Carroll Smith-Rosenberg, "The Female World of Love and Ritual: Relations between Women in Nineteenth-Century America," and "New Woman as Androgyne," in *Disorderly Conduct*, 53–76, 245–96, quotations on 59.

87. Laughlin, *Traveling through Life*, 144–45.

88. On middle-class birth-control practices and sexual intercourse among middle-class married couples, see D'Emilio and Freedman, *Intimate Matters*, 57–63, 171–83, 222–35. Taliaferro finally got to play Cinderella in the movies and even married Prince Charming, played by Thomas J. Carrigan. See "Miss Taliaferro a Secret Bride," *New York Morning Telegraph*, [?] June 1913, in Locke Scrapbook, series 2, vol. 22, TCNYPL.

89. "The Thompson's Celebrate," *New York Times*, 20 December 1909, 20.

90. In his response, Thompson denied the accusations; the judge awarded the divorce, finding Thompson "guilty of extreme and repeated cruelty toward" Taliaferro. See "Bill for Divorce," "Answer of Defendant," 11 December 1911, "Affidavit of Mabel Taliaferro Thompson," quotations on 3, 4, and "Decree," 18 December 1911, all in *Thompson v. Thompson*. Also see "Mabel Taliaferro Sues," *New York Times*, 3 December 1911, part 3, 4.

91. Laughlin, *Traveling through Life*, 154–56, quotation on 154.

92. "Thompson's Tete-a-Tete with Death," 18 January 1911, and "Frederic Thompson, Author and Manager Announces His Next Production," n.d., both published in *Frederic Thompson's Mile-a-Minute Specials*, in Thompson and Dundy clipping file, TCNYPL.

93. See "A Nice Thing Nicely Said," *Frederic Thompson's Mile-a-Minute Specials*, 30 October 1908, in Thompson and Dundy clipping file, TCNYPL.

94. Irving Kolodin, *The Metropolitan Opera, 1883–1966: A Candid History* (New York: Knopf, 1966), 185–86.

95. On *Salome* as a music-hall feature, see "'Salome' at the Manhattan Opera House," *Theatre* (March 1909), and "'I Had Set my Heart on Conquering America," *Musical America*, 20 November 1909, Robinson Locke Scrapbooks, series 1, vol. 227, TCNYPL. Also see the discussion of the "four versions" of the dance on display at one time in Chicago, in "Salome Dance Sets the Pace," *Chicago Inter-Ocean*, 23 June 1907, magazine section, 2.

96. Frederic Thompson, "After the Salome Dance—What?" *Success* 12 (March 1909): 157.

97. For an account of Hammerstein's production, see Vincent Sheean, *Oscar Hammerstein I: The Life and Exploits of an Impresario* (New York: Simon and Schuster, 1956), 267–71; John Frederick Cone, *Oscar Hammerstein's Manhattan Opera Company* (Norman: University of Oklahoma Press, 1966), 210-19, 225; Andreas Huyssen, "Mass Culture as Woman: Modernism's Other," in *After the Great Divide: Modernism, Mass Culture, Postmodernism* (Bloomington: Indiana University Press, 1986), 49.

98. Robert Hilliard, the actor whom Thompson cast in the role of the Fool, credited himself with originating the idea of the play. He claimed he took it to Browne, who returned two weeks later with a script; the next day Thompson reportedly bought the rights to produce it. Clipping from *Chicago Inter-Ocean*, 28 March 1909, in Locke envelope 871, TCNYPL. Also see Lynde Denig, "Vicissitudes of Play-

wright—No. 4: Porter Emerson Browne," *Theatre* 22 (August 1915): 71, 93–94; Robert Hilliard, "You Can't Fool the Public; It Knows Well What It Wants," *Chicago Tribune*, 17 October 1909, in Locke Scrapbook, vol. 270, TCNYPL.

99. W. Arthur Young, *A Dictionary of the Characters and Scenes in the Stories and Poems of Rudyard Kipling* (London: George Routledge and Sons, 1911), 211; Angus Wilson, *The Strange Ride of Rudyard Kipling: His Life and Works* (New York: Viking, 1977), 155.

100. See clipping of painting and poem from promotional material for *A Fool There Was*, in Locke Scrapbook, vol. 270, TCNYPL.

101. Porter Emerson Browne, "The Symbolism of 'A Fool There Was,'" in promotional brochure published for the play, 10 January 1910[?], in *A Fool There Was* clipping file, TCNYPL.

102. "'A Fool There Was,' Important as Drama of Mental Anguish," *Toledo News*, 18 February 1910, Locke Scrapbook, vol. 270, TCNYPL.

103. Ruth Crosby Dimmick, "Some of the Best Lines in 'A Fool There Was,'" *New York Sunday Telegraph*, 11 April 1909, clipping in Locke Scrapbook, vol. 270, TCNYPL. The following lines and descriptions, unless otherwise noted, are taken from this synopsis. A typescript of the play is available in the Billy Rose Theatre Collection, New York Public Library.

104. Various versions of Kipling's "Vampire" with conflicting punctuation and spelling are available. The text here appears in the play summary; an alternative, and more exclamatory, version appears in *A Choice of Kipling's Verse; Made by T. S. Eliot* (New York: Charles Scribner's Sons, 1943), 108–9.

105. Review of the play in *Toledo Blade*, 18 February 1910, Locke Scrapbook, vol. 270, TCNYPL; "A Fool There Was; No Doubt of That," *New York Times*, 25 March 1909, 9.

106. Browne, "Symbolism of 'A Fool There Was.'"

107. Huyssen, "Mass Culture as Woman," 52–53, 55.

108. "Are There Real Vampires? Lots of 'Em, Says Hilliard," *Chicago Tribune*, 31 October 1909, in Locke Scrapbook, vol. 270, TCNYPL.

109. Nina Auerbach, *Woman and the Demon: The Life of a Victorian Myth* (Cambridge, Mass.: Harvard University Press, 1982), 185, 65, 61–62; Michael Rogin, "'The Sword Became Flashing Vision': D. W. Griffith's *The Birth of a Nation*," in Rogin, *Ronald Reagan, the Movie; and Other Episodes in Political Demonology* (Berkeley and Los Angeles: University of California Press, 1987), 200.

110. Bram Dykstra, *Idols of Perversity: Fantasies of Feminine Evil in Fin-de-Siècle Culture* (New York: Oxford University Press, 1986), 401; Dykstra, *Evil Sisters: The Threat of Female Sexuality in Twentieth-Century Culture* (New York: Henry Holt, 1996), 6.

111. "Are There Real Vampires?"

112. Hilliard, "You Can't Fool the Public."

113. D'Emilio and Freedman, *Intimate Matters*, 66–73; G. J. Barker-Benfield, *The Horrors of the Half-Known Life: Male Attitudes toward Women and Sexuality in Nineteenth-Century America* (New York: Harper and Row, 1976), 135–226.

114. Quoted in promotional brochure for the play, Porter Emerson Browne clipping file, TCNYPL.

115. "Breaking Away from an Ungrateful [Vampire?]," *New York Tribune*, n.d., in Locke Scrapbook, series 2, vol. 263, TCNYPL.

116. Andrea Weiss, *Vampires and Violets: Lesbians in Film* (New York: Penguin, 1993), 84–108, quotation on 98; Janet Staiger, *Bad Women: Regulating Sexuality in Early American Cinema* (Minneapolis: University of Minnesota Press, 1995), 161, 148.
117. Review of the play in *Rochester Post*, [5?] February 1910, Locke Scrapbook, vol. 270, TCNYPL.
118. "Striking a Woman Allowed in Drama," *Pittsburgh Leader*, 12 March 1911, Locke Scrapbook, vol. 270, TCNYPL.
119. Richard Slotkin, *Gunfighter Nation: The Myth of the Frontier in Twentieth-Century America* (New York: Harper Perennial, 1992), 57, 10–16; on the "regenerative" force of defeat in American culture, see Slotkin, *The Fatal Environment: The Myth of the Frontier in the Age of Industrialization, 1800–1890* (New York: Atheneum, 1985), 7–12.
120. "Why Vampire's Easiest Part for Her," *New York Morning Telegraph*, 30 May 1909, Locke envelope 871, TCNYPL.
121. "Spring Flurry to Bring Many New Plays," *New York Times*, 10 April 1910, part 8, 1; typescript of *The Spendthrift* by Porter Emerson Browne, TCNYPL, act 1, 15, 20, 38; "'The Spendthrift' Faulty," *New York Times*, 12 April 1910, 11.
122. "Frederic Thompson, Enthusiast," *New York Dramatic Mirror* 64, 6 August 1910, 5; advertisement for play in *New York Times*, 10 April 1910, part 8, 3; review of *The Spendthrift* in *Saturday Post*, 5 November 1910, in Browne clipping file, TCNYPL. On race suicide and its connection to consumption, see Horowitz, *Morality of Spending*, esp. 67–108.
123. Gail Bederman, *Manliness and Civilization: A Cultural History of Gender and Race in the United States, 1880–1917* (Chicago: University of Chicago Press, 1995), 200–206, quotation on 200.
124. "Frederic Thompson, Enthusiast."
125. For account of teddy bear craze, see the article originally published in the April 1907 issue of the *Chicago Dry Goods Reporter*, reprinted as "A Short Teddy Bear Review," *Playthings* 5 (May 1907): 74–78; quotations are from "Teddy Bears in Clover," *Playthings* 5 (July 1907): 48; "Hurrah For Teddy Bears! Getting Lots of Free Advertising," *Playthings* 5 (August 1907): 56, 60. On the cuddly quality of teddy bears, see Stewart Culin, "Stewart Culin Talks of Toys," *Playthings* 25 (March 1927): 162. On the landmark importance of teddy bears to the toy industry, see Gary Cross, *Kids' Stuff: Toys and the Changing World of American Childhood* (Cambridge, Mass.: Harvard University Press, 1997), 94–97. See also William Leach, "Child World in the Promised Land," in *The Mythmaking Frame of Mind: Social Imagination and American Culture*, edited by James Gilbert et al. (Belmont, Calif.: Wadsworth, 1993), 209–38. I have been influenced here by Erica Carter's astute examination of narratives of transformation from agent of desire to bourgeois housewife in post–World War II German films. See Carter, "Deviant Pleasures? Women, Melodrama, and Consumer Nationalism in West Germany," in *Sex of Things*, 359–77, esp. 375.
126. "Dig up Yard in Search for 'Phantom Twins,'" *Chicago Herald and Examiner*, 18 October 1922, 1–2; quotations from "'Doll Mother' Freed on Twin Murder Charge," *Chicago Daily Tribune*, 21 October 1922, 2; "The New Ladies," *Chicago Daily Tribune*, 20 October 1922, 8.
127. "'Twin Doll' Case Still a Mystery Despite Acquittal," *Chicago Evening Post*, 21 Oc-

tober 1922, 1; "Says Dolls, Not Twins, Were Hidden by Mother," *New York Times*, 19 October 1922, 21; "Mystery Mother Freed of Murder," *Providence Journal*, 21 October 1922, 13; "The Twin Doll Mother," *Toys and Novelties* 19 (November 1922): 57.

128. Lears, *Fables of Abundance*, 38; see also Elizabeth Kowaleski-Wallace, *Consuming Subjects: Women, Shopping, and Business in the Eighteenth Century* (New York: Columbia University Press, 1997).

129. For a discussion of women and department stores, see William R. Leach, "Transformations in a Culture of Consumption: Women and Department Stores, 1890–1925," *Journal of American History* 71 (September 1984): 331–42; Susan Porter Benson, *Counter Cultures: Saleswomen, Managers, and Customers in American Department Stores, 1890–1940* (Urbana: University of Illinois Press, 1986), esp. 75–282; and Kathy Peiss, *Cheap Amusements: Working Women and Leisure in Turn-of-the-Century New York* (Philadelphia: Temple University Press, 1986). For an alternative view, see Elaine S. Abelson, *When Ladies Go a-Thieving: Middle-Class Shoplifters in the Victorian Department Store* (New York: Oxford University Press, 1989).

130. Quoted in promotional brochure for the play, Porter Emerson Browne clipping file, TCNYPL; see also Ada Patterson, "A Vampire Woman at Close Range," *Theatre* 10 (July 1909): 13–14, 16, vi. A photograph of Kaelred as the siren seductress accompanies the article.

131. See discussion of Campbell in chap. 3.

132. Stephen B. Johnson, *The Roof Gardens of Broadway Theatres, 1883–1942* (Ann Arbor, Mich.: UMI Research Press, 1985), 1–135.

133. Clipping, review of *Girlies* in *New York Dramatic Mirror*, 25 June 1910; "'Girlies' Lives Up to Its Title," *New York Morning Telegraph*, 14 June 1910, both in Locke Scrapbook, series 2, vol. 41, TCNYPL.

134. "Capacity Not Enough," *Variety* 19, 18 June 1910, 4.

135. See the contract files for *Girlies*, no. 33, and *The Spendthrift*, no. 117, both in series 3, Shubert Archive; quotation in untitled review in *New York Dramatic Mirror*.

136. The new productions included a follow-up summer musical to *Girlies* called *The Maid of the Moon*; a new drama by Porter Emerson Browne suggestively billed as *Money; A Fool's Comedy* by Hartley Manners; and a new play for Robert Hilliard, the star of *A Fool There Was*. Giving no hint of his troubled marriage, Thompson promised that Mabel Taliaferro would appear early in the coming season in yet another play by Porter Emerson Browne, *The Other Half*. Instead, Taliaferro appeared in the role of the unfortunate female lead in *My Man* by Forrest Halsey, when it opened at the Colonial Theatre in Boston in August. By the time the play reached Broadway in late September, she had left the cast. For an outline of these plans, see "Frederic Thompson, Enthusiast"; the New York cast of *My Man* is listed in Mantle and Sherwood, *Best Plays of 1909–1919*, 425. Mantle and Sherwood attribute the play to Halsey and Edith Ellis.

137. "Fred Thompson to Retire from Show Business," *New York Review*, 26 November 1910, in Thompson and Dundy clipping file, TCNYPL. The *Review* was an arm of the Shubert brothers. On the history of the *Review* and the *New York Morning Telegraph*, see Maryann Chach, "Behind the Scenes of *The New York Review*," *Passing Show* 12 (fall 1989): 2–6.

138. "Thompson Won't Desert Theatre," *New York Morning Telegraph*, 9 December 1910, in Thompson clipping file, TCNYPL.
139. Thomas P. Hughes, *American Genesis: A Century of Invention and Technological Enthusiasm, 1870–1970* (New York: Viking, 1989), 55–61, 101–4.
140. For Thompson's aviation plans and career, see untitled clipping from *New York Morning Telegraph*, 25 September 1910, in Thompson and Dundy clipping file, TCNYPL. See the following articles in the *New York Times*: "Panama's Lonely Navy Now at Anchor Here," 4 April 1905, 8; and "Co-Operative Boarding-House Proves to Be a Genuine Success," 3 December 1916, part 2, 11. See also "Another Monoplane Enters Chicago Race," *New York Times*, 24 September 1910, 3; "Would Hire Grahame-White," *New York Times*, 25 September 1910, 16; "Aero Trust Formed to Manage Fliers," *New York Times*, 11 November 1910, 4; and "Breaks Aviation Trust," *New York Times*, 12 November 1910, 1.
141. "Luna Park Burns in Part, with All Coney Island in Danger," *New York Morning Telegraph*, 12 December 1911, in Thompson and Dundy clipping file, TCNYPL; "Slice of Luna Park Eaten Out by Fire," *New York Times*, 12 December 1911, 2. The plays destroyed were *Elizabeth's Chauffeur* by John McIntyre, and *The Flyers* by George Barr McCutcheon.
142. "Theatrical Factory," *New York Morning Telegraph*, 11 October 1908, in Thompson and Dundy clipping file, TCNYPL.
143. "Frederic Thompson Ill with Neuritis," *New York Morning Telegraph*, 28 December 1911; "Fred Thompson Badly Off," *New York Review*, 3 February 1912; both clippings in Thompson and Dundy clipping file, TCNYPL.
144. See the following records for the assignment of the Luna Park Company in the Office of the County Clerk, King's County Court House, Brooklyn, New York: assignment of Luna Park Company, filed on 3 April 1912; list of assets and liabilities, filed on 6 April 1912; order to pay delinquent state taxes, 15 August 1913; testimony of Roman Debes from a hearing on 11 January 1918, filed with the court on 18 March 1918; and testimony of Edwin T. Taliaferro, dated 1 February 1918.
145. "Thompson Is Retained as Manager of Luna," *New York Morning Telegraph*, 11 April 1912, in Thompson and Dundy clipping file, TCNYPL; Thompson's salary is listed in the affidavit of Roman Debes, August 1912, *In the Matter of Frederic Thompson, Bankrupt*, United States District Court for the Eastern District of New York, Brooklyn, New York; these records are stored at the National Archives and Records Administration, Bayonne, New Jersey.
146. See the following documents from *In the Matter of Frederic Thompson, Bankrupt*, United States District Court for the Eastern District of New York, Brooklyn, New York: affidavit of Roman Debes; schedule of unsecured debts; list of properties and assets; and report of Trustee's attorney, 23 June 1913. "Thompson Has $7,831 But Owes $664,854," *New York Times*, 9 June 1912, 5; Thompson, quoted in Pilat and Ranson, *Sodom by the Sea*, 156.

### Chapter 6: We're Playing Games

1. Frank Morton Todd, *The Story of the Exposition: Being the Official History of the International Celebration Held at San Francisco in 1915 to Commemorate the Discovery of the Pacific Ocean and the Construction of the Panama Canal* (New York: G. P. Putnam's Sons, Knickerbocker Press, 1921), 1: 184–87, quotation on 187.

On Nordica, see Edward T. James, ed., *Notable American Women, 1607–1950* (Cambridge, Mass.: Harvard University Press, 1971), 2: 633–35. In 1911 the site of the fair had not yet been chosen, although Golden Gate Park was considered a favorite; as it turned out, however, Taft broke ground in the wrong place.

2. "Seeds of Toyland Planted; 'Kids' Revel in Rare Treat," *San Francisco Chronicle*, 14 October 1913, 4; "First Fair Concession Is Dedicated; Children Loath to Bury Pretty Toys," *San Francisco Examiner*, 14 October 1913, 3; Todd, *Story of the Exposition*, 2: 153.

3. On Victorian expositions, see James Gilbert, "World's Fairs as Historical Events," in *Fair Representations: World's Fairs and the Modern World*, edited by Robert W. Rydell and Nancy Gwinn (Amsterdam: VU University Press, 1994), 13–27. On expositions as "colossal" universities, see the discussion in chap. 2; the quotation appears in "Some Information Regarding the Pan-American Exposition," in the promotional release collected as Pan-American Exposition literature, New York Public Library.

4. Elizabeth N. Armstrong, "Hercules and the Muses: Public Art at the Fair," 114-15, quotation on 114, and George Starr, "Truth Unveiled: The Fair and Its Interpreters," 138–54, in *The Anthropology of World's Fairs: San Francisco's Panama Pacific International Exposition of 1915*, edited by Burton Benedict (London and Berkeley: Lowie Museum of Anthropology, Scolar Press, 1983).

5. Eugen Neuhaus, "The Architecture of the Exposition," *University of California Chronicle* 17 (July 1915): 292.

6. "'Toyland' at the Panama Fair," *Playthings* 12 (July 1914): 76.

7. "Toyland Grown Up," *New York World*, 28 September 1913, magazine, 12.

8. Fred Thompson, "Fooling the Public," *Delineator* 69 (February 1907): 265. For Thompson's marginality, see the discussion of the Pan-American exposition in chap. 2.

9. Pauline Jacobson, "Forty Winks at the Exposition," *San Francisco Bulletin*, 13 February 1915, 13.

10. Katherine Dunlap Cather, "Titania's Playground: A Glimpse of the Panama Exposition," *St. Nicholas* 42 (April 1915): 524.

11. Jacobson, "Forty Winks at the Exposition."

12. See, for instance, the description of the lighting as a "glimpse into fairyland" in James B. Haynes, *History of the Trans-Mississippi and International Exposition of 1898* (St. Louis: Woodward and Tieman Printing, 1910), 137.

13. "Salesgirls in Costume," *Playthings* 25 (October 1927): 69.

14. Todd, *Story of the Exposition*, 1: xv. For a description of some of the fair's executives, see Robert Rydell, *All the World's a Fair: Visions of Empire at American International Expositions, 1876–1916* (Chicago: University of Chicago Press, 1984), 213.

15. Neuhaus, "Architecture of the Exposition," 294.

16. Todd, *Story of the Exposition*, 1: 282–85, 300.

17. Bacon, quoted in "Gems of Art Will Bedeck San Francisco's Exposition Robe," *New York Tribune*, 27 October 1912, part 2, 1, 7, clipping in Architectural Commission file, carton 27, Panama-Pacific International Exposition Collection, Bancroft Library, University of California, Berkeley (hereinafter cited as PPIEBL); Gray Brechin, "Sailing to Byzantium: The Architecture of the Fair," in Benedict, *Anthropology of World's Fairs*, 94–113. Bernard Maybeck's Palace of Fine Arts, as many critics have observed, was a departure from the neoclassical

norm of the rest of the exposition city; Todd, *Story of the Exposition*, 1: 287–89, quotations on 288, 287.

18. Neuhaus, "Architecture of the Exposition," 294; Todd, *Story of the Exposition*, 2: 353–58, 364, 372.

19. "Chief of Concessions Named; Frank Burt of Denver Chosen," *San Francisco Call*, 17 October 1912, 3; Todd, *Story of the Exposition*, 2: 155.

20. Chester H. Liebs, *Main Street to Miracle Mile: American Roadside Architecture* (Baltimore: Johns Hopkins University Press, 1995), 49.

21. Walter D'Arcy Ryan, "Illumination of the Panama-Pacific International Exposition," *General Electric Review* 18 (June 1915): 579–80.

22. Todd, *Story of the Exposition*, 2: 155; for descriptions of the amusements, see 2: 350–67.

23. Stella G. S. Perry, *The Sculpture and Murals of the Panama-Pacific International Exposition* (San Francisco: Wahlgreen, 1915), 1.

24. Cora Lenore Williams, *The Fourth-Dimensional Reaches of the Exposition* (San Francisco: Paul Elder, 1915), 7–16, quotations on 16, 9.

25. "A City of Lovely Light," *San Francisco Examiner*, 21 February 1915, magazine, n.p.

26. "Fred Thompson's Reception," *New York Morning Telegraph*, 1 January 1913, Thompson and Dundy clipping file, TCNYPL.

27. "Fred Thompson Quits Luna Park and Moves to San Francisco," *New York Morning Telegraph*, 16[?] July 1913, and "Frederic Thompson Busy," *New York Morning Telegraph*, 29 August 1913, Thompson and Dundy clipping file, TCNYPL; Todd, *Story of the Exposition*, 2: 93, 148; Minutes of the Division of Concessions and Admissions, vol. 122, 16 and 22 July 1913, PPIEBL; "Frederic Thompson in Town," *New York Morning Telegraph*, 2 September 1913, Thompson and Dundy clipping file, TCNYPL.

28. Memorandum from Frank Burt to R. B. Hale, 26 November 1913, 2, in Concessions and Admissions file, October 1911–November 1916, carton 69, PPIEBL; "Interesting Incident," *Billboard*, 3 July 1915, 36; biography of Burt, 5 December 1914, in historian's file "Bios A-K," carton 163, PPIEBL; Todd, *Story of the Exposition*, 2: 93. Burt recommended that the exposition lend the Toyland Company money at several crucial junctures leading up to its opening. For example, see Burt's letter to M. J. Brandenstein, 14 May 1914, Concessions and Admissions file, carton 28, PPIEBL. According to a memorandum prepared by Burt, the centerpiece of Toyland was supposed to be Fire and Sword, which Thompson had staged at Luna in 1913, a circus hippodrome, and A Trip to the Moon. It is doubtful, however, that Thompson actually owned the Moon Trip amusement, which still was operating at Luna Park. Burt's memorandum of 26 November 1913 estimates Toyland's projected cost at $750,000; the Gates connection is cited in a letter from J. H. Bragg to R. B. Hale, 28 May 1915, in Concessions and Admissions file, carton 28, PPIEBL. For Gates's obituary, see "J. W. Gates Dead; Ill for Months in Paris," *New York Times*, 9 August 1911, 9.

29. Letters from F. S. Brittain to R. B. Hale, 15 and 19 May 1914, 27 October 1914, in Concessions and Admissions file, October 1911–November 1916, carton 69, PPIEBL; "Toyland Is Taken from Thompson," *San Francisco Examiner*, 15 May 1914, 3; "Toyland Is Thompson's Realm Again," *San Francisco Examiner*, 20 May 1914, 6.

30. *Final Financial Report in Condensed Exhibition of All Construction Costs, Operating Receipts and Disbursements, and Expenses of Liquidation and Site Restoration, Embracing the Transactions of Pre-Exposition Period—March 22, 1910, to Feb. 19, 1915; Exposition Period—February 20, 1915, to Dec. 4, 1915; Post-Exposition Period—Dec. 5, 1915, to Dec. 31, 1919* (San Francisco: Panama-Pacific International Exposition, 1921), 55, 63, 96. According to this document, the Toyland Company lost $73,386 with gross receipts of $80,584; the loss figure seems astonishingly low. I am grateful to the late Ronald Mahoney of the Henry Madden Library, California State University, Fresno, for providing me with this material.

31. Report of the Assistant Director, Division of Concessions and Admissions, Pre-Exposition Period, prepared for historian Todd, 13 December 1915, carton 28, PPIEBL.

32. Letter from Frederic Thompson to Charles C. Moore, 2 October 1913, C. C. Moore "Personal" file "T," carton 25, PPIEBL.

33. "First Fair Concession Is Dedicated."

34. "Frederic Thompson Busy."

35. "Toyland Grown Up," 12.

36. J. M. Barrie, *Peter Pan, or The Boy Who Would Not Grow Up*, act 4, in *The Plays of J. M. Barrie in One Volume* (New York: Charles Scribner's Sons, 1948), 74.

37. "'Toyland' at the Panama Fair," 76.

38. E. T. A. Hoffmann, *Nutcracker*, translated by Ralph Manheim (New York: Crown, 1984), 1–2, 8–10; quotation from the scenario reprinted in Roland John Wiley, *Tchaikovsky's Ballets: Swan Lake, Sleeping Beauty, Nutcracker* (Oxford: Clarendon Press, 1985), 335.

39. "Toyland Grown Up," 12; "Close Watch Kept on Fair Concessions," *San Francisco Examiner*, 26 December 1913, 34.

40. Jacobson, "Forty Winks at the Exposition."

41. "Joy Zone at Panama-Pacific International Exposition Vast and Entrancing Wonderland of Amusement Creations," *San Francisco Chronicle*, 16 January 1915, Exposition Joy Zone section, n.p.

42. Toyland letterhead can be seen in the letter from Frederic Thompson to C. C. Moore, 2 October 1913.

43. "Close Watch Kept on Fair Concessions."

44. See the illustrations "Toyland Grown-Up" and "Cafe of the Grand Hotel, Toyland," Department of Special Collections, Henry Madden Library, California State University, Fresno, (hereinafter cited as CSUF); see also illustrations accompanying "Toyland Grown Up," and especially the illustration printed with the Toyland advertisement "Frederic Thompson's Toyland Grown Up," *New York Sunday Telegraph*, 13 December 1914, section 4, 5; photographs in the Toyland photograph file, TCNYPL.

45. "Close Watch Kept on Fair Concessions."

46. See the following examples of Thompson's illustrations: "Toyland Grown-Up," "Band-Stand, Principality of Toyland G. U.," "The Town Pump, Principality of Toyland G. U.," CSUF; advertisement for "Frederic Thompson's Toyland Grown Up"; Gus R. Kinsley, "Playthings at the Panama Fair," *Playthings* 12 (October 1914): 96, 98. A photograph of Cobweb Lake in operation appears in "Toyland Grown-Up on May Day," *Toys and Novelties* 12 (May 1915): 27.

47. Quotation from "'Toyland' at the Panama Fair," 78. For illustrations of the Toy-

land Grand Hotel, see Thompson's sketch "Cafe of the Grand Hotel, Toyland;" "Toyland Grown Up;" and the photographs of Mother Hubbard's Cupboard in the photographic file for Toyland Grown Up, TCNYPL.

48. See illustration of "Toyland G. U. Hand Car Ride," CSUF. Even Thompson's sacrilege had its limitations; the church's steeple is topped with an asterisk instead of a cross.

49. "Monster Militant at Panama Fair," *Playthings* 12 (June 1914): 72; reprint of a letter from Charles T. Halliman to Frederick Thompson, 5 March 1915, in "The Billboard and Suffrage," *Billboard*, 10 April 1915, 43; clipping, "Fun at the Panama-Pacific Exposition," *Denver Post*, 28 February 1915, in Concessions and Admissions file, carton 28, PPIEBL.

50. See the following examples of Thompson's illustrations: "Toyland Grown-Up," "Band-Stand, Principality of Toyland G. U.," "The Town Pump, Principality of Toyland G. U.," "Toyland G. U. Hand Car Ride," CSUF.

51. See illustration of "Toyland Sausage Factory," San Francisco History Center, San Francisco Public Library, San Francisco, Calif.

52. Ralph H. Lutts, *The Nature Fakers: Wildlife, Science, and Sentiment* (Golden, Colo.: Fulcrum, 1990), esp. 69–100.

53. Benjamin Kline Hunnicutt, *Work without End: Abandoning Shorter Hours for the Right to Work* (Philadelphia: Temple University Press, 1988), 109–45.

54. See Richard Ohmann's chapter on the professional-managerial class in *Selling Culture: Magazines, Markets, and Class at the Turn of the Century* (London: Verso, 1996), 118–74.

55. Illustration, "The Wishing Well," CSUF.

56. Frederic Thompson, "Amusing People," *Metropolitan* 32 (August 1910): 607.

57. For a representation of the cultural primitivism of vanity, see one of the sculptural highlights of the fair, Robert I. Aitken's "Fountain of the Earth," which shows "Vanity" (a woman holding a mirror before her face) blind to the dangers that flank her: a male representation of "Greed," a man and woman embracing in "Sexual Love," and a woman alone with a child, demonstrating "mere Physical Parenthood without enlightenment." As the historian Todd interpreted the symbolic narrative, the "ultimate result" of this "complex, unending drama" was the victory of "reason and spirituality and ability for self-sacrifice." Typescript of meeting of the PPIE Architectural Commission, 14 August 1912, Architectural Commission file, carton 27, PPIEBL; Juliet James, *Palaces and Courts of the Exposition: A Handbook of the Architecture, Sculpture, and Mural Paintings, with Special Reference to the Symbolism* (San Francisco: California Book, 1915), 95–96 (photograph of "Dawn of Life" on 94); Stella G. S. Perry, *The Sculpture and Mural Decorations of the Exposition: A Pictorial Survey of the Art of the Panama-Pacific International Exposition* (San Francisco: Paul Elder, 1915), 74; Todd, *Story of the Exposition*, 2: 291-92.

58. "Playthings at the Panama Fair," 98.

59. Letter from F. S. Brittain to C. C. Moore, 19 February 1914, and Toyland Financing Statement, dated 18 February 1914, prepared by Frederic Thompson, both in Concessions and Admissions—Permit Policy file, carton 28, PPIEBL; letter from Frank Burt to M. J. Brandenstein, 14 May 1914.

60. Letters from F. S. Brittain to R. B. Hale, 15 and 19 May 1914, and 27 October 1914; "Toyland Is Taken from Thompson"; "Toyland Is Thompson's Realm Again."

61. Letter from Bragg to Hale, 28 May 1915. It is difficult to determine which of the amusements that Thompson planned were actually constructed. The promotions of Toyland published in the eastern press in late 1914 and the first six months of 1915 relied on the press material supplied by Thompson's publicity office, resulting in wholly unreliable descriptions such as that of Felix Koch in *Toys and Novelties*. The problem has been further complicated by the disposition of the Panama-Pacific's official records; many of the records relating to the Joy Zone have been destroyed.

62. Letter from E.W.A. Waterhouse to Harris H. D. Connick, 31 August 1914, Toyland concession file, carton 95, PPIEBL; letter from Bragg to Hale, 28 May 1915; letter from Burt to F. S. Brittain, 15 April 1915, Concessions and Admissions file, carton 69, PPIEBL. Burt, who stubbornly supported the Toyland concept, even traveled to Denver, where he had managed the Lakeside Park amusement park before going to San Francisco, to solicit investments from Colorado capitalists; he, too, found no buyers.

63. Todd, *Story of the Exposition*, 2: 350; "myth" quotation in letter from Burt to C. C. Moore, 16 July 1915, Concessions and Admissions file, carton 28, PPIEBL; "Fred Thompson Launches a Big Idea for Picturizing Stories from the Bible," *Brooklyn Daily Eagle*, 27 June 1915, section 2, 3; on Thompson's breakdown, see the following from Thompson and Dundy clipping file, TCNYPL: "Frederic Thompson Has Fighting Chance," *Brooklyn Daily Eagle*, 26 September 1915; "Fred Thompson in the Hospital," *New York Morning Telegraph*, 25 September 1915; "Frederic Thompson Is Operated Upon," *New York Morning Telegraph*, 12 October 1915; and untitled item from *New York Dramatic News*, 23 October 1915, stating that Thompson was cured and released from the hospital.

64. Report of the Assistant Director, Division of Concessions and Admissions, 13 December 1915.

65. Walter D'Arcy Ryan, "Illumination of the Panama-Pacific International Exposition," *Transactions of the Illuminating Engineering Society*, vol. 11, 30 August 1916, 631.

66. The best account of Guérin's career is Mark A. Hewitt, "Jules Guérin and the American Renaissance," in the exhibit catalogue, *Jules Guérin: Master Delineator* (Houston: Farish Gallery, Rice University, 1983), 5–13.

67. Todd, *Story of the Exposition*, 1: 347–53; Guérin, quoted in Elmer Grey, "The Panama-Pacific International Exposition of 1915," *Scribner's* 54 (July 1913): 48.

68. Todd, *Story of the Exposition*, 1: 289.

69. William Leach, *Land of Desire: Merchants, Power, and the Rise of a New American Culture* (New York: Pantheon, 1993), 75–78; Leach, "Strategists of Display and the Production of Desire," in *Consuming Visions: Accumulation and Display of Goods in America, 1880–1920*, edited by Simon J. Bronner (New York: W. W. Norton, 1989), 99–132; Matthew Luckiesh, *Color and Colors* (New York: D. Van Nostrand, 1938), 151–62; Edward L. Bernays, *Biography of an Idea: Memoirs of Public Relations Counsel Edward L. Bernays* (New York: Simon and Schuster, 1965), 306–9.

70. Rilla Evelyn Jackman, *American Arts* (Chicago: Rand McNally, 1929), 232.

71. Leach, *Land of Desire*, 108–11, Hichens quoted on 109.

72. Hewitt, "Jules Guérin and the American Renaissance," 13.

73. Grey, "Panama-Pacific International Exposition of 1915," 48.

74. Jesse Lynch Williams, "The Color Scheme at the Panama-Pacific Exposition: A New Departure," *Scribner's* 56 (September 1914): 279.

75. Todd, *Story of the Exposition*, 1: 349.

76. Ryan, "Illumination of the Panama-Pacific International Exposition," 579; Matthew Luckiesh, *Artificial Light: Its Influence upon Civilization* (New York: Century, 1920), 306–7.

77. Ryan, "Illumination of the Panama-Pacific International Exposition," *Transactions*, 632–39.

78. See letter from Walter D'Arcy Ryan to Robert Sibley, n.d., General Electric-Illumination file, carton 85, PPIEBL.

79. Markham, quoted in Todd, *Story of the Exposition*, 2: 343.

80. Ryan, "Illumination of the Panama-Pacific International Exposition," *Transactions*, quotations on 631–34.

81. Todd, *Story of the Exposition*; quotations on 2: 342-47.

82. Ryan, "Illumination of the Panama-Pacific International Exposition," *Transactions*, 631. Unpublished reactions to Ryan's work are rare. Doris Barr Stanislawski, a middle-class girl who was fourteen in 1915, viewed Ryan's work exactly as he wished, although she seems practically to have transcribed her diary reaction to the exposition lighting from the descriptions in official brochures; see Stanislawski, "Life Books," vol. 6, n.p., Bancroft Library, University of California, Berkeley.

83. "A City of Lovely Light."

84. "Daylight at Night for City's Center," *San Francisco Examiner*, 23 January 1916, 1N-2N, merchant quoted on 1N; "Thousands Cheer Beauties of Path of Gold; Gasp at Wonders of Fairy Street," *San Francisco Examiner*, 5 October 1916, 13–14.

85. "Thousands Cheer Beauties of Path of Gold," 13.

86. The descriptions and quotations that follow are in "Santa and Toyland to Move into City," *New York Sun*, 20 April 1919, 10.

87. "'Kuties' on 'Kiddie Kars,'" *Playthings* 14 (December 1916): 102. See also the photograph of the Ziegfeld Midnight Frolic girls on jumping sticks in advertisement for Pogo Jumping Sticks, *Toys and Novelties* 18 (December 1921): 23.

88. "How American Toys Made Good," *Playthings* 17 (April 1919): 87; "We Are Proud of Our Veteran Toy Men," *Toys and Novelties* 14 (April 1917): 49; "Buyers Boost American Toys," *Toys and Novelties* 12 (July 1915): 34; "The Toy Trade," editorial, *Playthings* 9 (July 1911): 51.

89. Richard O'Brien, *The Story of American Toys, from the Puritans to the Present* (New York: Abbeville, 1990), 72–76; "Playthings Pioneers," *Playthings* 15 (January 1918): 66-77; August Belden, "When the Side-line Becomes the Big Profit Maker," *Printers' Ink* 125, 6 December 1923, 73–76.

90. "The Toy Trade," 51; "Toys in America," editorial, *Playthings* 8 (June 1910): 79; Robert H. McCready, "The Toy Department," *Playthings* 15 (December 1917): 10; Thomas K. Black, "Feature Blood Building Toys!" *Playthings* 18 (May 1920): 99.

91. Susan Porter Benson, *Counter Cultures: Saleswomen, Managers, and Customers in American Department Stores, 1890–1940* (Urbana: University of Illinois Press, 1986), 31–74, 124–76; on the cost of female labor, see 23. Men who embodied these "womanly" qualities were conventionally denominated "sissies." See E. Anthony Rotundo, *American Manhood: Transformations in Masculinity from the Revolution to the Modern Era* (New York: Basic Books, 1993), 273.

92. On the problems of "sincerity" in the early republic, see Karen Halttunen, *Confidence Men and Painted Women: A Study of Middle-Class Culture in America, 1830–1870* (New Haven: Yale University Press, 1982), 33–55.

93. "The Toy Trade Today," *Playthings* 8 (November 1910): 36–41, quotation on 37.

94. On the effeminacy of milliners, see Roscoe Conkling's 1877 denunciation of liberal Republicans as "man-milliners, the dilettanti and carpet knights of politics" (quoted in Rotundo, *American Manhood*, 271); "The Question Box: That Man in the Department," *Toys and Novelties* 9 (September 1913): 36.

95. "Toys Bring Children's Trade; Why the Youngsters Are the Best Spenders," *Toys and Novelties* 9 (June 1913): 70; "Going After Toy Business," *Toys and Novelties* 12 (July 1915): 44–45; "What Has the Future in Store?" *Playthings* 9 (January 1911): 51–52; Robert H. McCready, "The American Toy Industry," *Playthings* 22 (January 1924): 308.

96. There are many sources on manhood and "enslavement." For a recent treatment in relation to "labor Republicanism," see Paul Krause, *The Battle for Homestead, 1880–1892: Politics, Culture, and Steel* (Pittsburgh: University of Pittsburgh Press, 1992).

97. "Editorial Comment," *Playthings* 17 (January 1920): 227–28; advertisement for Erector, *Toys and Novelties* 15 (January 1918): 19; "Toy Fair Wonderful Success," *Toys and Novelties* 17 (February 1920): 200; "At the Threshold of a New Era," *Toys and Novelties* 16 (January 1919): 129.

98. "The 'Oasis' of the Mercantile World," *Playthings* 7 (February 1909): 66.

99. Gail Bederman, *Manliness and Civilization: A Cultural History of Gender and Race in the United States, 1880–1917* (Chicago: University of Chicago Press, 1995), 37.

100. "Sentimental business" would have seemed unnatural in a culture that honored the independence of "masculine achievers." See Bruce Dorsey, "A Youthful and Useful Manhood: Young Men's Reform Societies in Jacksonian Philadelphia," paper presented at the 1993 conference of the Organization of American Historians (in author's possession).

101. Margaret Marsh, "Suburban Men and Masculine Domesticity, 1870–1915," in *Meanings for Manhood: Constructions of Masculinity in Victorian America*, edited by Mark C. Carnes and Clyde Griffen (Chicago: University of Chicago Press, 1990), 111–27.

102. L. Shoneman, "The Fourteenth Street Store (N.Y.) Toy Department," *Playthings* 7 (December 1909): 35; "Salesgirls in Costume," 69.

103. Thompson used the same formula at the Toyland groundbreaking in 1913 and the next year, when he marked the start of construction by having four grown "girls" rub an enormous Aladdin's lamp to conjure up his playland venture. See "Girls Rub Aladdin's Lamp; Toyland Looms," *San Francisco Examiner*, 2 July 1914, 5.

104. Leonard S. Marcus, *The American Store Window* (New York: Whitney Library of Design, 1978), 12–13; "To Suit Every Fancy," *New York Times*, 27 November 1888, 8.

105. Warfield Webb, "Christmas in Chicago," *Playthings* 10 (December 1912): 45; "Christmas Displays in New York," *Playthings* 10 (December 1912): 41–42; Sidney J. Rockwell, "The Christmas Displays of New York," *Playthings* 13 (December 1915): 52–58, quotations on 52, 55, 54.

106. On toy spectacles outside major cities, see "'Santa Claus Arrival' in Boonville,

Mo.," *Playthings* 11 (January 1913): 117–18. The Marshall Field store in Chicago was remarkable for its refusal to join in on the dramatization of toys and Christmas. Its toy merchandising perennially emphasized "a splendid, dignified simplicity which is the height of good taste." See "Marshall Field Merchandising," *Playthings* 10 (May 1912): 46–49, quotation on 46.

107. "Essentials in the Toy Department Interior," *Toys and Novelties* 9 (June 1913): 44; "Pointers from the Macy Toy Section," *Toys and Novelties* 9 (September 1913): 30. The word "sordid" was used frequently to describe merchandising outside the toy department. See "Little Schemes Which Draw the Children," *Toys and Novelties* 9 (July 1913): 26.

108. "From a Success Note Book," *Toys and Novelties* 9 (June 1913): 63; Bloomingdale's ad, *Toys and Novelties* 16 (January 1919): 128; "Capitalize Toy Atmosphere," *Playthings* 15 (March 1917): 78; "A 'Real Estate' Development," *Playthings* 14 (January 1916): 87–88.

109. Benson, *Counter Cultures*, 83.

110. "'Oasis' of the Mercantile World," 66; F. W. Trumpore, "Confessions of a Reformed Toy Buyer," *Toys and Novelties* 15 (February 1918): 157; "The 'Art' in Toy Selling," *Playthings* 25 (July 1927): 73; Miriam Formanek-Brunell, *Made to Play House: Dolls and the Commercialization of American Girhood, 1830–1930* (New Haven: Yale University Press, 1993), 57–58; Rotundo, *American Manhood*, 36–67.

111. The other eleven, from W. Barrett Hankins, "Toy Talks," *Toys and Novelties* 15 (August 1918): 42, were as follows:

   1. Love for children
   2. Patience
   3. Happy and friendly disposition
   4. Delight in seeing children happy
   5. Believe the child has a right to express his wants
   6. Can see enjoyment in toys, even though yourself a "grown-up"
   7. Believe you have some idea of what children think of and like at different ages
   8. Can forget the child's appearance—can see all children as children and love them for what they are
   9. Really want to aid in anything that will assist the child to develop physically, mentally and morally
  10. Believe the child is a national institution and the future of the American home depends upon what the child of today, is tomorrow—a grown-up
  11. Believe it good policy for any business to encourage a friendly relation with the child.

112. Warfield Webb, "Christmas in Chicago," *Playthings* 9 (December 1911): 56; "Flapper Filosofy by Sunshine Sue (The Girl behind the Toy Counter)," *Toys and Novelties* 26 (October 1929): 58; Marie H. Anderson, "You Must Put Heart Interest into Your Toy Advertising," *Playthings* 19 (August 1921): 86–87; "'Oasis' of the Mercantile World," 66.

113. Richard Wightman Fox, "The Discipline of Amusement," in *Inventing Times Square: Commerce and Culture at the Crossroads of the World*, edited by William R. Taylor (Baltimore: Johns Hopkins University Press, 1996), 97.

114. "The Fine Art of Helping Children Buy Toys," *Toys and Novelties* 24 (December

1927): 211. On lopsided friendships, see T. H. Breen and Stephen Innes, *"Myne Owne Ground": Race and Freedom on Virginia's Eastern Shore, 1640–1676* (New York: Oxford University Press, 1980), 32–35. I have been influenced by Donald Meyer's examination of Dale Carnegie and the era of salesmanship and administration in *The Positive Thinkers: Popular Religious Psychology from Mary Baker Eddy to Norman Vincent Peale and Ronald Reagan* (1965; reprint, Middletown, Conn.: Wesleyan University Press, 1988), esp. 177–94, and Warren Susman, "The Culture of the Thirties," in *Culture As History: The Transformation of American Society in the Twentieth Century* (New York: Pantheon, 1984), 150–83. See also Dale Carnegie, *How to Win Friends and Influence People* (1936; reprint, New York: Pocket Books, 1981), esp. 3–50.

115. "Cincinnati Store Pays Fine Tribute to Its Toy Buyer," *Toys and Novelties* 24 (November 1927): 66–67.

116. Robert H. McCready, "Children's Day a New Era in Toy Selling," *Playthings* 25 (July 1927): 146.

117. "The Little Girl's Doll," *Playthings* 8 (January 1910): 75; "A Little Knowledge Is a Dangerous Thing," *Playthings* 7 (January 1909): 63.

118. "Every Toy Salesman Should Know," *Playthings* 17 (November 1919): 94; "Toy Problems Get 'Lead-Editorial' Attention in Metropolitan Newspaper," *Playthings* 19 (January 1921): 352.

119. William Leach, "Child World in the Promised Land," in *The Mythmaking Frame of Mind: Social Imagination and American Culture*, edited by James Gilbert et al. (Belmont, Calif.: Wadsworth, 1993), 226–34.

120. "Editorial Comment," *Playthings* 18 (January 1920): 227-28; advertisement reprinted in *Toys and Novelties* 17 (December 1920): 130; on "useful play," see McCready, "American Toy Industry," 308. On the "manliness" of civilization, see Bederman, *Manliness and Civilization*.

121. These ads are reprinted in *Toys and Novelties* 16 (October 1919): 70–73.

122. "At the Threshold of a New Era," *Toys and Novelties* 16 (January 1919): 129; "Lord and Taylor Plans to Do Business Twelve Months a Year," *Toys and Novelties* 16 (April 1919): 59; H. E. Rodenbaugh, "New York Stores Have Greatest Toy Season," *Toys and Novelties* 16 (January 1919): 127; "Uninterrupted Toy Season Assured," *Toys and Novelties* 15 (September 1918): 29; "How American Toys Made Good," 87.

123. "Uninterrupted Toy Season Assured," 29; Rodenbaugh, "New York Stores Have Greatest Toy Season," 127; "Lord and Taylor Plans to Do Business Twelve Months a Year," 59; "How American Toys Made Good," 87; Ernest W. J. Hughes, "The American Child of Today Demands Better Toys," *Toys and Novelties* 17 (January 1920): 298.

124. According to "Why Doll Sales Are Increasing," *Toys and Novelties* 23 (March 1926): 138, 75 percent of domestic doll sales were foreign made prior to the war.

125. "Why the American Doll Leads the World," *Toys and Novelties* 20 (May 1923): 51. See also Dorothy Lucas, "Dolls No Longer Mere Dolls—They are 'Humans,'" *Toys and Novelties* 23 (January 1926): 291–92; "How American Toys Made Good," 87.

126. M. Michtom, "Must Educate Public to Superiority of the American Product," *Toys and Novelties* 15 (June 1918): 46. Also see "Why the American Doll Leads the World," 51–52.

127. "How American Toys Made Good," 88–89. Such discourse about "real" and "unreal" dolls also reflected the more general movement within the industry, between 1860 and 1930, toward an aesthetic of realism in doll making. See Formanek-Brunell, *Made to Play House*, 1-4, 35–60, 135–60.

128. "Salesgirls in Costume," 69; Anderson, "You Must Put Heart Interest into Your Toy Advertising," 86–87. As one "Successful Middle Western Toy Buyer" claimed, it was a mistake to try to sell adults on the "constructive" qualities of toys, how they "would help the children grow up to be sturdy men and women.... The vast majority of toys, I feel sure, are purchased by the grown folks because the purchasers feel that the toys will please and amuse the youngsters." See "What I've Learned by My Mistakes," *Toys and Novelties* 20 (March 1923): 107.

129. Advertisement for Structo, *Toys and Novelties* 14 (April 1917): 32–33.

130. Advertisement for Gilbert Toys, *New York Times*, 19 December 1920, part 7, 5. Erector, like its competitor Structo, reflected and encouraged the imperial ambitions of American culture during that era. An ad for Structo in 1915 hailed playing boys as "Empire Builders." See *Toys and Novelties* 12 (November 1915): 45.

131. A. C. Gilbert with Marshall McClintock, *The Man Who Lives in Paradise: The Autobiography of A. C. Gilbert* (New York: Rinehart, 1954), 150–156, quotation on 156.

132. Gilbert, *Man Who Lives in Paradise*, 18, 16.

133. Gilbert, *Man Who Lives in Paradise*, 19, 21.

134. Gilbert, *Man Who Lives in Paradise*, 69-85, 104–16, quotations on 83. Alfred C. Gilbert, "Are You a Booster or a Knocker?" *Playthings* 18 (February 1920): 231.

135. Gilbert, *Man Who Lives in Paradise*, 19, Mysto ad on 106. See the following catalogues collected on microfilm as "Conjuring: A Collection of Pamphlets" (1979) in TCNYPL: the Mysto Manufacturing Company, *Mysto Magic* (New Haven, Conn.: Mysto Manufacturing, 1911), cover, 2–3; "pleasant fraud" in Donald Holmes Alsdorf, *Tricks and Conjuring Apparatus for Parlor and Stage* (Kansas City, Mo.: Donald Holmes Alsdorf, 1916), 2, and Hornmann Magic Company, *The Twentieth-Century Wonders, Illustrated and Descriptive: The Latest European Novelties, Magical Effects, etc., the Latest Books, Music, and Stage Instructions* (New York: Hornmann Magic Company, 1916).

136. Gilbert, *Man Who Lives in Paradise*, 115, quotations on 119, 123. A slightly different account attributing the inspiration to "an overhead signal stand of structural iron" appears in "Fine Tribute to A. C. Gilbert by American Magazine," *Toys and Novelties* 20 (December 1923): 165.

137. Gilbert, *Man Who Lives in Paradise*, 135-39; Roland Cole, "Gilbert, Maker of Scientific Toys," *Printers' Ink Monthly* 2 (January 1921): 96.

138. See Erector ad reprinted in *Playthings* 14 (October 1916): 82; Gilbert, *Man Who Lives in Paradise*, 130, 131; Cole, "Gilbert, Maker of Scientific Toys," 96; "Gilbert Talks on Scientific Toys," *Playthings* 18 (April 1920): 89. Gilbert's secret, so he claimed, was that he was a boy at heart; when he announced innovations to Erector in 1924, he explained that "for these last two years I have been a boy again, building models which far surpass any models ever built with any construction toy." See ad in *Playthings* 22 (January 1924): 35.

139. "Toys Are 'Essential' So Long As There Are Children in the World," *Toys and Novelties* 15 (July 1918): 26; advertisement for Gilbert Toys, *Toys and Novelties* 15 (August 1918): 21; "This Is the Revised Order of the Council of National De-

fense," *Toys and Novelties* 15 (September 1918): 29; Gilbert, *Man Who Lives in Paradise*, 145–57, quotations on 155, 156, 157. Gilbert used essentially the same strategy in 1921 in testifying for tariff protection for the American toy industry against German competition. "It is our purpose to couple fun and education," he told the Senate Committee on Finance. Robert McCready, editor of *Playthings*, similarly argued that American toys "lay the foundation for lives of usefulness" and deserve protection from cheap German manufacturing. See United States Senate, *Hearings on the Proposed Tariff Act of 1921*, 67th Congress, 2d session, 1921–22, Senate Documents, vol. 5, part 5 (Washington, D.C.: Government Printing Office, 1922), 4088, 4095.

140. "Fine Tribute to A. C. Gilbert by American Magazine," 166.

141. John Monk Saunders, "Tony Sarg Has Never Done a Stroke of Work in His Life," *American* 101 (May 1926): 27–28; *The Tony Sarg Marionette Book* (New York: Huebsch, 1921), 3.

142. Anne Stoddard, "The Renaissance of the Puppet Play," *Century* 96 (June 1918): 177; *Tony Sarg Marionette Book*, 4–6.

143. *Tony Sarg Marionette Book*, 6.

144. "The Little Theatre," *International Drama* 47 (October 1912): lxviii; Mary Cass Canfield, "Reflections on Tony Sarg's Marionettes," in *Grotesques and Other Reflections* (New York: Harper and Bros., 1927), 191.

145. A good example of the open highway between high and low culture was the midget troupe Ames hired in 1914 for *Snow White and the Seven Dwarfs* at the Little Theatre. The midgets had appeared the previous summer at Luna Park; after *Snow White*, they were heading to San Francisco for a forty-week engagement at Toyland Grown Up. "P.P.I.E. News," *Billboard* 37, 30 January 1915, 15; "Midgets for Thompson's Toyland," *Billboard* 27, 6 February 1915, 28.

146. See programs for the Neighborhood Playhouse, 29–30 December 1917, and 5–6 January 1918, in Tony Sarg Scrapbook, TCNYPL; Fred J. McIsaac, "Tony Sarg," *Drama* 12 (December 1921): 83, in Tony Sarg Scrapbook, TCNYPL; Tamara Robin Hunt, *Tony Sarg: Puppeteer in America, 1915–1942* (North Vancouver, B.C.: Charlemagne Press, 1988), 42, 55; Stoddard, "Renaissance," 174, 175.

147. *Tony Sarg Marionette Book*, 8; Hunt, *Tony Sarg*, 13; "A Man Who Plays with Dolls, and Admits It," *Literary Digest* 94, 30 July 1927, 60.

148. "Dolls As Fads," *Toys and Novelties* 19 (March 1922): 81.

149. Clayton Hamilton, "In Praise of Puppet-Theatres," *Seen on the Stage* (New York: Henry Holt, 1920), 112; Saunders, "Tony Sarg Has Never Done a Stroke of Work in His Life," 26; Phil C. Humphrey, "Tony Sarg Talks about Puppets and Chalk," *Institute Magazine* (n.d.), 17, in Tony Sarg Collection, 1905–63, Museum Archives, Detroit Institute of Arts, Detroit, Michigan (hereinafter cited as TSC); "How Puppets Surpass Our Human Actors," *Current Opinion* 64 (April 1918): 257.

150. Clipping, Redfern Mason, "Marionettes in Rip Van Winkle Delight Crowd," *San Francisco Examiner*, 20[?] December 1925 [?], TSC.

151. See the following in *New York Times*: "Childhood Tales Brought to Life," 26 November 1923, 17; Macy's advertisement, 24 November 1923, 5; "Greet Santa Claus As 'King of Kiddies,'" 28 November 1924, 15; "Santa Claus Appears in Christmas Parade," 27 November 1925, 2; "Alters Macy Parade Plan," 23 November 1926, 19; Macy's advertisement, 25 November 1926, 17. See also Harriet Thorndyke, "Tony and the Balloons," *Family Circle*, 23 November 1934, in TSC.

On the origins of Macy's balloons, see Bil Baird, *The Art of the Puppet* (New York: Macmillan, 1965), 179–80; Baird worked for Sarg during this period and coordinated the balloon productions.

152. Saunders, "Tony Sarg Has Never Done a Stroke of Work in His Life," 105–6; Anne Stoddard, "The Story of Tony Sarg and His Varied Art Activities," *Mentor* 16 (May 1928): 25.

153. See various promotional material in TSC, including "Tony Sarg Grotesques," "Tony Sarg's Little Theatre," and flyer advertising Sarg as a speaker and humorist. Also, "Tony Sarg," *Industrian* (n.d.), in TSC; clipping of Sarg advertisement for Dairylea evaporated milk, in TSC; clipping of "Magic Midget Theater," *New York Sun*, 25 March 1928[?], in TSC; and Stoddard, "Story of Tony Sarg," 23–30. On cereal, Camel, Franklin Simon, and Macy's, see Hunt, *Tony Sarg*, 34–35, 148. On Bullock's, see "Treasure Trove Is Bullock's Feature," *Toy World* 1 (November 1927): 25.

154. Hunt, *Tony Sarg*, 62–63, 66; Baird, *Art of the Puppet*, 181. Hunt reports another estimate that ten million people watched the Century of Progress shows.

155. Saunders, "Tony Sarg Has Never Done a Stroke of Work in His Life," 26; testimonials given at the death of Sarg by Bil Baird, Jean Gros, Helen Livers, Hettie Louise Mick, Dave Pritchard, and Ellen Van Volkenburg, 1–5, TSC.

156. Saunders, "Tony Sarg Has Never Done a Stroke of Work in His Life," 28.

*Chapter 7: A Kindergarten Preacher in Toys*

1. On Thompson's death, see "Frederic Thompson Operated on Again," *New York Times*, 3 June 1919, 13; "Frederic Thompson Worse," *New York Times*, 4 June 1919, 17; "Frederic Thompson, Show Builder, Dies," *New York Times*, 7 June 1919, 13; "Frederic Thompson Dies in Hospital," *New York Sun*, 7 June 1919, 9; "Mr. Frederic W. Thompson, Who Built the Hippodrome and Luna Park, Dies," *New York Herald*, 7 June 1919, 4; "Frederic Thompson, Luna Builder, Dies after 17 operations," *New York Tribune*, 7 June 1919, 8.

2. See untitled clipping from *New York Star*, 7 April 1920, in Thompson and Dundy clipping file, TCNYPL.

3. "Honor Thompson, Amusement Builder," *New York Times*, 7 June 1922, 6. The inscription was taken from the monument, which can be found with the assistance of the Woodlawn Cemetery staff.

4. Frances A. Groff, "Exposition Moths," *Sunset* 35 (July 1915): 135, 138.

5. The Report of the Westchester County Park Commission to the Board of Supervisors of the County of Westchester, State of New York, 1928, 10, identifies the total appropriation of $4.1 million for the project, which included a much larger park. Newspaper accounts, however, put a higher price tag on Playland: "New $5,000,000 Playground Is Opened at Rye," *New York Tribune*, 27 May 1928, Playland Opening file, folder 10, Westchester County Property Records, Westchester County Historical Society (hereinafter cited as WCHS).

6. On suburbanization in general, see Kenneth T. Jackson, *Crabgrass Frontier: The Suburbanization of the United States* (New York: Oxford University Press, 1985); on "automobility" and Westchester parkways, see 157–71.

7. On the collaboration of governments with private consumer industries, see William Leach, *Land of Desire: Merchants, Power, and the Rise of a New American Culture* (New York: Pantheon, 1993) 349–78.

8.  Frederic Thompson, "Amusing People," *Metropolitan* 32 (August 1910): 601; Jean Robertson, "Press Day at Playland Reveals Park's Wonders," *Bronxville Press*, 29 May 1928, Park Commission clippings, WCHS.

9.  "The Kiddie Park," *Showman* 1, 30 May 1925, 24.

10. "New $5,000,000 Playground Is Opened at Rye"; letter, chief engineer to George H. Covey, superintendent, 3d district, Katonah, New York, 8 May 1928, Playland Opening file, folder 10, Westchester County Property Records, WCHS.

11. "Well What's This?" *New York World*, 17 May 1908, Locke Scrapbook, vol. 448, TCNYPL.

12. Report of the Westchester County Park Commission to the Board of Supervisors of the County of Westchester, State of New York, 1928, 31.

13. William Leach, "Child World in the Promised Land," in *The Mythmaking Frame of Mind: Social Imagination and American Culture*, edited by James Gilbert et al. (Belmont, Calif: Wadsworth, 1993) 212–13.

14. Memorandum to Jay Downer, chief engineer of Westchester County Park Commission, from Frank Darling, 2 August 1929, Parks Department Property Records, series 149; "Coney Island of the Future," *Rye Chronicle*, 15 August 1927, Park Commission clippings, WCHS.

15. For views and descriptions of the park and information on its "landmark" designation, see the Rye Playland website: http://www.ryeplayland.org/.

16. See "Downer Advocates More Widespread Building of Parks," *Hastings News*, n.d., Park Commission clippings, WCHS.

17. The bet appeared initially to pay off. In 1930 alone, 4.6 million clicked the turnstiles; most were from the leafy northern suburbs rather than from the crowded inner city of New York. Report of the Westchester County Park Commission to the Board of Supervisors of the County of Westchester, State of New York 1930, 104, WCHS.

18. Cindy S. Aron, *Working at Play: A History of Vacations in the United States* (New York: Oxford University Press, 1999).

19. For a recent and brief account of Disneyland, see Steven Watts, *The Magic Kingdom: Walt Disney and the American Way of Life* (Boston: Houghton Mifflin, 1997), 383–403, quotation on 389.

20. Martha Wolfenstein, "The Emergence of Fun Morality," reprinted in *Mass Leisure*, edited by Eric Larrabee and Rolf Meyersohn (Glencoe, Ill.: Free Press, 1958), 86–96, quotation on 92. Wolfenstein based most of her argument on 1940s child-rearing literature, especially the *Infant Care* bulletin of the federal Children's Bureau.

21. Barbara Ehrenreich, *The Hearts of Men: American Dreams and the Flight from Commitment* (Garden City, N.Y.: Anchor Books, 1983), esp. 42–51, quotations on 11–12, 50.

22. Ehrenreich, *Hearts of Men*, 46; Thompson, "Amusing People," 602.

23. On the evolution of this idea of passionate male friendships in the twentieth century, see E. Anthony Rotundo, *American Manhood: Transformations in Masculinity from the Revolution to the Modern Era* (New York: Basic Books, 1993), esp. 239–44; for an older, "Enlightenment" ideal of friendship, see Frank Lambert, "Subscribing for Profits and Piety: The Friendship of Benjamin Franklin and George Whitefield," *William and Mary Quarterly*, 3d series, 50 (July 1993): 544–48.

24. Ehrenreich, *Hearts of Men*, 51; on "American Girl," see Thompson, "Amusing People," 601.

25. William J. O'Malley, "The Peter Pan Syndrome," *Spirituality for Today* 1, no. 2 (1995), http://www.spirituality.org/issue02/page06.html.

26. Dan Kiley, *The Peter Pan Syndrome: Men Who Have Never Grown Up* (New York: Dodd, Mead, 1983), 22–37, quotations on 22–23, 28, 30.

27. Kiley, *Peter Pan Syndrome*, 215-23, quotations on 223, 218.

28. Larry's story appears in the chapter "For the Victims," in Kiley, *Peter Pan Syndrome*, 254-74, quotations on 271, 272, 274.

29. "Dan Kiley, 54, Dies; Wrote 'Peter Pan Syndrome,'" *New York Times*, 27 February, 1996, B7.

30. John Bradshaw, *Homecoming: Reclaiming and Championing Your Inner Child* (New York: Bantam, 1992).

31. Bradshaw, *Homecoming*, x-xvi, quotations on x, xv.

32. Bradshaw, *Homecoming*, 31–33, 193–201, quotations on 33, 198. Bradshaw does not claim to have invented the term "inner child." An early precursor (which is listed in Bradshaw's bibliography) was W. Hugh Missildine, *Your Inner Child of the Past*, originally published in 1963 (New York: Simon and Schuster). It, too, was a big seller; the dust jacket on my 1963 edition claims "over 150,000 copies sold." Missildine and Bradshaw have much in common, but the earlier author, with his advice on "setting firm limits" on the "inner child" and his assertion that "life itself is filled with struggle, its satisfactions are achieved in struggle," betrays concerns about scarcity and limitation that are largely missing from *Homecoming*; see *Your Inner Child of the Past*, 311, 305.

33. Bradshaw, *Homecoming*, 204, 175–76. The links between recovering the inner child, consumption, and personal power are underscored in the 2001 catalogue for the home furnishings retailer IKEA, which is subtitled, "Uncover your inner home." IKEA claims to bring inner and outer home into an empowering harmony: "Make the best use of your living space and you create a better space for living. Freeing your home of clutter makes it easy to get around, find what you need, feel like you're in control—and, in a very real way, provides true peace of mind" (5).

34. Lary May, *Screening Out the Past: The Birth of Mass Culture and the Motion Picture Industry* (Chicago: University of Chicago Press, 1983), 96–146.

35. In 1999, *Forbes* magazine listed Hanks, Spielberg, and Williams in the top twelve of its "Celebrity 100" list; in 2000, Hanks and Spielberg were in the top ten. For the lists, see the *Forbes* website: http://www.forbes.com.

36. On skeptical critics, see Philip M. Taylor, *Steven Spielberg: The Man, His Movies, and Their Meaning* (New York: Continuum, 1994), 19–227; Joseph McBride, *Steven Spielberg: A Biography* (New York: Da Capo, 1999), 258–59, 426–27; Richard Corliss and Jeffrey Ressner, "Peter Pan Grows Up," *Time* 149, 19 May 1997, 75–82.

37. According to the *Los Angeles Times*, the film grossed in excess of a hundred million dollars. See "Best Box Office in 1988," 8 January 1989, in *Big* clipping file, TCNYPL.

38. Anne Spielberg conjectured in *Premiere* magazine, "maybe I'm always writing about Steve." See review, *Village Voice*, 7 June 1988, in Collection of Newspaper Clippings of Moving Picture Criticism, 1988 A-B, TCNYPL. For reviews, see the

articles collected in *Big* clipping file, TCNYPL, including, for a dissenting review, Lloyd Sachs, "'Big' Yields Small Returns Despite Its Talented Cast," *Chicago Sun-Times*, 3 June 1988. On the "hidden child," see Janet Maslin, "Tom Hanks as a Thirteen-Year-Old, in 'Big,'" *New York Times*, 3 June 1988; review, *Variety*, 1 June 1988; review, David Denby, *New York*, 13 June 1988, all in Collection of Newspaper Clippings, TCNYPL.

39. See the Book of Isaiah, 9:6.

40. Nina Darnton, "Penny's Big Break," *New York Post*, 2 June 1988, *Big* clipping file, TCNYPL.

41. Sachs, "'Big' Yields Small Returns."

42. On Spielberg's "Peter Pan Syndrome," see McBride, *Steven Spielberg*, 42–43.

43. Corliss and Ressner, "Peter Pan Grows Up," 82.

44. Thomas Postlewait, "From Melodrama to Realism: The Suspect History of American Drama," in *Melodrama: The Cultural Emergence of a Genre*, edited by Michael Hays and Anastasia Nikolopoulou (New York: St. Martin's, 1996), 41–49. On Spielberg's history of television watching, see McBride, *Steven Spielberg*, 62–64.

45. Quotations about *Schindler's List* are in McBride, *Steven Spielberg*, 415. See also Corliss and Ressner, "Peter Pan Grows Up," 75–76.

46. Terrence Rafferty, "Fear of Flying," *New Yorker*, 30 December 1991, *Hook* clipping file, TCNYPL.

47. McBride, *Steven Spielberg*, 400.

48. Descriptions and quotations are from *Hook*, TriStar Pictures, Amblin Entertainment, director Steven Spielberg, 1991, DVD.

49. Hilary de Vries, "A 'Peter Pan' for the 90's," *New York Times*, 8 December 1991, *Hook* clipping file, TCNYPL.

50. De Vries, "A 'Peter Pan' for the 90's."

51. Corliss and Ressner, "Peter Pan Grows Up," 76.

52. This message also was related to the backlash against feminism in the 1990s. For one, it suggests that men, in order to find themselves and become heroes in the eyes of their sons, must return to an all-male, prefeminist Never Land. For a parallel and contemporaneous prescription for male revitalization, see Robert Bly, *Iron John: A Book about Men* (New York: Vintage, 1990). See also the chapter "The Incredible Shrinking He(r)man: Male Regression, the Male Body, and Film," in Tania Modleski, *Feminism without Women: Culture and Criticism in a "Postfeminist" Age* (New York: Routledge, 1991), 90–111.

53. Janet Maslin, "'Saving Private Ryan': A Soberly Magnificent New War Film," *New York Times*, 24 July 1998, E1. Ambrose's quotation comes from "Into the Breach: Saving Private Ryan," on *Saving Private Ryan* "special edition" DVD, DreamWorks Pictures and Paramount Pictures and Amblin Entertainment, director Steven Spielberg, 1999, DVD.

54. Tom Brokaw, *The Greatest Generation* (New York: Random House, 1998). On the anxieties of "postheroic generations" of American men, see George B. Forgie, *Patricide in the House Divided: A Psychological Interpretation of Lincoln and His Age* (New York: W. W. Norton, 1979), esp. 13–53.

55. Brokaw, quoted in Maureen Dowd, "Our Retro Patriotism," *New York Times*, 6 December 1998, section 4, 19. *The Greatest Generation* has encouraged a number of books, usually by sons and about their war-generation fathers, and has

boosted popular support and interest in the National D-Day Museum in New Orleans, a special project of the historian Stephen Ambrose. For example, see James Bradley and Ron Powers, *Flags of Our Fathers* (New York: Bantam, 2000), and Bob Greene, *Duty: A Father, His Son, and the Man Who Won the War* (New York: William Morrow, 2000). On the museum, see the official website, http://ddaymuseum.org/about_us/from_our_founder.htm. The site's online bookstore of the museum demonstrates the promotional circuitry connecting Spielberg, Ambrose, and Brokaw in particular: other than a biography of the New Orleans native who invented the boats used in the Allied landing, the only books offered for sale on 21 August 2000 were either by Ambrose and Brokaw or about *Saving Private Ryan*. The only films for sale were the DVD and video-tape editions of Spielberg's movie.

56. "Into the Breach: Saving Private Ryan."

57. Corliss and Ressner, "Peter Pan Grows Up," 78.

58. Janice Maloney, "Perlmania," *Wired* 7 (July 1999), available online at http://www.wired.com:80/wired/archive/7.07/perlman.html.

59. Darnton, "Penny's Big Break." This observation is not meant to suggest that women cannot claim Peter Pan for themselves. On the contrary, Maude Adams and other female actors associated with the part have been notoriously posses-sive of the role. In 1920 and 1921, for instance, when she was approaching fifty, Adams was planning to make and star in a filmed version of *Peter Pan*; in 1934, she performed three radio broadcasts of the play, when she was in her early six-ties. See Phyllis Robbins, *Maude Adams, An Intimate Portrait* (New York: Put-nam, 1956), 206–11, 242. While Adams rejected feminism, other women claimed Peter Pan for themselves in ways that explicitly challenged dominant sexual and social orthodoxies. For instance, see the socialist and writer Frances Maule's representation of herself as Peter Pan, which she contributed to a 1920 photo album of the feminist Heterodoxy Club, a "little band of willful" and "un-ruly" women who for thirty years gathered in Greenwich Village, New York City. See the image and Judith Schwarz's introduction to the photographs in *Passion and Power: Sexuality in History*, edited by Kathy Peiss and Christina Simmons (Philadelphia: Temple University Press, 1989), 120, 135.

60. Roman Polanski pleaded guilty to unlawful intercourse with a minor and fled the country before completing his sentence. His legal troubles were well cov-ered in newspapers between March 1977 and March 1978; see, for instance, "Polanski, Facing Court Sentence, Flies to Europe; Warrant Issued," *New York Times*, 2 February 1978, section 2, 5.